EXECUTIVE POWER

The prerogative has long been a mystery to most observers; this book demystifies it.

It explains each of the prerogative powers in separate chapters. It clarifies the respective roles of government, Parliament and the courts in defining the extent of prerogative powers, and in regulating their use. It also looks at which powers should be codified in statute, which should be regulated by convention, and which could be left at large.

The book is very timely in contributing to current debates. The fevered parliamentary debates over Brexit thrust the prerogative centre-stage. Recent controversies have ranged from the role of Parliament in assenting to treaties, to the prorogation and dissolution of Parliament, to the grant or withholding of royal assent to bills.

In their 2019 election manifesto, the Conservative Party stated that 'After Brexit we also need to look at the broader aspects of our constitution, the relationship between the Government, Parliament and the courts; the functioning of the Royal Prerogative …'.

The book covers the whole range of prerogative powers, from going to war and ratifying treaties, appointing and dismissing ministers, regulating the civil service and public appointments, to the grant of honours and pardons and the issue of passports. Its 19 chapters provide a comprehensive guide to the operation of the prerogative – past, present, and future – together with suggestions for reform.

Executive Power

The Prerogative, Past, Present and Future

Robert Hazell
and
Timothy Foot

•HART•
OXFORD • LONDON • NEW YORK • NEW DELHI • SYDNEY

HART PUBLISHING

Bloomsbury Publishing Plc

Kemp House, Chawley Park, Cumnor Hill, Oxford, OX2 9PH, UK

1385 Broadway, New York, NY 10018, USA

29 Earlsfort Terrace, Dublin 2, Ireland

HART PUBLISHING, the Hart/Stag logo, BLOOMSBURY and the Diana logo are trademarks of Bloomsbury Publishing Plc

First published in Great Britain 2022

A catalogue record for this book is available from the British Library.

A catalogue record for this book is available from the Library of Congress.

Library of Congress Control Number: 2022940534

ISBN: HB: 978-1-50995-144-4
ePDF: 978-1-50995-146-8
ePub: 978-1-50995-145-1

Typeset by Compuscript Ltd, Shannon

PREFACE

This book has had a long gestation, and there are many people to thank who have finally helped it to be born. I first conceived the idea of writing about the prerogative in 2014: it was to be an academic article, challenging the common refrain that the prerogative was the last unreformed bastion of the UK constitution, by showing how many of the prerogative powers were now regulated or codified. An article was drafted, with the help of Jake Rylett, but put to one side when it was already becoming over long.

My interest was rekindled when I was invited by Prof Philippe Lagassé to be one of the UK partners on his big five-year comparative study of the prerogative in Australia, Canada, New Zealand and the UK. I wrote a paper for the inaugural workshop in Ottawa in 2019, thinking it might subsequently be published as a Constitution Unit report. That text has gradually grown longer and longer, until eventually emerging as this book of 19 chapters.

But the purpose has remained the same: to demystify the prerogative, still a source of mystery to most observers: to explain its origins, its evolution, and its continuing relevance today. And along the way to challenge the widespread misconception that the prerogative is a medieval relic, exemplifying all that is wrong with our unwritten constitution, which has no equivalent elsewhere. Hence the inclusion of two comparative chapters, showing that the prerogative indeed has equivalents in the reserve powers in countries with written constitutions: constitutions just as reliant on conventions as our own. But neither should this book be seen as a defence of the prerogative. Our purpose is to clarify the respective roles of government, Parliament and the courts, in defining the extent of prerogative powers, and in regulating their use in specific cases. And in the concluding section of each chapter, it is to consider proposals for change: to make the prerogative more transparent and more accountable, less of a mystery to those who exercise it, and to the public at large.

In bringing this work to fruition, the first people I have to thank are my co-author Tim Foot and our researcher Charlotte Sayers-Carter. Both are research volunteers with the Constitution Unit; but both have gone way beyond that. Tim has written all the legal chapters in the book, which is half the total; Charlotte has written two chapters (16 and 18), as well as the bibliography, and copy edited all the rest. They have continued to work on the book despite going on to other occupations, they have been inexhaustible and meticulous researchers (as the footnotes will show), and the book could not possibly have happened without them. Their scholarship is superb, and I owe both of them a huge debt of gratitude.

Tim and Charlotte are not the only research volunteers to thank. Previous volunteers who have helped research different aspects of the prerogative and compile bibliographies include Natacha Folliguet, James Fowler, Zachariah Pullar, Harrison Shaylor, Daniel Skeffington, and Holly Sommers. They too have made important contributions which they will recognise in the pages which follow, and I hope they are pleased with the result.

Each of the chapters has been read by at least two reviewers, who have saved us from error, patiently explained how things work, and turned round drafts in record time. Special thanks for their comments and corrections go to Margaret Aldred, Sir David Beamish, Prof Rodney Brazier, Sir David Calvert-Smith, Matthew Congreve, Prof Mark Elliott, Paul Evans, Catherine Haddon, Sir Richard Heaton, Lord (Michael) Jay, Sir Jonathan Jones, Richard Kelly, Prof Philippe Lagassé, Arabella Lang, Sir Brian Leveson, Baroness (Eliza) Manningham-Buller, Ciaran Martin, Bob Morris, Sir David Natzler, Sir David Normington, Sir David Omand, Sir Hayden Phillips, Lord (Nicholas) Phillips, Prof Tom Poole, Sir Peter Riddell, Prof Meg Russell, Jonathan Slater, Martin Stanley, Jack Straw, Prof Anne Twomey, Robert Ward QC, Ian Watmore, Prof Albert Weale, Tony Wright, Ben Yong, Paul Yowell; and others who wished to remain anonymous.

Others who have helped with advice and support include Ronan Cormacain, Prof Peter Hennessy, Lord (Robin) Janvrin, Prof Alison Young, Bob Morris, Prof Petra Schleiter; and from the Royal Archives Bill Stockting, who kindly released the papers on the Lascelles principles on dissolution. In the Constitution Unit I owe thanks to Meg Russell, Alan Renwick and Rachel Cronkshaw for their unfailing support; and at Hart Publishing to Rosie Mearns and Kate Whetter for their patience and their professionalism. Any remaining errors in the book are down to us, the authors; while we have allowed a few subsequent developments to creep in, we have endeavoured to bring the text as a whole up to date to 31 December 2021.

Last but by no means least I owe heartfelt thanks to my wife Alison Richards, for her forbearance during long periods while this book has been my main preoccupation. I look forward to spending more time together, with a promise not to write another one; or at any rate, not for a while.

Robert Hazell
February 2022

Addendum

The text of this book was finalised before the death of Queen Elizabeth II in September 2022. We ask for readers' understanding that we have been unable to update the text to reflect the accession of King Charles III; what we have to say on the powers and responsibilities of the late Queen applies just as much to the new King. The late Queen was an exemplary constitutional monarch, and upon his accession the King committed himself to 'strive to follow the inspiring example I have been set in upholding constitutional government'.

September 2022

CONTENTS

PART 2
THE MONARCH'S PERSONAL PREROGATIVES

PART 3
PREROGATIVE POWERS OF THE EXECUTIVE

PART 5
REFORM OF THE PREROGATIVE

PART 1

Introduction

1

Why the Prerogative Matters

> The royal prerogative has no place in a modern western democracy … Ministers have been insufficiently accountable for their executive decisions as a result of their use of prerogative powers. By the same token, the monarchy has been scarcely accountable at all for its conduct of this crucial institution at the heart of our constitutional arrangements.
>
> Jack Straw (1994)[1]

> … with specific prerogatives, it is often in their flexibility that they exhibit their greatest utility. It is in their origins in the ancient powers of kingship that they manifest a unique, immanent and valuable aid to executive government, whose abolition could well cause more problems than their retention.
>
> Noel Cox (2020)[2]

The Prerogative and Brexit

On 28 August 2019, in the Library at Balmoral Castle, the Queen held a meeting of her Most Honourable Privy Council. Three Privy Counsellors were present, led by the Lord President, Jacob Rees-Mogg. By tradition, meetings of the Privy Council are held standing up, and this one was particularly brief, with only two items of business. The first was to approve orders appointing two new members of the Privy Council. The second was to order the prorogation of Parliament, which was promulgated as follows:

> At the Court at Balmoral
>
> THE 28th DAY OF AUGUST 2019
>
> PRESENT, THE QUEEN'S MOST EXCELLENT MAJESTY IN COUNCIL
>
> It is this day ordered by Her Majesty in Council that the Parliament be prorogued on a day no earlier than Monday the 9th day of September and no later than Thursday the 12th day of September 2019 to Monday the 14th day of October 2019, to be then

[1] J Straw, 'Abolish the Royal Prerogative' in A Barnett (ed), *Power and the Throne: The Monarchy Debate* (London, Vintage, 1994), 125–9.

[2] N Cox, *The Royal Prerogative and Constitutional Law: A Search for the Quintessence of Executive Power* (Oxford, Routledge, 2020), 221.

> holden for the despatch of divers urgent and important affairs, and that the Right Honourable the Lord High Chancellor of Great Britain do cause a Commission to be prepared and issued in the usual manner for proroguing the Parliament accordingly.

There followed a storm of protest against Parliament being closed down for five weeks, when in the view of many parliamentarians it had a lot of 'divers urgent and important affairs' about the Brexit negotiations demanding its immediate attention. There also followed a dramatic court challenge, which led to the Supreme Court declaring that the order of prorogation was null, void and of no effect.[3] And there followed a lot of questioning about prorogation, and the prerogative powers more generally. How is it in a modern democracy that Parliament can be closed down by the monarch on the advice of the Prime Minister? What other prerogative powers does the monarch have, and the government? And in what ways can they be better controlled?

That is what this book is about: the royal prerogative, what the main prerogative powers are, and how they might be reformed. Until Brexit the prerogative had seldom been the subject of much political attention. It has long been shrouded in mystery, even to lawyers: one of the cobwebs of the constitution which might need sweeping one day, but could be left to moulder in a dark corner until that day came. Then Brexit came and shone a terrible spotlight on this dark and dusty corner. Obscure powers which had been of interest only to obscure constitutionalists suddenly became the talk of parliamentarians and newspaper leader writers. There was fierce debate over whether Parliament should be allowed a meaningful vote over the European Union (EU) Withdrawal Agreement, spilling over from Parliament into the courts.[4] This was followed by wild speculation that the Queen might be advised to withhold royal assent from the European Union (Withdrawal) (No. 2) Act 2019 (the Benn Act), passed against the government's wishes. Then there was speculation (which turned out to be less wild) that Boris Johnson might prorogue Parliament to prevent it heading off a no deal Brexit. And finally, there were repeated votes as Johnson sought to find a way round the Fixed-term Parliaments Act 2011 to dissolve Parliament and hold a general election.

Underlying all these different aspects of the prerogative are questions about the fundamental balance of power between Parliament and the executive; and about the role of the courts. How much power should Parliament have to scrutinise and approve (or block) the ratification of treaties, traditionally a prerogative of the executive? How much say should the courts have in adjudicating on that question? Is royal assent a legislative function, the Crown certifying that a law has been duly passed by Parliament; or an executive function, exercised by the Crown acting on ministerial advice? Is prorogation a discretionary reserve power of the Crown; or is the Queen bound to follow the Prime Minister's advice? And who should decide when Parliament is dissolved: the government, or Parliament itself?

[3] *R (Miller) v The Prime Minister; Cherry v Advocate General* [2019] UKSC 41.
[4] *R (Miller) v Secretary of State for Exiting the European Union* [2017] UKSC 5.

Campaigns to Reform the Prerogative

These episodes from the Brexit battles of 2019 were not the first time that parliamentarians have taken an interest in the prerogative; but they were certainly the first time that it became thrust centre stage, as an increasingly frustrated government sought every reserve power available to get its Brexit business through a divided and fractious Parliament. Up until this time the prerogative had been a fringe interest, associated with groups like Charter 88, the organisation spawned by the *New Statesman* in 1988 to campaign for fundamental constitutional reforms, leading up to a written constitution. Item two in their ten-point manifesto was to 'subject executive powers and prerogatives, by whomsoever exercised, to the rule of law'.[5] The prerogative was identified as exemplifying everything that was wrong with the archaic, secretive, and centralised nature of power in the British constitution:

> The cushioning, conveniencing, excluding powers of the prerogative crop up throughout our system of government … Its exercise lies close to the heart of whatever in British government is most arbitrary, most secretive, and least accountable … It is crown prerogative which enables prime ministers and their chosen subordinates to order the country to war, to make treaties, to give up national territory, to staff the commanding heights of political life, the church and the law, to dish out honours … Even today the Queen retains the ancient prerogatives of choosing or dismissing the prime minister and deciding whether or not parliament should be dissolved.[6]

But reform of the prerogative proved a difficult cause around which to muster support because of its diffuse and sprawling nature. Easier to grasp and identify with were Charter 88's more specific demands: devolution to Scotland and Wales, a bill of rights, reform of the House of Lords, and freedom of information. After New Labour had enacted these high-profile items, Charter 88 struggled to maintain interest in the rest of its campaign. The prerogative was too mysterious, elusive, hard to pin down.

Pinning down the prerogative became the objective in the next stage of campaigning, which shifted to Parliament under the leadership of Tony Wright, chairman of the House of Commons Public Administration Select Committee (PASC). PASC's main interest was in the prerogative powers exercised by ministers, and finding the government unable to provide a comprehensive list, its first task was simply to enumerate them. In its 2004 report, *Taming the Prerogative: Strengthening Ministerial Accountability to Parliament*, the main powers were identified as follows: making and ratifying treaties; the conduct of diplomacy and foreign relations; deployment of the armed forces; the grant of peerages and honours; organisation of the civil service; the issue and revocation of passports;

[5] D Erdos, 'Charter 88 and the Constitutional Reform Movement' (2009) 62 *Parliamentary Affairs* 537, 539.

[6] D McKie, 'How Ministers exercise Arbitrary Power', *The Guardian* (London, 6 December 2000).

and the grant of pardons. These powers historically had belonged to the Crown, but over the years their exercise had gradually passed to the government, so that for all practical purposes these powers now lay in the hands of ministers.

Quite separate are the prerogative powers of the monarch, known as the monarch's personal prerogatives, or reserve powers. These powers were summarised by PASC as follows:

> the rights to advise, encourage and warn Ministers in private; to appoint the Prime Minister and other Ministers; to assent to legislation; to prorogue or to dissolve Parliament; and (in grave constitutional crisis) to act contrary to or without Ministerial advice.[7]

At the time these reserve powers were of less interest to PASC, but during the parliamentary skirmishing over Brexit it was the personal prerogatives of the monarch which were invoked as much as the prerogative powers of ministers. And it was both sets of prerogative powers which the Conservative Party had in mind when they stated in their 2019 election manifesto that 'After Brexit we also need to look at the broader aspects of our constitution, the relationship between the Government, Parliament and the courts; the functioning of the Royal Prerogative …'.[8]

The Purpose of this Book

Our purpose in writing this book is similar to that of PASC. First and foremost, it is to demystify the prerogative, still a source of mystery to most observers: to explain its origins, its evolution, and its continuing relevance today. Second, it is to clarify the respective roles of government, Parliament and the courts, in defining the extent of prerogative powers, and in regulating their use in specific cases. Third, it is to consider proposals for change: which powers should be codified in statute; which should be regulated by convention, or by specialist watchdogs; and which could be left at large. In particular, we examine proposals for Parliament to have a stronger role: if that is to happen, we consider what additional powers or resources Parliament might need to exercise that role effectively and responsibly.

Not everyone believes that Parliament should have a stronger role. One of the sceptics is Noel Cox, a staunch defender of the prerogative, who maintains that:

> There is no clear argument, however, as to why majoritarian representative democracy, operating through members of Parliament, should necessarily provide a greater mandate for executive government action than the legitimacy derived from ancient prerogatives of the Crown.[9]

[7] Fourth Report from the House of Commons Public Administration Select Committee, *Taming the Prerogative: Strengthening Ministerial Accountability to Parliament* HC 422 (2003–04), para 5.

[8] Conservative Party, *Get Brexit Done: Unleash Britain's Potential* (2019), 48.

[9] Cox, above n 2 at 221.

Cox might find few supporters nowadays in claiming that the ancient prerogatives of the Crown somehow convey their own legitimacy. He might find a few more supporters in his view, quoted in the epigraph above, that the prerogative powers 'manifest a unique, immanent and valuable aid to executive government'.[10] One would be Timothy Endicott, arguing that a strong, general purpose executive is necessary for the public good.[11] The prerogative has certainly proved a valuable aid to those in executive government, which is why reformers have found it so difficult to loosen the executive's grip. The underlying issue in all the debates about the prerogative is about power: how much autonomy the executive should have to wield that power; with what degree of supervision (if any) from Parliament or the courts; or (more rarely) from the monarch.

Prerogative Powers and Executive Autonomy

With the underlying issue being a struggle for power, we do not need sophisticated theory to understand the tug-of-war for control of the prerogative. One way of understanding it is through David Howarth's Whitehall versus Westminster models. Howarth posited two different views of the constitution and the way the political system operates:

> According to the Westminster view, Parliament, and especially the House of Commons, sits at the centre of the system … The other view, the Whitehall view, posits that the Crown, now largely in the form of its ministers, is the centre of the system. Effective government requires ministers to be able to act quickly and authoritatively.[12]

These competing views are not merely about the centre of power, but from where that power derives its legitimacy, and to whom it is accountable. On the Westminster model, the government derives its democratic legitimacy, and authority, from Parliament. The government is chosen by Parliament and is accountable to Parliament: this is the classic model of responsible government. In the Whitehall model, the government derives its democratic legitimacy from the people. Long before Brexit, Anthony Birch showed how the rise of mass political parties with the doctrine of an electoral mandate has endowed governments with a sense of legitimacy, independently of that derived from Parliament: people feel they have a direct channel of communication to the government, and the government feels

[10] ibid.

[11] T Endicott, *The Stubborn Stain Theory of Executive Power* (Policy Exchange, 2017).

[12] D Howarth, 'Westminster versus Whitehall: Two Incompatible Views of the Constitution' (*UK Constitutional Law Association Blog*, 10 April 2019) www.ukconstitutionallaw.org/2019/04/10/david-howarth-westminster-versus-whitehall-two-incompatible-views-of-the-constitution/. For a longer exegesis, see D Howarth, 'Westminster versus Whitehall: What the Brexit Debate Revealed About an Unresolved Conflict at the Heart of the British Constitution' in O Doyle, A McHarg and J Murkens (eds), *The Brexit Challenge for Ireland and the United Kingdom* (Cambridge, Cambridge University Press, 2021).

directly accountable to the people. Birch called this direct relationship between government and the people representative government.[13]

Brexit served to throw these competing models into particularly sharp relief, with the 2016 referendum seen as a mandate from the people to the government, which had to respect the people's will. The contrast was vividly illustrated when Theresa May said at the Conservative Party conference that those who maintained the approval of Parliament was necessary before initiating the process for leaving the EU were not standing up for democracy but trying to subvert it.[14] The Prime Minister relied on the referendum result as her democratic mandate, and the prerogative as the source of her unfettered executive power to withdraw from treaties as well as make them. In *R (Miller) v Secretary of State for Exiting the European Union* (*Miller 1*), the Supreme Court ruled that she needed the approval of Parliament before triggering Article 50 of the Treaty on European Union, thus upholding the Westminster view of the constitution.[15]

The Whitehall view, with the requirement for ministers to be able to act quickly and authoritatively, is the classic defence of prerogative power. Executive autonomy is another way to express this: the need for the executive to be able to act effectively and decisively, without interference from Parliament or the courts. It may have particularly strong appeal in the UK, where a similar justification is given for the first past the post voting system – namely, that it delivers strong and effective government. The Whitehall view has been clearly espoused by the Johnson government, sensing that the Westminster view has been discredited by the travails of the Brexit Parliament; it is the *leitmotif* underlying the constitutional reform proposals of the Conservative 2019 election manifesto, and the constitutional changes initiated by the government once in office.[16]

The Structure of this Book

Executive autonomy is also the thread which runs through every chapter in this book: its justification, whether it can be constrained, by whom, and in what circumstances. The book is divided into five parts. Part one provides the background, with chapter two giving the historical and legal background: describing the evolution of the prerogative from the Middle Ages to the twentieth century,

[13] AH Birch, *Representative and Responsible Government: An Essay on the British Constitution* (London, Allen & Unwin, 1964).

[14] BBC, 'Theresa May's Conservative Conference Speech: Key Quotes' (*BBC News*, 2 October 2016) www.bbc.co.uk/news/uk-politics-37535527.

[15] *Miller* [2017], above n 4.

[16] A McHarg and A Young, 'The Resilience of the (*Old*) British Constitution' (*UK Constitutional Law Association Blog*, 8 September 2021) www.ukconstitutionallaw.org/2021/09/08/aileen-mcharg-and-alison-l-young-the-resilience-of-the-old-british-constitution/.

and closer review by the courts from the late twentieth century onwards. Chapter three gives the political background, with tighter regulation of the prerogative by Parliament over the last 20 years; but with executive pushback just in the last two years, with the Johnson government seeking to revive the prerogative power of dissolution, and to restrict judicial review.

Part two of the book covers the personal prerogatives of the monarch, in three chapters. The monarch is the ultimate guardian of the constitution, with power in exceptional circumstances to refuse a request for dissolution or prorogation, to withhold royal assent from legislation, and to dismiss a Prime Minister. But the monarch's powers are closely circumscribed by conventions. Chapter four explains the prerogative power to appoint and dismiss the Prime Minister, and other ministers, and the soft law codification of the conventions on government formation which regulate the monarch's choice of Prime Minister. Chapter five is about how much control the executive should have over summoning, dissolving and proroguing Parliament, vividly illustrated in the prorogation crisis of 2019; and in the tussles over the Fixed-term Parliaments Act 2011, which transferred the power of dissolution to the House of Commons, but has now been repealed and power transferred back to the executive by reviving the prerogative power. Chapter six is about royal assent to legislation: whether the monarch retains any discretionary power to veto legislation passed by Parliament, whether the government could advise the monarch to exercise such a veto, and other ways in which the executive can block legislation without needing a veto.

Part three of the book examines the prerogative powers in the hands of the executive, and is the longest section, with eight chapters. They show how with some prerogative powers, the executive still enjoys unfettered autonomy; with others, there has been greater supervision by Parliament or the courts; but even where the prerogative has been codified in statute, the executive may still enjoy significant autonomy, depending on the nature of codification. Chapter seven, on the war-making power, examines the growing pressure from Parliament to have a vote before engaging in military action overseas, and the debates on whether that should be governed by statute, by resolution of the House of Commons, or merely by convention. Chapter eight, on making and ratifying treaties, records how the convention that treaties should be laid before Parliament before ratification was put into statute in 2010; but Parliament's continuing weakness in scrutinising treaties has been exposed by Brexit and subsequent trade agreements. Chapter nine records how regulation of the civil service was also put on a statutory footing in 2010, but how that has done little to prevent further creeping politicisation of the civil service. Chapter ten, on public appointments, compares the constraints on executive autonomy exercised by three regulatory bodies: the Judicial Appointments Commission, which is statutory; the Commissioner for Public Appointments, created by Order in Council; and the House of Lords Appointments Commission, created under the prerogative.

The next four chapters in part three examine lesser-known prerogative powers exercised by the executive. Chapter eleven looks at the prerogative of mercy, which now offers very little scope for executive autonomy: its use has declined greatly since the establishment of the Court of Appeal, and growth in the powers of the Criminal Cases Review Commission. Chapter twelve shows the reverse: the issue and withdrawal of passports is still governed almost entirely by the prerogative, with minimal scope for intervention by watchdogs or by Parliament. Chapter thirteen is about the grant of honours, where executive autonomy has been constrained by recent initiatives to make the Honours Advisory Committees more independent, but there remains scope for executive discretion and abuse. Chapter fourteen, about public inquiries, discusses how inquiries can still be established outside the Inquiries Act 2005, illustrating non-statutory powers' advantage of flexibility.

Part four of the book looks at the prerogative in a comparative context, with two chapters. Australia, Canada and New Zealand have all retained the prerogative, and chapter fifteen describes how much executive autonomy they still enjoy, and their attempts at tighter regulation. This is examined through the lens of four case studies, looking at prorogation and dissolution, the war making power, judicial appointments, and ratification of treaties. Chapter sixteen widens the comparative lens to explore the parallels between the prerogative and reserve powers in six countries with written constitutions; again, the central issue is executive autonomy, the balance of power between the legislature and executive, and reserve powers as a form of executive veto.

The final part of the book, part five, draws the threads together in three concluding chapters. Chapter seventeen looks at the role of the courts, and the growth in their willingness to review both the scope, and the exercise of prerogative powers. Chapter eighteen examines the role of Parliament, and its growing assertiveness over war powers, and treaties, but also the limitations of parliamentary scrutiny in terms of time, information, expertise and resources. The final chapter, chapter nineteen, asks whether the prerogative can ever be fully codified, as some reformers have proposed, by going through each of the prerogative powers, and analysing the scope for codification in statute, in soft law, or by stronger and clearer conventions. Our conclusion is that complete codification is unachievable. Codification of the major prerogative powers is certainly desirable; but it will never fully resolve tensions between government, Parliament and the courts, because in any constitution and political system the balance of power is continually being adjusted and re-negotiated.

2

History of the Prerogative

> The 'prerogative' appears to be both historically and as a matter of actual fact nothing else than the residue of discretionary or arbitrary authority, which at any given time is legally left in the hands of the Crown.
>
> Albert Venn Dicey (1885)[1]

> The stubborn stain theory, with its centuries-old tradition of indiscriminate suggestions that there is something generally wrong with constitutional executive power, is a mistake because there are … further constitutional principles …
>
> Timothy Endicott (2017)[2]

Introduction

Prerogative power is a part of governmental power. Sometimes it is exercised by the Queen on the advice of her ministers; sometimes it is exercised by ministers directly. However, prerogative power has its roots in *royal* power – the ceremony and the prestige of the prerogative in the modern day recalls and relives that history.[3] The story of its evolution to the present day is part of the story of the curtailment of royal power and the emergence of the modern state. Each prerogative power has developed in its own way as part of that overall story. In later chapters, we address those individual developments before zooming out again to look at thematic developments in the recent past. This chapter stands as a broad-brush prologue to that story of the more recent past.

The two quotations standing as an epigraph to this chapter represent two ways of reading the history of the prerogative. Albert Venn Dicey's description exposes the prerogative to the impression that it is a 'relic of a past age',[4] or a 'stubborn stain' that needs to be washed out.[5] Timothy Endicott argues that 'the great historical

[1] AV Dicey, *Introduction to the Study of the Law of the Constitution*, 9th edn (London, Macmillan, 1939), 424.

[2] T Endicott, *The Stubborn Stain Theory of Executive Power* (Policy Exchange, 2017), 22.

[3] See T Poole, 'The Strange Death of Prerogative in England' (2018) 43 *University of Western Australia Law Review* 42, 46.

[4] *Burmah Oil Co (Burma Trading) Ltd v Lord Advocate* [1965] AC 75, 101.

[5] See Endicott, above n 2.

successes in taking power away from the executive have been great for *particular* reasons, and it is equally important not to take away the powers that the executive ought to have'.[6] At the end of this chapter, we explore this danger with historical overviews such as the one we are about to give. Indeed, throughout this book, we are mindful that the future of the prerogative's continued evolution must be debated as a matter of principle, not taken as a matter of course.

Medieval Origins

The prerogative powers of the Crown have their roots in the ancient royal powers of the monarch. Their existence and their scope depended as much on practicality and political power as on fine legal distinctions or constitutional theory. 'The breadth or width of [the King's] assertion from time to time depended on high politics and it varied from time to time depending on considerations of power and of expediency. The history of [the prerogative's] changes lies not in legal history but in political history.'[7]

Yet that political history has always been accompanied by legal commentary. From Bracton, in the thirteenth century, we have the principle that the King was *sub lege* (under the law) and *sub Deo* (under God), even if not *sub homine* (under man).[8] The King could do 'nothing save what he can do *de jure*'.[9] Thus, when the King acted rightfully, no one could question his act, but 'if it is wrongful it will not then be the deed of the King'.[10] Here perhaps is the first exposition of that famous maxim that the 'King can do no wrong'. Importantly, for Bracton it does not act as a shield for indiscriminate royal power, although the King was also not to be subject to enforcement of law. Rather, he should submit himself *voluntarily* to law (*lex*) just as did Christ and the Virgin Mary.[11] For one thing, the King was king by virtue of law.[12] As a later statement in the yearbooks puts it: 'si le ley ne fuit, nul Roi, ny nul inheritance sera'.[13]

This idea of *voluntary* royal submission to the law eventually disappeared. Royal power became less and less arbitrary, controlled by other institutions within the constitution. John Fortescue, writing in the fifteenth century, outlined the difference between what he called the 'purely regal' kingship (ie absolute monarchy) of France and the 'regal and political' kingship (ie constitutional monarchy)

[6] ibid at 9.

[7] *New South Wales v Commonwealth* (1975) 135 CLR 337, 489 (Jacobs J).

[8] H Bracton, *On the Laws and Customs of England*, vol 2 (Samuel Thorne tr, Cambridge, Harvard University Press, 1968), 33.

[9] ibid at 305.

[10] ibid at 159.

[11] ibid at 33.

[12] ibid at 33 and 206.

[13] 'If the law did not exist, there would be no King, nor any inheritance [of the King]': YB ET 19 Hen VI, 63.

of England. The latter was, he claimed, by far the better because it prevented the extremes of poverty seen in France.[14] He describes how 'the statutes of England are established not only by the prince's will but by the assent of the whole kingdom' and 'in the kingdom of England, the kings do not make laws nor impose subsidies on their subjects without the consent of the three estates of their kingdoms' (ie Parliament).[15]

By the time the Tudor dynasty came to power, England was a 'limited monarchy … Everyone, including the king, was subject to the law; and new law could only be made by Parliament'.[16] This was not entirely lost, despite the centralising dynamics of Tudor politics. For example, the Statute of Proclamations 1539,[17] which appeared to give the monarch's proclamations the force of law, was enacted in response to judicial concerns. It reinforced the long-established rule that proclamations were restricted to being *declaratory* of existing statute or common law, including the prerogative. This continued to be taught as law into the late sixteenth century.[18]

That is not to say that everything was plain sailing. There were frequent tensions between – as well as amongst – the royal administration, Parliament and the judges. For instance, Queen Elizabeth I tried (and failed) to instigate a doctrine that it was not for Parliament to debate military or foreign policy.[19]

The Seventeenth Century

These struggles between and among political and legal institutions continued into the seventeenth century. In particular, the arrival of the Stuarts brought a new urgency, as central government struggled for power and challenged Parliament's roles in legislating and approving taxation. The pre-Civil War tensions are visible in a string of legal cases, including *The Case of Monopolies*, *The Case of Prohibitions del Roy*, *Bate's Case*, *Dr Bonham's Case*, and *The Case of Ship Money*.[20]

Perhaps the most often cited of these is *The Case of Proclamations*, including the famous dictum: 'the King has no prerogative but that which the law of the

[14] J Fortescue, *The Difference between an Absolute and a Limited Monarchy* (Charles Plummer ed, Oxford, Oxford University Press, 1885), 112-5.

[15] J Fortescue, *De Laudibus Legum Angliae* (Andrew Amos ed, London, Butterworths, 1825), 18; J Fortescue, *De Natura Legis Naturae*, vol 1 (Lord Clermont ed, 1869), 16; See SB Chrimes, *English Constitutional Ideas in the Fifteenth Century* (Cambridge, Cambridge University Press, 1936), 59-60.

[16] J Baker, *The Reinvention of Magna Carta 1216-1616* (Cambridge, Cambridge University Press, 2017), 63.

[17] 31 Hen 8 c 8.

[18] Baker, above n 16 at 64 and 151.

[19] G Parry, 'Foreign Policy and the Parliament of 1576' (2015) 34 *Parliamentary History* 62, 63-4.

[20] *Darcy v Allin* (1601) 11 Co Rep 84; *Prohibitions del Roy* (1607) 12 Co Rep 63; *Case of Impositions* (1606) 2 St Tr 271; *Bonham v College of Physicians* (1610) 8 Co Rep 113; *R v Hampden* (1637) 3 St Tr 825; *cf* S Sedley, *Lions Under the Throne: Essays on the History of English Public Law* (Cambridge, Cambridge University Press, 2015), 123-42.

land allows him'.[21] King James I had issued proclamations including a prohibition on new buildings in and about London. This prohibition could be lifted by payment of a fine – ie the aim was to bring in a new tax. Sir Edward Coke, Chief Justice of the Common Pleas, stated that it was not within the King's prerogative to issue such a proclamation: the King could not by his proclamation change 'any part of the common law, or statute law or customs of the realm'.[22] *Proclamations* was not just about the contest between the King and the courts. Coke (and the Lord Chancellor, Lord Ellesmere) was advising the King on how to respond to the House of Commons' opposition to the proclamation. Furthermore, it came in the context of another dispute, in which Coke and Ellesmere were two of the main protagonists, between the common law courts and other courts.[23] It was a battle that Coke, Parliament and the common lawyers largely won, even if it was to take a Civil War and a Glorious Revolution.

Following the parliamentarians' victory in the Civil War, the entire machinery of government was wrested from the hands of the monarchy. This included powers previously exercised as part of the prerogative. No longer was warfare a matter for a monarch; instead, it was devolved to a committee of parliamentarians.[24] Once Cromwell's regime collapsed, the prerogative powers of the monarch were reasserted. King James II even succeeded in obtaining judicial acquiescence to a royal power of dispensing with Parliamentary legislation.[25]

On the coat-tails of the Glorious Revolution, the Bill of Rights 1689 assertively codified much of what judges and parliamentarians had won with their words and their muskets: the monarch was to have no power of dispensing with the law; levying money 'by pretence of Prerogative without Grant of Parlyament' was illegal; and no standing army might be kept (in peacetime) except 'with Consente of Parlyament'.[26] Most importantly, there was to be freedom of speech in Parliament without fear of external sanction, and 'for Redresse of all Grievances and for the amending strengthening and preserveing of the Lawes Parlyaments ought to be held frequently'.[27] In Scotland, the Claim of Right Act 1689 asserted the same, renewed role for Parliament.

Throughout this period, and on into the following centuries, there is a persistent problem with tracking the tale of 'the prerogative'. Often, 'It is hard to say what executive power is because sometimes it is whatever it needs to be.'[28] The question

[21] *Case of Proclamations* (1610) 77 ER 1352; (1611) 12 Co Rep 74.

[22] *Case of Proclamations* (1611) 12 Co Rep 74, [75]; 77 ER 1352, 1353.

[23] Baker, above n 16 at 206-7 and 213. J Goldsworthy, *Parliamentary Sovereignty: Contemporary Debates* (Cambridge, Cambridge University Press, 2010), 27-30.

[24] Under the various names of the Committee of Safety, the Committee of Both Kingdoms, the Derby House Committee and the Council of State. See R Joseph, *The War Prerogative: History, Reform and Constitutional Design* (Oxford, Oxford University Press, 2013), 46.

[25] *Godden v Hales* (1686) 11 St Tr 1165.

[26] Bill of Rights 1689, arts 1-2, 4, 6.

[27] ibid at arts 9 and 13.

[28] C Moore, *Crown and Sword: Executive power and the use of force by the Australian Defence Force* (Acton, ANU Press, 2017), 51.

of the extent of executive power was a political question as much as a legal one. Although the common law had taken a hold on the prerogative, the constitutional authors of the seventeenth and eighteenth centuries continued to refer to it as a political concept. For theorists like John Locke, a 'prerogative is nothing but the power of doing public good without a rule'.[29] For common lawyers like Sir Matthew Hale, on the other hand, the tendency was 'to carve up and classify prerogative into a bundle of particular, bespoke *prerogatives*'.[30] The legal and the political concepts of 'the prerogative' did not always align.

The Modern State

Among the many alterations in our constitution over the centuries since 1689, perhaps the most significant is the emergence of responsible government: the transition from monarchical power to government by ministers, who were accountable to Parliament. With that change, the powers once wielded by the monarch alone became – in effect – separated between the monarch and ministers. As the principle developed and solidified into a set of conventions, and later adapted to fit a new democratic basis, the monarch ceased to play an active role: with the exception of the reserve powers considered in part two of this book.[31] This coincided with a vast expansion in Britain's international power. As a result, the growth of the British Empire and global trade – in the running of which the prerogative played no small part – had at its helm a powerful system of government dominated by ministers, not monarchs.[32]

For ministers, the prerogative powers have remained potent elements of executive government. Yet over time, individual powers have been subsumed by statute. A famous example is the disappearance of the power of requisitioning property without compensation under the weight of nineteenth-century Defence Acts.[33] This is a trend that has continued into recent times. The powers to dissolve Parliament and to regulate the civil service have been subsumed, although not necessarily permanently, by statute (see chapters five and nine).[34] Furthermore, conventions have sprung up to regulate the use of particular powers. For instance, from the 1920s until its codification in the Constitutional Reform and Governance Act 2010, the 'Ponsonby Rule' required the government to lay newly signed treaties before the Commons at least 21 days before ratification (see chapter eight).

[29] J Locke, *Essay concerning the True Original, Extent and End of Civil Government*, 4th edn (London, 1713), 316.

[30] Poole, above n 3 at 42 and 49.

[31] As part two explains, these are deep reserve powers, to be used in last resort by the monarch as ultimate guardian of the constitution.

[32] See T Poole, *Reason of State: Law, Prerogative and Empire* (Cambridge, Cambridge University Press, 2015), chs 5-6.

[33] *Attorney General v De Keyser's Royal Hotel Ltd* [1920] AC 508.

[34] Constitutional Reform and Governance Act 2010; Fixed-term Parliaments Act 2011.

The Modern Courts

Until the 1970s, judges took the view that judicial review did not extend to the exercise of prerogative powers. They would go no further than determining the existence and extent of a power, including the questions of whether it had been superseded by statute or was being used contrary to common law. However, during the 1970s, there was a marked shift in the courts' approach. In *Laker Airways Ltd v Department for Trade*, Lord Denning suggested that review of a prerogative power should be little different to that of a statutory power.[35] The House of Lords finally recognised in *Council of Civil Service Unions v Minister for the Civil Service* (*GCHQ*) that the source of executive power (prerogative or statute) was irrelevant to the question of justiciability, although the manner of exercise of some prerogative powers remained unreviewable because of their subject-matter.[36]

Since *GCHQ*, therefore, there has been a divide between those prerogative powers falling within the 'excluded categories'[37] (sometimes termed 'high policy') and those that lie open to the full scope of judicial review. Lord Roskill gave a helpful list of non-justiciable powers: 'the making of treaties, the defence of the realm, the prerogative of mercy, the grant of honours, the dissolution of Parliament and the appointment of ministers as well as others'.[38] On the other side of the divide, the courts have found little trouble with the justiciability of, for example, passport powers.[39] Yet the simple, subject-matter based test of justiciability has not been entirely stable. The prerogative of mercy (pardon powers) has subsequently been recognised as justiciable (see chapter eleven). Even where ministers make 'high policy' decisions, the courts may intervene 'to cure … actual bad faith' in decision-making.[40] This tightening of control is not uncontroversial. When commissioning the Independent Review of Administrative Law in 2020, the Johnson government made clear its concern that the law on justiciability was fast intruding on the proper realm of executive autonomy.[41]

Even the more traditional limits on the prerogative have been tightened. For example, in *R v Secretary of State for the Home Department, ex parte Fire Brigades Union* (*FBU*), the House of Lords held that the Home Secretary had a statutory discretion as to *when* to make a commencement order for a new, statutory compensation scheme (replacing one run under the prerogative), but not *whether* to do so. The prerogative power had been 'curtailed' even though the statute was not yet in force.[42] This has been said to give rise to the principle that the prerogative 'cannot

[35] *Laker Airways Ltd v Department of Trade* [1997] QB 643, 705-707.

[36] *Council of Civil Service Unions v Minister for the Civil Service* [1985] AC 374.

[37] ibid at 418 (Lord Roskill).

[38] ibid.

[39] *R v Secretary of State for Foreign and Commonwealth Affairs, ex parte Everett* [1989] QB 811, 817.

[40] *R (Marchiori) v The Environment Agency* [2002] EWCA Civ 3, [40].

[41] Independent Review of Administrative Law, *Terms of Reference* (2020), para 2.

[42] *R v Secretary of State for the Home Department, ex parte Fire Brigades Union* [1995] 2 AC 513, 576 (Lord Nicholls).

frustrate the purpose of a statute or a statutory provision, for example by emptying it of content or preventing its effectual operation'.[43] This 'frustration principle' is clearly connected to the more traditional limit imposed on the prerogative when it is subsumed by statute, but signals a development that may have much more wide-reaching effects.

The two most famous constitutional cases of recent times have both concerned prerogative powers. Each demonstrates the same tightening of judicial control. In *R (Miller) v Secretary of State for Exiting the European Union* (*Miller 1*) (the Article 50 case), the Supreme Court held that ministers could not bring about 'such a far-reaching change to the UK constitutional arrangements' as withdrawal from the European Union (under Article 50 of the Treaty on European Union) without an Act of Parliament.[44] Some have seen this as an example of the 'frustration principle' derived from *FBU*.[45] It certainly represents something of a development from the two traditional limits on the prerogative – the common law and statute. *Miller 1* looked to the constitutional principles underlying those limits, and made an assertion about the proper place of Parliament as part of the UK's constitutional order.[46]

In *R (Miller) v The Prime Minister* (*Miller 2*) (the prorogation case), the Supreme Court *explicitly* framed the limits of the prerogative as constitutional principle, in that case the principle of 'parliamentary accountability'. The Prime Minister could not lawfully advise the Queen to prorogue Parliament if:

> the prorogation has the effect of frustrating or preventing, without reasonable justification, the ability of Parliament to carry out its constitutional functions as a legislature and as the body responsible for the supervision of the executive.[47]

Since the Prime Minister had not given the court *any* justification for the prorogation, and since the prorogation stymied Parliament's abilities, the prorogation was annulled: 'it was as if the Commissioners had walked into Parliament with a blank sheet of paper'.[48] Of course, it would be foolish to assert that constitutional principle is a newcomer to the tale of the prerogative: even our brief overview of history belies that. Yet its emergence as an *explicit* ground of judicial control demonstrates that, even three and a half centuries on from 1689, the prerogative continues to raise questions of the distribution of power between the Crown and Parliament. The tale of that tug-of-war is *both* legal *and* political.

[43] *R (Miller) v Secretary of State for Exiting the European Union* [2017] UKSC 5, [51].
[44] ibid at [80]-[82].
[45] P Craig, 'Epilogue: *Miller*, the Legislature and the Executive' in S Juss and M Sunkin (eds), *Landmark Cases in Public Law* (Oxford, Hart Publishing, 2017), 311.
[46] A Twomey, '*Miller* and the Prerogative' in M Elliott, J Williams and A Young, *The UK Constitution After Miller: Brexit and Beyond* (Oxford, Hart Publishing, 2017), 85-6.
[47] *R (Miller) v The Prime Minister; Cherry v Advocate General* [2019] UKSC 41, [50].
[48] ibid at [69].

What is the Prerogative?

The result of these centuries of history is a prerogative that – while still providing potent powers in a limited number of areas – is part of the common law, that must give way to parliamentary statute, that cannot exceed the bounds put upon it by law, and that is seemingly ever dwindling in scope.

Is the prerogative, then, merely a 'relic of a past age' (Lord Reid) or a 'residue of discretionary or arbitrary authority' (Dicey)?[49] There are two ways to answer this question. The first is the technical: what is a prerogative power in law? The second is more substantive: is the prerogative something *more* than a relic? In this book, we are primarily concerned with the latter of these two questions. However, it would be imprudent not to attempt some answer to the first before beginning upon our central enterprise.

As a preliminary observation, Dicey's description (quoted more fully in the epigraph to this chapter) 'does not take us very far',[50] because it does not help positively to define the prerogative. Although it has found some judicial support,[51] its breadth encompasses powers that are not usually considered to be 'prerogatives', such as the powers to make contracts or to convey land. In short, it is better at telling us what the prerogative is *not* than what it *is*. A narrower definition was adopted by William Wade: '"Prerogative" power is, properly speaking, *legal* power that appertains to the Crown but not to its subjects.'[52]

There are two elements to this definition. First, drawing on William Blackstone,[53] Wade attributes 'prerogative' power uniquely to the Crown. For him, the prerogative does not include, for example, setting up a trust to distribute money to the victims of crime.[54] Second, it must be a '*legal* power' capable of altering people's rights, duties and status. This definition leaves space for a third sort of executive power, beyond statute and the prerogative, sometimes called the Crown's 'administrative powers'.[55] These powers are 'a necessary and incidental part of the ordinary business of central government'.[56] However, the definition does exclude some powers that have often been classed as prerogatives (and some of which appear in this book). For example, the granting of passports is not a legal power

[49] *Burmah Oil Co*, above n 4 at 101.

[50] ibid at 99 (Lord Reid); *Council of Civil Service Unions*, above n 36 at 416 (Lord Diplock).

[51] *De Keyser*, above n 33 at 526; *Council of Civil Service Unions*, above n 36 at 398 (Lord Fraser); *Privacy International v Secretary of State for Foreign and Commonwealth Affairs* [2021] EWCA Civ 330, [80].

[52] HWR Wade and C Forsyth, *Administrative Law*, 4th edn (Oxford, Oxford University Press, 2004), 216.

[53] W Blackstone, *Commentaries on the Laws of England*, vol 1 (London, S Sweet, 1836), 239.

[54] See *R v Panel on Take-overs and Mergers, ex parte Datafin plc* [1987] QB 815, 848 (Lloyd LJ), approving Wade's analysis of *R v Criminal Injuries Compensation Board, ex parte Lain* [1967] 2 QB 864.

[55] A Perry, 'The Crown's Administrative Powers' (2015) 131 *Law Quarterly Review* 652.

[56] *Shrewsbury and Atcham BC v Secretary of State for Communities and Local Government* [2008] EWCA Civ 148, [49]; *cf R (New College London) v Secretary of State for the Home Department* [2013] UKSC 51, [28].

but an administrative one (see chapter eleven)[57] and anyone may set up an inquiry (see chapter fourteen).[58]

In this book, we are primarily concerned with the legal and political questions of how the prerogative has and should (or should not) be made subject to scrutiny and oversight by Parliament, the courts and others. For those purposes, the important thing to note is the tension between these two definitions: Dicey is too expansive; Wade perhaps narrower than expected. As a result of its origin in the murky world of political power, 'the prerogative' does not have clean edges.

Conclusion

We wish to make two final observations, both relating to the dangers of overviews such as in this chapter. The first is about the use of history. Judges in constitutional cases, and authors writing chapters such as this, seek to draw a thread of connection from Bracton to the present day. There is, of course, a great benefit from taking the long view. Our institutions and practices have not arisen overnight but over the course of a long history. However, there is a risk of entering 'into a world of apples and oranges', that 'the very process of narrative [history] adjusts the concept in the telling'.[59] Judges are not unaware of that risk.[60] The greatest element of that risk is that we stop asking the substantial political questions of what the scope and potency of the prerogative should be in our time. To some extent, that requires an historical examination of principles previously established. For example, Bracton's lengthy explanation of the monarch's voluntary subjugation to law is unpalatable in modern Britain: 'the proposition that the executive obey the law as a matter of grace and not as a matter of necessity [is] a proposition which would reverse the result of the Civil War'.[61] Yet it is also a matter of political decision-making and constitution-forming in the present day. This book is a (small) contribution to that process.

That brings us to our second observation. This is about the nature of historical sketches. An historical overview, including this one, is a sketch of developments. Its focus is change. What is often overlooked in that sketch is the space between the pencilled lines – the constant background without which there is no picture. There are important, continuing reasons for the preservation of many prerogative powers. To return to Endicott's imagery, in the epigraph to this chapter, we should not be misled into thinking that the evolution of the prerogative is a matter of trying to remove a 'stubborn stain'. However, the context in which those powers

[57] *cf* HWR Wade, *Constitutional Fundamentals* (London, Stevens, 1980), 51.

[58] Although designation as a 'public' inquiry may require ministerial sanction.

[59] R Gordon, '*Entick v Carrington* [1765] Revisited: All the King's Horse' in Juss and Sunkin, above n 45 at 6.

[60] See *Rahmatullah (No. 2) v Ministry of Defence and another* [2017] UKSC 1, [15].

[61] *M v Home Office* [1994] 1 AC 377, 395 (Lord Templeman).

are held and are exercised changes over time and the reasons for their preservation must continually be revisited. Such a revisitation can be seen in cases like *Miller 1*, where the majority recognised that the prerogative was *not* 'anomalous or anachronistic' and that 'There are important areas of governmental activity which, today as in the past, are essential to the effective operation of the state and which are not covered, or at least not completely covered, by statute.'[62] However, they also thought that, in the rather unique circumstances of withdrawal from the European Union, the prerogative could not be used to make 'such a far-reaching change to the UK constitutional arrangements'.[63] That returns us to the aim of this book: to set out where we are with the prerogative, how we got here, and where we might be going.

[62] *Miller* [2017], above n 43 at [49].
[63] ibid at [80]-[81].

3

Recent Political Developments

> We want a balance of rights, rules and entitlements ... After Brexit we also need to look at the broader aspects of our constitution: the relationship between the Government, Parliament and the courts; the functioning of the Royal Prerogative ...
>
> Conservative Party (2019)[1]

Introduction

Although the royal prerogative featured on the agenda of some constitutional reformers in the last two decades of the twentieth century, including campaigning organisations like Charter 88 and academics like Rodney Brazier (see chapter one), it was not until the twenty-first century that these reform proposals gained any traction. But in the first two decades of the new century, the prerogative powers finally made it onto the parliamentary and political agenda.

These political developments can be divided into five phases. In the first phase, the House of Commons Public Administration Select Committee (PASC) developed a clear agenda for reform of the prerogative, particularly in relation to the war-making power, the ratification of treaties, and the regulation of the civil service.

In the second phase, the Brown government published bold plans in 2007 for statutory codification of the prerogative, but in the event succeeded in putting on a statutory footing only the powers in relation to treaties and the civil service.

The third phase, with the formation of the Conservative-Liberal Democrat coalition in 2010, saw codification of the personal prerogatives of the Sovereign, not in statute but in the Cabinet Manual.

In the fourth phase, the parliamentary battles over Brexit from 2016–19 stress tested dramatically the prerogative powers over treaties, royal assent to legislation and prorogation of Parliament, with significant court challenges adding to the parliamentary fray.

[1] Conservative Party, *Get Brexit Done: Unleash Britain's Potential* (2019), 48.

The fifth phase is still unfolding, with the Johnson government formed in 2019 seeking to curb the jurisdiction of the courts to review prerogative powers, and to restore the prerogative power of dissolution in place of the Fixed-term Parliaments Act 2011.

Phase 1: PASC Sets the Agenda

The House of Commons Public Administration Select Committee (PASC), chaired by Tony Wright, developed an enviable reputation for not just scrutinising the policies of the executive, but for proposing its own policy initiatives. It had already conducted searching inquiries into the patronage state,[2] and the need for a Civil Service Act.[3] In 2004 it widened these out into a sustained campaign to reform the prerogative, launched in its report *Taming the Prerogative: Strengthening Ministerial Accountability to Parliament.*[4]

The report considered the prerogative powers exercised by ministers, not those of the Sovereign. After recording the main prerogative powers in the hands of the executive, it recognised that – though they are necessary for effective administration, especially in times of national emergency – they should be subject to more systematic parliamentary oversight. The committee concluded that the case for reform was unanswerable. It recommended legislation to require the government to list the prerogative powers exercised by ministers. The list would then be considered by a parliamentary committee, and legislation framed to put in place statutory safeguards where necessary.

A paper and draft Bill appended to the report, prepared by specialist adviser to the inquiry Professor Rodney Brazier, contained these provisions. It also set out proposals for early legislative action in the case of three specific prerogative powers: armed conflict, treaties and passports. The report concluded by recommending that the government should, before the end of the parliamentary session, initiate a public consultation exercise on the prerogative powers of ministers. The government's response rejected this approach:

> It is often possible to make out a case for either the transfer of prerogative powers to a statutory basis, or for an increase in the level of non-statutory parliamentary scrutiny … These changes are best made on a case-by-case basis, as circumstances change. It does not therefore agree with the recommendation for a wide-ranging consultation exercise.[5]

[2] Fourth Report from the House of Commons Public Administration Select Committee, *Government by Appointment: Opening up the Patronage State* HC 165 (2002–03).

[3] First Report from the House of Commons Public Administration Select Committee, *A Draft Civil Service Bill: Completing the Reform* HC 128-I (2003–04).

[4] Fourth Report from the House of Commons Public Administration Select Committee, *Taming the Prerogative: Strengthening Ministerial Accountability to Parliament* HC 422 (2003–04).

[5] Department for Constitutional Affairs, *Government response to the Public Administration Select Committee's Fourth Report of Session 2003–04: Taming the Prerogative: Strengthening Ministerial Accountability to Parliament* (Cm 6187, 2004).

Meanwhile in the House of Lords, Lord Lester of Herne Hill mounted a similar campaign through parliamentary questions asking ministers to list the prerogative powers, and Private Member's Bills to reform them. In 2004, he introduced an Executive Powers and Civil Service Bill, and in 2006 a Constitutional Reform (Prerogative Powers and Civil Service etc) Bill, both with similar provisions. Neither Bill proceeded beyond second reading, but they served to keep up the pressure; as did the further report from PASC in March 2007 which contained a chapter on a Civil Service Bill.[6] But just three months later, the campaign finally bore fruit when Gordon Brown became Prime Minister with a pent-up zeal for constitutional reform.

Phase 2: The Brown Government – Big Plans, Lesser Delivery

Unlike most of his Cabinet colleagues (including Tony Blair), Gordon Brown had a longstanding interest and commitment to constitutional reform, which he had to keep suppressed during his ten years as Chancellor of the Exchequer.[7] But when he became Prime Minister in June 2007, his interest came bursting out. Brown's first Cabinet meeting was devoted to a three hour discussion of constitutional reform and within a week he had published an ambitious agenda in the Green Paper *The Governance of Britain*.[8] This had been prepared in draft in the months following Tony Blair's announcement of his retirement, and extended even to a British Bill of Rights and a written constitution.[9]

The Green Paper set out plans for wide-reaching constitutional reforms, stating that 'in general the prerogative powers should be put on a statutory basis'.[10] In particular, the government outlined plans to reform ten powers, declaring:

> The Government will seek to surrender or limit powers which it considers should not, in a modern democracy, be exercised exclusively by the executive … These include powers to:
>
> - deploy troops abroad;
> - request the dissolution of Parliament;
> - request the recall of Parliament;
> - ratify international treaties without decision by Parliament;

[6] Third Report from the House of Commons Public Administration Select Committee, *Politics and Administration: Ministers and Civil Servants* HC 122 (2006–07).

[7] With one exception: his speech to Charter 88 delivered 12 weeks after New Labour's election victory. See G Brown, 'Speech to Charter 88' (Charter 88, London, 12 July 1997).

[8] Ministry of Justice, *The Governance of Britain* (Cm 7170, 2007).

[9] ibid at paras 204–212; The main architect of the proposals was Michael Wills. See G Brown, My *Life, Our Times* (London, Vintage, 2018), ch 10; In 2009, Brown told the House of Commons 'I personally favour a written constitution': *Hansard*, HC Deb Vol 493, col 798 (10 June 2009).

[10] Ministry of Justice, above n 8 at para 24.

- determine the rules governing entitlement to passports and for the granting of pardons;
- restrict parliamentary oversight of the intelligence services;
- choose bishops;
- have a say in the appointment of judges;
- direct prosecutors in individual criminal cases; and
- establish the rules governing the Civil Service.[11]

The Green Paper then went on to explain why the government was proposing to limit its powers:

> The flow of power from the people to government should be balanced by the ability of Parliament to hold government to account. However, when the executive relies on the powers of the royal prerogative – powers where government acts upon the Monarch's authority – it is difficult for Parliament to scrutinise and challenge government's actions …
>
> It is important that the key decisions that affect the whole country – such as the decision to send troops into armed conflict – are made in the right way, and with Parliament's consent. The same is true of treaties that the UK makes with its partners in Europe and across the world … In a modern 21st century parliamentary democracy, the Government considers that basing these powers on the prerogative is out of date. It will therefore seek to limit its own power by placing the most important of these prerogative powers onto a more formal footing, conferring power on Parliament to determine how they are exercised in future.[12]

Included in the Green Paper was the announcement that the government would undertake a wider review of the prerogative powers held by ministers. This led to the publication of a White Paper and draft Bill in March 2008.[13] The draft Bill addressed some areas of the prerogative, restricting the powers of the Attorney General, placing the civil service on a statutory basis, and formalising in statute the parliamentary procedure for scrutinising treaties. On war powers, the White Paper proposed a House of Commons resolution setting out the processes Parliament should follow in order to approve military action, and appended a detailed draft resolution. On passports, the government said that it intended to remove the prerogative power and instead introduce comprehensive legislation regulating the issue of passports. For the remainder, the government reported that it was conducting an internal scoping exercise of the executive prerogative powers, and would launch a consultation in due course.

The draft Bill and White Paper were scrutinised by a parliamentary Joint Committee under the chairmanship of Michael Jabez Foster. PASC also published a report on the White Paper.[14] The Joint Committee welcomed the wider review of

[11] ibid at 6.

[12] ibid at paras 15 and 17.

[13] On the role of the Attorney General, see Ministry of Justice, above n 8 at paras 32–98.

[14] Tenth Report from the House of Commons Public Administration Select Committee, *Constitutional Renewal: Draft Bill and White Paper* HC 499 (2007–08).

prerogative powers but observed that matters like the issue of passports were not included in the draft Bill, and commented that 'Ideally, reform of the prerogative should be approached in a coherent manner, not in a piecemeal fashion.'[15]

In October 2009, the government finally published the review of prerogative powers first promised two years earlier in the *Governance of Britain* Green Paper.[16] It was the product of an exhaustive survey conducted over six months across 64 government departments and agencies, and resulted in a comprehensive list of all the prerogative powers, ancient and modern, set out in a detailed list at the end of the report. The body of the report was devoted to explaining why, despite the government's initial intention of codifying all the prerogative powers, in practice that was not feasible or desirable. In some cases, such as the conduct of diplomacy or regulation of the armed forces, statutory and prerogative powers were so intertwined that it was impossible to disentangle them.[17] In others, such as emergency powers, largely covered by the Civil Contingencies Act 2004, it was desirable to keep the prerogative for extreme emergencies where immediate action was required before emergency regulations could be made. And, although major inquiries would be held under the Inquiries Act 2005, inquiries convened under the prerogative had the advantage of being cheaper and quicker, and more suitable for localised or smaller inquiries, or those where all parties were willing to co-operate.

Although further action was promised on war powers, passports, and the dissolution and recall of Parliament, the review concluded:

> The changes now in train will deal with the most serious concerns about the remaining manifestations of the executive prerogative powers. The Government has concluded that it is unnecessary, and would be inappropriate, to propose further major reform at present. Our constitution has developed organically over many centuries and change should not be proposed for change's sake. Without ruling out further changes aimed at increasing Parliamentary oversight of the prerogative powers exercised by Ministers, the Government believes that any further reforms in this area should be considered on a case-by-case basis, in the light of changing circumstances.[18]

On war powers, the review reaffirmed the government's promise to introduce a detailed House of Commons resolution.[19] Passports were to be the subject of comprehensive legislation, but this was unlikely to be introduced before the next Parliament.[20] And, on dissolution, the review proposed that the Prime Minister

[15] *Report from the Joint Committee on the Draft Constitutional Renewal Bill* HL 166-I HC 551-I (2007–08), para 254.

[16] Ministry of Justice, *The Governance of Britain: Review of the Executive Royal Prerogative Powers: Final Report* (2009).

[17] To give one example, the Defence Council is appointed by the Queen under the prerogative, and by Letters Patent given responsibility for the command of the armed forces. But it also has statutory responsibilities, for example deployment of the armed forces within the UK in an emergency. For details, see ibid at para 51.

[18] ibid at para 112.

[19] ibid at para 37.

[20] ibid at para 38.

should be required to seek the approval of the House of Commons before asking the monarch for a dissolution; on recall, that the Speaker should be able to recall the House on receiving a request from over half the MPs.[21]

Other prerogative powers were to be regulated by legislation in the Constitutional Reform and Governance Bill which had been introduced in July 2009. Like the Draft Constitutional Renewal Bill of 2008, it included provisions to formalise the procedure for Parliament to scrutinise treaties prior to ratification, place the civil service Commissioners onto a statutory footing, and enshrine in statute the core values of the civil service. The proposed reforms to the role of the Attorney General were dropped because they could be achieved without legislation; but the 2009 Bill included provisions to phase out the hereditary peers from the House of Lords and make it possible for its members to resign or be disqualified, expelled or suspended. Late in the Bill's passage through the Commons, the government added clauses on a referendum on the voting system used for parliamentary elections; substantial amendments to the Parliamentary Standards Act 2009; new provisions concerning the tax status of MPs and members of the House of Lords; and amendments to the Public Records Act 1958 and the Freedom of Information Act 2000.

Time was running out by the time the Bill reached the House of Lords in March 2010, because the Parliament had only weeks left to run. The House of Lords Constitution Committee were fiercely critical of the long delays, first between publication of the draft Bill in March 2008 and the Bill itself in July 2009, and then of the Bill's passage through the Commons because of the government piling on amendments.[22] This allowed very little time for proper scrutiny. As the committee anticipated, the Bill had not completed all its stages by the time Gordon Brown asked the Queen for a dissolution on 6 April. The wash-up proceedings in the Lords went into the small hours of the next day, with then Lord Chancellor Jack Straw, from the steps of the Throne, having to make immediate decisions on what to leave out to get the Bill through. The Bill was severely stripped down to gain consent to its passage, leaving only Part 1 (on the regulation of the civil service), and Part 2 (on parliamentary scrutiny of treaties) when the Constitutional Reform and Governance Act 2010 (CRAG) was finally enacted.

Thus it was that Gordon Brown's bold plans in *The Governance of Britain* for comprehensive reform of the prerogative ended in a whimper. The war powers resolution, legislation on passports, restricting the Prime Minister's powers over the dissolution and recall of Parliament, and reforming the office of the Attorney General – all had been abandoned. To be fair, after the financial crisis of 2008 Brown's main political energies had been elsewhere; the minister charged with delivering the reforms, the Justice Secretary Jack Straw, had other distractions; and no ministers shared Brown's enthusiasm. The MPs' expenses scandal in 2008, and

[21] ibid at para 39.

[22] Eleventh Report from the House of Lords Constitution Committee, *Report on Constitutional Reform and Governance Bill* HL 98 (2009–10), paras 38–47.

Brown's creation in 2009 of a Democratic Renewal Council (in reality a glorified Cabinet committee) provided the opportunity for renewed focus and impetus. But as successive parliamentary committees commented, the reforms continued to be ad hoc and piecemeal with no strategic plan or set of guiding constitutional principles;[23] and as time went on, the reforms became more and more of a ragbag, as evidenced in the miscellaneous provisions of the Constitutional Reform and Governance Bill.

Phase 3: The Cabinet Manual and the Fixed-term Parliaments Act 2011

The next phase in codification of the royal prerogative had a very different genesis, in which the UCL Constitution Unit played a part. It began in the dying days of the Brown government. In 2009 the Unit had embarked on a comparative study of governing in a hung Parliament, focusing on the lessons to be learned from minority and coalition governments in Australia, Canada, New Zealand and Scotland.[24] The Unit's report warned of the risks from the mystery surrounding the monarch's prerogative powers of dissolving Parliament and appointing a Prime Minister, and emphasised the need for a clear and published set of rules.[25] The report pointed to the Cabinet Manual of New Zealand as a model to follow, and copies of the New Zealand Manual were sent with the Unit's report to the Cabinet Secretary and the Palace.[26]

There was no time before the 2010 election to produce a full version of the Cabinet Manual, but on 26 February the Cabinet Office published a draft of the key chapter on elections and government formation,[27] which was then the subject of a quick inquiry by the House of Commons Justice Committee.[28] The sections on the principles of government formation and hung Parliaments codified the conventions governing the Queen's exercise of her prerogative powers, previously known only to a few constitutional lawyers and senior civil servants. When the May 2010 election delivered a hung Parliament, the draft chapter proved invaluable in helping explain to politicians and the media that the Queen had no discretion but would appoint as Prime Minister the person most likely to be able to command the

[23] Eleventh Report from the House of Commons Justice Committee, *Constitutional Reform and Renewal* HC 923 (2008–09), paras 86–92.

[24] R Hazell and A Paun (eds), *Making Minority Government Work: Hung Parliaments and the Challenges for Westminster and Whitehall* (London, Constitution Unit, 2009).

[25] ibid at paras 6.3.1–6.3.5.

[26] New Zealand Cabinet Office, *Cabinet Manual*, 6th edn (2017).

[27] Cabinet Office, *Chapter 6: Elections and Government Formation (DRAFT)* (February 2010).

[28] Fifth Report from the House of Commons Justice Committee, *Constitutional processes following a general election* HC 396 (2009–10).

confidence of Parliament, once the political parties had concluded their negotiations and determined who that person was.[29]

There were three key principles which the Cabinet Manual helped to explain:

- the continuity principle, that after the election the incumbent Prime Minister is expected to remain in office until it is clear who can command confidence in the new Parliament;
- the caretaker principle, that the previous government must not take decisions or initiate policies which might tie the hands of a new government; and
- the confidence principle, that a Prime Minister who cannot command the confidence of Parliament is required by convention to resign, or request a dissolution.

These conventions had been poorly understood, and still proved contentious even when set out in the draft chapter of the Cabinet Manual. The Cabinet Office proceeded cautiously in drafting the full Cabinet Manual, working with a small group of constitutional experts to publish a full draft for public consultation in December 2010. The draft Manual was stated to be 'lore, not law': a 'guide to the laws, conventions, and rules on the operation of government',[30] with chapters on the Sovereign, elections and government formation, the executive, collective Cabinet decision-making, ministers and Parliament, the law, the civil service, relations with the devolved administrations and the European Union (EU), government finance and official information.

The main purpose of the consultation was to ensure that the Manual reflected an agreed position on important constitutional conventions, including those governing the prerogative. Three parliamentary committees scrutinised the draft, approaching it with varying degrees of suspicion. One concern related to the ownership and status of the document: on this the government was clear, it was *by* the executive, *for* the executive, and did not require endorsement from Parliament, let alone joint ownership.[31] Another related to how the Manual should record conventions which were disputed: for example, experts could not agree on whether the incumbent Prime Minister had a duty to remain in office until it was clear who could command confidence in his place, or was merely expected to do so.[32] A third related to omissions from the Manual, such as military action;

[29] G O'Donnell, 'Cabinet Secretary Speech on the Cabinet Manual' (Constitution Unit, London, 26 February 2011) assets.publishing.service.gov.uk/government/uploads/system/uploads/attachment_data/file/60644/speech-cabinet-manual-24feb2011.pdf.

[30] G O'Donnell, 'Foreword' in Cabinet Office, *The Cabinet Manual – Draft* (December 2010).

[31] Twelfth Report from the House of Lords Constitution Committee, *The Cabinet Manual* HL 107 (2010–11), para 39; Cabinet Office, *Government Response to the House of Lords Constitution Committee, Political and Constitutional Reform Committee and Public Administration Select Committee on the Cabinet Manual and Committee Reports of Session 2010–12* (Cm 8213, 2011).

[32] House of Lords Constitution Committee, ibid at para 59.

whether there was a convention requiring the prior approval of Parliament was also the subject of dispute (see chapter seven).

After careful consideration of all of the responses to the consultation, from the public as well as the parliamentary committees, the Cabinet Office published the final version of the Cabinet Manual in October 2011.[33] Chapter one, on the Sovereign, contains only one short paragraph on the royal prerogative, which does not mention the Sovereign's reserve powers; but there is a detailed section on the operation of the Privy Council, which approves legislation made under the prerogative.[34] Changes had been made to chapter two, on elections and government formation, to take account of the Fixed-term Parliaments Act 2011 (FTPA), and to soften the wording about certain conventions which were contested. Chapter three, on the executive, contains six paragraphs about the royal prerogative, explaining the distinction between the personal or constitutional prerogatives of the Sovereign and the executive prerogative powers exercised by ministers, as well as the role of the courts in determining the existence and extent of the prerogative.[35]

Publication of the final version of the Cabinet Manual was delayed to take account of the FTPA, enacted in September 2011. The Act introduced five-year fixed terms, and on dissolution went further than Gordon Brown had proposed (see pages 25–26): it abolished the prerogative power of dissolution, transferring power to call an early election from the executive to Parliament. It was introduced in part to strengthen the Conservative-Liberal Democrat Coalition by removing from the Prime Minister the power to cut and run. But it is a myth that the FTPA came into being simply for that reason. The proposal had been made for decades previously in several Private Members' Bills, before appearing in the 2010 Labour and Liberal Democrat election manifestos.[36] The Conservative Party meanwhile had included a more general pledge in 2010 to make 'the use of the Royal Prerogative subject to greater democratic control so that Parliament is properly involved in all big national decisions'.

When introducing the Fixed-term Parliaments Bill, ministers emphasised three explicit objectives:

- to limit the power of the executive, which was too dominant in relation to the legislature;
- to remove the right of a Prime Minister to choose the date of the next election for partisan advantage; and
- to increase certainty, and end debilitating speculation about the date of the next election.[37]

[33] Cabinet Office, *The Cabinet Manual*, 1st edn (2011).
[34] ibid at paras 1.10–19.
[35] ibid at paras 3.33–38.
[36] R Hazell, *Fixed Term Parliaments* (London, Constitution Unit, 2010), 22–5.
[37] *Hansard*, HC Deb Vol 515, col 621 (13 September 2010) (Nick Clegg)

The Conservative Party manifesto of 2015 celebrated the first objective as an achievement of the FTPA, stating that 'We also passed the Fixed-Term Parliaments Act, an unprecedented transfer of Executive power.'[38] But after the difficulties of persuading the 2017–19 Parliament to vote for early dissolution, the Conservatives changed their minds and their 2019 manifesto contained a commitment to repeal the FTPA and restore the prerogative power of dissolution (discussed further below).

Phase 4: The Brexit Battleground

The difficulties in obtaining an early dissolution were not the only constitutional wrangle resulting from Brexit, which shone a fierce spotlight on several different aspects of the prerogative. Obscure powers which had been of interest only to a small band of constitutional experts suddenly became the talk of parliamentarians and writers of newspaper editorials. Could Parliament have a meaningful say over the EU Withdrawal Treaty? Could the Queen be advised by ministers to withhold royal assent from legislation passed against the government's wishes? Could Boris Johnson prorogue Parliament to prevent scrutiny of his Brexit plans? Could he find a way round the FTPA to dissolve Parliament and hold a general election?

All these episodes illustrate different aspects of the prerogative. The first, the power to sign and ratify treaties, had been codified in Part 2 of the Constitutional Reform and Governance Act 2010 (CRAG), which put on a statutory footing the convention that treaties should be laid before Parliament for 21 days before they could be ratified. Treaty making in itself remained a prerogative power, but was henceforth subject to parliamentary approval. Yet, CRAG was silent about the process of unmaking a treaty, which was the first stage of Brexit. The Prime Minister Theresa May proposed to trigger Article 50 of the Treaty on European Union, giving formal notice to the EU of the UK's departure without reference to Parliament. This was the subject of Gina Miller's first court challenge before the Supreme Court, which ruled that notice of withdrawal did require parliamentary approval by legislation because withdrawal from the EU treaties was such a fundamental change to the UK's constitutional arrangements.[39] How much say Parliament could subsequently have in scrutinising and approving the EU Withdrawal Treaty was later the subject of much procedural wrangling in the House of Commons, with a plethora of EU (Withdrawal) Acts enacted before Parliament eventually passed the EU (Future Relationship) Act in a single day on 30 December 2020.

[38] Conservative Party, *Strong Leadership. A Clear Economic Plan. A Brighter, More Secure Future* (2015).

[39] *R (Miller) v Secretary of State for Exiting the European Union* [2017] UKSC 5.

Two of those EU (Withdrawal) Acts illustrate a second aspect of the prerogative, in the grant of royal assent to legislation. The EU (Withdrawal) Act 2019 (the Cooper-Letwin Act) and the EU (Withdrawal) (No 2) Act 2019 (the Benn Act), were both passed against the wishes of Theresa May's minority government. Opponents of the government's rushed approach to Brexit had succeeded in seizing control of the Commons agenda to pass legislation requiring the government to seek an extension of the timetable.[40] This was accompanied by fevered speculation as to whether the government might advise the Queen to withhold royal assent in order to prevent these unwelcome Bills from becoming law. We do not know whether the government considered giving such advice, nor what would have happened if it had. In the event, royal assent was granted: in the case of the Benn Act on 9 September 2019, the last day before Parliament stood prorogued for five weeks until 14 October.

Prorogation is the third aspect of the prerogative which came into play during the Brexit saga. Prorogation normally happens at the end of the parliamentary year to bring that session to an end. It had generally been exercised without any controversy. That changed dramatically when, in August 2019, the new Prime Minister Boris Johnson advised the Queen to prorogue Parliament for five weeks, leading to accusations that he was closing down Parliament in order to avoid scrutiny of his Brexit plans. Gina Miller's second court challenge led the Supreme Court to declare not merely that the advice to prorogue for such a lengthy period was unlawful, but that the prorogation order itself was null and void.[41] Parliament resumed sitting on the day after the court judgment, and the subsequent prorogation to end the session in October was for a more normal period of just three sitting days.

The dissolution of Parliament also became very controversial during the Brexit process. The prerogative power of dissolution had been abolished by the FTPA, which transferred responsibility for dissolving Parliament from the executive to the legislature. The Act allowed a mid-term dissolution following a successful no confidence motion, or if the House of Commons voted for early dissolution by a two thirds majority. Frustrated by the endless procedural shenanigans over Brexit, Boris Johnson sought three times to persuade the House of Commons to vote for early dissolution, on 4 September, 9 September and 28 October 2019, but on each occasion failed to reach the necessary two thirds majority. Eventually Parliament was dissolved by the government introducing separate legislation, the Early Parliamentary General Election Act 2019, which provided that the next election would be held on 12 December. In the ensuing election, the Conservatives won a landslide majority of 80 seats.

[40] T Fleming, 'Parliamentary Procedure under Theresa May: Nothing has Changed?' (2021) 74 *Parliamentary Affairs* 943, 948–9.

[41] *R (Miller) v The Prime Minister; Cherry v Advocate General* [2019] UKSC 41.

Phase 5: The Executive Fights Back

The Conservative Party's 2019 election manifesto has to be read in the light of the Brexit saga, and the Party's determination to remove or reduce the institutional and procedural obstacles to Brexit. Under the heading 'We will protect our democracy', page 48 of the manifesto contained the following analysis:

> The failure of Parliament to deliver Brexit – the way so many MPs have devoted themselves to thwarting the democratic decision of the British people in the 2016 referendum – has opened up a destabilising and potentially extremely damaging rift between politicians and people. If the Brexit chaos continues … they will lose faith even further …
>
> We want a balance of rights, rules and entitlements … After Brexit we also need to look at the broader aspects of our constitution: the relationship between the Government, Parliament and the courts; the functioning of the Royal Prerogative; the role of the House of Lords; and access to justice for ordinary people.[42]

And, in terms of specific commitments, the manifesto promised:

> We will get rid of the Fixed Term Parliaments Act – it has led to paralysis at a time the country needed decisive action … We will update the Human Rights Act and administrative law to ensure that there is a proper balance between the rights of individuals, our vital national security and effective government. We will ensure that judicial review is available to protect the rights of the individuals against an overbearing state, while ensuring that it is not abused to conduct politics by another means or to create needless delays. In our first year we will set up a Constitution, Democracy & Rights Commission that will examine these issues in depth, and come up with proposals to restore trust in our institutions and in how our democracy operates.[43]

Although the language in the manifesto was couched in seemingly neutral terms, most commentators understood the re-balancing called for to be in favour of the executive, after the difficulties caused by Parliament and the courts. Writing before she was appointed as Attorney General, Suella Braverman explained why 'we must take back control, not just from the EU, but from the judiciary':

> Traditionally, Parliament made the law and judges applied it. But today, our courts exercise a form of political power. Questions that fell hitherto exclusively within the prerogative of elected Ministers have yielded to judicial activism: foreign policy, conduct of our armed forces abroad, application of international treaties and, of course, the decision to prorogue Parliament …
>
> The political has been captured by the legal. Decisions of an executive, legislative and democratic nature have been assumed by our courts. Prorogation and the triggering of Article 50 were merely the latest examples of a chronic and steady encroachment by the judges.[44]

[42] Conservative Party, above n 1 at 48.

[43] ibid.

[44] S Braverman, 'People we elect must take back control from people we don't. Who include the judges', (*ConservativeHome*, 27 January 2020) www.conservativehome.com/platform/2020/01/suella-braverman-people-we-elect-must-take-back-control-from-people-we-dont-who-include-the-judges.html.

Ministers were equally contemptuous of Parliament. Delivering the keynote speech to the Conservative Party conference, Boris Johnson said:

> There is one part of the British system that seems to be on the blink. If Parliament were a laptop, then the screen would be showing the pizza wheel of doom. If Parliament were a school, Ofsted would be shutting it down.[45]

In government it fell initially to Michael Gove, Chancellor of the Duchy of Lancaster and Minister for the Cabinet Office, to deliver on the Conservative manifesto commitments, supported by the Lord Chancellor Robert Buckland on the legal aspects. The promised Constitution, Democracy and Rights Commission, which might have looked at the relationship between government, Parliament and the courts, and the functioning of the royal prerogative was quietly abandoned.[46] Instead, the government initiated discrete reviews of different aspects. The first, the Independent Review of Administrative Law (IRAL), chaired by former government minister, Lord Faulks, must have disappointed the government, concluding that it would be a mistake to codify judicial review or to limit by statute the grounds on which judicial review was available.[47] The subsequent Judicial Review and Courts Bill 2021 did not attempt to restrict judicial review, but introduced minor procedural changes which if anything might slightly increase judicial power.[48] The second review, chaired by former Court of Appeal judge Sir Peter Gross, was initiated in December 2020 to look at whether the Human Rights Act 1998 strikes the right balance between the courts, government and Parliament.[49] Before the review had reported, the new Lord Chancellor Dominic Raab promised to overhaul the 1998 Act and end 'the licence given to courts to adopt through judicial legislation ever more elastic interpretation of rights'.[50]

One of the issues to be examined in these reviews was whether any powers of the executive, including prerogative powers, should be non-justiciable. IRAL's terms of reference expressly invited the panel to 'focus its consideration

[45] R Mason, 'Boris Johnson's speech to the Tory party conference' *The Guardian* (2 October 2019).

[46] R Buckland, *Oral evidence to the House of Commons Public Administration and Constitutional Affairs Committee* HC 829 (8 December 2020), QQ 119–20.

[47] *Report from the Independent Review of Administrative Law* (CP 407, 2021); E Faulks, 'Parliament has the right to reverse judicial decisions, but governments must be careful not to undermine the important role the courts play as a check and balance in our constitution' (*Constitution Unit Blog*, 27 August 2021) www.constitution-unit.com/2021/08/27/the-judicial-review-and-courts-bill-must-not-undermine-the-important-role-the-courts-play-as-one-of-the-checks-and-balance-that-exist-in-our-unwritten-constitution/.

[48] T Hickman, 'Quashing Orders and the Judicial Review and Courts Act' (*UK Constitutional Law Association Blog*, 26 July 2021) www.ukconstitutionallaw.org/2021/07/26/tom-hickman-qc-quashing-orders-and-the-judicial-review-and-courts-act/; J Varuhas, 'Remedial Reform Part 1: Rationale' (*UK Constitutional Law Association Blog*, 3 November 2021) www.ukconstitutionallaw.org/2021/11/03/jason-varuhas-remedial-reform-part-1-rationale; J Varuhas, 'Remedies Reform Part 2: Discretionary Factors' (*UK Constitutional Law Association Blog*, 9 November 2021) www.ukconstitutionallaw.org/2021/11/09/jason-varuhas-remedies-reform-part-2-discretionary-factors/.

[49] *Hansard*, HC cWS (7 December 2020) (Robert Buckland).

[50] J Rozenberg, 'Things can only get better: Dominic Raab struggles to say the right thing' (*A Lawyer Writes*, 8 October 2021) www.rozenberg.substack.com/p/things-can-only-get-better.

of justiciability … to the prerogative executive powers'.[51] But the overwhelming majority of submissions from outside government were opposed to legislation on the issue of non-justiciability, and the panel concluded that questions of justiciability should properly be left to the courts.[52]

Much of the government's language around these reviews appeared to be political rhetoric, without any clear or specific outcome in mind other than to cut the courts down to size. By contrast, the manifesto commitment to repeal the FTPA was quite specific. But if some had assumed that a one-line repeal Bill was sufficient, the Draft Fixed-term Parliaments Act 2011 (Repeal) Bill published in December 2020 showed that it was not so easy to turn the clock back. The government wished to restore the prerogative power of dissolution and return to the Prime Minister the decision over the timing of the next election. But the evidence received by the parliamentary Joint Committee to review the FTPA raised a host of objections and uncertainties: was the restored power of dissolution now a statutory power; was it right to transfer the power back to the executive; could the Queen still refuse an untimely request?

As described in chapter five, the Joint Committee was strongly critical of the Draft Fixed-term Parliaments Act 2011 (Repeal) Bill and accompanying Dissolution Principles.[53] But the only concessions the government made were to acknowledge that the Prime Minister can only request, rather than advise dissolution and to change the title of the Bill. The ensuing Dissolution and Calling of Parliament Bill had its second reading in July 2021, and passed its remaining Commons stages in a single day in September. The government remained determined to revive the prerogative power of dissolution with as few fetters as possible: its declared purpose was to 'enable governments … to call a general election at the time of their choosing',[54] with no need for a vote in Parliament, and any risk of challenge in the courts excluded by a sweeping ouster clause. In vain did commentators and PACAC argue that a vote in Parliament was the best protection against court challenge, and avoiding the monarch being dragged into political controversy.[55] The only check remains the right of the monarch to refuse an untimely request. But that would be quite exceptional, and would generate a major constitutional crisis if it ever happened.

[51] Independent Review of Administrative Law, *Terms of Reference* (2020), para D www.assets.publishing.service.gov.uk/media/5f27d3128fa8f57ac14f693e/independent-review-of-administrative-law-tor.pdf.

[52] Independent Review of Administrative Law, above n 47 at paras 2.58 and 2.70–78.

[53] *First Report from the Joint Committee on Fixed-Term Parliaments Act* HC 1046 HL 253 (2019–21).

[54] Explanatory Notes to the Dissolution and Calling of Parliament Bill HL (2021–22) 51, para 3.

[55] Letter from William Wragg to Chloe Smith (21 July 2021), 7; M Russell, G Phillipson and P Schleiter, 'The Dissolution and Calling of Parliament Bill: Why the House of Commons should retain control over dissolution' (*Constitution Unit Blog*, 8 September 2021) www.constitution-unit.com/2021/09/08/the-dissolution-and-calling-of-parliament-bill-why-the-house-of-commons-should-retain-control-over-dissolution/.

Conclusion: Reforms Wax and Wane

Anyone reading the first three parts of this chapter might reasonably assume that reform of the prerogative was going in only one direction, with an incremental programme of closer regulation through statutory control by Parliament and soft law codification. First came the civil service, put on a statutory footing; then parliamentary approval of treaties; then abolition of the prerogative power of dissolution; and codification of the monarch's personal prerogatives in the Cabinet Manual. Parliamentary control of war powers seemed to be on a similar trajectory, with the Brown government's bold plans for a House of Commons resolution, and equally bold declarations by experts that prior parliamentary approval was a new constitutional convention after the parliamentary votes on Iraq in 2003, Libya in 2011 and Syria in 2013.[56]

But then the pendulum stalled, and began to swing backwards. Despite report after report from different parliamentary committees (see chapter seven) recommending codification of the war powers convention, at least in a House of Commons resolution, successive governments failed to act. And then, in April 2018, Theresa May appeared to repudiate the convention, in not allowing even a retrospective vote in Parliament following her decision over bombing in Syria. The earlier votes to approve military action seemed in retrospect to be a high-water mark of parliamentary involvement, from which the executive was now rowing back.

So it was also with the Johnson government's plans to repeal the FTPA, and restore the prerogative power of dissolution. Although Lord Justice Diplock famously stated of the courts, 'It is 350 years and a civil war too late for the Queen's courts to broaden the prerogative',[57] the Dissolution and Calling of Parliament Act 2022 has re-created a prerogative power once thought to have been abolished. Codification of the prerogative does not all run one way.

[56] G Phillipson, '"Historic" Commons' Syria vote: the constitutional significance (Part I)' (*UK Constitutional Law Association Blog*, 19 September 2013) www.ukconstitutionallaw.org/2013/09/19/gavin-phillipson-historic-commons-syria-vote-the-constitutional-significance-part-i/. See also G Phillipson, '"Historic" Commons' Syria vote: the constitutional significance (Part II – the way forward)' (*UK Constitutional Law Association Blog*, 29 November 2013) www.ukconstitutionallaw.org/2013/11/29/gavin-phillipson-historic-commons-syria-vote-the-constitutional-significance-part-ii-the-way-forward/; G Phillipson, 'Voting on Military Action in Syria: A Reply' (*UK Constitutional Law Association Blog*, 2 December 2015) www.ukconstitutionallaw.org/2015/12/02/gavin-phillipson-voting-on-military-action-in-syria-a-reply/.

[57] *BBC v Johns* [1965] Ch 32, 79.

PART 2

The Monarch's Personal Prerogatives

4

Appointing and Dismissing Ministers

> The office of Prime Minister exists by virtue of the royal prerogative. The Sovereign could lawfully appoint anyone to be Prime Minister, but is guided by constitutional conventions when making a choice.
>
> Rodney Brazier (2020)[1]

The Personal Prerogatives of the Monarch

Part two of this book is about the personal prerogatives of the monarch, known variously as her reserve powers, constitutional powers, or the personal prerogatives (a term first coined by Sir Ivor Jennings).[2] These powers are distinct from the prerogative powers exercised by ministers, considered in part three. The most important constitutional powers of the monarch are:

- to appoint and dismiss ministers, in particular the Prime Minister;
- to summon, prorogue and dissolve Parliament; and
- to give royal assent to bills passed by Parliament.

This chapter is about the appointment and dismissal of ministers. The power to summon and dissolve Parliament is considered in chapter five, and royal assent to legislation in chapter six. In addition, the monarch has certain other discretionary powers, for example in relation to those honours bestowed in her personal gift, considered in chapter thirteen.

The monarch's reserve powers have been defined by Anne Twomey as 'the discretionary powers of the head of state that may be used to uphold and maintain the fundamental constitutional principles of the system of government'.[3] As she goes on to explain, the reserve powers are fundamental to maintaining not merely constitutional principles, but the system of government itself. They are essential

[1] R Brazier, *Choosing a Prime Minister: The Transfer of Power in Britain* (Oxford, Oxford University Press, 2020), 167.

[2] I Jennings, *Cabinet Government* (Cambridge, Cambridge University Press, 1959), 394.

[3] A Twomey, *The Veiled Sceptre: Reserve Powers of Heads of State in Westminster Systems* (Cambridge, Cambridge University Press, 2018), 1.

to the operation of Parliament, providing for its summoning and dissolution, and the promulgation of its laws. They are also essential to the operation of the executive, providing for the appointment and replacement of the Prime Minister. These tend to be regarded as formalities because they are governed by longstanding conventions. But formally they remain discretionary, and the monarch remains the ultimate guardian of the constitution. The monarch therefore retains the formal power to dismiss the Prime Minister, to deny a request for dissolution or prorogation, or to withhold royal assent. Whether these powers might ever need to be exercised, and in what circumstances, will be discussed in the chapters which follow.

For Twomey, the mere existence of the reserve powers, however remote the possibility of their exercise, acts as a constraint on political actors. And for her it does not matter that people struggle to define when they might be used: the uncertainty is part of their mystique and their potency. Hence the title of her book, *The Veiled Sceptre*:

> The uncertainty regarding the scope and application of the reserve powers might be regarded as important to their effectiveness. If it is accepted … that the reserve powers are most effective when they are not formally used, but the prospect of their use causes constitutional actors to moderate their behaviour, then the doubt as to the extent of their potential operation may be beneficial. It is in this context that the reserve powers may be envisaged as a veiled sceptre …[4]

Appointment of the Prime Minister: Remnants of Discretion

Appointment of the Prime Minister is done in person, in an audience with the Queen. In July 2019, the Queen delayed going to Balmoral for her summer holiday so that when Boris Johnson was elected as the new Conservative Party leader, he could be appointed Prime Minister at an audience in Buckingham Palace. He succeeded Theresa May as the head of a minority government in circumstances where the government was struggling to maintain the confidence of the House of Commons.

The Queen has no formal adviser when it comes to appointing a new Prime Minister. Because hung Parliaments have been relatively rare, there is no tradition (unlike in states such as Belgium, or the Netherlands) of appointing an *informateur* or *formateur* to guide her choice. The outgoing Prime Minister is occasionally consulted, but his or her advice is not binding. The Queen is bound by a strong convention that she will appoint that person who holds, or is most likely to hold, the confidence of the House of Commons. So, in practice she has little or no

[4] ibid at 43.

discretion: it is the members of the House of Commons that determine who will be Prime Minister, and the Queen who formally appoints that person.

The power to appoint a Prime Minister used to retain a discretionary element, but that is now gone. King George V persuaded a reluctant Ramsay MacDonald not to resign in 1931 when his Labour government broke up, but to head a national government dominated by the Conservatives. A small discretionary element remained in the case of a mid-term change of Prime Minister in the days when Conservative Party leaders were anointed rather than elected. In those circumstances, the monarch took advice from the outgoing Prime Minister and party grandees to ascertain who would command the confidence of the parliamentary party, and hence of the House of Commons. The last occasions upon which this occurred were in 1955, 1957 and 1963, as related below.

When Sir Winston Churchill resigned as Prime Minister in 1955, he stated that he observed the constitutional proprieties by not recommending a successor, although there was no real competitor other than Sir Anthony Eden.[5] However, when Eden in turn resigned in 1957, he recommended Rab Butler as the best person to succeed him.[6] The Queen sought informal advice from Lord Salisbury and Winston Churchill. Lord Salisbury and Lord Kilmuir interviewed the Cabinet and other senior Conservative figures, and reported that the Party preferred Harold Macmillan, who was then appointed.[7] When Macmillan resigned in 1963, Rab Butler was the favourite to succeed him amongst several contenders; but Macmillan advised the Queen from his hospital bed to appoint Lord Home. Given the differences within the Conservative Party, Home was initially invited to see if he could form a government. When only two Cabinet colleagues refused to serve under him, he confirmed that he could, and the next day was appointed Prime Minister.[8] The choice of Home over Butler was controversial, and the magic circle of old Etonians who engineered it were heavily criticised by Iain Macleod in a famous article in *The Spectator*.[9]

1963 was the last occasion when the Queen had to choose a new leader for the Conservative Party. The parliamentary Labour Party had always elected its leader, and stung by the 'magic circle' criticism, the Conservatives introduced election of the leader by the parliamentary party in 1965. In a series of further steps, the Conservative and Labour parties have since extended voting rights to all party members. The Labour Party introduced three electoral colleges in 1981 (for the trade unions, constituency parties, and party members), and then 'one member, one vote' in 2014. Voting rights were extended also to 'registered supporters', and to stand for election an MP had to obtain the written support of at least 10 per cent

[5] B Pimlott, *The Queen: Elizabeth II and the Monarchy* (London, Harper Collins, 2001), 232.
[6] ibid at 259.
[7] ibid at 260.
[8] Brazier, above n 1 at 92–4.
[9] I Macleod, 'The Tory Leadership' *The Spectator* (London, 17 January 1964), 65–6.

of the parliamentary Labour Party, increased to 20 per cent by the party conference in 2021. In 1998, the Conservative Party introduced a postal ballot of all party members (who must have been paid members for three months), after an initial selection of two candidates by the parliamentary party.[10]

Extending voting rights to the whole party membership means that leadership elections take much longer than when the leader was chosen simply by the parliamentary party. The consequence is that when a Prime Minister decides to resign mid-term, they must remain in office for several weeks while the party elects a new leader, and it becomes clear who can command the confidence of Parliament in their place. When Theresa May announced her intention to resign on 23 May 2019, she officially resigned as Conservative leader on 7 June, but continued as Prime Minister for a further five weeks until Boris Johnson had won the ensuing Conservative Party leadership election and was appointed Prime Minister on 14 July.

If the Queen is out of the UK when a new Prime Minister might need to be appointed, she must return as Counsellors of State are not able to exercise powers that involve royal discretion.[11] This occurred in February 1974. When Edward Heath called a snap election while the Queen was on tour in New Zealand, she had to fly back from Australia in order to be present to appoint the new Prime Minister. It was not immediately obvious who should be appointed, with no party winning an overall majority. Labour won fewer votes than the Conservatives, but more seats (301 to the Conservatives' 297), and the Liberals held the balance with 14 seats. Over the weekend, the Conservative Prime Minister Edward Heath tried to do a deal with the Liberal leader Jeremy Thorpe. When that failed, he offered his resignation to the Queen, who appointed the Labour leader Harold Wilson to be Prime Minister as head of a minority government.[12]

Codification in the Cabinet Manual

The key constitutional convention, stated in all the constitutional law textbooks, is that the Queen will appoint as Prime Minister the person who is most likely to command the confidence of the House of Commons. When a party wins an overall majority in a general election, the result is clear and the Queen appoints the party's leader as Prime Minister. But the textbooks were less clear on how the Queen is to identify who is most likely to command confidence in a hung Parliament where no party has an overall majority. To fill that gap, in the run up to the 2010

[10] Brazier, above n 1 at 89–103.

[11] The Regency Act 1937, s 6(1) specifies only the award of peerages as a function that may not be delegated, but additional restrictions are specified in Letters Patent appointing the Counsellors of State. The Buckingham Palace website states that the following duties cannot be undertaken by Counsellors of State: Commonwealth matters; the dissolving of Parliament, except on the Queen's express instruction; the creation of peers; and appointing a Prime Minister. See Buckingham Palace, 'Counsellors of State' (*The Royal Family*) www.royal.uk/counsellors-state.

[12] The events are described in detail in Robert Armstrong's note for the record: 'Events leading to the resignation of Mr Heath's administration 4 March 1974' TNA PREM 16/231.

election, when a hung Parliament was expected, the Cabinet Secretary published guidance in the form of an advance chapter of a wider Cabinet Manual.[13] The guidance made it clear that it was for the political parties first to negotiate to determine who could command confidence in the event of a hung Parliament, and the Queen would then appoint that person. A full draft of the Cabinet Manual was published after the election, and after minor revision following scrutiny by three parliamentary committees, the first edition of the Cabinet Manual was published in October 2011.[14] It follows quite closely the Cabinet Manual of New Zealand, which is now in its sixth edition.[15]

Chapter two of the Cabinet Manual, on elections and government formation, codifies the constitutional conventions about the appointment of the Prime Minister. The key paragraphs about a hung Parliament are as follows:

> **Parliaments with no overall majority in the House of Commons**
>
> 2.12 Where an election does not result in an overall majority for a single party, the incumbent government remains in office unless and until the Prime Minister tenders his or her resignation and the Government's resignation to the Sovereign. An incumbent government is entitled to wait until the new Parliament has met to see if it can command the confidence of the House of Commons, but is expected to resign if it becomes clear that it is unlikely to be able to command that confidence and there is a clear alternative.
>
> 2.13 Where a range of different administrations could potentially be formed, political parties may wish to hold discussions to establish who is best able to command the confidence of the House of Commons and should form the next government. The Sovereign would not expect to become involved in any negotiations, although there are responsibilities on those involved in the process to keep the Palace informed …[16]

The Cabinet Manual goes on to describe what happens if the Prime Minister resigns mid-term, stating that it is for the party or parties in government to identify who can be chosen as the successor.[17] So, the monarch is left with no discretion in any circumstances in which she may be required to appoint a Prime Minister, whether post-election or mid-term. Indeed, the Cabinet Manual makes clear that the whole purpose is to remove any residual discretion:

> In modern times the convention has been that the Sovereign should not be drawn into party politics, and if there is doubt it is the responsibility of those involved in the political process, and in particular the parties represented in Parliament, to seek to determine and communicate clearly to the Sovereign who is best placed to be able to command the confidence of the House of Commons.[18]

[13] Cabinet Office, *Chapter 6: Elections and Government Formation (DRAFT)* (2010).
[14] Cabinet Office, *The Cabinet Manual – Draft* (2010); Cabinet Office, *The Cabinet Manual*, 1st edn (2011).
[15] New Zealand Cabinet Office, *Cabinet Manual*, 6th edn (2017).
[16] Cabinet Office, *The Cabinet Manual*, above n 14 at paras 2.12–2.13.
[17] ibid at para 2.18.
[18] ibid at para 2.9.

In 2010, the draft chapter of the Cabinet Manual worked well in helping explain to politicians, the media and the public that the incumbent government remained in office until it was clear who could command confidence in the new Parliament; that it was for the political parties to establish who was best able to command confidence; and then to communicate that information to the Sovereign. During the 'five days in May', the Queen distanced herself from the negotiations by announcing she would spend the weekend at Windsor while the parties negotiated in London.[19] But not all the media understood the need to allow the political parties time to negotiate. Two days after the election, *The Sun* newspaper splashed the headline 'Squatter holed up in No 10' to put pressure on Gordon Brown to resign when the negotiations had only just got under way.[20] And not all the public accepted the outcome. Amongst voters so used to single party majority government, it became a familiar refrain to hear people say 'but no one voted for a coalition'.

One further reform could help to clarify for everyone how the Prime Minister is chosen when there is a hung Parliament and help voters to understand the two-stage process of government formation in a parliamentary system: first voters elect MPs, and then the House of Commons determines who should form the government. The reform would be to hold a vote on the floor of the House of Commons as the first piece of business after an election, to determine who commands the confidence of the newly elected House. This is the practice followed in Scotland and Wales, and would help more clearly to distance the monarch from the political process. In Scotland and Wales, the Parliament must within 28 days of an election nominate one of its members as First Minister, and the Presiding Officer then recommends the appointment of that person to the Queen.[21] Such a reform has been advocated by the Institute for Government and the House of Commons Political and Constitutional Reform Committee, as well as the Constitution Unit.[22] But it has not yet found favour at Westminster, with the House of Lords Constitution Committee advising against its recommendation:

> We do not recommend the creation of an investiture vote for a Prime Minister after an election. It would result in our system of government becoming more presidential and would be a step away from the principle that the Government as a whole should command the confidence of the House of Commons.[23]

[19] R Wilson, *Five Days to Power: The Journey to Coalition Britain* (London, Biteback, 2010).

[20] T Newton-Dunn, 'Squatter Holed up in No 10' *The Sun* (London, 8 May 2010).

[21] Scotland Act 1998, s 46; Government of Wales Act 2006, s 47.

[22] Tenth Report from the House of Commons Political and Constitutional Reform Committee, *Government formation post-election* HC 1023 (2014–15), paras 62–3; Institute for Government, *Written evidence to the House of Commons Political and Constitutional Reform Committee* HC 1023 GFE0003 (16 February 2015), para 16; R Hazell, *Written evidence to House of Commons Political and Constitutional Reform Committee* HC1023 GFE0004 (16 February 2015), paras 10–2; P Schleiter, V Belu and R Hazell, *Forming a government in the event of a hung parliament: The UK's recognition rules in comparative context* (London, Constitution Unit, 2016). See also M Taylor, 'Parliamentary Confirmation of Ministerial Nominations' (*UK Constitutional Law Association Blog*, 11 March 2021) www.ukconstitutionallaw.org/2021/03/11/max-taylor-parliamentary-confirmation-of-ministerial-nominations/.

[23] Fifth Report from the House of Lords Constitution Committee, *Constitutional implications of coalition government* HL 130 (2013–14), para 52.

Death or Incapacity of the Prime Minister

One lacuna in the Cabinet Manual is what should happen in the case of the death or sudden incapacity of the Prime Minister. There would be no time to wait for a couple of months while the governing party went through the process of electing a new leader. But equally there would be no wish to go back to what happened in 1957 and 1963, with the Queen making a decision based on secret soundings, that was in effect binding on the Conservative Party as to who should be its leader. Three Cabinet Secretaries (Sir Robert Armstrong, Sir Robin Butler and Sir Andrew Turnbull) thought hard about this after the attempt to assassinate Margaret Thatcher in the Brighton bombing of 1984, and then the IRA mortar attack on Downing Street in 1991. They concluded that the Queen would need to appoint an interim Prime Minister, pending the election of a new party leader. And the person appointed should be a senior figure who was not a contender to be party leader. But how should the Queen identify such a figure? Philip Norton concluded that the Queen's Private Secretary could take soundings, but it would be better if the Cabinet were asked to advise the Queen what to do.[24]

Similar concerns arose when Boris Johnson was infected with Covid-19 and admitted into intensive care in April 2020. He had asked his First Secretary of State Dominic Raab to lead the government in his absence. But what if he had failed to recover?[25] There is no presumption that Raab would necessarily have succeeded him as Prime Minister. He might have continued in temporary charge of the government until a new party leader was elected; but if he was himself a candidate for the succession, another senior Cabinet minister would have had to take temporary charge. Rodney Brazier has codified the rules on choosing a new Prime Minister into a detailed draft code covering every eventuality, including the PM's death or sudden incapacity.[26] In this case, Brazier explains that the Cabinet would have had to decide on a caretaker Prime Minister and advise the Queen accordingly.

The Appointment and Dismissal of Other Ministers

The monarch's appointment and dismissal of other ministers is made on the advice of the Prime Minister. The days are gone when the monarch had an influence on the composition of the government. Queen Victoria was able to express strong preferences, and veto certain appointments; but during her long reign the scope

[24] P Norton 'A Temporary Occupant of No.10? Prime ministerial succession in the event of the death of the incumbent' [2016] *Public Law* 18, 18–34.

[25] R Hazell, 'What happens when the Prime Minister is incapacitated?' (*Constitution Unit Blog*, 9 April 2020) www.constitution-unit.com/2020/04/09/what-happens-when-the-prime-minister-is-incapacitated/.

[26] Brazier, above n 1 at 167–76.

of the prerogative shrank dramatically. With the extension of the franchise and rise of political parties, the power of Parliament grew and the monarch's powers of patronage and discretion were correspondingly diminished. Her successors were markedly less interventionist. The last recorded case of a monarch influencing a Prime Minister's selection of his Cabinet colleagues was King George VI persuading Clement Attlee to appoint Ernest Bevin rather than Hugh Dalton as Foreign Secretary in 1945. But it remains uncertain how significant the King's advice was; the King's earlier attempt to warn Winston Churchill against appointing Lord Beaverbrook to be Minister of Aircraft Production in 1940 had gone unheeded.[27]

The monarch's remaining involvement in the appointment process is ceremonial, presiding at meetings of the Privy Council when new Secretaries of State are sworn in, and giving them their seals of office. The Cabinet Manual explains the protocol as follows:

> 3.18 Senior ministers are required to take oaths of office under the Promissory Oaths Act 1868 and all Cabinet members are made Privy Counsellors.
>
> 3.19 Secretaries of state and some other ministers (for example, the Lord Privy Seal) also receive seals of office. Their appointments take effect by the delivery of those seals by the Sovereign … Appointments of other ministers generally take effect from when the Sovereign accepts the Prime Minister's recommendation of the appointment.

All this can and has been done virtually during the Covid-19 pandemic, as have the Queen's other meetings and audiences. In cases of scandal or controversy, the Prime Minister has the final decision whether a minister should be dismissed, as 'the ultimate judge of the standards of behaviour expected of a Minister' under the Ministerial Code;[28] in practice, a minister is usually persuaded to resign rather than face dismissal. The Prime Minister can now seek advice from the Independent Adviser on Ministers' Interests, a new role created in 2006.[29] The Independent Adviser can only act upon the request of the Prime Minister. In 2021, the Committee on Standards in Public Life recommended that the Adviser be put on a statutory basis, with power to initiate his own investigations, and to determine whether the Code had been breached.[30] In 2020, Sir Alex Allan had resigned as Independent Adviser when the Prime Minister decided that the Home Secretary Priti Patel had not breached the Ministerial Code, after Sir Alex found that she had through her bullying behaviour.[31] In 2022 his successor Lord Geidt resigned in frustration at the Prime Minister's lack of support for his role.

[27] A Seldon, *The Impossible Office? The History of the British Prime Minister* (Cambridge, Cambridge University Press, 2021), 242.

[28] Cabinet Office, *Ministerial Code* (2019), para 1.6.

[29] H Armstrong and C Rhodes, *The Ministerial Code and the Independent Adviser on Ministers' Interests* (House of Commons Library Briefing Paper 03750, August 2021).

[30] Committee on Standards in Public Life, *Upholding Standards in Public Life* (November 2021), ch 3.

[31] Armstrong and Rhodes, above n 29 at 32–4.

The Dismissal of Ministers

The last time a Prime Minister was dismissed by the monarch was in 1834, when King William IV dismissed Lord Melbourne and installed a Tory government led by Sir Robert Peel. It was not a happy precedent: in 1835, the King had to re-appoint Melbourne in order to reflect the Whig majority in the House of Commons. The Cabinet Manual records, 'Historically, the Sovereign has made use of reserve powers to dismiss a Prime Minister or to make a personal choice of successor, although this was last used in 1834 and was regarded as having undermined the Sovereign.'[32]

Few would maintain that the power might be exercised today, save as a deep reserve power.[33] It is a reserve power, in that it can be exercised without advice: as happened when the Australian Governor General Sir John Kerr dismissed Gough Whitlam in 1975 after he had failed to achieve supply, and failed to request a dissolution. That proved deeply controversial at the time, and ever since; but no one questioned that formally the Governor General had the power to dismiss the Prime Minister.[34] Denial of a dissolution can also amount effectively to dismissal, as happened with the King-Byng affair in Canada in 1926.[35]

In evidence to the House of Lords Constitution Committee in 2011, the former Cabinet Secretary Lord Armstrong said:

> I believe that the Sovereign also retains the power to dismiss a Prime Minister, but it is difficult to envisage circumstances in which it might be exercised. It seems to me that it could be exercised only if there were compelling and generally accepted reasons for exercising it: if (for instance) a Prime Minister was generally recognised to be acting with persistent and dangerous irrationality or with deliberate and persistent disregard of constitutional conventions and was refusing to resign, and then only after consultations with other senior political figures.[36]

Lord Armstrong added, 'The very existence of the power should serve to ensure that it never needs to be exercised.'[37] That reflects Anne Twomey's concept of the veiled sceptre, that the mere existence of reserve powers should act as a constraint on political actors.[38] But in the febrile parliamentary endgame over Brexit, with

[32] Cabinet Office, *The Cabinet Manual*, above n 14 at 14.

[33] Robert Blackburn, in an article aimed at restricting any discretionary use of the monarch's personal prerogatives, suggested that 'A monarch is duty bound to reject prime ministerial advice, and dismiss the Prime Minister from office, when the Prime Minister is acting in manifest breach of convention.' The example he gave was if a Prime Minister, after a successful no confidence motion, refused to resign or call a general election: R Blackburn, 'Monarchy and the Personal Prerogatives' [2004] *Public Law* 546, 551.

[34] J Kerr, *Matters for Judgement: An Autobiography* (London, Macmillan, 1978); P Kelly and T Bramston, *The Dismissal: In the Queen's Name* (Melbourne, Viking, 2015).

[35] Twomey, above n 3 at 388–402.

[36] R Armstrong, *Supplementary memorandum to the House of Lords Constitution Committee* HL 107 DCM1 (8 February 2011).

[37] ibid.

[38] Twomey, above n 3.

Boris Johnson desperate to obtain a dissolution to break the deadlock but also facing the risk of a formal no confidence motion, *The Sunday Times* had the histrionic headline on 6 October 2019, '"Sack me if you dare", Boris Johnson will tell the Queen.' The story quoted an unnamed senior Cabinet minister as saying, 'Our opponents have flouted convention and there is nothing in the Fixed-term Parliaments Act that says you have to resign. The Queen is not going to fire the prime minister. She would dissolve parliament and let the people decide.'[39]

That reflected a serious misunderstanding of the Fixed-term Parliaments Act 2011, which had removed the Queen's power to dissolve Parliament and transferred the power of dissolution to the House of Commons (see chapter five). But, if Boris Johnson had been defeated on a formal no confidence motion, and it was clear that an alternative Prime Minister could command confidence, but Johnson refused to resign, then the Queen would have had to dismiss him. In practice, it would not have come to that. Despite his bluster, when faced with the veiled sceptre, Johnson would have had no option but to resign.

Conclusion

The appointment and dismissal of ministers remains formally one of the reserve powers of the monarch. Over the last century, any remaining discretion in the hands of the monarch has disappeared. The last time the monarch exercised any personal choice in the appointment of the Prime Minister was when King George V pressured Ramsay MacDonald to remain in office in 1931. No one supposes Queen Elizabeth II was exercising any personal choice when she appointed Macmillan as Prime Minister in 1957, or Douglas-Home in 1963. She was acting on the advice of the party elders, and soon after that, when the Conservatives followed the other parties in introducing a system for electing their leader, there was no need any longer to consult the elders. But when a Prime Minister resigns mid-term, there is need to allow several weeks for the governing party to elect a successor who will then become the new Prime Minister.

The conventions guiding the monarch's choice of a Prime Minister remained opaque until published in the draft Cabinet Manual in 2010. That made it clear that the monarch must appoint the person who is best able to command the confidence of the House of Commons. In a hung Parliament, it is for the parties to negotiate and determine who is best able to command confidence and so form a government, and then to communicate that information to the monarch. One further reform which would further distance the monarch from the political process could be to hold an investiture vote as the first piece of business in a newly elected House of Commons, as in Scotland and Wales; but that has not yet found favour at Westminster.

[39] T Shipman and C Wheeler, '"Sack me if you dare," Boris Johnson will tell the Queen' *The Sunday Times* (London, 6 October 2019).

5

Summoning, Dissolving and Proroguing Parliament

The constitutional history of this country is the history of the prerogative powers of the Crown being made subject to the overriding powers of the democratically elected legislature as the sovereign body.

Lord Browne-Wilkinson (1995)[1]

Introduction

Historically, the monarch has controlled the sittings of the legislature through the prerogative power to summon, dissolve, and prorogue Parliament. Dissolution brings a Parliament to an end, leading to a general election. The summons is made by proclamation commanding the newly elected Parliament to convene on an appointed day. Prorogation brings a parliamentary session to an end, and normally lasts less than a week before the new parliamentary session begins, with the new legislative programme announced in the Queen's Speech. A session normally lasts a year. By contrast, adjournment is decided by Parliament itself with a motion for the adjournment at the end of each day in the House of Commons, and with motions deciding the Christmas, Easter, Whitsun, summer and autumn recesses which punctuate the parliamentary calendar. Recall during the recess is decided not by Parliament, but by the government asking the Speaker.

The prerogative powers are essential to the operation of Parliament: if Parliament is dissolved or prorogued, it cannot function. This enabled the Stuarts to rule without Parliament for prolonged periods. King Charles I managed 11 years of personal rule from 1629–40; King Charles II ruled without Parliament from 1679–85; and King James II continuously prorogued the Parliament elected in 1685 for more than a year and a half until he dissolved it in 1687. The Bill of

[1] *R v Secretary of State for the Home Department, ex parte Fire Brigades Union* [1995] UKHL 3, 552.

Rights 1689 sought to remedy this by calling for frequent Parliaments, as well as the better-known claims of free elections and freedom of speech in Parliament:

> And that for Redresse of all Grievances and for the amending strengthening and preserveing of the Lawes Parlyaments ought to be held frequently.[2]

Since that time, the prerogative power has become constrained by convention, by legislation, and most recently, by the courts. The main legislative changes have been to control the length of Parliaments, with the Triennial Act 1694 introducing three-year Parliaments, extended to seven years by the Septennial Act 1715, and then reduced to five years by the Parliament Act 1911. The power of dissolution, which had been governed by convention, was changed fundamentally by the Fixed-term Parliaments Act 2011 (FTPA), which transferred the power from the executive to Parliament. But the Johnson government elected in 2019 was committed to repeal the FTPA and revive the prerogative power. The fundamental question underlying debates about the power of dissolution and of prorogation is about the balance of power and the respective roles of executive and legislature. Is it right for the executive to control the sittings of Parliament, or should Parliament decide for itself when it should sit, and for how long?

Dissolution of Parliament

Before the FTPA: The Prerogative Power of Dissolution

Under the Septennial Act 1715, as amended by the Parliament Act 1911, a Parliament was dissolved after a maximum of five years from the date of its first meeting. In practice, the Prime Minister normally requested a dissolution from the monarch before that date. This being a reserve power, the monarch was not obliged to grant a dissolution. The draft Cabinet Manual published in December 2010 summarised the pre-FTPA understanding of the conventions governing the reserve power as follows:

> A Prime Minister may request that the Monarch dissolves Parliament so that an election takes place. The Monarch is not bound to accept such a request, although in practice it would only be in very limited circumstances that consideration is likely to be given to the exercise of the reserve power to refuse it, including when such a request is made very soon after a previous dissolution. In those circumstances, the Monarch would normally wish to know before granting dissolution that those involved in the political process had ascertained that there was no potential government that would be likely to command the confidence of the House of Commons.[3]

[2] Bill of Rights 1689, art 13.
[3] Cabinet Office, *The Cabinet Manual – Draft* (2010), para 58.

So far as we know, in the UK no request for dissolution has been refused in modern times. But after the Labour government saw its majority slashed to just five seats in the 1950 election, there was speculation whether its leader Clement Attlee might properly seek a second election. This prompted Sir Alan Lascelles, Private Secretary to King George VI, to write a letter to *The Times* (under the pseudonym Senex) explaining that the monarch might justifiably refuse dissolution in three circumstances:

> Sir, It is surely indisputable (and common sense) that a Prime Minister may ask – not demand – that his Sovereign will grant him a dissolution of Parliament; and that the Sovereign, if he so chooses, may refuse to grant this request. The problem of such a choice is entirely personal to the Sovereign, though he is, of course, free to seek informal advice from anybody whom he thinks fit to consult.
>
> In so far as this matter can be publicly discussed, it can be properly assumed that no wise Sovereign – that is, one who has at heart the true interest of the country, the constitution, and the Monarchy – would deny a dissolution to his Prime Minister unless he were satisfied that: (1) the existing Parliament was still vital, viable, and capable of doing its job; (2) a General Election would be detrimental to the national economy; (3) he could rely on finding another Prime Minister who could carry on his Government, for a reasonable period, with a working majority in the House of Commons. When Sir Patrick Duncan refused a dissolution to his Prime Minister in South Africa in 1939, all these conditions were satisfied: when Lord Byng did the same in Canada in 1926, they appeared to be, but in the event the third proved illusory.[4]

Sir Patrick Duncan had first consulted with the South African Minister of Justice, Jan Smuts, before refusing a dissolution to Prime Minister Hertzog, thus satisfying condition three. Lord Byng had similarly consulted the leader of the opposition, Arthur Meighen, before refusing a dissolution to the Canadian Prime Minister, Mackenzie King, but the reassurance that Meighen could rely on support from the Agricultural Party proved ill founded. Lascelles had followed these events closely, commenting on them and seeking advice from a wide range of constitutional experts, and was eventually moved to write to *The Times* because he was 'so fed up with the vapouring of Lord Simon and Lord Chorley'.[5]

Until 1918, Prime Ministers consulted the Cabinet before seeking a dissolution; thereafter, they decided alone. The Prime Minister would choose a date which seemed most opportune to their chances of re-election. In modern times, that would often be after the Parliament had run for four years (Margaret Thatcher in 1983 and 1987, and Tony Blair in 2001 and 2005). But if their poll ratings did not look good, they would sometimes allow the Parliament to run for five years

[4] A Lascelles, 'Dissolution of Parliament: Factors in Crown's Choice' *The Times* (London, 2 May 1950).

[5] 'I was so fed up with the vapouring of Lord Simon and Lord Chorley and the way they obscure what … is a fairly plain and simple issue (The Crown and a Dissolution), that I took up my pen and did a thing which I hope won't make Lord Stamfordham turn in his grave – I wrote to the Times newspaper': Letter from Alan Lascelles to Michael Adeane (3 May 1950) Royal Archives PS/PSO/GVI/C/320/37.

hoping for something to turn up; it seldom did (John Major in 1997, and Gordon Brown in 2010).

An involuntary dissolution and election could also occur if the government lost a vote of confidence in the House of Commons. The most recent example was in March 1979 when an Opposition motion of no confidence in the Callaghan government was carried with a majority of one.[6] The result led to James Callaghan requesting an immediate dissolution, and the victory of Margaret Thatcher in the following general election.

The Prerogative Power is Called into Question

From the 1990s onwards, the unfairness of allowing the incumbent Prime Minister to choose the timing of the next election was increasingly called into question, with proposals for fixed terms, or for allowing Parliament to vote on dissolution. Gordon Brown's 2007 Green Paper *The Governance of Britain* (see chapter three) included a proposal that the Prime Minister should have to seek the approval of the House of Commons before asking the monarch to dissolve Parliament. After consultation, any change would be announced to Parliament and would become through precedent, a new convention.[7] The House of Commons Modernisation Committee subsequently initiated an inquiry into the dissolution and recall of Parliament, which received submissions but did not hold evidence sessions or issue a report. Like so many of Brown's initiatives to reform the prerogative, this one ran into the sand.[8]

Meanwhile, fixed-term Parliaments were gaining greater currency. It was a prominent pledge for Labour in 1992, and fixed-term Parliaments featured in the Liberal Democrat manifesto for 1992 and 1997. Three Private Member's Bills were introduced, by Tony Banks in 1992, Jeff Rooker in 1994, and David Howarth in 2007, but all without success.

Fixed terms were being successfully introduced elsewhere in the Westminster world.[9] All the state Parliaments in Australia except Tasmania have introduced fixed terms, starting with New South Wales in 1995, the latest being Queensland, which legislated to do so in 2015. In Canada all the provincial legislatures except Nova Scotia have also introduced fixed terms, starting with British Columbia in 2001, and the most recent being Quebec in 2013. The federal Parliament in

[6] *Hansard*, HC Deb Vol 965, cols 461–590 (28 March 1979); This episode was dramatised in J Graham 'This House' (2012).

[7] Ministry of Justice, *The Governance of Britain* (Cm 7170, 2007), paras 34–36.

[8] House of Commons Modernisation Committee, 'Press Notice' (11 October 2007); For further details of the government's proposal, see *Memorandum from the Leader of the House of Commons* (M58) (February 2008).

[9] R Hazell, *Written evidence to the Joint Committee on the Fixed-Term Parliaments Act* HC 1046 HL 253 FTP0013 (January 2021).

Ottawa also introduced fixed-term legislation in 2007. Closer to home, the Labour government had introduced fixed terms for the devolved legislatures in Scotland, Wales and Northern Ireland in the devolution legislation passed in 1998.

The arguments for fixed terms were the same around the Westminster world: that allowing the incumbent government to decide the timing of elections was unfair; it gave the executive too much power over Parliament; fixed terms enabled better civil service planning and long-term thinking; they were better also for political parties, for electoral administrators, and for regulating election spending.[10] In the 2010 election, the arguments returned to Westminster, with both the Liberal Democrats and Labour renewing pledges to introduce fixed-term Parliaments. The Conservatives did not make this specific commitment, but had a more general pledge 'to make the Royal Prerogative subject to greater democratic control so that Parliament is directly involved'.[11]

The Fixed-term Parliaments Act 2011

When a Conservative-Liberal Democrat coalition was formed after the 2010 election, fixed-term Parliaments became one of the main items in their programme for government. A government Bill was swiftly introduced, with ministers emphasising three explicit objectives:

- to limit the power of the executive, which was too dominant in relation to the legislature;
- to remove the right of a Prime Minister to choose the date of the next election for partisan advantage; and
- to increase certainty, and end debilitating speculation about the date of the next election.[12]

But the coalition government's haste allowed no time for public consultation or debate: there was no Green or White Paper, and no pre-legislative scrutiny. This haste was criticised at the time, and subsequently.[13] The Bill was heavily criticised during its passage in the House of Lords and, to fend off a sunset clause, the government inserted a last-minute amendment providing for a full review of the legislation in 2020.

The Fixed-term Parliaments Act 2011 transferred the power of dissolution from the executive to Parliament, and in so doing abolished the prerogative power.

[10] For an eloquent account of the advantages of fixed-term legislation, see A Twomey, *Oral evidence to the Joint Committee on the Fixed-Term Parliaments Act* HC 1046 HL 253 (21 January 2021), Q 189.

[11] Conservative Party, *Invitation to Join the Government of Britain* (2010), 67.

[12] *Hansard*, HC Deb Vol 515, col 621 (13 September 2010) (Nick Clegg).

[13] R Hazell, *Fixed Term Parliaments* (London, Constitution Unit, 2010); *First Report from the Joint Committee on the Fixed-Term Parliaments Act* HC 1046 HL 253 (2019–21), para 6.

It provided for five-year Parliaments, with polling on the first Thursday in May five years after the previous general election; and automatic dissolution 17 working days before the election (later extended to 25 days by the Electoral Registration and Administration Act 2013). Section 3(2) baldly stated that 'Parliament cannot otherwise be dissolved', thus abolishing the prerogative power.

There was provision for an early dissolution in section 2, but again by statute not under the prerogative. Section 2 allowed for early dissolution in only two circumstances. The first was if two thirds of all MPs voted for an early general election. The second was if the House passed a formal no confidence motion 'that this House has no confidence in Her Majesty's Government', and no alternative government which could command confidence was formed within 14 days.

After the 2010 Parliament ran for a full fixed term, the Conservative Party in 2015 celebrated the achievement, stating that 'We have also passed the Fixed Term Parliament Act, an unprecedented transfer of Executive power.'[14] But all that was to change with the bitter struggles over Brexit in the Parliaments which followed. Theresa May found herself unable to deliver her flagship policy because of the deep divisions within the Conservative Party, but Labour could not muster the numbers to carry a formal no confidence motion. In April 2017, May persuaded the House of Commons to vote for an early dissolution by 522 votes to 13, but lost her majority in the subsequent election. To try to break the gridlock, May's successor Boris Johnson also sought an early dissolution but on three occasions failed to obtain the two-thirds majority required by the FTPA. In desperation, he eventually sidestepped the FTPA with bespoke legislation in the Early Parliamentary General Election Bill introduced in October 2019. It was passed by simple majority, leading to a second early election in December 2019.

Review of the Fixed-term Parliaments Act

These difficulties brought the FTPA into disrepute, leading both Labour and Conservatives to commit to its repeal. In their 2019 election manifesto, the Conservative Party pledged: 'We will get rid of the Fixed Term Parliaments Act – it has led to paralysis when the country needed decisive action.'[15] The manifesto pledge seemed oblivious to the fact that the FTPA contained in section 7 a requirement that the Prime Minister in 2020 should make arrangements for a committee to review the operation of the Act.

The government sought to pre-empt the statutory review by publishing a Draft Fixed-term Parliaments Act 2011 (Repeal) Bill a week after the Joint Committee

[14] Conservative Party, *Strong Leadership. A Clear Economic Plan. A Brighter, More Secure Future.* (2015), 49.

[15] Conservative Party, *Get Brexit Done: Unleash Britain's Potential* (2019), 48.

was established. The Bill reverted to the previous system and restored the prerogative power of dissolution. As the government's foreword explained:

> The Bill makes express provision to revive the prerogative power to dissolve Parliament. This means once more Parliament will be dissolved by the Sovereign, on the advice of the Prime Minister. This will enable Governments, within the life of a Parliament, to call a general election at the time of their choosing.[16]

The committee inevitably focused a lot of attention on the government's draft repeal Bill. But their report published in March 2021 devoted almost equal space to the FTPA and how it might be amended, in case a future government and Parliament ever wished to re-introduce fixed terms.

The committee's review opened with a reminder of the principled rationale for fixed terms:

- that allowing the government to decide the timing of elections gives it an unfair incumbency advantage;
- that it also confers disproportionate power on the executive over Parliament;
- that a fixed election cycle is better for civil service planning and long term thinking, as well as planning parliamentary business; and
- that fixed terms are also better for political parties, and for regulating election spending.[17]

Next, the committee critiqued the FTPA itself. The two thirds requirement for an early dissolution in section 2(1) FTPA risked parliamentary gridlock, while the existence of a statutory no-confidence motion in section 2(4) had undermined shared understandings of the conventions on confidence. Any replacement, the committee argued, should substitute a simple majority as the threshold for triggering an early general election; and remove the 'no-confidence' mechanism from the statute.

The Government's Draft Repeal Bill

The Joint Committee was equally critical of the government's draft Bill, which would repeal the FTPA, and restore the prerogative power of dissolution. But it would go beyond simple restoration of the previous system, by adding an ouster clause to prevent any judicial oversight of the power, and a statement of Dissolution Principles enabling the Prime Minister to advise rather than request a dissolution. The committee was strongly critical of both.

Witnesses had argued that the ouster was unnecessary, and undesirable. Its extraordinary breadth might lead to it being 'read down' by the courts, and

[16] Cabinet Office, *Draft Fixed Term Parliaments Act 2011 (Repeal) Bill* (CP 322, 2020).
[17] Joint Committee on the Fixed-Term Parliaments Act, above n 13 at para 17.

non-justiciability could equally be achieved by requiring a vote of the House of Commons for an early dissolution. Nonetheless, the majority were satisfied with the inclusion of an ouster clause, arguing: 'An early dissolution puts power in the hands of the electorate so, if an ouster is ever appropriate, it is appropriate in this case.'[18]

The government's statement of Dissolution Principles was deemed to be seriously inadequate. Reflecting the Lascelles principles, witnesses suggested that a dissolution could be refused if a Prime Minister, having lost his majority in an election, requested another election, when there was an alternative government which could be formed; or if an election might be damaging in the midst of an emergency such as a pandemic, war or economic crisis. The committee's report summarised their understanding of the conventions surrounding the prerogative of dissolution, with a detailed codification in 20 paragraphs.[19]

On several key issues the committee's report went against the weight of evidence received. The main recommendation where this happened was on the central issue of whether dissolution should be decided by the executive or by Parliament. As the committee acknowledged, 'Retaining a role for the House of Commons commanded a great deal of support in evidence to this Committee as well as PACAC and the Constitution Committee.'[20] Retaining a vote for the House of Commons would resolve two other central concerns: it would protect the monarch from controversy; and it would ensure that the decision to dissolve was non-justiciable, obviating the need for any ouster clause. It is perhaps surprising that a parliamentary committee was not braver in asserting a stronger role for the legislature: a point we return to in the conclusion.

The Dissolution and Calling of Parliament Act 2022

In May 2021, the government introduced its Bill to repeal the FTPA, with only two changes. One was to change the title to the Dissolution and Calling of Parliament Bill. The other was tacitly to withdraw the statement of Dissolution Principles, with the government declining to set out when the Sovereign might reasonably refuse a dissolution request.[21] The issues raised on second reading in July were the same as those rehearsed before the Joint Committee, and the Bill passed its remaining Commons stages in a single day in September.[22]

On second reading in the Lords, Lord True explained the government's objectives as follows:

> The Bill seeks to return to the tried and tested position of the past over many centuries, replacing the 2011 Act with arrangements more in keeping with our best constitutional

[18] ibid at 5; see also ibid at paras 160–2.

[19] ibid at 61–4.

[20] ibid at 84.

[21] See C Smith, *Oral evidence to the House of Commons Public Administration and Constitutional Affairs Committee* HC 376 (23 June 2021), QQ 62-64.

[22] R Kelly, *Recall of Parliament* (House of Commons Library Briefing Paper 1186, 2021).

> practices: delivering stable and effective government; upholding proper parliamentary accountability and public confidence in our democratic arrangements; and, above all, placing the British people at the heart of the resolution of any great national crisis.[23]

In the ensuing debate, most peers who spoke supported the repeal of the FTPA. But there was fierce criticism of the ouster clause from all sides, including from the Conservatives. Despite this, an amendment to remove the ouster clause was defeated at the report stage of the Bill. But an additional amendment was inserted to require a vote in the House of Commons before Parliament could be dissolved. Moving the amendment, Lord Judge explained that its purpose was to ensure that the ultimate power of dissolution lay with Parliament, and not the executive; and to avoid the need for the monarch or the courts becoming involved. He invited the Commons to have second thoughts, while acknowledging that the view of the elected chamber must prevail.[24] After the amendments were rejected by the Commons, the Dissolution and Calling of Parliament Act was granted royal assent in March 2022.

Prorogation

Before the committee stage of the 2021 Bill in the Commons, Chris Bryant tried to raise the issue of prorogation, even though it was not within the scope of the Bill. Prorogation is usually a brief intermission, which brings a parliamentary session to an end before the next one begins. The effect of prorogation is to suspend parliamentary activity. MPs and peers cannot debate government policy and legislation, table motions or parliamentary questions, or scrutinise government activity through select committees. There is therefore a risk of abuse. Canada has a long history of controversial prorogations, from 1873 to 2020.[25] One of the most controversial occurred in December 2008 when the Prime Minister Stephen Harper, heading a minority government and facing an imminent no confidence motion, sought a prorogation. The Governor General kept the Prime Minister waiting while she consulted constitutional experts, and it later emerged that she granted prorogation on two conditions. First, that Parliament should reconvene soon after Christmas and second, the government should present its budget, which would be an issue of confidence. (In the event the opposition coalition collapsed, and the government's revised budget passed).[26]

Until 2019, prorogation in the UK had generally been exercised without the kind of controversy which has occurred in Canada. That changed dramatically

[23] *Hansard*, HC Deb Vol 704, col 1278 (30 November 2021).

[24] *Hansard*, HL Deb Vol 818, col 1585 (9 February 2022).

[25] For a useful summary, see 'Prorogation in Canada' (*Wikipedia*, 6 April 2021) www.en.wikipedia.org/wiki/Prorogation_in_Canada.

[26] P Russell and L Sossin (eds), *Parliamentary Democracy in Crisis* (Toronto, University of Toronto Press, 2009).

when, in August 2019, the new Prime Minister Boris Johnson advised the Queen to prorogue Parliament for five weeks, leading to accusations that he was closing down Parliament in order to avoid scrutiny of his Brexit plans. The Speaker of the House of Commons, John Bercow, described such a long prorogation as an 'act of executive fiat', and there were opposition boycotts of the prorogation ceremony in the House of Lords. Court challenges were mounted in England by Gina Miller, and in Scotland by a cross-party group of 75 MPs and peers. The Divisional Court in England, headed by the Lord Chief Justice, concluded that the matter was not justiciable, and that the exercise of the power to prorogue Parliament was not susceptible to legal standards.[27] By contrast, the Inner House of the Court of Session in Scotland found that the prorogation was justiciable, and that it was an unlawful exercise of the prerogative: the power had on this occasion been exercised for the improper purpose of 'stymying Parliament'.[28]

Both cases were fast tracked on appeal to the Supreme Court. In *R (Miller) v The Prime Minister* (*Miller 2*), a full court of 11 Justices ruled unanimously that the prerogative power of prorogation was justiciable, and unlawful. But it set the legal test differently from the Scottish court, based not upon the purpose of prorogation, but its effect. Baroness Hale held that such a long prorogation significantly interfered with the fundamental constitutional principles of parliamentary sovereignty and parliamentary accountability:

> The court is bound to conclude that the decision to advise Her Majesty to prorogue Parliament was unlawful, because it had the effect of frustrating or preventing the ability of Parliament to carry out its constitutional functions without reasonable justification. Accordingly the advice to prorogue for such a lengthy period was unlawful, and the prorogation order itself was null and void.[29]

The court ruling evoked a fierce response from the government, with the Leader of the House of Commons Jacob Rees-Mogg calling it a 'constitutional coup', and the Prime Minister saying he strongly disagreed with it: 'I don't think this was the right decision. I think that the prerogative of prorogation has been used for centuries without this kind of challenge. It's perfectly usual to have a Queen's Speech. That's what we want to do.'[30] Brexit supporting newspapers were similarly indignant, with headlines like 'Boris blasts: Who runs Britain?'.[31] Papers on the other side hailed the judgment for reaffirming the principle of parliamentary sovereignty, with the

[27] *R (Miller) v The Prime Minister* [2019] EWHC 2381. The judges were Lord Burnett of Maldon CJ, Sir Terence Etherton MR, and Dame Victoria Sharp P.

[28] *Cherry v Lord Advocate* [2019] CSIH 49.

[29] *R (on the application of Miller) v The Prime Minister; Cherry v Advocate General* [2019] UKSC 41; For commentary, see A McHarg, 'The Supreme Court's Prorogation Judgment: Guardian of the Constitution or Architect of the Constitution?' (2020) 21 *Edinburgh Law Review* 88.

[30] M Honeycombe-Foster, 'Boris Johnson slams judges but confirms Parliament will return after court rules his suspension was unlawful' (*PoliticsHome*, 24 September 2019) www.politicshome.com/news/article/boris-johnson-slams-judges-but-confirms-parliament-will-return-after-court-rules-his-suspension-was-unlawful.

[31] J Groves, 'Boris Blasts: Who Runs Britain?' *The Daily Mail* (London, 25 September 2019).

Financial Times saying it underscored the constitutional significance of reinforcing the power of Parliament 'in the face of an often powerful governing executive'.[32]

As a result of the court ruling, Parliament immediately resumed sitting, and the subsequent prorogation to end the session in October was for just three sitting days. The Supreme Court confidently asserted that the case had arisen in circumstances which were unlikely ever to recur. But if in future a Prime Minister has the temerity to take a chance, the court laid down clear guidelines by which to judge any questionable request:

> … the relevant limit on the power to prorogue is this: that a decision to prorogue (or advise the monarch to prorogue) will be unlawful if the prorogation has the effect of frustrating or preventing, without reasonable justification, the ability of Parliament to carry out its constitutional functions as a legislature and as the body responsible for the supervision of the executive. In judging any justification which might be put forward, the court must of course be sensitive to the responsibilities and experience of the Prime Minister and proceed with appropriate caution.[33]

Those guidelines will apply as much to the monarch considering any future request for prorogation, as to a court adjudicating on that request. But, following the intense controversy over the 2019 prorogation, the courts might lose their jurisdiction to adjudicate in such cases. This could happen if the government introduced legislation to make prorogation non-justiciable, as it has proposed for dissolution. The extreme breadth of the ouster clause in the Dissolution and Calling of Parliament Act was justified by explicit reference to the *Miller 2* judgment[34] and it is conceivable that the ouster might be extended to prorogation.

This would be a severely retrograde step. The UK is already an outlier among European parliamentary democracies in allowing the executive to suspend Parliament through prorogation. In a study of 26 European countries, Thomas Fleming and Petra Schleiter found only one other country (Greece) similar to the UK. In all other European democracies, Parliament cannot be suspended against its will. In nearly all these countries, the suspension of Parliament is protected against executive encroachment in the constitution; where this protection is not constitutionally enshrined, it is regulated in parliamentary procedure. They conclude:

> Overall, the comparison with international practice shows that the UK's prorogation rules sit far outside the European norm. In particular, the UK parliament, unusually, lacks the power to insist on sitting against the wishes of the executive, or to un-prorogue itself once suspended.[35]

[32] J Blitz and J Croft, 'Parliament the winner in prorogation case, say lawyers' *Financial Times* (24 September 2019) www.ft.com/content/ba8a6afc-dede-11e9-b112-9624ec9edc59.

[33] *R (on the application of Miller) v The Prime Minister; Cherry v Advocate General*, UKSC Press Summary, 2.

[34] Explanatory Notes to the Dissolution and Calling of Parliament Bill HC (2021–2022) 8, paras 21–3; 'Explanatory Notes' in Cabinet Office, above n 16 at paras 16, 17.

[35] T Fleming and P Schletier, 'Prorogation: Comparative Context and Reform' (2021) 74 *Parliamentary Affairs* 964.

Fleming and Schleiter are not alone in arguing that prorogation should require parliamentary consent. In 2020, the House of Lords Constitution Committee suggested, 'As part of the statutory review of the Fixed-term Parliaments Act 2011, Parliament may wish to consider whether the prorogation of Parliament should require its approval in the same way the Commons approves its recess dates.'[36] During the passage of the FTPA, an amendment to include prorogation and make it subject to decision by the House of Commons had been debated, but defeated.[37] Similar suggestions were made in evidence to the parliamentary Joint Committee reviewing the FTPA.[38] Had the committee risen to the challenge, two possible changes could have been considered. First, the power of prorogation could be given to Parliament so that Parliament itself would decide when it was suspended. Second, the power could remain with the executive, but Parliament could have the power to veto prorogation or to un-prorogue itself. As with dissolution, giving Parliament control over prorogation would have the advantage of removing the risk of challenge in the courts, because as a proceeding of Parliament it would be shielded by Article 9 of the Bill of Rights 1689; and it would remove the risk of the monarch being drawn into political controversy, avoiding a repeat of what happened in 2019.

Recall of Parliament

The power to recall Parliament is not a prerogative power, but is worth mentioning briefly here. Parliament has been recalled 34 times during the recess since 1948.[39] Under Standing Order 13, the House of Commons is recalled during a recess only when the government proposes a recall, and the Speaker agrees. So the initiative lies with the government. As Prime Minister, Gordon Brown proposed that a majority of MPs should also have the right to request a recall.[40] The proposal was referred to the House of Commons Modernisation Committee, who initiated but did not complete an inquiry, so it was not implemented (see page 52). Delivering a lecture to the Hansard Society in 2017, the Commons Speaker John Bercow revived the idea that Parliament should be able to propose a recall as well as the government.[41] It would require a minimum number of MPs to request a recall, and perhaps a minimum number from each of the different parties.[42]

[36] Twelfth Report from the House of Lords Constitution Committee, *A Question of Confidence? The Fixed-term Parliaments Act 2011* HL 121 (2019–21), para 144.

[37] *Hansard*, HC Deb Vol 521, cols 733-811 (18 January 2011).

[38] R Hazell and M Russell, *Written evidence to the Joint Committee on the Fixed-Term Parliaments Act* HC 1046 HL 253 FTP0003 (December 2020), paras 31–32.

[39] Kelly, above n 22.

[40] Ministry of Justice, above n 7 at paras 37–39.

[41] J Bercow, 'Opening up the Usual channels: next steps for reform of the House of Commons' (Hansard Society, London, 11 October 2017).

[42] Kelly, above n 22 at ch 3.

Summoning Parliament

Following every dissolution, the Crown will summon the new Parliament by Proclamation, and appoint the first day on which Parliament is to meet following a General Election. Here is the text of the Proclamation issued before the 2019 general election:

> BY THE QUEEN A PROCLAMATION FOR DECLARING THE CALLING OF A NEW PARLIAMENT ELIZABETH R.
>
> Whereas We, by and with the advice of Our Privy Council, being desirous and resolved, as soon as may be, to meet Our People, and to have their Advice in Parliament, do publish this, Our Royal Proclamation, and do hereby make known to all Our loving Subjects Our Royal Will and Pleasure to call a new Parliament to be holden at Westminster on Tuesday the seventeenth day of December next: And We do hereby also, by this Our Royal Proclamation under Our Great Seal of Our Realm, require Writs to be issued by Our Lord High Chancellor for causing the Lords Spiritual and Temporal who are to serve in the said Parliament to give their Attendance in Our said Parliament on the said date.
>
> Given at Our Court at Buckingham Palace, this sixth day of November in the Year of our Lord two thousand and nineteen and in the sixty-eighth year of Our Reign.
>
> **GOD SAVE THE QUEEN**

In 2019, the date of the election was specified by Parliament in the Early Parliamentary General Election Act 2019. But, if an early general election were held under the FTPA, section 2(7) provides that the Queen appoints the date for the poll by proclamation on the recommendation of the Prime Minister. This was uncontroversial in 2017, when the House of Commons voted on 19 April for an early election under section 2(2) FTPA, in the knowledge that Theresa May was proposing the election be held on 8 June. But leaving the choice of election date with the Prime Minister became deeply controversial in September 2019. It was one of the reasons why the House of Commons was reluctant to grant Boris Johnson an early dissolution under the FTPA, or to pass a vote of no confidence, fearful that he might postpone polling day until after the deadline for the UK leaving the European Union, then set at 31 October.

Under the Dissolution and Calling of Parliament Act 2022, the new arrangements for setting the date of polling day, and of the first meeting of the new Parliament are as follows. To avoid the theoretical possibility that Parliament could be dissolved without triggering an election, the Act provides that dissolution will trigger the statutory election timetable.[43] It thus provides certainty that when a dissolution is granted, the poll will be held 25 working days later. The Joint Committee on the Fixed-Term Parliaments Act recommended legislation to ensure that a proclamation summoning a new Parliament must be made at the

[43] Dissolution and Calling of Parliament HC Bill (2021–22) 8, sch para 7.

same time as, or immediately after dissolution.[44] But the government did not feel it necessary to specify this in legislation, arguing that 'any government would not wish to delay the first meeting of parliament, but would want to commence its legislative programme at the earliest opportunity'.[45]

The Proclamation specifies the date when the new Parliament will meet. This generally used to be six days after the election. But, in 2007, the House of Commons Modernisation Committee recommended an interval of 12 days, to allow more time for induction of new MPs.[46] This was the practice followed in 2010 and 2015. But, in 2017 and 2019, Parliament met five days after the election. As there was an urgent need to approve the EU Withdrawal Agreement before the Brexit deadline, the House of Commons was recalled during the Christmas recess to do so, passing the European Union (Future Relationship) Bill through all its stages on 30 December 2019.[47]

Conclusion

This chapter has been about the prerogative power to summon, dissolve, and prorogue Parliament. Underlying it are fundamental differences of view about where the power lies, where it should lie, and how it should be exercised. The evidence submitted to the Joint Committee on the Fixed-Term Parliaments Act disclosed two broad camps: those who maintain the power should rest with the executive, and those who believe it should be transferred to Parliament, or at least be subject to some form of parliamentary control. These views can be represented as the Whitehall view and the Westminster view, with the majority of the evidence supporting the Westminster view. Historically the two views derive from different ideas about where authority ultimately lies in the British constitution, in the Crown-in-Parliament (now largely represented by ministers), or in the sovereignty of Parliament (now mainly represented by the House of Commons).[48]

This binary divide is an over-simplification in two respects: it leaves out the courts, and it leaves out the Crown as an independent actor. But that is what the government has proposed in the Dissolution and Calling of Parliament Act. The courts would be excluded by the ouster clause, and it was clear from the statement of Dissolution Principles that in the government's mind the Crown would

[44] Joint Committee on the Fixed-Term Parliaments Act, above n 13 at para 188.

[45] Cabinet Office, *Government Response to the Joint Committee on the Fixed-Term Parliament Act Report* (CP 430, 2021), 13.

[46] First Report from the House of Commons Modernisation Committee, *Revitalising the Chamber: the role of the back bench Member* HC 337 (2006–07), paras 36–39.

[47] *Hansard*, HC Deb Vol 686, cols 595-599 (30 December 2019).

[48] D Howarth, 'Westminster versus Whitehall: Two Incompatible Views of the Constitution' (*UK Constitutional Law Association Blog*, 10 April 2019) www.ukconstitutionallaw.org/2019/04/10/david-howarth-westminster-versus-whitehall-two-incompatible-views-of-the-constitution/.

be expected always to follow the advice of ministers. We might describe this as an extreme Whitehall view, leaving the executive in complete control of when Parliament should sit. It is also an extreme view in comparative terms. As Fleming and Schleiter have shown, it would leave Westminster as almost the only Parliament in Europe unable to control its own sittings.

Those who reject the extreme Whitehall view may nevertheless feel uncomfortable about involving the Crown or the courts as a check on untrammelled executive power because of the risk of dragging them into political controversy. But, as several witnesses argued to the Joint Committee, and as the committee later acknowledged in their report, there is an alternative solution: to leave the decision on dissolution (and prorogation) with the House of Commons. This would obviate the need for the monarch to act as constitutional umpire and as a proceeding in Parliament, it would exclude the jurisdiction of the courts.

Defenders of the Whitehall view point to the risk of a zombie government, unable to govern, in a Parliament unable or unwilling to put it out of its misery, as happened in 2017–19. The argument then becomes one about the balance of risks. How likely is it that such a toxic combination of circumstances might recur, with a minority government unable to deliver its flagship policy; compared with the risk that future Prime Ministers allowed to choose the election date will choose one favourable to their party? And if fixed terms are brought into the equation, it becomes an argument about potential benefits as well as risks. Fixed terms bring multiple benefits, to the civil service, to business, to political parties and electoral administrators (see page 53). It is harder to compile an equivalent list of benefits from restoring the royal prerogative. The arguments of principle, cogently laid out by the Supreme Court in *Miller 2*, tend to favour the Westminster view. And so do the arguments about the balance of risk.

6

Royal Assent and Executive Veto of Legislation

> An astonishing rumour has been current of late. A certain section of the Unionist party is said to be encouraging the idea that it is possible, as a matter of practical politics, for the King to refuse the Royal Assent to the Home Rule Bill next May, when for the third time it has passed the House of Commons and has complied with all the requirements of the Parliament Act.
>
> *Fortnightly Review* (1913)[1]

Introduction

This third and final chapter on the personal prerogatives, or reserve powers, of the monarch, is about the grant of royal assent to legislation. First, we explain the process for granting royal assent, and the history of monarchs refusing royal assent, before considering whether a modern monarch might ever refuse royal assent; and if so, in what circumstances. Second, we explain the completely separate requirement, found at the start rather than the end of the legislative process, of Queen's consent to the introduction of legislation which affects the prerogative. Third, we consider more broadly the question of the executive veto: whether there are other ways at Westminster for the executive to veto legislation, and how it is done.

The Process and History of Royal Assent

The process of royal assent is as follows. Once a Bill has passed through all its stages in both Houses of Parliament, it must be submitted for royal assent; without royal assent, it does not become law. Laws are made by the Crown-in-Parliament, not Parliament alone. The grant of royal assent is an elaborate four stage process. First, the Clerk of the Parliaments prepares a list of Bills which have been passed by both Houses and sends it to the Crown Office in the Ministry of Justice. Next, the

[1] Auditor Tantum, 'The Veto of the Crown', *Fortnightly Review* (London, September 1913), 424.

Lord Chancellor submits the list to the Queen, requesting that a warrant be issued for affixing the Great Seal to Letters Patent to indicate the grant of royal assent. Third, the Queen signs the warrant and Letters Patent to give her assent; she does not sign each Bill. Finally, the process returns to Westminster for royal assent to be communicated to both Houses. Royal assent used to be given in person by the monarch sitting on the throne in the House of Lords, but the last monarch to do so was Queen Victoria in 1854. In the absence of the monarch, royal assent was given by Commissioners; but since the Royal Assent Act 1967, it is notified to each House by the Speaker. The exception is the prorogation ceremony at the end of a session, when royal assent is still given by Commissioners: following a recitation of the short title of each Act, the Clerk of the Parliaments signifies royal assent in the Norman French formula 'La Reyne le veult'.[2]

As the Norman French implies, the history of royal assent goes back to the origins of Parliament itself. In the fourteenth and fifteenth centuries, Parliament petitioned the King for the redress of grievances and medieval Kings treated the petitions they received as negotiable, often using the formula 'Le Roy s'avisera' ('the King will consider it') to withhold responding to the request directly. This practice continued when petitions became Bills. If the King did not wish to give royal assent to a Bill, he would use the old temporising formula. Withholding royal assent was common under the Tudors, but gradually declined under the Stuarts, with the last royal veto being in 1708. Queen Elizabeth I vetoed 72 Bills during her long reign and her successor King James I vetoed six Bills. King Charles I vetoed just one, but the royal veto became a key issue in the 1640 Parliament over issues such as legislation on control of the militia.[3]

The veto was re-asserted at the restoration of the Stuart monarchy in 1660, and Charles II vetoed five Bills during his reign. But this aroused parliamentary protests, and he resorted to other stratagems to prevent unwelcome Bills being presented for royal assent. Despite these protests, the veto survived the revolution of 1689, and King William and Queen Mary exercised the veto seven times: but again, in the face of growing parliamentary opposition. The veto was becoming unsustainable by the end of their reign, and its solitary use by Queen Anne – the last occasion when it was used – was in exceptional circumstances. The Scottish Militia Bill was passed by the new Parliament of Great Britain in the first year after the Act of Union 1707 in order to equip and arm the Scottish militia. But on the day when it was due to receive royal assent, news came that a French and Jacobite force had set sail from Dunkirk to land in Scotland. Queen Anne announced news

[2] This is a simplified account of the process – money bills have a different formula; R Brazier, 'Royal Assent to Legislation' (2013) 129 *Law Quarterly Review* 184, 188; *cf* Francis Bennion says that it is not the Lord Chancellor, but the Clerk of the Crown in Chancery (his Permanent Secretary) who acts as intermediary between the Clerk of the Parliaments and the Palace: F Bennion, 'Modern Royal Assent Procedure at Westminster' (1981) 2(3) *Statute Law Review* 133.

[3] P Seaward, 'The Veto' (*History of Parliament Trust Blog*, 15 April 2019) www.historyofparliament-blog.wordpress.com/2019/04/15/the-veto/.

of the invasion to the House of Lords when granting assent to 11 other Bills, but when the title of the Scottish Militia Bill was read out, the Clerk pronounced the fateful words, 'La Reyne s'avisera'. Continuation of an armed militia in Scotland, whose loyalty was uncertain, seemed unwise and so the veto was exercised with ministers' agreement and with no complaint from Parliament.[4]

Although that was the last occasion when royal assent was refused, the threat of a veto from King George III held up Catholic emancipation for decades, and there was talk of Queen Victoria refusing royal assent to the Irish Church Act 1869, which disestablished the Anglican church in Ireland.[5] Albert Venn Dicey described the use of the veto as practically obsolete in 1885, but in 1914, it was nearly revived in response to the Irish Home Rule crisis which prompted the epigraph to this chapter. Diehard Unionists had urged King George V to refuse royal assent to the third Irish Home Rule Bill on the grounds that so fundamental a change to the country ought to be submitted to a general election. As the Parliament Act 1911 meant that the House of Lords could no longer veto the Bill, only the King's veto could force the issue. The King came under intense pressure, but ultimately granted royal assent. The First World War then forced the issue in a different way, with the Government of Ireland Act 1914 being suspended for the duration of the war.

Could the Queen Refuse Royal Assent?

Royal assent has occasionally been withheld by other European monarchs, but mainly on grounds of individual conscience. King Baudouin of the Belgians declined to grant royal assent to legislation decriminalising abortion in 1990; instead abdicating for a day while the Council of Ministers granted royal assent on his behalf.[6] In 2008, Grand Duke Henri of Luxembourg refused to sign a Bill legalising euthanasia and the Constitution was consequently changed to remove the requirement for royal assent. In the Netherlands, Queen Juliana twice withheld royal assent: in refusing to sign the death penalty for certain war criminals after the Second World War, and later in refusing to approve legislation to reduce the size of the Dutch royal family. The consequence was different from that in Luxembourg: the death sentences of the criminals were commuted to life imprisonment, and the 1971 legislation reducing the size of the royal family was quietly dropped.[7]

It is hard to conceive that the British monarch would withhold royal assent on grounds of conscience, although the play *King Charles III* is predicated on the

[4] Brazier, above n 2 at 188–9.

[5] G Wheeler, 'Royal Assent in the British Constitution' (2016) 132 *Law Quarterly Review* 495, 497.

[6] Strictly, Baudouin did not abdicate: at his request, the Council of Ministers declared the King incapable of exercising his powers and the next day the Parliament declared him capable again.

[7] R Andeweg, 'Constitutional Functions in the Netherlands' in R Hazell and B Morris (eds), *The Role of Monarchy in Modern Democracy* (Oxford, Hart Publishing, 2020), 39.

future King refusing assent to a Bill curtailing freedom of the press.[8] In Britain, academic debate has focused on whether the royal veto still exists when it has not been formally exercised for over 300 years; and if it does exist, the circumstances in which the monarch might justifiably withhold royal assent. King George V certainly took the view that he had the legal power and constitutional right to refuse assent and was supported by constitutional experts Sir William Anson and Albert Venn Dicey. The argument was made and rejected in 1914 that the power to refuse royal assent had fallen into desuetude. The ardent Unionist and former Conservative Prime Minister Arthur Balfour rejected the argument on logical grounds: 'It is surely obvious that if a prerogative *ought* rarely to be used, it cannot become obsolete, *merely because* it is rarely used.'[9] And Rodney Brazier has rejected the argument on legal grounds: royal assent is part of the royal prerogative, which is part of the common law, and 'no part of the common law loses its legal effect through desuetude'.[10] But the reluctance of the May and Johnson governments to deploy the royal veto in 2019 (discussed further below) adds further instances of non-use, and greater weight to the argument that it is now unusable.

Anne Twomey's work shows that even if the royal veto has not been exercised in the UK for over 300 years, it continues to be used elsewhere. As late as 1980, the Queen was advised (by the UK government) to refuse assent to a Bill passed by the Parliament of New South Wales, the Privy Council Appeals Abolition Bill, on constitutional grounds. Rather than face the royal veto, the New South Wales government let the Bill lapse.[11] This illustrates a point made by both Twomey and Brazier: that the threat of exercising the royal veto can be more powerful than the actuality.

Anne Twomey also provides a useful analysis of the underlying constitutional principles of royal assent. The main ones are representative government and responsible government. Pursuant to the principle of representative government, it can be argued that the Queen, as a constituent part of the Crown-in-Parliament, is performing a *legislative act* in giving assent, and acts on the advice of the Houses of Parliament. That is how assent is recorded in the opening words of Acts of Parliament:

> Be it enacted by the Queen's most Excellent Majesty, by and with the consent of the Lords Spiritual and Temporal, and Commons, in this present Parliament assembled, and by the authority of the same, as follows …

On the other hand, it can be argued that the Queen forms part of the executive, and in giving assent to a Bill, is performing an *executive act* upon the advice of

[8] M Bartlett, *King Charles III* (2014).

[9] Balfour Papers, BL Add MS 49869, fos 123–4 quoted in V Bogdanor, *The Monarchy and the Constitution* (Oxford, Oxford University Press, 1995), 127.

[10] Brazier, above n 2 at 199.

[11] A Twomey, *The Veiled Sceptre: Reserve Powers of Heads of State in Westminster Systems* (Cambridge, Cambridge University Press, 2018), 638, 656.

responsible ministers, pursuant to the principle of responsible government.[12] Most of the time there is no conflict between these principles because ministers command the confidence of Parliament, and will want the Queen to assent to legislation passed by Parliament. The dilemma arises when Parliament passes legislation against the government's wishes, and ministers advise against the grant of royal assent. Upon whose advice does the Queen then rely: that of the Houses of Parliament, or the ministers who are responsible to them?

A more extreme dilemma may conceivably arise if ministers and a compliant Parliament pass legislation which the monarch regards as unconscionable (as in *King Charles III*). In what circumstances might the monarch withhold royal assent on her own initiative as the ultimate guardian of the constitution? Academic writers have struggled to think of plausible scenarios. One example given is if Parliament ignored a manner and form requirement in previous legislation.[13] A current instance could be the section 1 provision in the Scotland Act 2016 that the Scottish government and Parliament are not to be abolished except by referendum. If Westminster subsequently legislated to abolish the Scottish Parliament without a referendum, would the monarch be justified in withholding royal assent? A second example given is a Bill that indefinitely suspended parliamentary elections, or that extended the life of a Parliament beyond the five-year statutory maximum.[14] Would the monarch be justified in vetoing such a Bill in order to uphold parliamentary democracy? In either case, what is more likely is that the monarch would warn against passing such legislation before it reached the point of exercising a formal veto. Rodney Brazier makes a similar point to Anne Twomey: 'in practice a Sovereign's concerns about any legislation actually expressed in private might be of greater constitutional importance than the legal possibility of a royal veto'.[15]

The more likely dilemma is how the monarch should respond if advised by ministers to veto legislation that has been passed by Parliament against the government's wishes. This question seemed hypothetical in the UK with its long history of single party majority government.[16] But then came the Brexit referendum, shortly followed by Theresa May's minority government struggling and failing to find a majority for her Brexit deal. On two occasions, parliamentary rebels succeeded in temporarily seizing control of the Commons agenda and passing legislation to force the government's hand. In April 2019, the Cooper-Letwin Bill was passed (by a majority of one vote in the Commons) to become the European

[12] ibid at 617.

[13] G Marshall, *Constitutional Conventions: The Rules and Forms of Political Accountability* (Oxford, Oxford University Press, 1984), 22–3.

[14] Under the Parliament Act 1911, extending the life of a Parliament is subject to a veto by the House of Lords. See also P Joseph, *Constitutional and Administrative Law in New Zealand*, 4th edn (London, Thomson Reuters, 2014), 742, who gives the same two examples, of ignoring a manner and form requirement or suspending parliamentary elections; Wheeler, above n 5 at 498.

[15] Brazier, above n 2 at 202.

[16] For the hypothetical debate, see R Blackburn, 'Monarchy and the Personal Prerogatives' [2004] *Public Law* 546, 554; and Brazier, above n 2 at 45–7.

Union (Withdrawal) Act 2019, requiring the government to seek an extension to the two-year negotiating period. And, in September 2019, Parliament passed the EU Withdrawal (No.2) Act, known as the 'Benn Act', which forced the government to seek a further extension to stop a no-deal Brexit on 31 October.

Withholding royal assent seemed to offer a last-ditch means of preventing such unwelcome Bills becoming law. We do not know whether Theresa May or Boris Johnson ever considered advising the Queen to withhold royal assent; but in 2019 the legal blogosphere went wild with speculation that they might. Commentators were divided, with John Finnis, Richard Ekins and Michael Detmold asserting that the government could advise the Queen to do so,[17] and Mark Elliott, Jeff King and others[18] countering that this would amount to executive hegemony, effectively subverting the sovereignty of Parliament:

> Once a Bill has been passed by Parliament the Queen's role is purely ceremonial. And this is for good reason. Any attempt to advise refusal of Royal Assent to a Bill passed by Parliament would stand constitutional principle on its head. It would presume a governmental power to override Parliament, yet it is in Parliament, not the Executive, that sovereignty resides.[19]

The division of opinion depended on the underlying issues identified above: on the principle of representative versus responsible government, and on whether royal assent was seen as a legislative or executive act. In the remainder of this section, we seek to argue that royal assent is a legislative function, the Crown certifying that a Bill has been properly passed by Parliament, and not an executive function relying on ministerial advice. We do so by combining past precedents with arguments of principle, concluding that in the UK there is no longer any scope for a royal veto.

Precedent first, starting with one of the EU Withdrawal Bills passed against the government's wishes in 2019. The speed with which royal assent was granted to the Cooper-Letwin Bill supports the impression that it is a legislative function. After a series of votes on Lords amendments, the Bill was finally passed by the

[17] R Ekins, 'Constitutional Government, Parliamentary Democracy and Judicial Power' (*Policy Exchange*, 5 April 2019) www,policyexchange.org.uk/constitutional-government-parliamentary-democracy-and-judicial-power/; J Finnis, 'Only one option remains with Brexit – prorogue Parliament and allow us out of the EU with no deal', *Daily Telegraph* (London, 1 April 2019); M Detmold 'The Proper Denial of Royal Assent' (*UK Constitutional Law Association Blog*, 5 September 2019) www.ukconstitutionallaw.org/2019/09/05/michael-detmold-the-proper-denial-of-royal-assent/.

[18] M Elliott, 'Can the Government veto legislation by advising the Queen to withhold royal assent?' (*Public Law for Everyone*, 21 January 2019) www.publiclawforeveryone.com/2019/01/21/can-the-government-veto-legislation-by-advising-the-queen-to-withhold-royal-assent/; J King, 'Can Royal Assent to a Bill be withheld if so advised by Ministers?' (*UK Constitutional Law Association Blog*, 5 April 2019) www.ukconstitutionallaw.org/2019/04/05/jeff-king-can-royal-assent-to-a-bill-be-withheld-if-so-advised-by-ministers/.

[19] P Craig, B Dickson, S Douglas-Scott, M Elliott, T Hickman, D Howarth, J King, A Le Sueur, R Masterman, C McCrudden, A McHarg, C O'Cinneide, P Pannick, G Phillipson, T Poole, T Prosser, D Rose, M Russell, M Sunkin, R Thomas and H White, 'Royal Assent: A Letter to The Times' *The Times* (London, 3 April 2019).

Commons at 10.35pm on 8 April 2019.[20] At 11.05pm that same evening, royal assent was signified in the House of Lords.[21] It is hard to believe that the elaborate four stage process for obtaining royal assent described at the beginning of this chapter could be achieved in half an hour, or that the Lord Chancellor as a minister of the executive could have had any real involvement. This is confirmed by senior officials involved in the process of granting royal assent, who regard themselves as carrying out an automatic function, as officers of Parliament, with no scope for ministerial interference.

There seems to be some doubt as to whether the Lord Chancellor has any role in this process.[22] Anne Twomey records official correspondence from the Office of the Lord Chancellor in 1972 as being corrected to delete any reference to ministerial advice. The circumstance was a challenge by an early Brexiteer, Ross McWhirter,[23] who contended that the Queen should refuse assent to the European Communities Bill (on the ground that it would fetter the powers of Parliament and thus violate her Coronation Oath). Twomey reports her findings from the archives as follows:

> The first draft of a response to this complaint stated that it is an 'established constitutional convention that the Royal Assent will not be refused to Bills which have been passed by both Houses of Parliament and which ministers advise should receive assent'. This was later corrected, upon the advice of the Lord Chancellor's Office, on the ground that ministerial advice is not tendered in relation to the grant of royal assent. The letter, as altered to state the correct position, provided that 'it is an established constitutional convention – indeed (it might be said) a custom of the realm – that the Royal Assent is not withheld from Bills which have been passed by both Houses of Parliament'.[24]

The third piece of evidence about precedent comes from guidance published by the Office of Parliamentary Counsel. In their booklet about Queen's consent, it baldly states that 'Royal Assent is of course never refused for a Bill that has successfully made its way through Parliament.'[25] Parliamentary Counsel's specialism is careful and precise language; such a categorical statement would not have been made lightly. And a fourth piece comes from Graham Wheeler, of the Government Legal Department (but writing in a personal capacity), who says 'The stark fact is that ministers *do not* advise the sovereign on Royal Assent. There is not even any formal process by which they might do so …'.[26]

[20] *Hansard*, HC Deb Vol 658, cols 134–144 (8 April 2019).

[21] *Hansard*, HC Deb Vol 797, col 442 (8 April 2019).

[22] It is only Brazier who ascribes a role to the Lord Chancellor. Bennion says the go-between role is performed by the Clerk of the Crown in Chancery, see above n 2.

[23] Ross McWhirter was one of the founders of the National Association for Freedom, now the Freedom Association. He was murdered by the Provisional IRA in 1975.

[24] Twomey, above n 11 at 628–9; Letter by Mr De Winton (Law Officers' Department) to Lord Bridges (5 September 1972) TNA PREM 15/1183; Draft Letter by No 10 Downing Street (Prime Minister's Office) to Mr McWhirter (21 September 1972) TNA PREM 15/1183.

[25] Office of Parliamentary Counsel, *Queen's or Prince's Consent* (September 2018), para 7.12.

[26] Wheeler, above n 5 at 500.

So, precedent suggests there is no scope for ministers to advise on the grant of royal assent. This suggestion is supported by the arguments of principle. Those who argue that the Queen must accept the advice of her ministers on royal assent do so by analogy with the executive royal prerogatives, discussed in part three of this book. But there is a fundamental problem with applying the convention on ministerial advice in the context of withholding royal assent. As Graham Wheeler has observed:

> The purpose of the convention is to ensure that the sovereign acts in accordance with the wishes of elected politicians. Yet the effect of following a minister's advice to veto a Bill would be to frustrate the will of the much larger number of elected politicians who had voted in favour of it.[27]

Nick Barber makes a similar argument:

> But does this reason justify the inclusion of royal assent within the group of prerogative powers that are exercised on ministerial advice? It is hard to see that it does. Now the convention is operating against democratic values, rather than upholding them. Rather than supporting parliamentary government, it would undermine it … Just as it would be undemocratic to allow one person – the Monarch – to veto legislation, so too it would be undemocratic to give this power to the Prime Minister.[28]

The principle of responsible government depends on ministers being responsible to Parliament and commanding the confidence of the House of Commons. But, if ministers have failed to prevent Parliament from passing a Bill against their wishes, it raises the question of whether they can command confidence; if they cannot, they are no longer entitled to give binding advice. As Twomey has said,

> The whole *raison d'être* of responsible government is to give primacy to Parliament by ensuring executive accountability to it. It would seem illogical, therefore, for the principles of responsible government to be relied upon to override the will of Parliament.[29]

Simply put, the will of Parliament has a higher constitutional status than that of the executive.

In conclusion, there is no longer any scope for an executive veto through the withholding of royal assent to legislation. Principle suggests that ministers should not be able to override the will of Parliament; and so too does precedent, with the Office of the Lord Chancellor in 1972 recognising that ministers no longer have a role. The latest precedent, from 2019, confirms that if ever there was an occasion to deploy the royal veto, urged on by the Brexiteers and their supporters, then this was it – but ministers declined to do so. In declining to do so, it has been tacitly

[27] ibid.
[28] N Barber, 'Can Royal Assent be Refused on the Advice of the Prime Minister?' (*UK Constitutional Law Association Blog*, 25 September 2013) www.ukconstitutionallaw.org/2013/09/25/nick-barber-can-royal-assent-be-refused-on-the-advice-of-the-prime-minster/.
[29] Twomey, above n 11 at 626.

recognised that royal assent is a legislative act, with no role for the executive. Paul Evans comes to the same conclusion:

> For all practical purposes, the absence of any attempt to advise against royal assent by the May and Johnson administrations in the cases of the Cooper-Letwin and Benn-Burt Acts has confirmed that the idea that it could be withheld is no longer a thing. At the only moment in modern times when it might have been attempted to revive a veto power no such attempt was made … If we were to seek to clarify our constitutional vocabulary it would be more accurate to describe royal assent as 'promulgation'.[30]

Royal Consent to Bills Affecting the Prerogative and Personal Interests of the Crown

Quite separate from the process of royal assent is the requirement for Queen's and Prince's consent to Bills affecting the prerogative, as well as Bills concerning the hereditary revenues, property and personal interests of the Crown and the Duchy of Cornwall. This requirement applies at the start of the legislative process, for introduction of a Bill, not as the final stage. And it applies only to those Bills which affect the prerogative or the interests of the Crown. The Clerk of Legislation in each House determine whether Queen's consent is required for a Bill, and if so, it must be signified by a Privy Counsellor before the Bill's third reading can be moved. At first blush, Queen's consent would appear to represent another form of executive veto. It may potentially be more powerful, since failure to obtain consent can prevent Parliament debating a Bill.

Queen's consent is a little known requirement which gave rise to controversy in 2013 when its scope became known following a freedom of information (FOI) request that saw *The Guardian* newspaper criticise the wide range of Bills (including tuition fees, identity cards, paternity pay and child maintenance) which were subject to Queen's or Prince's consent.[31] The article reported that 39 Bills had required consent, and quoted Andrew George MP saying that

> It shows the royals are playing an active role in the democratic process and we need greater transparency in parliament so we can be fully appraised of whether these powers of influence and veto are really appropriate.

Academic criticism followed, with Thomas Adams saying on the UK Constitutional Law Association Blog:

> Quite apart from its scope it is worth emphasising that the content of the power is absolutely damning: it is not simply that the relevant bill fails to become law if consent

[30] P Evans, *Braking the Law: Is there, or should there be, an Executive Veto in the UK Constitution?* (London, Constitution Unit, 2020), 10–1.

[31] R Booth, 'Secret papers show extent of senior Royals' veto over bills' *The Guardian* (14 January 2013) www.theguardian.com/uk/2013/jan/14/secret-papers-royals-veto-bills.

> is not given, although this is implied. It is that the bill cannot even be properly debated by our elected politicians.[32]

But it soon became clear that the Queen's or Prince's consent is only granted or refused on advice from ministers. Buckingham Palace quickly issued a statement to this effect. When the House of Commons Political and Constitutional Reform Committee (PCRC) launched an inquiry, their main concern was to ascertain whether the consent requirement gave the Palace any influence over the content of legislation and whether ministers have ever used it as a means of blocking Private Member's Bills. The PCRC report provides a useful account of the process involved in seeking Queen's consent, an exploration of its rationale, and analysis of its effects.[33]

The most detailed guidance is contained in a 32-page pamphlet about Queen's and Prince's consent, coincidentally published in 2013 by the Office of Parliamentary Counsel in response to a separate FOI request.[34] When drafting a Bill, Parliamentary Counsel take an initial view as to whether Queen's consent is required, which they then check with the Clerk of Legislation in each House. If consent is required, the lead government department is informed, and the department must write to the royal household accordingly. The letter to the Palace must enclose two copies of the Bill, explain its purpose, how it affects the prerogative or interests of the Crown, and ask for consent. The letter is copied to Farrer & Co, the royal family's legal advisers, who advise the Palace on the nature of the legislation and its potential impact.[35]

Even in the case of Private Member's Bills, it is still the department, not the individual MP, which writes to request consent. Queen's consent is subject to the convention that the Queen must follow ministerial advice; so a request for consent carries with it by implication advice that consent should be granted. Ministers who wish to block a Bill would not normally advise the Queen to withhold consent; they would simply not seek consent in the first place.[36] The effect would be the same: without consent, the Bill could not progress.

The PCRC found that Private Member's Bills were occasionally blocked by refusing to seek the Queen's consent, the most brazen case being Tam Dalyell's 1999 Military Action against Iraq (Parliamentary Approval) Bill.[37] But, in evidence to the committee, the Leader of the House of Commons explained that the government would only block a Bill if it had no hope of making further progress:

> The Government will generally seek consent for Private Member's Bills, even where it opposes the bill, on the basis that Parliament should not be prevented from debating

[32] T Adams, 'Royal Consent and Hidden Power' (*UK Constitutional Law Association Blog*, 26 January 2013) www.ukconstitutionallaw.org/2013/01/26/tom-adams-royal-consent-and-hidden-power/.

[33] Eleventh Report from the House of Commons Political and Constitutional Reform Committee, *The Impact of Queen's and Prince's Consent on the Legislative Process* HC 784 (2013–14).

[34] Office of Parliamentary Counsel, above n 25.

[35] Cabinet Office, *Guide to Making Legislation* (July 2014), ch 17.

[36] House of Commons Political and Constitutional Reform Committee, above n 33 at para 11.

[37] For four other examples, see ibid at para 22.

> a matter on account of consent not having been obtained … The Government of the day has on occasion not sought consent for bills they opposed (and did not wish to be proceeded with), on the basis that there was no realistic opportunity for the bill in question to be debated.[38]

In their respective evidence, the Clerks of both Houses deplored this as a misuse of process. Five years later, they could have pointed to a possible solution. In a 2019 article, the Clerk of Legislation in the Lords, Andrew Makower, disclosed that as late as 1952 it was the normal practice for the Houses to make a direct request to the Sovereign for consent through an Address to the Crown in the case of Private Members' Bills.[39] Another option would be to pass a resolution dispensing with the requirement for consent. As Paul Evans has noted:

> The requirement of consent is a self-imposed parliamentary rule, which parliament can dispense with. The relatively recent delegation of the mechanics of seeking consent to the government where it is required for a PMB could at any point be withdrawn, and parliament could seek the consent through its own channels (which it is perfectly well equipped to do).[40]

A second question explored by the PCRC inquiry is whether the process of seeking Queen's consent gave the Palace undue influence over legislation. The PCRC found no such evidence:

> When the Queen or the Prince of Wales grant their Consent to Bills, they do so on the advice of the Government. We have no evidence to suggest that legislation is ever altered as part of the Consent process. The fact that the Prince of Wales has in the past both granted his Consent to a Bill, in a constitutional capacity, and petitioned against it, in a personal capacity, indicates the formal nature of the process … In reality, it is a veto that could be operated by the Government, rather than the monarchy.[41]

In 2021, *The Guardian* returned to the charge with an article headed 'Royals vetted more than 1,000 laws via Queen's consent: secretive procedure used to review laws ranging from Brexit trade deal to inheritance and land policy.'[42] The Palace replied with the routine defence, that consent is granted solely on the advice of ministers, with a spokesperson saying:

> Queen's consent is a parliamentary process, with the role of the sovereign purely formal. Consent is always granted by the monarch where requested by government. Any assertion that the sovereign has blocked legislation is simply incorrect.[43]

[38] ibid at para 25.

[39] A Makower, 'Queen's Consent' (2019) 87 *The Table: The Journal of the Society of Clerks-at-the-Table in Commonwealth Parliaments* 35, 38.

[40] Evans, above n 30 at 18.

[41] House of Commons Political and Constitutional Reform Committee, above n 33 at para 35.

[42] D Pegg and R Evans, 'Queen lobbied for changes to three more laws, documents reveal' *The Guardian* (8 February 2021) www.theguardian.com/uk-news/2021/feb/08/queen-lobbied-for-changes-to-three-more-laws-documents-reveal.

[43] ibid.

The Palace did not respond directly to the charge of undue influence, but in further articles *The Guardian* gave details of Bills which had been altered at the request of the Palace before they were introduced. These included a Companies Bill in 1973, amended to enable the Queen to keep her shareholdings secret; legislation in 1982 on national monuments, amended to preserve the Royal Commission on Historic Monuments of England; and a road safety Bill in 1968, amended to ensure it did not apply to the Queen's private estates.[44] In July 2021, *The Guardian* returned to the charge yet again, revealing that Scottish legislation was subject to a similar requirement of Crown consent, with the Queen being consulted about 67 Bills before their introduction into the Scottish Parliament.[45] But, in October 2021, in response to a parliamentary question about Queen's consent, the Paymaster General Michael Ellis gave the deadpan reply: 'Consent to Bills has never been refused by the Monarch in modern times and legislation is not amended in order to ensure Queen's Consent.'[46]

In response to *The Guardian*'s earlier disclosures, Adam Tucker was quoted as saying: 'If it was a purely formal process, which it's supposed to be, then no documentation like this would exist at all. There would be no substantive conversations about changing legislation.'[47] Given that the process involves writing to the Palace with copies of the Bill, and forwarding a side copy to Farrer's, it would be naïve to suppose that Farrer's never advise on ways in which the Queen's interests should be protected, or that the Palace never seek to do so. The question which then arises is, does this count as undue or improper influence; and what is the justification for giving the Palace advance sight of legislation which affects the prerogative or the Queen's private interests and which confers, in the words of Thomas Adams, 'the kind of influence over legislation that lobbyists would only dream on'?[48]

The PCRC pressed several witnesses about the origins of Queen's consent in their inquiry, and asked for a modern justification. Adam Tucker and Robert Blackburn suggested it was a relic from the past, with no constitutional justification in the present day.[49] Officials talked about comity: it was a courtesy to the Queen, as a constituent part of the Crown-in-Parliament, to be consulted about forthcoming legislation.[50] If they had been pressed (which they were not) about the influence which this conferred, they might have said it formed part of

[44] ibid; D Pegg and R Evans, 'Queen lobbied for change in law to hide her private wealth' *The Guardian* (7 February 2021) www.theguardian.com/uk-news/2021/feb/07/revealed-queen-lobbied-for-change-in-law-to-hide-her-private-wealth.

[45] S Carrell, R Evans, A Hughes and D Pegg, 'Queen vetted 67 laws before Scottish Parliament could pass them' *The Guardian* (28 July 2021) www.theguardian.com/uk-news/2021/jul/28/revealed-queen-vetted-67-laws-before-scottish-parliament-pass-them; S Carrell and R Evans, 'Scottish government refuses to publish details about Queen's secret lobbying' *The Guardian* (29 July 2021) www.theguardian.com/uk-news/2021/jul/29/scottish-government-refuses-to-publish-details-about-queens-secret-lobbying.

[46] Question tabled by Charlotte Nichols UIN 56265 (answered on 25 October 2021).

[47] Pegg and Evans, above n 42.

[48] ibid.

[49] House of Commons Political and Constitutional Reform Committee, above n 33 at paras 36 and 38.

[50] ibid at paras 39–40.

the Queen's wider rights to be consulted, to encourage and to warn. The committee remained unconvinced, and concluded:

> The United Kingdom is a constitutional monarchy. The Queen has the right to be consulted, to advise and to warn. But beyond that she should have no role in the legislative process. Consent serves to remind us that Parliament has three elements – the House of Commons, the House of Lords, and the Queen-in-Parliament – and its existence could be regarded as a matter of courtesy between the three parts of Parliament. Whether this is a compelling justification for its continuance is a matter of opinion.[51]

Stronger justifications were offered by Philippe Lagassé in a three-part defence of Queen's consent. First, despite references to a 'royal veto', consent is always granted on ministerial advice: it is ultimately a decision for ministers whether to agree to any concessions in response to lobbying from the Palace. Second, the rationale for prerogative consent is to protect the constitutional powers of the Sovereign: 'a bill that attempted to terminate the Sovereign's power to dismiss a prime minister might not be given the Crown's consent unless it included alternative means of removing a head of government under certain situations'. Third, for Bills that affect the Crown Estate, and the personal interests and property of the monarch, Lagassé argues that Crown consent exists to safeguard the political independence of the Sovereign: 'interest consent exists to guarantee that parliamentarians are unable to target the Crown Estate or the personal property of the Queen or Prince in an effort to coerce or threaten the Sovereign or Prince of Wales'.[52]

The third limb may seem far-fetched, but Spain has seen funding for the monarchy being reduced, and a minority of a select committee in 1971 argued for making Palace staff civil servants.[53] Another argument could be that the Queen *qua* private citizen has no vote, and is unrepresented in Parliament; but again, this will strike some observers as fanciful. The strongest defence of consent remains that it is only granted on ministerial advice: the Queen's interests are privileged because she receives advance notice of legislation – but any special protection of those interests must be agreed by ministers. Yet, this special protection is negotiated in secret: any changes to the Bill are made before its introduction, and ministers are not required to disclose what changes have been agreed.

The final question addressed in the PCRC inquiry is whether the requirement of Queen's consent should continue. The quotation above suggests that the committee were ambivalent about this. What was in no doubt for the committee was that Parliament could dispense with the requirement if it felt minded to do so:

> Consent is a matter of parliamentary procedure. If the two Houses of Parliament were minded to abolish Consent, they could do so by means of addresses to the Crown, followed by a resolution of each House. Legislation would not be needed.[54]

[51] ibid at para 41.

[52] P Lagassé, 'On Crown Consent', (*Phillipe Lagassé*, 13 August 2013) www.lagassep.com/2013/08/13/on-crown-consent/.

[53] D Houghton, 'Memorandum: Proposal to set up a Department of the Crown' in *First Report from the Select Committee on the Civil List* HC 529 (1971–72), App 3.

[54] House of Commons Political and Constitutional Reform Committee, above n 33 at para 20.

We began this section by suggesting that Queen's consent would appear to represent a potential form of executive veto. The PCRC inquiry found that it is seldom deployed as such; but should it ever be abused by the Crown, or by the government, the committee were clear that the remedy lies in Parliament's hands. The rule is self-imposed by Parliament, not by a fundamental constitutional principle. If Parliament were minded to abolish consent, the two Houses could readily do so. And if Parliament wanted to reduce the secrecy around Queen's consent, to learn more about the changes made to a Bill at the request of the royal households, Parliament could request that the government routinely published any correspondence with the royal households concerning consent.

The Rule of Crown Initiative

The rule of Crown initiative forms no part of the royal prerogative but is included here for completeness because it offers another means for the executive to veto legislation. To ensure fiscal discipline, Parliament cannot propose new public spending or revenue raising: only the Crown (meaning the government) can do so. Any Bill (and any new clause of a Bill) which would entail new expenditure or revenue raising must be sanctioned by a separate financial resolution, as must any amendment.

The absence of a money resolution blocks the progress of such a Bill beyond second reading. This is what provides the executive with a veto, because under Standing Orders 48 to 52, a motion for a money resolution can only be moved by a minister. There used to be a convention that if a Private Member's Bill obtained a second reading, the government would subsequently bring forward a money resolution if required.[55] But in recent years that has broken down, in a tit-for-tat under the Coalition over Private Members' Bills introduced by Bob Neill and Andrew George; and in the 2017–19 Parliament over a Private Members' Bill from Afzal Khan to reverse the impending reduction in the size of the House of Commons from 650 to 600 MPs. Afzal Khan's Bill secured its second reading by 229 votes to 44, with a lot of support from the government's own backbenchers; so denying it a money resolution was an effective way of stifling at birth a Bill which appeared to have a good chance of being passed.[56]

Paul Evans' detailed study of the executive veto at Westminster concludes that the government's key defence against the risk of Parliament passing unwelcome legislation remains its control over the House of Commons agenda under Standing Order 14. The Cooper-Letwin and Benn Bills were the first ever non-government Bills to be passed against the wishes of the government by seizing control of the

[55] Evans, above n 30 at 21.
[56] ibid.

agenda and timetable. They were lucky in that they did not require Queen's consent, and the Speaker ruled that they did not require a money resolution. Denial of royal assent was the only veto card remaining, and the government's failure to play that card suggests it is no longer available. In other circumstances, Evans concludes that denial of a money resolution is likely to be the most effective way for the government to block a Bill of which it disapproves.

Conclusion

This chapter has examined three ways in which the executive can potentially veto legislation at Westminster. The first way is through the government advising the Queen to withhold royal assent after a Bill has been passed by Parliament. After examining recent precedents alongside the arguments of principle, we conclude that royal assent is a legislative act with no role for the government: it does not provide an executive veto. The second way is through refusing to apply for Queen's consent for Bills which affect the prerogative or the property and personal interests of the Crown. These Bills form only a minority of total legislation, and the requirement of consent is a self-imposed parliamentary rule, which Parliament could modify, or dispense with altogether. Parliament could impose requirements of greater transparency; or waive the requirement, either for an individual Bill, or for all such Bills. So, Queen's consent also does not provide a reliable executive veto.

The third way of blocking legislation is by denying a money resolution to Bills which increase spending or taxation. This is likely to be the most effective form of executive veto, so long as the Bill has spending or revenue implications. We have not questioned in this chapter whether it is right for the government to be able to ignore or override the wishes of a legislative majority. Whether the government needs a reserve power to veto legislation, how the veto works in other countries, and whether it should be capable of being overridden, are all issues that we consider in chapter sixteen.

PART 3

Prerogative Powers of the Executive

7

The War-Making Power

> If there be a prerogative of the Crown which no one has ever challenged, it is the prerogative of the Crown to declare peace or war without the interference of Parliament, by her Majesty alone, under the advice of her responsible Ministers.
>
> Benjamin Disraeli (1864)[1]

Introduction

The prerogative powers of waging war are some of the most potent the government possesses. Although the Queen remains Commander-in-Chief of the armed forces, ultimate de facto decision-making as to the deployment of troops rests with the Prime Minister. The position of Parliament is, at present, uncertain. Although the approval of Parliament was once required to provide the supply (ie money) for wars, that approval has since been reduced to a matter of routine. This chapter examines a much more forensic mechanism for Parliament's scrutiny of the war-making power: a 'convention' that the government will put military deployments to a vote before they are begun (except in certain special circumstances).[2] This convention was conceived as a statement of principle by Tony Blair in 2003, and later affirmed by David Cameron's administration in 2011, but whether it still exists in any meaningful sense is highly questionable.

The story of the last 20 years of debate as to whether Parliament should be given a prior vote on military deployments has been often told. This strand of control over the war-making power does not stand alone, but is one element in a more complex picture, dominated by international law.[3] However, it is the richest seam for exploring the interactions between government and Parliament in regulating the prerogative. Furthermore, the debate is ongoing. As matters stand, there is a high degree of uncertainty as to what rules bind the Prime Minister in the exercise

[1] *Hansard*, HC Deb Vol 173, cols 97-8 (4 February 1864).

[2] We use the term 'convention' because the rule is described as such in the Cabinet Manual. However, as we set out below, it is questionable what the content of the convention currently is and to what extent the government believes that it is bound by it.

[3] P Scott, *The National Security Constitution* (Oxford, Hart Publishing, 2018), 109.

of the war-making power. The shape of that control will depend, in the words of a recent commentator, 'on individual attitudes, immediate circumstances and on party politics'.[4] As a result, this chapter takes the form of a narrative, followed by observations on the current position of the convention.

Before embarking upon this parliamentary tale, it is important to note that there is very little question of the war-making power being challenged in the courts. It is the epitome of 'high policy'; that category of prerogative powers in which the courts will not intervene.[5] As Richards J put it in 2002, 'it is unthinkable that the national courts would entertain a challenge to a government decision to declare war or to authorise the use of armed force against a third country. That is a classic example of a non-justiciable decision.'[6] That is despite the fact that the war-making power can have domestic legal effects – and drastic ones. Whether the UK is 'at war' is a matter of fact (as certified by the Foreign Secretary),[7] and that fact can have dramatic consequences on individuals: actions that were previously lawful may become treasonable, and some individuals will become enemy aliens, whose property is liable to confiscation.[8] However, aside from the ballot box, Parliament is the only forum in which the government is held accountable for decisions to go to war at a national level.

Parliamentary Scrutiny before 2003

Parliament has long had an interest in military affairs because wars have historically been some of the most expensive enterprises undertaken by government. Before the establishment of a standing army in 1689,[9] the House of Commons held direct control over whether the Crown could pursue a particular military goal: they held the purse-strings. From 1323 to 1639, 'only one significant war started without the meeting of a Parliament, and that was because the king had promised not to ask for a subsidy for one year'.[10] Indeed, even after 1689, the vast sums required to keep a standing army – in past centuries by far the greatest call on the public purse – led to the development in the late seventeenth century of the principle of 'appropriation', whereby the moneys voted by Parliament for a particular purpose could not

[4] J Strong, 'Did Theresa May Kill the War Powers Convention? Comparing Parliamentary Debates on UK Intervention in Syria in 2013 and 2018' (2021) 00 *Parliamentary Affairs* 1, 2.

[5] *Council of Civil Service Unions v Minister for the Civil Service* [1985] AC 374, 417-418 (Lord Roskill).

[6] *Campaign for Nuclear Disarmament v Prime Minister* [2002] EWHC 2777 (Admin), 59.

[7] *R v Bottrill, ex parte Kuechenmeister* [1947] 1 KB 41, 50.

[8] *Porter v Freudenberg* [1915] 1 KB 857, 869–70; See *R (Miller) v Secretary of State for Exiting the European Union* [2017] UKSC 5, [53]; A Twomey, '*Miller* and the Prerogative' in M Elliott, J Williams and A Young (eds), *The UK Constitution After Miller: Brexit and Beyond* (Oxford, Hart Publishing, 2018), 74–5; Scott, above n 3 at 111–2.

[9] Mutiny Act 1689, s 1.

[10] R Joseph, *The War Prerogative: History, Reform and Constitutional Design* (Oxford, Oxford University Press, 2013), 97.

be put to another.[11] Initially, the Commons 'took upon themselves the authority of judging as well of the nature, as of the *quantum*, of the particular services recommended to them by the Crown'[12] – ie performing substantive scrutiny of proposed military and foreign policy. However, this practice declined over the course of the next two centuries, to such an extent that one MP in 1857 called such debates 'all moonshine'.[13]

Though Parliament might have a say over monetary matters, constitutional orthodoxy has always held that the power to make war or peace is the Crown's. As the Court of Exchequer Chamber said in 1608, '*bellum indicere* [waging war] belongeth only and wholly to the king'.[14] The basic premise that the direction of war and peace should be for the executive has been passed down through the hands of John Locke, William Blackstone, Joseph Chitty, Walter Bagehot, Albert Venn Dicey and the entire gamut of British constitutional writers through four centuries. It was even something of which Montesquieu approved: 'Once an army is established, it ought not to depend immediately on the legislative, but on the executive power; and this from the very nature of the thing; its business consisting more in action than in deliberation.'[15]

One of the few dissenting voices came from across the Atlantic. Article 1(8) of the United States (US) Constitution (ratified in 1788) states that 'The Congress shall have the power to declare war', although Article 2(2) declares that 'the President shall be Commander in Chief of the Army and Navy of the United States'. This division of power has been subverted by the fact that, in modern warfare, declarations of war are rarely made and the Presidential power under Article 2(2) has been relied upon for troop deployments (see chapter sixteen). For present purposes, it suffices to note that the drafters of the US Constitution sought to place the war-making power in the hands of the legislature.[16] As James Madison wrote:

> [The Constitution] supposes, what the History of all Governments demonstrates, that the Executive is the branch of power most interested in war, & most prone to it. It has accordingly with studied care, vested the question of war in the Legislature.[17]

The US founding fathers consciously departed from the constitutional arrangement in Britain, where the King had the 'supreme command and directive of the military'.[18] However, despite the firm position of British constitutional theorists, the Parliaments following the Restoration – though they did not take upon

[11] J Redlich, *The Procedure of the House of Commons*, vol 3 (London, Constable, 1908), 168–69.

[12] J Hatsell *Precedents of Proceedings in the House of Commons*, vol 3, 2nd edn (London, T Payne, 1796), 180.

[13] *Hansard*, HC Deb Vol 146, cols 1577-652 (16 July 1857).

[14] *Calvin's Case* (1608) 7 Co Rep 25ba. See also Joseph, above n 10 at 16–8.

[15] C Montesquieu, *L'Espirit des Lois* (Thomas Nugent tr, London, J Nourse, 1777), 221–37.

[16] See M McConnell, *The President Who Would Not Be King: Executive Power Under the Constitution* (New Jersey, Princeton University Press, 2020), 188–201.

[17] Letter from James Madison to Thomas Jefferson (2 April 1798) in Joseph, above n 10 at 22.

[18] A Hamilton, 'The Federalist No 69' in A Hamilton, J Madison and J Jay, *The Federalist Papers* (Ian Shapiro ed, New Haven, Yale University Press, 2009), 349.

themselves the mantle of actual military command (as during the Civil Wars)[19] – shed the (contested) pre-Civil War belief that it was not Parliament's place to debate military or foreign policy.[20] Indeed, the Bill of Rights (also enacted in 1689) prohibited keeping a standing army without the consent of Parliament.[21] Today, the consent of Parliament is still required every five years for continuation of the Army.[22]

Some parliamentarians in the immediate aftermath of Oliver Cromwell's rule even suggested the existence of a convention that they would be consulted before a declaration of war, protesting that the Third Dutch War had been declared while Parliament was not sitting.[23] However, as Rosara Joseph has charted, the intensity of this parliamentary scrutiny declined dramatically in the nineteenth century and on into the twentieth.[24] While George Canning could declare as Foreign Secretary that the House of Commons was 'as essential a part of the national council as it is of the national authority',[25] Lord Palmerston – speaking 50 years later as Prime Minister – would stress that Parliament could only expect to be consulted when war was considered against one of the 'great powers' involving 'serious consequences', not against 'a remote country, a conflict with which is not likely to entail upon us any considerable efforts'.[26] Any other practice, said Palmerston, would be a 'burlesque on our constitutional forms'. It is always astounding how quickly assertions about constitutional arrangements attract striking rhetoric.

Perhaps unsurprisingly, those in government had a very different approach to those in opposition. No example is more conspicuous than William Gladstone. Speaking against Palmerston's decision not to consult Parliament over the Persian War in 1857, Gladstone was sternly critical of those who said Parliament had no place in such decisions.[27] Speaking some years later as Prime Minister in 1880, he had rather changed his tune:

> Parliament puts into the hands of the Executive Government the use of the military and naval power within certain limits … yet we are not prepared to say … that on

[19] When parliaments had taken military command under various guises: the Committee of Safety, the Committee of Both Kingdoms, the Derby House Committee, the Council of State.

[20] DL Keir, *The Constitutional History of Modern Britain 1485–1937* (London, A and C Black, 1938), 231, 233; For Queen Elizabeth I's (failed) assertion of this doctrine, see G Parry, 'Foreign Policy and the Parliament of 1576' (2015) 34 *Parliamentary History* 62, 63–4.

[21] Bill of Rights 1689, art 6.

[22] The usual mechanism is to amend s 382 of the Armed Forces Act 2006 to extend its duration for a further five years. The most recent amendment was by the Armed Forces Act 2021. The RAF is permanently constituted under the Air Force (Constitution) Act 1917. The Navy is still raised under the prerogative: Fourth Report from the House of Commons Public Administration Select Committee, *Taming the Prerogative: Strengthening Ministerial Accountability to Parliament* HC 422 (2003–04), para 9.

[23] PS Lachs, 'Advise and Consent: Parliament and Foreign Policy under the Later Stuarts' (1975) 7 *Albion* 41.

[24] Joseph, above n 10 at 100–2.

[25] S Low, 'The Foreign Office Autocracy' (1912) 91 *Fortnightly Review* 1, 3.

[26] *Hansard*, HC Deb Vol 144, cols 167-8 (3 February 1857).

[27] *Hansard*, HC Deb Vol 146, col 1637 (16 July 1857).

> no condition should it be exercised … until Parliament had been called together and consulted at the very outset as to the origin of the measure.[28]

The First and Second World Wars saw a rapid expansion in government power and discretion: the 'heightened coordinating functions accrued by the state during wartime were substantially carried over into its constitutional structure during the peace'.[29] Furthermore, warfare itself changed after 1945. The UK's last declaration of war was in 1942. Whether or not there is a state of war in a particular area now depends on the question of whether there is an armed conflict. This means that the dividing line between peace and war does not crystallise – at least on the domestic plane – in a single moment so readily as it used to. For example, troops may be deployed before war begins, but almost immediately get caught up in conflict. The difficulty in determining at what point Parliament *could* (let alone *should*) get a vote exacerbated the already rapid decline in prospective parliamentary scrutiny.

That is not to say that the government believed that it could act with impunity. Since the Second World War, it has been de rigueur for the Commons to be given an opportunity to express its view on military engagements after the event, although most commonly through debates on motions to adjourn rather than substantive motions. For example, in 1950, Clement Attlee came to the Commons to seek approval for UK involvement in the UN-approved mission in Korea.[30] In support of the motion, Winston Churchill noted the importance of a vote to avoid 'false impressions' abroad that the Commons did not support the government's action.[31] A 2019 parliamentary report has even asserted that after the war there arose 'a convention … that the Government will consult the House of Commons to ensure that the Government's policy on armed conflict reflects the will of the House of Commons'.[32] However, while the aim of that report was to stress continuity in its proposed approach to *prospective* parliamentary control, it is also important to remember that all of the parliamentary debates before 2003 were *retrospective* and that few ever culminated in a vote.[33] Unlike in Canada and Australia, where senior political figures were proposing prospective parliamentary votes on deployments from the 1950s onwards (see chapter fifteen), the post-war period up to 2003 in the UK continued to a great extent the low-point in prospective parliamentary scrutiny that had been reached in the late nineteenth century.

[28] *Hansard*, HC Deb Vol 256, col 1326 (4 September 1880).

[29] T Poole, *Reason of State: Law, Prerogative and Empire* (Cambridge, Cambridge University Press, 2015), 216.

[30] *Hansard*, HC Deb Vol 477, col 485 (5 July 1950).

[31] *Hansard*, HC Deb Vol 477, col 495 (5 July 1950).

[32] Twentieth Report from the House of Commons Public Administration and Constitutional Affairs Committee, *The Role of Parliament in the UK Constitution: Authorising Military Force* HC 1891 (2017–19), para 41.

[33] ibid at paras 36–8.

The Birth of the Convention

On 18 March 2003, after a nine and a half hour debate, the House of Commons approved a motion supporting military action in Iraq. The motion noted the House's previous endorsement of UN Security Council Resolution 1441, recognised that Iraq posed 'a threat to international peace and security', and supported the government's decision that 'the United Kingdom should use all means necessary to ensure the disarmament of Iraq's weapons of mass destruction'.[34] In his opening speech, Tony Blair stated that it was right that the Commons should have a say in the issue: 'that is the democracy that is our right, but that others struggle for in vain'.[35] It was also, of course, politically convenient: the Commons vote gave the deployment a (specific) legitimacy it had failed to achieve through the UN. Nonetheless, no previous decision to go to war in modern times had been backed by *prior* parliamentary approval on a *substantive motion*. The 2003 vote represented 'something of a turning point'.[36] Ever since, it has stood as a precedent for the consultation of Parliament before the deployment of military forces.

However, that 2003 vote became infamous for other reasons. First, the briefing paper summarising the legal basis of the invasion was, as Rosara Joseph has put it, 'revealed to be a selective and misleading summary of the Attorney General's full opinion'.[37] Equally, it is questionable whether Parliament had a genuine choice – 40,000 troops had already been mobilised in the region, and it would have been impossible for Britain to withdraw without a massive loss of credibility.[38] As a precedent for substantive parliamentary control, the 2003 vote left considerable room for development.

Yet, Blair's statement was immediately seized on by the House of Commons Public Administration Select Committee (PASC) in their report, *Taming the Prerogative: Strengthening Ministerial Accountability to Parliament*.[39] This was a major report covering all aspects of prerogative power (see chapter eighteen). PASC suggested 'that any decision to engage in armed conflict should be approved by Parliament, if not before military action then as soon as possible afterwards'.[40] Furthermore, the committee advocated legislation to enforce this practice, particularly favouring a draft Bill proposed by Rodney Brazier.[41]

Despite the Prime Minister's apparent zeal in 2003, the government's willingness for reform did not match PASC's enthusiasm. In June 2006, troops were deployed to Helmand province in Afghanistan, albeit to support ongoing

[34] *Hansard*, HC Deb Vol 401, cols 760–858 (18 March 2003).

[35] ibid.

[36] House of Commons Public Administration and Constitutional Affairs Committee, above n 32 at para 48, quoting David Lidington MP.

[37] Joseph, above n 10 at 105.

[38] *Hansard*, HC Deb Vol 401, cols 829, 840-1 (18 March 2003).

[39] House of Commons Public Administration Select Committee, above n 22.

[40] ibid at para 57.

[41] ibid at para 56.

operations. A subsequent vote supporting the 'continued deployment of UK armed forces in Afghanistan' was passed only four years later in September 2010.[42] Three Private Member's Bills – including Lord Lester's Constitutional Reform (Prerogative Powers and Civil Service etc.) Bill – were brought in this period, attempting to give Parliament a greater role in the exercise of the royal prerogative. All of them failed.

In 2006, the House of Lords Constitution Committee published their own report, *Waging War: Parliament's role and responsibility*.[43] In contrast to PASC, *Waging War* engaged in detail with the technical issues surrounding increased parliamentary involvement. Convinced that parliamentary approval afforded combat decisions 'legitimacy', but mindful of the difficulties of legislating, the committee recommended formalising the convention in a parliamentary resolution.[44] In exceptional circumstances of emergency, the government could seek *retrospective* parliamentary approval within seven days.[45] However, the Blair administration was unconvinced by the need to codify the matter further.[46]

The Brown Government and *The Governance of Britain*

When Gordon Brown became Prime Minister in 2007, the nascent war powers convention had one precedent (Iraq in 2003) and had scant support in government statements. However, as related in chapter three, Gordon Brown took a much more proactive attitude towards reform of the prerogative than Tony Blair (or indeed any other Prime Minister). In May 2007, the Commons had passed a (government drafted) resolution acknowledging the 2004 and 2006 reports and stating that 'it is inconceivable that any Government would in practice depart from this precedent [Iraq in 2003]'.[47] The resolution also invited the government to 'come forward with more detailed proposals for Parliament to consider'. On 3 July 2007, the newly appointed Prime Minister announced that 'the Government will now consult on a resolution to guarantee that on the grave issue of peace and war it is ultimately this House of Commons that will make the decision'.[48]

These consultations began in the *Governance of Britain* Green Paper, supplemented by a separate paper on *War Powers and Treaties*, and culminated in the

[42] *Hansard*, HC Deb Vol 515, cols 494–570 (9 September 2010).
[43] Fifteenth Report from the House of Lords Constitution Committee, *Waging War: Parliament's role and responsibility* HL 236-I (2005–06).
[44] ibid at para 108.
[45] ibid at para 110.
[46] Department for Constitutional Affairs, *Government Response to the House of Lords Constitution Committee's Fifteenth Report of Session 2005–06: Waging War: Parliament's role and responsibility* (Cm 6923, 2006).
[47] *Hansard*, HC Deb Vol 460, cols 492, 578 (15 May 2007).
[48] *Hansard*, HC Deb Vol 462, col 816 (3 July 2007).

Constitutional Renewal White Paper in 2008 and a *Final Report* in 2009.[49] On the war prerogative, the government concluded that the problems associated with legislation – the changing nature of military warfare, the risk of exposing the power to judicial review – were too great to overcome, and suggested 'that a detailed resolution is the best way forward'.[50] A draft resolution was drawn up which required the approval of the Commons for a 'conflict decision' except in three circumstances:

- 'The emergency condition' – when there is not sufficient time for prior parliamentary approval.
- 'The security condition' – where public disclosure of information about the decision could prejudice either (a) the effectiveness of the decision or (b) the security or safety of troops.
- Where the decision covered special forces.[51]

For emergencies, the draft resolution required a retrospective vote. However, when the security condition applied – at least for as long as it remained satisfied – no vote was to take place, even after a deployment. The involvement of special forces would take the conflict decision out of the purview of Parliament altogether.

The draft resolution was never finished. Time and other priorities overtook it, and the Brown government lost office in 2010. There were several reasons why this issue slipped down the agenda in favour of (for example) reform to treaty scrutiny. The content of the resolution remained controversial, and the drafting difficult. Many suggestions were mooted for defining 'armed conflict'. The government adopted a legal approach: a 'conflict decision' would be a decision to authorise the use of force by UK troops abroad that 'would be regulated by the law of armed conflict' in international law.[52] Other deployments, such as in support of peacekeeping operations, would be excluded. Another unresolved issue was the use of secret information (the 'security condition'). This had been rather glossed over by the House of Lords Constitution Committee in 2006, but has since become one of the key concerns in developing the convention.[53]

Although the Brown-era reports did little to really move the dial on the development of the convention, the detailed concerns they identified underlie much of the later debate. They are an important bridge between the general, aspirational statement by Tony Blair in 2003 and the more challenging relationship between the government and Parliament that was to emerge in the next decade.

[49] Ministry of Justice, *The Governance of Britain* (Cm 7170, 2007); Ministry of Defence and Foreign & Commonwealth Office, *War Powers and Treaties: Limiting Executive Powers* (Cm 7239, 2007); Ministry of Justice, *The Governance of Britain – Constitutional Renewal* (Cm 7342, 2008); Ministry of Justice, *Review of the Executive Royal Prerogative Powers: Final Report* (2009).

[50] Ministry of Justice, *The Governance of Britain – Constitutional Renewal*, ibid at para 215.

[51] ibid at 53-6 (Annex A).

[52] ibid at 53.

[53] House of Lords Constitution Committee, above n 43 at para 101; *cf* House of Commons Public Administration and Constitutional Affairs Committee, above n 32 at para 64.

The Cameron Government

Libya and the Cabinet Manual (2011)

In 2011, the Arab Spring brought the prospect of UK military engagement once again to the fore. On 10 March 2011, when asked by Edward Leigh MP for a guarantee of a parliamentary vote before engagements *of any kind* with Colonel Gaddafi in Libya, Sir George Young, then Leader of the House, replied:

> A convention has developed in the House that *before troops are committed*, the House should have an opportunity to debate the matter. We propose to observe that convention except when there is an emergency and such action would not be appropriate. As with the Iraq war and other events, we propose to give the House the opportunity to debate the matter before troops are committed.[54] (emphasis added)

Just over one week later, on Saturday 19 March, the government ordered a missile strike on Colonel Gaddafi's forces. On the Monday *after* the strike the Prime Minister sought the Commons' approval for UK support of the No Fly Zone under UN Security Council Resolution 1973.[55] The motion won a sweeping majority of 557 to 13 votes. It was presumably because the air-strikes on Libya were not troop deployments that they were thought not to come within the convention of *prior* parliamentary approval. However, the vote – particularly in the context of Sir George Young's statement – was suggestive of a shift in attitude in government. Parliamentary approval was now an expectation. As Gavin Phillipson has noted, the second of Sir Ivor Jennings' famous criteria for the existence of a convention appeared to have been fulfilled: the political actors now believed that they were bound by a rule.[56]

Yet the convention was carefully circumscribed. Sir George Young confined his recognition of a convention to troop deployments, rather than military engagements in general, and that caution persisted throughout the government.[57] The only government member to break ranks was the then Foreign Secretary, William Hague, who said on 21 March, 'We will also enshrine in law for the future the necessity of consulting Parliament on military action.'[58] This appeared to promise statutory crystallisation of the nascent convention upon very broad terms.

[54] *Hansard*, HC Deb Vol 524, col 1066 (10 March 2011).

[55] *Hansard*, HC Deb Vol 525, col 700 (21 March 2011).

[56] G Phillipson, "Historic' Commons' Syria vote: the constitutional significance (Part I)' (*UK Constitutional Law Association Blog*, 19 September 2013) www.ukconstitutionallaw.org/2013/09/19/gavin-phillipson-historic-commons-syria-vote-the-constitutional-significance-part-i/.

[57] See the formulation of Gus O'Donnell quoted in Eighth Report from the House of Commons Political and Constitutional Reform Committee, *Parliament's role in conflict decisions* HC 923 (2010–12), 4.

[58] *Hansard*, HC Deb Vol 525, col 799 (21 March 2011).

As in 2003, parliamentary actors leapt upon these government statements. In May 2011, the House of Commons Political and Constitutional Reform Committee (PCRC) published a short report, *Parliament's role in conflict decisions*, calling 'on the current Government urgently to bring forward a text for parliamentary decision' given the lack of progress since 2007.[59] The Committee also recommended that the Cabinet Manual should include a clear reference to Parliament's role in conflict decisions. The government's response was non-committal: the matter was complex and there was no case for urgency.

However, when the Cabinet Manual was published later in the year, it stated that: 'In 2011, the government acknowledged that a convention had developed in Parliament that before troops were committed the House of Commons should have an opportunity to debate.'[60] This reflected the careful terms used by Young, and remains the most authoritative (although not the most complete) statement of the new convention to date. Arriving at this point required both the insistence of parliamentary actors and government acceptance, but concrete precedents were still hard to identify. Notably, the Cabinet Manual still includes references to pre-2003 examples of non-binding (and retrospective) adjournment debates to bolster the credibility of the convention.[61]

Syria (2013)

The most potent precedent for a war powers convention came in mid-2013. On 11 July 2013, the House of Commons Backbench Business Committee enabled the tabling of a motion 'That this House believes no lethal support should be provided to anti-government forces in Syria without the explicit prior consent of Parliament.' It passed by 114 votes to 1.[62] The House of Lords Constitution Committee, who produced a report on the convention on 17 July, placed heavy emphasis on this Commons resolution in concluding that 'the existing convention … provides the best framework for the House of Commons to exercise political control over, and confer legitimacy upon, such decisions'.[63]

By August, the question had become of more than academic interest. Tensions with Damascus were running high and the regime of President Assad had reportedly used chemical weapons on its own people. The Prime Minister came to the Commons and proposed a motion:

> That this House … Agrees that a strong humanitarian response is required from the international community and that this may, if necessary, require military action that

[59] House of Commons Political and Constitutional Reform Committee, above n 57 at 3.

[60] Cabinet Office, *Cabinet Manual*, 1st edn (2011), para 5.38.

[61] ibid at para 5.36.

[62] *Hansard*, HC Deb Vol 566, cols 627–8 (11 July 2013).

[63] Second Report from the House of Lords Constitution Committee, *Constitutional arrangements for the use of armed force* HL 46 (2013–14), para 64.

> is legal, proportionate and focused on saving lives by preventing and deterring further use of Syria's chemical weapons; Notes the failure of the United Nations Security Council over the last two years to take united action in response to the Syrian crisis; … Believes … that every effort should be made to secure a Security Council Resolution backing military action before any such action is taken, and *notes that before any direct British involvement in such action a further vote of the House of Commons will take place…*[64] (emphasis added).

The House was presented with a Joint Intelligence Committee report concluding that it was 'highly likely' that Assad's regime was responsible for the chemical weapons attacks in Syria, as well as the Attorney General's reasons for thinking intervention legal (despite the motion's strong criticism of the UN).[65] Furthermore, the motion did not (ostensibly) seek to give final Commons approval to troop deployments, which would be subject to a further vote. Despite this, the motion was defeated by 272 to 285. The Prime Minister was forced to drop his plans.

The media did not treat David Cameron kindly. The loss was a 'blow to Cameron's authority' on the national and international stage.[66] The legacy of the Syria vote can be found in debates in Parliaments around the world.[67] Furthermore, it emboldened the PCRC to produce a further report, expressing their irritation at lack of progress: they were frustrated that no minister had responsibility to deal with the issue, and found it 'hard to believe that the Government does not possess the expertise to draft an Act of Parliament or parliamentary resolution that would satisfactorily define those decisions on which Parliament should be consulted on, or approve'.[68]

Whether the Prime Minister had been forced into consulting Parliament because of the motion on 11 July[69] or whether he was motivated by his duty under the convention referred to in the Cabinet Manual, the force – both real and symbolic – of that August 2013 vote was substantial. Not only did it stop the government in its tracks in deploying troops; it was also hailed as the moment at which the convention of prior parliamentary approval gained its 'teeth'. As one commentator immediately put it, 'it is now hard to see how any UK Government

[64] *Hansard*, HC Deb Vol 566, col 1425-6 (29 August 2013).

[65] J Day, 'Memo to the Prime Minister' (Jp 115, 29 August 2013) www.gov.uk/government/uploads/system/uploads/attachment_data/file/235094/Jp_115_JD_PM_Syria_Reported_Chemical_Weapon_Use_with_annex.pdf; Prime Minister's Office, *Chemical weapon use by Syrian regime: UK government legal position* (29 August 2013) www.gov.uk/government/publications/chemical-weapon-use-by-syrian-regime-uk-government-legal-position/chemical-weapon-use-by-syrian-regime-uk-government-legal-position-html-version.

[66] N Watt, R Mason and N Hopkins, 'Blow to Cameron's authority as MPs rule out British assault on Syria' (*The Guardian*, 30 August 2013) www.theguardian.com/politics/2013/aug/30/cameron-mps-syria.

[67] *New Zealand Hansard*, Vol 703, 1830 (24 February 2015).

[68] Twelfth Report from the House of Commons Political and Constitutional Reform Committee, *Parliament's role in conflict decisions: a way forward* HC 892 (2013–14), para 34.

[69] P Lagassé, 'Parliament and the War Prerogative in the United Kingdom and Canada: Explaining Variations in Institutional Change and Legislative Control' (2017) 70 *Parliamentary Affairs* 280, 289.

could undertake significant military action without the support of Parliament, or indeed of the wider public'.[70]

Post 2013: Syria, Iraq and Targeted Killings

On 26 September 2014, David Cameron once again consulted the Commons, this time for air strikes against ISIS in Iraq. The September motion explicitly ruled out the deployment of ground troops in combat operations as well as any air strikes in Syria without approval of the House.[71] In presenting his case, the Prime Minister was more wary than in the previous year. He explicitly acknowledged the convention but also made clear that the government retained authority to act in times of emergency.[72] The motion was carried by a landslide of 542 to 43.[73]

However, in August 2015, the UK and US carried out drone strikes in Syria as targeted killings of two ISIS organisers, Reyaad Khan and Junaid Hussain,[74] without a further vote in the Commons and therefore apparently against the September 2014 resolution. The government's purported reason for not seeking the prior approval of the House was that the strike was not part of armed conflict, despite the fact that the justification given for the strikes in international law was that they *were* part of an armed conflict to which the law of war applied (the defence of Iraq).[75] Later in 2015, the government did approach the Commons for its blessing to extend military action in Syria. Once again, the Prime Minister set out the arguments and this time the House approved the motion, which notably ruled out explicitly any deployment of troops on the ground.[76]

The May Government

By the time Theresa May entered Downing Street in 2016, the war powers convention was firmly lodged in the political consciousness, chiefly because of the 2013 Syria vote. However, during her years as Prime Minister, May oversaw

[70] M Chalmers, 'Parliament's decision on Syria: pulling our punches' (*Royal United Services Institute*, 30 August 2013) www.rusi.org/explore-our-research/publications/commentary/parliaments-decision-syria-pulling-our-punches.

[71] Note that UK troops had been deployed to Iraq for humanitarian operations in August.

[72] *Hansard*, HC Deb Vol 585, col 663 (8 September 2014); *Hansard*, HC Deb Vol 585, col 1193 (12 September 2014).

[73] *Hansard*, HC Deb Vol 585, col 1360 (26 September 2014).

[74] See Intelligence and Security Committee of Parliament, *UK Lethal Drone Strikes in Syria* (HC 1152, 26 April 2017), paras 28–30.

[75] Second Report from the Joint Committee on Human Rights, *The Government's policy on the use of drones for targeted killing* HL 141 HC 574 (2015–16), para 2.25; Scott, above n 3 at 145.

[76] *Hansard*, HC Deb Vol 603, cols 323–499 (2 December 2015).

the destabilisation of the convention to such an extent that its very existence was under threat.[77] In part, this was due to developing circumstances. ISIS had still not been contained, the internal war in Syria was carrying on apace, and the UK's military contributions had shifted away from troop deployments towards drone-operated and other airstrikes.

On 13 April 2018, the UN Security Council met for the fourth time in a week, to discuss the ongoing use of chemical weapons in Syria. Chemical weapon attacks had occurred in January, February, and April of that year. Since 2013, Human Rights Watch had documented 85 chemical weapons attacks in Syria.[78] On 14 April, France, UK, and the United States executed coordinated airstrikes on Syria's chemical weapons facilities. No direct authorisation had been granted by the UN, although the Security Council rejected a proposal to condemn the attack.

The lack of UN authorisation made the attacks contentious internationally as well as domestically, although the government's stated legal basis for the strikes was to relieve humanitarian suffering.[79] As with the Libyan airstrikes in 2011, the government lacked prior authorisation from the Commons in launching the strikes. However, the Prime Minister argued her case on different grounds, perhaps unable to exclude airstrikes from the convention because of her predecessor's September 2014 vote. She said that – Parliament having been in recess at the time – it would have been impossible to recall the House to discuss the issue before the attack because 'the speed with which we acted was essential in co-operating with our partners to alleviate further humanitarian suffering and to maintain the vital security of our operations'.[80]

However, May went further. She suggested that prior authorisation would not in any case have been desirable because of a need to keep 'intelligence and information' sources secret; these 'could not be shared with Parliament'.[81] Picking up her predecessor's language from September 2014, the Prime Minister stressed that the government had 'the right to act quickly in the national interest'.[82] In such circumstances, she said, retrospective scrutiny was sufficient. The Labour leader, Jeremy Corbyn, disagreed. In his very short opening response, he moved quickly from the substantive issue to the question of Parliament's rights. The Prime Minister, he said, should not be accountable 'to the whims of the US President' but to Parliament, and it was now necessary to bring forward a 'war powers Act … to transform a now broken convention into a legal obligation'.[83]

[77] Strong, above n 4.

[78] Human Rights Watch, 'Syria: A Year On, Chemical Weapons Attacks Persist' (*Human Rights Watch*, 4 April 2018) www.hrw.org/news/2018/04/04/syria-year-chemical-weapons-attacks-persist.

[79] *Hansard*, HC Deb Vol 639, cols 40–1 (16 April 2018).

[80] *Hansard*, HC Deb Vol 639, col 42 (16 April 2018).

[81] ibid.

[82] ibid.

[83] *Hansard*, HC Deb Vol 639, col 44 (16 April 2018).

Despite Theresa May's protestations to the contrary, the 2018 debate was clearly a departure from the convention. Not only was the debate *after* the deployment (unlike with the Syria airstrikes in 2014); it did not even end in a vote (unlike with the Libya airstrikes in 2011). The only opportunity for MPs to vote came in a subsequent emergency debate on Syria, called by opposition members on a motion that 'this House has considered the current situation in Syria and the UK Government's approach'.[84] Even that, therefore, was not retrospective *approval* of the deployment. The Prime Minister tried to reshape the scope of the convention in her speech. She argued that 'the assumption that the convention means that no decision can be taken without parliamentary approval is incorrect – it is the wrong interpretation of the convention'.[85] There was a distinction, she said, between military deployments in which action was taken over a few weeks and those where it was effectively decided and effected in a couple of days.[86] In so doing, the Prime Minister asserted a novel exception to the convention, in which the 'nature and scale' of the conflict will preclude parliamentary involvement.[87]

The Convention in 2022

The most recent parliamentary report into the war powers convention was published by the House of Commons Public Administration and Constitutional Affairs Committee (PACAC) on 23 July 2019, a year after Theresa May's Syria deployment (which it mentions only briefly).[88] The report made two crucial analytical points. First, it recognised that the content of the convention was fundamentally in the hands of the government and was seriously unstable.[89] Second, it suggested that in a democratic society, the legitimacy of the government's use of the war-making power stems from maintaining the confidence of the House. The government may be responsible, but the government is also accountable to Parliament.[90] PACAC concluded that the instability of the content of the convention was undermining the government's accountability to Parliament and recommended that a resolution be put to the Commons to update the codification of the convention.

The most notable way in which the convention was unstable was in defining exceptions to the general rule that there would be a prior vote. Although the only

[84] *Hansard*, HC Deb Vol 639, col 105 (16 April 2018).
[85] *Hansard*, HC Deb Vol 639, col 201 (17 April 2018).
[86] *Hansard*, HC Deb Vol 639, col 203 (17 April 2018).
[87] V Fikfak and HJ Hooper, 'Whither the War Powers Convention? What Next for Parliamentary Control of Armed Conflict after Syria?' (*UK Constitutional Law Association Blog*, 20 April 2018) www.ukconstitutionallaw.org/2018/04/20/veronika-fikfak-and-hayley-j-hooper-whither-the-war-powers-convention-what-next-for-parliamentary-control-of-armed-conflict-after-syria.
[88] House of Commons Public Administration and Constitutional Affairs Committee, above n 32.
[89] ibid at para 63.
[90] ibid at para 81.

exception referred to in the Cabinet Manual is for emergencies, the government submitted in evidence to the committee that there were four broad exceptions to the convention:

- where a vote could compromise effectiveness;
- to protect secret intelligence sources;
- so as to not undermine security of operational partners; and
- where the legal basis of the deployment has been previously agreed by Parliament.[91]

However, this list is clearly incomplete. The government's list did not even include the 'scale and nature' exception outlined by Theresa May. It appears that the following exceptions exist in addition to those identified by the government and by the Cabinet Manual:

- troop deployments not governed by the law of armed conflict;[92]
- deployments of Special Forces;
- drone attacks;[93] and
- circumstances where the 'nature and scale' of the conflict is such that it is not appropriate to consult the House.

In 2022, then, the convention appears to be rather patchy. There are further areas where recent precedents conflict: for example, airstrikes did not appear to be covered by the convention in 2011 or (perhaps) 2018, but were in 2014. To some extent, this patchiness is to be expected in a nascent convention,[94] particularly one arising as much from policy as practice. The outline of the exceptions is clear, but more work needs to be done in defining them. PACAC invited the government to hold debates and consultations with Parliament,[95] but the government was unwilling to engage, stressing that there was no need for urgency and that 'current arrangements strike an appropriate balance between respecting the role of Parliament … and allowing the government to act flexibly as circumstances demand'.[96]

[91] ibid at para 64.

[92] UK troops were deployed in non-combat roles to Mali in January 2013, and to Iraq in August 2014. Some have questioned whether 'mission creep' might lead such deployments to undermine the war powers convention: eg, *Hansard*, HC Deb Vol 557, cols 783–4 (29 January 2013) (Jim Murphy).

[93] V Fikfak and HJ Hooper, *Parliament's Secret War* (Oxford, Hart Publishing, 2018), 95–100.

[94] Strong, above n 4 at 17.

[95] House of Commons Public Administration and Constitutional Affairs Committee, above n 32 at para 119.

[96] First Special Report from the Public Administration and Constitutional Affairs Committee, *Government Response to the Committee's 20th Report of Session 2017–19: The Role of Parliament in the UK Constitution: Authorising the Use of Military Force* HC 251 (2019), 11.

The Future of the Convention: Some Observations

Codification

At a surface level, the principal issue is codification of the nascent convention whose evolution we have set out in this chapter. There have been attempts to codify it ever since Tony Blair's declaration of principle in 2003. Parliamentary committees, backbenchers and the Brown government have all drafted either legislation or parliamentary resolutions. PACAC followed suit in 2019 with its own draft resolution.[97] In our view, the need for proper codification is evident: in particular, the inadequate account in the Cabinet Manual is misleading and, because it is widely accepted as inaccurate, lacks 'bite' (even as a guideline).

However, we make three observations. First, the process of codification has already begun. Imperfect as it is, the Cabinet Manual does attempt to codify the convention, stating both the general rule and the major exception thought to exist in 2011. As PACAC recommended, that description should be updated to reflect changes since 2011.[98] We should speak more of amending or updating the current codification than codifying the convention de novo.

Second, the process of updating the codification would be better effected by Parliament and government together than by government alone. The Cabinet Manual should reflect the expectations Parliament has of ministers, but cannot stand alone. At the very least, Parliament will require its own rules as to, for example, what role its committees (including the Defence Committee, the Intelligence and Security Committee and the Joint Committee on National Security Strategy) are to play in performing detailed scrutiny, or how (select) parliamentarians might be allowed to examine sensitive material. While this does not necessarily require a resolution of the Commons, that is by far the cleanest solution, ensuring that the codified convention is commonly understood by both parliamentarians and ministers. Furthermore, the convention is, at its heart, a means of parliamentary scrutiny of government. Parliament has a legitimate role in determining what the shape of that scrutiny should be. PACAC's 2019 report demonstrates a cooperative attitude by parliamentarians, open to making accommodations for the government's need to keep some matters secret and options flexible. It proposes development of a shared vision between Parliament and the government on what kind of military intervention is acceptable and how the government should approach conflict decisions.

Third, it is notable that PACAC did not favour statutory reform, wary of placing too rigid a shackle on government action and of the possibility of increased

[97] House of Commons Public Administration and Constitutional Affairs Committee, above n 32 at para 134.

[98] ibid at paras 134 and 41.

judicial review.[99] The difficulties of drafting legislation are even greater than with a parliamentary resolution, which can be more 'open-textured'. Furthermore, as the repeal of the Fixed-term Parliaments Act 2011 has recently demonstrated, legislation does not stand in the way of a change in government policy.

A Convention or a Matter of Policy?

One important aspect of the development of the convention is that it has arisen as much from policy as practice. It originated in a declaration of principle in 2003, evolved through governmental and parliamentary reports (especially under Gordon Brown) and was recognised at the despatch box in 2011 – all before it had ever really been evident in practice. Concurrently, across the Atlantic, the Canadian Conservative Party made a commitment to introduce prior parliamentary votes on deployments in its 2006 manifesto.[100] It is, of course, perfectly possible for a convention to arise from policy: the Ponsonby Rule on treaties shows that (see chapter eight). However, two points flow from that. First, constructing a convention in the abstract is inherently difficult and imprecise – and leaves any general rule a hostage to fortune. That is one reason why the convention has been so unstable.

Second, matters of policy are rarely brought to fruition for purely altruistic reasons. Tony Blair's statement of principle in 2003 was part of securing parliamentary backing for a war which was looking unlikely to receive specific UN sanction. Receiving Conservative Party backing also meant that a controversial war was less toxic at the ballot box. David Cameron's government in 2011 was a coalition with the Liberal Democrats, a party that had opposed the Iraq War. Codifying the terms of government action – and particularly placing controls on warfare – was a central part of the coalition-building exercise. In Canada, Stephen Harper has used parliamentary votes both to 'launder controversial policies through the Commons' and to force the opposition to 'take a clear position on an issue that divided the wider party faithful'.[101] On the other side of the aisle, the New Zealand Labour Party (in opposition) has sought to exploit divisions in the governing National Party by demanding a parliamentary vote (see chapter fifteen). As with other important constitutional developments (eg the Fixed-term Parliaments Act 2011: see chapter five), the convention is the product of both principled debate and political expediency.

Does this matter? We think that it does. For so long as the convention remains more a matter of government policy than a commonly accepted principle, it will be vulnerable to a change in personnel. Successive governments' concern for

[99] ibid at para 81.
[100] Conservative Party of Canada, *Stand Up for Canada: Federal Election Platform* (2006), 5.
[101] N Hillmer and P Lagassé, 'Parliament will decide: an interplay of politics and principle' (2016) 71 *International Journal* 328, 335–6.

flexibility and executive autonomy has hindered the emergence of a predictable convention. The Johnson government, in its 2019 election manifesto, espoused a desire to 'look at the broader aspects of our constitution', including the 'functioning of the Royal Prerogative'.[102] The thrust of its initial reforms has been the polar opposite of those under Gordon Brown, seeking to defend executive power rather than place more controls upon it.

Furthermore, the convention risks being dislocated from the actual practice of going to war. Such decisions occur much more rarely than, for example, new treaties. Each time the question arises, warfare has progressed a little further. Veronika Fikfak and Hayley Hooper have shown how the emergence of drone warfare appears to have created a further exception to the convention.[103] That is supported by the lack of a parliamentary vote on the targeted killings in August 2015. As drone technology develops, the application of the convention to airstrikes – already precarious following Theresa May's refusal to hold a vote on the 2018 mission in Syria – may become more doubtful still.

Conclusion

Since 2018, new UK troop deployments have been restricted to peacekeeping and humanitarian missions.[104] The approach that would be taken by the current Prime Minister when sending troops into armed conflict is therefore uncertain. The convention is beginning to look decidedly battle-scarred, and it is unclear that it would itself survive another deployment. Born of a government announcement in 2003, the convention has survived in a state of dependency on the pronouncements and attitudes of successive governments. This has led to a wide range of 'exceptions', given shape according to the priorities of each Prime Minister. On the other hand, the convention's rare outings have had a strong impact: the memory of David Cameron's 2013 defeat will take a long time to die out.

Parliament and its committees have played a decisive role. At every stage, parliamentarians have seized on government statements and pushed ahead to the next step. Without those early reports after Blair's statement of principle in 2003, it is doubtful that the Brown government would have placed so much weight on the matter, or that it would then have been declared a convention in 2011. Through PACAC's latest report, Parliament continues to play that role. However, it is the weaker partner, unable to bring about greater codification on its own. Furthermore, the convention has struggled to get off the ground: unlike with treaties, which are relatively frequent occurrences, new troop deployments to armed conflicts are few

[102] Conservative Party, *Get Brexit Done: Unleash Britain's Potential* (2019), 48.
[103] Fikfak and Hooper, above n 93 at 95–100.
[104] Eg, the deployment of the UK Task Force to support the UN peacekeeping operation (MINUSMA) in Mali in 2020.

and far between. The war powers convention has existed as much in the realms of theory as of practice. It may, of course, take considerable political capital to erase the legacy of the 2013 Syria vote, but the instability of the convention's content and form, the inconsistency of its precedents and contextual developments in warfare leave it vulnerable to yet further erosion by future governments less persuaded by the convention's underlying principles.

8

Treaties

> Treaties are quite as important as most law, and to require the elaborate assent of representative assemblies to every word of the law, and not to consult them even as to the essence of the treaty, is prima facie ludicrous.
>
> Walter Bagehot (1872)[1]

Introduction

International relations traditionally represent a matter of 'high politics' par excellence. It is therefore unsurprising that, as a matter of domestic law, the conclusion of treaties on behalf of the UK is a prerogative power of the Crown. Moreover, the power to conclude treaties is a prerogative that has long been regarded as outside the scope of judicial review.[2] Scrutiny, or such scrutiny as is available, is instead performed by Parliament.

When we speak of the prerogative power to conclude treaties, the term 'treaty' is used to cover a multitude of sins. The UK signs a wide variety of international instruments under this power, including unilateral and bilateral treaties, agreements requiring ratification and those that do not, legally binding documents and non-binding understandings. International instruments also range across a wide field of subject areas. Following Brexit, attention has recently been focussed on trade agreements, but the UK is a signatory to over 14,000 treaties, including international human rights instruments, environmental pledges and data-sharing arrangements.

However, the treaty-making power cannot change obligations or rights in domestic law, even if it places the UK under obligations in international law.[3] That principle of dualism has long been established.[4] Where a treaty

[1] W Bagehot, *The English Constitution*, 2nd edn (London, 1872), xxxix.

[2] *Council of Civil Service Unions v Minister for the Civil Service* [1985] AC 374, 417-418.

[3] For the limited lawful effects of treaties on domestic law, see A Twomey, 'Miller and the Prerogative' in M Elliott, J Williams and A Young (eds), *The UK Constitution After Miller: Brexit and Beyond* (Oxford, Hart Publishing, 2017), 76-80.

[4] Eg, In *Walker v Baird* [1892] AC 491, the Crown's conclusion with France of an agreement on lobster fishing in Newfoundland could not itself alter the rights of lobster fishermen.

obligation requires a change in UK domestic law, the executive must either turn to Parliament for primary legislation or make the necessary changes through their powers to make secondary legislation.[5] Where such a treaty requires ratification, it is government practice not to ratify the treaty before the domestic legislation is in place.[6]

Treaty scrutiny in Parliament is largely restricted to treaties that require ratification. Furthermore, it has traditionally been restricted to the post-negotiation, pre-ratification period. The last twenty years and more have seen consistent calls from parliamentary committees and others to strengthen this scrutiny and to expand its scope to other types of agreements and to different stages of the treaty-making process. For the past few decades, some further limited scrutiny was afforded through the structures of the European Union (EU). Although the EU never had full competence over foreign policy, its ability to conclude trade agreements on behalf of the Member States has relieved the negotiating burden on the UK while the UK was a member. Furthermore, the European Parliament has significant powers of treaty scrutiny, with a veto power, a power to propose amendments to treaties, and the right to information and consultation during negotiations.[7] The UK's exit from the EU means that these democratic scrutiny mechanisms no longer apply. This shift in circumstances has unleashed a renewed parliamentary interest in reforming our own domestic provisions.[8] This chapter examines the case for Parliament's role in scrutinising new treaties. We trace the history of its involvement, lay out the reasons why we think greater involvement is now needed, and finally sketch the outlines of some realistic proposals for reform.

Foreign Policy in Parliament: An Historical Perspective

Parliament's claim to the right to scrutinise treaties is not new. Before social and other domestic policy began to dominate government business and the parliamentary agenda, foreign policy was one of the central matters that occupied parliamentary sessions, along with Parliament's traditional role in approving

[5] *JH Rayner (Mincing Lane) Ltd v Department of Trade and Industry* [1990] 2 AC 418.

[6] HM Government, *Government Response to the Constitution Committee Report: Parliamentary Scrutiny of Treaties* (July 2019), 8; *Reference on the Continuity Bill* [2018] UKSC 64, [29].

[7] Treaty on the Functioning of the European Union, art 218(6).

[8] Eg, Sixth Report from the House of Commons Exiting the European Union Committee, *Parliamentary Scrutiny and approval of the Withdrawal Agreement and negotiations on a future relationship* HC 1240 (2017-19); Seventeenth Report from the Joint Committee on Human Rights, *Human Rights Protections in International Agreements* HC 1833 HL 310 (2017-19); Twentieth Report from the House of Lords Constitution Committee, *Parliamentary Scrutiny of Treaties* HL 345 (2017-19); Eleventh Report from the House of Lords European Union Committee, *Treaty scrutiny: working practices* HL 97 (2019-21), paras 19-29.

taxation and public expenditure. By the eighteenth century, 'The centre of gravity of the action of the House of Commons lay in the region of foreign and colonial policy and the financial measures rendered necessary by the decisions on such subjects.'[9]

Long gone were the days when Queen Elizabeth I had tried (unsuccessfully) to curb discussion of foreign policy in Parliament.[10] As the Duke of Bedford put it in a debate in the House of Lords in 1752:

> Although his majesty has by his prerogative the sole power of making peace and war, and of concluding such treaties as he may at any time think necessary, yet no one doubts, but that by our constitution this House, which is the sovereign's supreme and highest council, may interpose and may advise his majesty to make such treaties as we may think necessary, or not to conclude any treaty, which may then be supposed to be upon the anvil.[11]

However, as the Earl Granville was keen to point out in that same debate, Parliament was wary of overstepping the mark and intruding upon business that belonged properly to the King's ministers.[12] In such business, as Joseph Chitty wrote in 1820:

> One of the chief excellencies of the constitution consists in the harmony with which it combines all that strength and dispatch in the executive department of the state, which might be expected only from a despotic government; with every liberty and right of interference on the part of the subject which is not inconsistent with the public welfare.[13]

The appropriate balance between executive flexibility and parliamentary scrutiny have continued to be the focal point of debate. However, the factors to be weighed upon that balance have been altered. For one thing, the justification for parliamentary scrutiny has changed. Alongside concerns for individual liberty and national revenue, matters over which Parliament has long extended its reach, the centuries since Chitty have seen a marked growth in democratic justifications for ministerial accountability to Parliament.

The conduct of foreign affairs has also changed. International agreements now play a greater role in constraining government action and have an important impact on our daily lives. Until the middle of the nineteenth century, international treaties were dominated by the drawing up of alliances, the ending of wars, and the definition of territorial borders. In the modern day, treaties cover (and are predominantly concentrated on) a vast range of other subjects, from trade to climate change to human rights protection. This shift demands not only a more

[9] J Redlich, *The Procedure of the House of Commons*, vol 1 (London, Constable, 1908), 66.
[10] G Parry, 'Foreign Policy and the Parliament of 1576' (2015) 34 *Parliamentary History* 62, 63-4.
[11] W Cobbett, *Parliamentary History of England*, vol 14 (London, TC Hansard, 1813), col 1176.
[12] ibid at cols 1184-5.
[13] J Chitty, *A Treatise on the Law of the Prerogatives of the Crown* (London, Butterworths, 1820), 39.

intense form of scrutiny, but also a more sophisticated set of mechanisms to effect it: we might expect, for example, the importance of speed and secrecy in negotiating a peace treaty or military alliance to differ from negotiations on a multilateral climate change agreement (as at the recent and much-publicised 2021 United Nations Climate Change Conference (COP26)).

On the other hand, the numbers of treaties now made means that there needs to be some filter to ensure that the limited capacity of Parliament is not overwhelmed. Indeed, it may be no coincidence that the nineteenth-century explosion in the numbers of international treaties globally coincided with an erosion of parliamentary scrutiny.[14] Any proposals for reform must be sustainable, given the constraints of parliamentary resources.

From Ponsonby to CRAG

The Ponsonby Rule

The beginnings of a more structured approach to the scrutiny of treaties lie in the turn of the twentieth century. Although Parliament had always been able to debate treaties, scrutiny was hampered by the facts that negotiations were often conducted in secret and that the contents of treaties themselves might remain secret, even after ratification.[15] This was attacked on two fronts: first domestically, then internationally. It became late nineteenth-century practice for the government to lay concluded and ratified treaties before Parliament, permitting post-ratification scrutiny.[16] This was bolstered on the international plane by developments following the hostile American reaction to the web of secret arrangements that underlay the lead-up to (and conduct of) the First World War. First Article 18 of the Covenant of the League of Nations and now Article 102 of the UN Charter require members to register their agreements with the Secretariat for publication.

A more deliberate approach to pre-ratification scrutiny was set out in 1924. In the first, short-lived Labour administration of Ramsay Macdonald, the Parliamentary Under-Secretary of State for Foreign Affairs, Arthur Ponsonby, stated that: 'it is the intention of His Majesty's Government to lay on the table of both Houses of Parliament every treaty, when signed, for a period of 21 days, after which the treaty will be ratified'.[17] Ponsonby had been an opponent of British involvement in the First World War, calling it a 'diplomatists' war and not

[14] See E Keene, 'The Treaty-Making Revolution of the Nineteenth Century' (2012) 32 *The International History Review* 475.

[15] To the rancour of parliamentarians: J Black, *Parliament and Foreign Policy in the Eighteenth Century* (Cambridge, Cambridge University Press, 2004), 237.

[16] J Redlich, *The Procedure of the House of Commons*, vol 2 (London, Constable, 1908), 43.

[17] *Hansard*, HC Deb Vol 171, cols 2000-05 (1 April 1924).

a peoples' war'.[18] In 1915, he had published a book, *Democracy and Diplomacy*, strongly arguing for enhanced democratic control of foreign policy. In government, the policy announced by Ponsonby applied only to treaties that required ratification, as a later Foreign Secretary (Selwyn Lloyd) reiterated in 1957.[19] The House of Commons would be kept informed of other agreements, except those of a 'purely technical' nature. However, the Ponsonby Rule (as it became known) was only ever a 'negative resolution' procedure. That is, the 'absence of disapproval [would] be accepted as sanction'.[20] That reflected Ponsonby's major objective: building in compulsory delays to treaty ratification so that governments could not use the same fait accompli tactic he had so objected to in 1914.[21] Despite initial rejection by the subsequent Baldwin administration, the Ponsonby Rule became the benchmark for parliamentary scrutiny of treaties from its reassertion in 1929.

The Ponsonby Rule as a convention was followed almost invariably from 1929 to 2009,[22] although a modification was made in 1981 to exclude double taxation treaties.[23] In 1997, the convention expanded to include the provision of explanatory memoranda to Parliament upon the presentation of a treaty.[24] From the 1990s, there was a growing campaign further to codify the convention and to render its obligations binding under statute. The campaign was led by Lord Lester, who introduced Private Member's Bills in 1996, 2003 and 2006, and was supported by various Select Committee reports from 1994 to 2004.[25] It also found support from the Conservative Party's Democracy Taskforce, who espoused the 'belief that ratification should be removed from the Prerogative and made subject to Parliamentary consent'.[26]

Constitutional Reform and Governance Act 2010

Calls for the codification of the Ponsonby Rule in statute were eventually adopted by Gordon Brown as Prime Minister, as part of his wide-ranging review of

[18] *Hansard*, HC Deb Vol 65, cols 2089-90 (6 August 1914).

[19] *Hansard*, HC Deb Vol 171, col 2005 (1 April 1924); *Hansard*, HC Deb Vol 579, col 370 (4 December 1957).

[20] *Hansard*, HC Deb Vol 171, cols 1999-2005 (1 April 1924).

[21] A Ponsonby, *Democracy and Diplomacy: A Plea for Popular Control of Foreign Policy* (London, Meuthen, 1915), 84-5; see also J Stöckmann, 'The First World War and the Democratic Control of Foreign Policy' (2020) 249 *Past & Present* 121, 152-3.

[22] Despite some exceptions: *Hansard*, HC Deb Vol 651, cols 942-3 (18 December 1961).

[23] *Hansard*, HC Deb Vol 4, col 82W (6 May 1981). The Commons has to approve such agreements affirmatively in any case, since they concerned taxation: Inheritance Tax Act 1984, s 158; Taxation (International and Other Provisions) Act 2010, s 5.

[24] *Hansard*, HC Deb Vol 287, col 430W (16 December 1996); *Hansard*, HL Deb Vol 576, col WA101 (16 December 1996).

[25] The Treaties (Parliamentary Approval) Bill [HL] 1996; Executive Powers and Civil Service Bill [HL] 2003; Constitutional Reform (Prerogative Powers and Civil Service etc.) Bill [HL] 2006; see Ministry of Justice, *The Governance of Britain – War powers and treaties: Limiting Executive powers* (Cm 7239, 2007), 74-7.

[26] Conservative Democracy Task Force, *Power to the People: Rebuilding Parliament* (2007), 8.

prerogative powers (see chapter three). Following his reforms, the principal mechanism of parliamentary treaty scrutiny is the Constitutional Reform and Governance Act 2010 (CRAG). Under Part 2 of CRAG, the government is under a statutory duty to lay before Parliament any treaty that is subject to ratification.[27] Further, an explanatory memorandum must be included, containing the name of the responsible minister, the financial implications of the treaty and the means required to implement it, among other matters.[28] The government cannot usually ratify a treaty for 21 sitting days after it was laid before Parliament.[29]

In this way, the convention that developed around the Ponsonby Rule has been transformed into a statutory scheme. Notably, although CRAG formalised the 'negative resolution' model of the Ponsonby Rule, it only grants Parliament the power to *delay* ratification, not to veto it. If the House of Commons resolves against ratification, the government may only ratify if it sets out its reasons for desiring ratification in a statement and waits a further period of 21 sitting days.[30] If the Commons objects again within those 21 days, the process repeats. This may in theory continue indefinitely, so long as the Commons continues to pass negative resolutions. If the House of Lords alone objects, the government may ratify in any case, once it has laid an explanatory statement.[31]

CRAG did not, therefore, add very much meat to the bones of the pre-existing convention. Indeed, it did not entirely codify the convention, because the definition of 'treaties' contained in section 25 of CRAG to which its procedures apply is narrower than Ponsonby's.[32] Furthermore, by setting out that the consequence of a negative resolution is (at most) to *delay* ratification, it may have weakened the previous position. Ponsonby's 1924 statement envisaged the Commons' negative resolution being the final word – at least a political *veto* over ratification. Although Parliament has some sort of veto (at least in theory) when a treaty requires implementing legislation,[33] the only power the Commons has under CRAG is to delay ratification, and the Lords does not even have that. What is more, neither House regularly debates new treaties, especially where no implementing legislation is required.[34] There is no requirement for a debate to be held, and no special mechanism to ensure that a debate does take place if parliamentarians want one.

Nor did CRAG add any new mechanisms for scrutiny. Despite a Foreign Office undertaking to give them relevant information,[35] Commons departmental select committees have played only a limited role, at least until recently. Before Brexit,

[27] Constitutional Reform and Governance Act 2010, s 20.
[28] ibid at s 24.
[29] A treaty may be ratified earlier in 'exceptional' cases: ibid at s 22.
[30] ibid at s 20(4).
[31] ibid at s 20(7)-(8).
[32] House of Lords European Union Committee, above n 8 at para 105.
[33] Since the government does not ratify treaties until the implementing legislation has been passed: HM Government, above n 6 at 8; *Reference on the Continuity Bill*, above n 6 at para [29].
[34] A Lang, *Parliament's Role in Ratifying Treaties* (House of Commons Library Briefing Paper 5855, February 2017), 10.
[35] *Hansard*, HL Deb Vol 707, col 796 (31 January 2008).

the Joint Committee on Human Rights was the most active, screening all proposed human rights treaties and others with human rights implications.[36] However, Brexit has stimulated a more proactive approach elsewhere. The Lords committees have recently been restructured. Initially constituted as a sub-committee of the House of Lords European Union Committee (although with terms of reference not limited to treaties with the EU),[37] the International Agreements Committee (IAC) became a full sessional committee of the House of Lords in January 2021, with terms of reference 'To consider matters relating to the negotiation, conclusion and implementation of international agreements, and to report on treaties laid before Parliament in accordance with Part 2 of the Constitutional Reform and Governance Act 2010.'[38]

The IAC is the first time Parliament has had a dedicated treaty scrutiny committee, and it has been kept extremely busy, conducting six inquiries as a sub-committee in 2020 and publishing 13 reports in 2021. Furthermore, the committee has been able to receive confidential progress reports covering several trade negotiations.[39] However, the IAC is not a joint committee of both houses, nor does it have any particular powers to set aside time for debate in the House. According to its chair, Lord Goldsmith, the IAC's 'hands are tied while we wait for legislative change', although it has demonstrated considerable dexterity in exerting pressure on government through a wide variety of formal and informal channels.[40]

Specific Scrutiny Provisions

Notwithstanding the general position under the Ponsonby Rule and CRAG, Parliament has from time to time legislated for greater controls over specific treaties. The most notable recent example is the series of successful amendments proposed by Dominic Grieve to the European Union (Withdrawal) Bill in 2018. By section 13(1) of the 2018 Act, the UK's withdrawal agreement with the EU could only be ratified upon a positive resolution of the House of Commons (the so-called 'meaningful vote') and the passage of an Act of Parliament containing provision for the implementation of the agreement. The well-known failure of Theresa May to win a meaningful vote led directly to her resignation as Prime Minister.

[36] First Report from the Joint Committee on Human Rights, *Protocol No. 14 to the European Convention on Human Rights* HL 8 HC 106 (2004-5), paras 5-7.

[37] *First Report from the House of Lords Procedure Committee* HL 29 (2019-21), 6-7.

[38] Fifth Report from the House of Lords Liaison Committee, *Review of investigative and scrutiny committees: strengthening the thematic structure through the appointment of new committees* HL 193 (2019-21), 15-7.

[39] Seventh Report from the House of Lords International Agreements Committee, *Working Practices: One Year On* HL 75 (2021-22), para 46.

[40] P Goldsmith, 'International agreements affect us all. They deserve to be scrutinised' (*Prospect Magazine*, 12 February 2021) www.prospectmagazine.co.uk/world/peter-goldsmith-lords-international-agreements-select-committee-brexit-trade.

Further provisions in section 13 of the 2018 Act set out that a statement of the government's intentions should be made and voted upon should the Prime Minister conclude that no withdrawal agreement could be achieved,[41] or if no agreement in principle had been reached by 21 January 2019.[42] This laid the groundwork for potential future control of the negotiating agenda by Parliament. Indeed, section 1 of the European Union (Withdrawal) (No. 2) Act 2019 (the 'Benn Act') required the Prime Minister to seek an extension to the negotiating period prior to UK exit under Article 50(3) Treaty on European Union.

Should Parliament Have an Enhanced Role?

Despite some recent changes in parliamentary committee structures, the position of parliamentary scrutiny of treaties under CRAG is still rudimentary. In those circumstances, it is important to re-examine the reasons why Parliament may need to have greater input in future, and then to explore possible routes for reform.

First and foremost, treaties are of great importance to the determination of the rights, freedoms and practices of all citizens. As Walter Bagehot put it in the epigraph to this chapter:

> Treaties are quite as important as most law, and to require the elaborate assent of representative assemblies to every word of the law, and not to consult them even as to the essence of the treaty, is prima facie ludicrous.[43]

No longer are treaties confined to matters of war and peace, but range across the entire spectrum of governmental policy.

Whether it is the European Convention on Human Rights (especially since the Human Rights Act 1998), a double taxation treaty or a trade agreement, the policy choices made by the government on the international plane are of profound consequence for UK citizens and residents. Indeed, in *R (Miller) v Secretary of State for Exiting the European Union* (*Miller 1*), the Supreme Court found that the prerogative power could not be used to curtail individuals' legal rights, although this should be regarded as a special case: repealing the European Communities Act 1972 – which breached the 'dualist' divide and gave direct effect to EU law in UK domestic law – was 'such a far-reaching change to the UK constitutional arrangements' that it could not 'be brought about by ministerial decision … alone'.[44] Although not an entirely comparable situation, some have argued that the courts would find that Parliament's consent was required before any withdrawal from the European Convention on Human Rights.[45]

[41] European Union (Withdrawal) Act 2018, s 13(7)-(9).
[42] ibid at s 13(10)-(12).
[43] Bagehot, above n 1 at xxxix.
[44] *R (Miller) v Secretary of State for Exiting the European Union* [2017] UKSC 5, [80]-[81].
[45] J Williams, 'Miller and the Human Rights Act 1998: can the Government withdraw the UK from the ECHR by the royal prerogative?' (*Public Sector Blog*, 28 February 2017) www.publicsectorblog.

Brexit has brought the importance of treaties, particularly trade agreements, to the fore. Despite the principle of 'dualism', some of our most personally and economically significant rights rest, for their content as well as for the practical means of their exercise, on acts of the prerogative rather than Acts of Parliament. The continued lack of parliamentary control of the treaty-making prerogative in an age of ever-expanding horizons for international diplomacy threatens the usurpation of Parliament's role in the determination of rights by the prerogative.

Second, when Parliament is presented with the implementing legislation for a treaty that has been agreed, albeit not ratified, it has no real choice but to acquiesce. In many cases, it will not even be able to amend the legislation because of the terms already agreed by the government. Given the current limits on parliamentary scrutiny of those underlying terms, the usual powers of Parliament to determine the content of legislation are severely curtailed. In such circumstances, Parliament legislates with a metaphorical gun to its figurative head and its ability to perform meaningful democratic scrutiny of such legislation is very limited.

Moreover, this gun-to-the-head approach to legislating is not the only way in which international commitments shape domestic law. Despite our dualist separation of international and domestic law, the courts do refer to treaty provisions as part of the process of statutory interpretation. Where a court is seeking to interpret legislation enacted to give effect in domestic law to the UK's obligations under international law, the court may use a treaty-compliant interpretation where the language of the statute is ambiguous, 'for there is a *prima facie* presumption that Parliament does not intend to act in breach of international law, including therein specific treaty obligations'.[46] It is telling that Lord Justice Diplock, just before setting out this principle, used the phrase 'Once *the Government* has legislated' (emphasis added). While justifiable on its own terms, the rule demonstrates the government's ability to exert influence over domestic law by means of a prerogative power.

Third – moving beyond Parliament's role as legislator – the status quo threatens Parliament's ability to scrutinise government policy. Governments bind themselves and future governments (at least in international law) to particular policy positions in international treaties over the content of which Parliament gets little say. Even where there is no domestic mechanism, such as the Human Rights Act 1998, to enforce the obligation, ministers must abide by their commitments under international law.[47] Perhaps most obviously in recent years, successive governments have

practicallaw.com/miller-and-the-human-rights-act-1998-can-the-government-withdraw-the-uk-from-the-echr-by-the-royal-prerogative; A Peplow, 'Withdrawal from the ECHR after Miller – A Matter of Prerogative?' (*UK Constitutional Law Association Blog*, 28 February 2017) www.ukconstitutionallaw.org/2017/02/28/alex-peplow-withdrawal-from-the-echr-after-miller-a-matter-of-prerogative. Others deem this unlikely: G Phillipson and A Young, 'Would Use of the Prerogative to Denounce the ECHR "Frustrate" the Human Rights Act? Lessons from Miller' [2017] *Public Law* 150.

[46] *Salomon v Customs and Excise Commissioners* [1967] 2 QB 116, 143 (Diplock LJ); *cf* D Feldman, D Bailey, and L Norbury, *Bennion, Bailey and Norbury on Statutory Interpretation*, 8th edn (LexisNexis Butterworths, 2020), s 24.16.

[47] Cabinet Office, *Cabinet Manual*, 1st edn (2011), para 3.46.

made commitments on climate change under the Paris Agreement. Although these have been found to be ineffective when it comes to judicial review in the domestic courts,[48] they nonetheless act (until 2050 in the case of the Paris Agreement) as practical limits on future governments' and Parliament's ability to alter the course of domestic policy.

Finally, giving greater voice to Parliament in shaping and scrutinising the formation of foreign policy – particularly when it comes to the making of binding treaties – is both constitutionally and practically prudent. While a negotiating position may be weakened by being shackled to an unworkable mandate, it may equally suffer from a lack of domestic consensus (as Theresa May found to her cost). Present arrangements privilege the former concern over the latter. Such a monoptic view belongs to the age of Chitty, who wrote in 1820 that:

> When the rights in question are concentrated in one department of the state, and the power of the realm is wielded by one hand, the execution of public measures will inspire the people with confidence, and strike into the enemies of the country that awe, that dread of its activity and power, which it is the constant endeavour of good policy to create.[49]

Although retaining a rhetorical strength, that view is now deeply inconsistent with the modern reality. Governments are as accountable to Parliament and the electorate on matters of foreign policy as on any other matter. Moreover, diplomatic strength often relies upon 'a predictably durable consensus'.[50] To turn that idea around, a negotiating position is weakened if the other party or parties believe that there is a good chance that any agreement will be undermined by a change in government or public opinion. It is therefore disappointing to read the following passage from the government's response to the House of Lords Constitution Committee report in 2019:

> [The treaties prerogative] is not only the result of centuries of constitutional practice but also serves an important function: it enables the UK to speak clearly, with a single voice, as a unitary actor under international law. It ensures that partners understand the United Kingdom's views and are able to have faith that the position as presented formally in negotiations is the position of the United Kingdom.[51]

That statement may as well have been written by Chitty in 1820. It overlooks the very important point that international partners can only have faith that the government 'speaks clearly' for the UK when they are sure that the executive has the support of the legislature and electorate in doing so. One of the 'chief excellencies' of the British constitution, as Chitty recognised elsewhere, is the 'harmony'

[48] *R (Plan B Earth) v Secretary of State for Transport* [2020] UKSC 52; *R (Packham) v Secretary of State for Transport* [2020] EWCA Civ 1004.

[49] Chitty, above n 13 at 39-40.

[50] E Smith, A Lang and E Bjorge, 'Treaties, Parliament and the constitution' [2020] *Public Law* 508, 519.

[51] HM Government, above n 6 at 5-6.

between the government and Parliament.[52] It is hard to achieve such harmony when the government is playing the tuba and Parliament a piccolo.

Control by the Courts

A further reason why Parliament should have greater powers to scrutinise treaties is that the courts do not generally have jurisdiction over how the government exercises the treaty-making power.[53] In *Miller 1*, the Supreme Court went to great lengths to emphasise the unique circumstances that led them to intervene and reaffirmed that the courts would only police the *boundaries* of such prerogative powers rather than the *manner* of their exercise (see chapter seventeen).[54]

Notwithstanding the clarity of repeated judicial dicta, litigants have repeatedly invited the courts to review the exercise of the treaty-making power. For example, in *R v Secretary of State for Foreign and Commonwealth Affairs, ex parte Rees-Mogg*, the Eurosceptic former editor of *The Times* argued that the Secretary of State was unlawfully limiting his discretion by signing up to Title V of the Maastricht Treaty (which contained the Common Foreign and Social Policy).[55] The Court of Appeal held that it did not have jurisdiction over this exercise of the prerogative. Lord Justice Lloyd cited Lord Denning MR in *Blackburn v Attorney-General* – a challenge to accession to the EEC Treaty – who said:

> The treaty-making power of this country rests not in the courts, but in the Crown; that is, Her Majesty acting upon the advice of her Ministers. When her Ministers negotiate and sign a treaty, even a treaty of such paramount importance as this proposed one, they act on behalf of the country as a whole. … Their action in so doing cannot be challenged or questioned in these courts.[56]

The courts have also been asked (unsuccessfully) to break the dualist divide and enforce treaty commitments directly. In *R (Plan B Earth) v Secretary of State for Transport*, environmental campaigners attempted to show that the Secretary of State for Transport had unlawfully failed to take account of the Paris Agreement on climate change (2015) when making his decision to grant planning permission to Heathrow Airport to develop a third runway, contrary to his statutory duty under section 5(8) of the Planning Act 2008.[57] The central question was whether

[52] Chitty, above n 13 at 39.

[53] *Council of Civil Service Unions v Minister for the Civil Service*, above n 2 at 417-418. An (exceptional) contrary view was given by Lord Denning in *Laker Airway Ltd v Department of Trade* [1997] QB 643.

[54] *R (Miller and another) v Secretary of State for Exiting the European Union* [2017] UKSC 5.

[55] *R v Secretary of State for Foreign and Commonwealth Affairs, ex parte Rees-Mogg* [1994] QB 552, 570. However, the court did make obiter remarks drawing an analogy with the UN and NATO, membership of which could surely not be unlawful either.

[56] *Blackburn v Attorney-General* [1971] 1 WLR 1037, 1040.

[57] *R (Plan B Earth) v Secretary of State for Transport* above n 48.

the Paris Agreement could constitute government 'policy' for the purposes of that Act. Lords Hodge and Sales reasserted the dualism of the UK's approach to international and domestic law:

> The fact that the United Kingdom had ratified the Paris Agreement is not of itself a statement of Government policy in the requisite sense. Ratification is an act on the international plane. … Ratification does not constitute a commitment operating on the plane of domestic law to perform obligations under the treaty.[58]

This accords with constitutional orthodoxy: treaties do not form part of domestic law unless they are incorporated by legislation.[59] Nor may a court decide whether the government has correctly understood an obligation in an unincorporated treaty.[60] The Supreme Court may have left room for future argument following *Plan B Earth* based on the doctrine of legitimate expectations (see paragraphs [106]-[108]),[61] but the case stands as solid authority for the separation of domestic and international law. The domestic courts only have authority to rule on the former and, unlike Parliament, cannot provide effective scrutiny of treaty-making or treaty-keeping.

Reform

Despite this strong case for greater parliamentary involvement in foreign policy decision-making, especially the conclusion of treaties, very little has changed since 1929. With the renewed interest in reform following Brexit, it is to be hoped that long overdue developments will progress. There are three broad areas in which reforms are now needed: in scrutiny during the negotiation of treaties; in scrutiny after negotiations but before ratification; and in the relationship between central and devolved governments and Parliaments. In each area, it will be necessary to consider whether there is the political will, the capacity and the institutional competence to succeed.

Scrutiny During Negotiations

There is an obvious need for secrecy and flexibility during some sorts of negotiations. However, this must be balanced by ongoing scrutiny if Parliament is to be presented with any real choice at all in approving the content of concluded treaties

[58] ibid at para 108. This overturned a surprising Court of Appeal victory for the campaigners ([2020] EWCA Civ 214), which the Court of Appeal itself showed no desire to follow in *R (Packham) v Secretary of State for Transport*, above n 48.

[59] *JH Rayner (Mincing Lane) Ltd v Department of Trade and Industry* [1990] 2 AC 418.

[60] *R (JS) v Secretary of State for Work and Pensions* [2015] 1 WLR 1449, [90]; *cf* A Mills, 'Judicial Pushback – National Airports Policy Grounded' (2020) 79 *Cambridge Law Journal* 208.

[61] For older authorities on which, see Twomey, above n 3 at 78.

and any implementing legislation. Such oversight will not only improve democratic accountability but will also secure greater diplomatic strength by building consensus.[62] Change here is occurring, although slowly and disjointedly.

The most obvious way in which Parliament can balance the need for secrecy with the transparency required for scrutiny is through committees. Each House already has some capacity for pre-ratification scrutiny by committees, which are sometimes able to perform ongoing scrutiny during negotiations. For example, the IAC has received evidence in private and had access to confidential briefings on the progress of certain trade negotiations.[63] Unsurprisingly, given the context of Brexit, most progress has been made on trade negotiations. Theresa May's government agreed that there is a need for greater information-sharing in this context.[64] In 2019, the Department for International Trade set out the processes that would enable scrutiny of future free trade agreements, which include the provision of sensitive information to committees during the course of negotiations on a confidential basis.[65] In addition, the government promised to set out its outline approach at an early stage. These formal processes are complemented by the informal exchange of information during negotiations.[66] However, as the IAC has noted, the Johnson government has refused to say which of these commitments it stands by.[67]

However, the government has not accepted that these processes should apply to other types of treaties, despite the repeated recommendations of parliamentary committees.[68] Furthermore, the government has resisted any general principle or 'presumption' of transparency,[69] which had been suggested by both the House of Lords Constitution Committee and the House of Commons Liaison Committee.[70] Instead, it has made more limited promises, such as improvements to the explanatory memoranda accompanying treaties.[71] The overriding theme of the government's approach is that greater information-sharing may bring benefits, but must remain at the discretion of the executive.

At present, treaty scrutiny is fragmented, dealt with separately by each House and further split across the departmental select committees in the Commons (at least in theory). In its 2008 report, the Joint Committee on the Draft

[62] Smith, Lang and Bjorge, above n 50 at 523.

[63] House of Lords International Agreements Committee, above n 39 at para 46.

[64] HM Government, above n 6 at 4.

[65] Department for International Trade, *Processes for making free trade agreements after the United Kingdom has left the European Union* (CP 63, February 2019).

[66] HM Government, above n 6 at 7-8.

[67] House of Lords International Agreements Committee, above n 39 at para 28.

[68] House of Lords Constitution Committee, above n 8 at paras 80 and 98; House of Lords European Union Committee, above n 8 at para 82.

[69] HM Government, above n 6 at 7.

[70] Fourth Report from the House of Commons Liaison Committee, *The Effectiveness and Influence of the Select Committee System* HC 1860 (2017-19), para 89; House of Lords Constitution Committee, above n 8 at para 90.

[71] House of Lords European Union Committee, above n 8 at paras 71-2.

Constitutional Renewal Bill recommended the formation of a joint committee of both Houses to scrutinise treaties.[72] This suggestion has recently been taken up again, and the House of Commons Liaison Committee noted in their 2019 report the need to work closely with its House of Lords counterpart to discuss future options, including a joint committee.[73] A joint committee would address the current discrepancy between the predominant weight of actual scrutiny being performed by the Lords and the predominant strength of the powers under CRAG resting in the Commons. Furthermore, it might well be better resourced, with a team of legal advisers and good working relations with government, much like the Joint Committee on Human Rights.

Australia adopted a joint committee structure in 1996 (see chapter fifteen). The Joint Standing Committee on Treaties (JSCOT) assesses treaties according to their significance (following categorisation by the government), and produces reports on the most important. However, JSCOT does not currently have oversight during negotiations, although it has recently called for greater government transparency in that regard.[74]

On the other hand, as the House of Lords Constitution Committee recognised, 'there are advantages and disadvantages to any model'.[75] The working practices, procedures and power dynamics of the Commons and the Lords differ widely. It would not be an easy matter for a joint committee to straddle that divide. Furthermore, a joint committee would have to find its place alongside the more subject-specialist expertise of the Commons departmental select committees. The current approach, with subject specialism in the Commons and overall oversight in the Lords IAC, may afford greater coverage than a unified committee. Given that the IAC was only constituted in 2021, it is perhaps only fair to defer judgment on the question of a joint committee to a later date. By that time, it is to be hoped that the Commons select committees (beyond the International Trade Committee) will have begun to engage with treaty scrutiny more energetically.

Pre-Ratification Scrutiny

Separately to reforms to scrutiny during the negotiating process, the House of Lords Constitution Committee and IAC have suggested that the current provisions of CRAG for scrutiny between the conclusion of negotiations and ratification are deficient.[76]

[72] *First Report from the Joint Committee on the Draft Constitutional Renewal Bill* HL 166 HC 551 (2007-08), para 238.

[73] House of Commons Liaison Committee, above n 70 at para 84.

[74] Australian Parliament Joint Standing Committee on Treaties, *Strengthening the Trade Agreement and Treaty-Making Process in Australia* (Report 193, August 2021), 28.

[75] House of Lords Constitution Committee, above n 8 at para 67.

[76] ibid at para 33; House of Lords International Agreements Committee, above n 39.

First, the CRAG rules produce an extremely short timetable of just 21 sitting days for the relevant committee to scrutinise the treaty and produce a report.[77] If a debate is to take place as well, time is under even greater pressure. For example, the Lords EU Committee was only able to conduct a full inquiry into the 2019 trade agreement with the Republic of Korea, including a call for written evidence, because of the extraordinary circumstances of the purported prorogation of Parliament in September of that year and the concomitant effect on sitting days.[78] The chair of the sub-committee that scrutinised the agreement, Baroness Donaghy, called for the 21-day period to be extended to allow this greater level of scrutiny to be applied in future.[79] Ministers already possess the power, under section 21 of CRAG, to extend the period, and the Lords Constitution and International Agreements Committees have repeatedly invited the government to commit to agree extensions to allow for proper scrutiny.[80]

Second, the negative resolution model means that only some treaties are debated on the floor of the House and few parliamentarians are truly involved in scrutiny. One possible reform is to shift to an 'affirmative resolution' model.[81] However, parliamentary capacity is extremely limited and there would need to be a filter to select the most important treaties for consideration. As Holger Hestermeyer notes, there is a 'need to be realistic' about the amount of parliamentary time that can be dedicated to treaty scrutiny, which is evident in the constitutional provisions of those countries that require legislative approval for ratification.[82] For example, Article 80 of the Italian Constitution provides that 'Parliament shall authorise by law the ratification of such international treaties as have a political nature, require arbitration or a legal settlement, entail change of borders, spending or new legislation.'

Such an approach sits uneasily in a UK context. Using such vague terms as 'political' would risk intervention by the courts. A solution more consonant with UK practice would be to retain the current negative resolution model but to change the provisions of CRAG to give powers to those committees charged with treaty scrutiny in each House (or to any joint committee) to recommend debates on particular treaties. This was the preferred solution of the Lords Constitution Committee.[83] The IAC already has the power to draw particular treaties to the

[77] Constitutional Reform and Governance Act 2010, s 20.

[78] Third Report from the House of Lords Liaison Committee, *Review of House of Lords investigative and scrutiny committee activity in 2019-20* HL 103 (2019-21), para 26.

[79] R Donaghy, 'We must address the scrutiny gap in Brexit-related international agreements' (*PoliticsHome*, 28 October 2019) www.politicshome.com/news/uk/foreign-affairs/brexit/house/house-magazine/107549/baroness-donaghy-we-must-address-scrutiny.

[80] House of Lords Constitution Committee, above n 8 at para 116; House of Lords International Agreements Committee, above n 39 at 33.

[81] Lang, above n 34 at 16.

[82] H Hestermeyer, 'Parliament and treaty-making: from CRAG to a meaningful vote?' (*Constitution Unit Blog*, 14 March 2019) www.constitution-unit.com/2019/03/14/parliament-and-treaty-making-from-crag-to-a-meaningful-vote/.

[83] House of Lords Constitution Committee, above n 8 at para 104.

attention of the House, but not all of these are debated in the chamber.[84] An alternative would be to give each House the power to hold a debate upon the proposition of a certain number of members.[85] We suggest that either of these solutions would be preferable to a further alternative, currently used in New Zealand, which requires treaties to be listed on the order paper for debate, but with a very low priority (such that they are commonly timed out) and with a great deal of government control over the timetable.[86] Such powers would reflect the spirit behind Arthur Ponsonby's original promise that the government would make time for treaties to be debated upon request by the opposition, whilst permitting Parliament to determine for itself the appropriate criteria for holding a debate.[87] At present, however, the government appears wary of losing control of the parliamentary agenda.[88]

Third, CRAG only gives the House of Commons the power to delay ratification, not to veto it. There is therefore a mismatch between treaties that require implementing legislation, which parliamentary opposition may significantly stymie, and other treaties falling under CRAG. Moreover, the Commons' delaying power is rather theoretical: while government controls parliamentary time, it will remain difficult to hold one vote, let alone multiple votes every 21 sitting days. While the delaying power has some political force, therefore, it lacks real 'teeth'. Parliament's position is weaker as a result, unable to make any real demands on government when it comes to scrutiny before or during negotiations. A power of veto would give Parliament the necessary 'teeth' – although we envisage that the Commons would exercise its bark more than its bite.

Fourth, CRAG does not apply to any international agreement that is not binding under international law, nor to any 'regulation, rule, measure, decision or similar instrument made under a treaty (other than one that amends or replaces the treaty (in whole or in part))'.[89] That is contrary to Ponsonby's 1924 promise to draw to Parliament's attention

> other agreements, commitments and understandings which may in any way bind the nation to specific action in certain circumstances and which may involve international obligations of a serious character, although no signed sealed document may exist.[90]

In short, CRAG does not cover non-binding agreements (including those with international organisations) or amendments made to binding treaties. There is a significant 'scrutiny gap' here.[91]

[84] House of Lords International Agreements Committee, above n 39 at para 16.
[85] Joint Committee on the Draft Constitutional Renewal Bill, above n 72 at para 331.
[86] See chapter fifteen. Standing Orders (NZ) 254(2), 74(4); D McGee, *Parliamentary Practice in New Zealand*, 4th edn (Mary Harris and David Wilson eds, Auckland, Oratia, 2017), 691.
[87] Forty-second Report from the House of Lords European Union Committee, *Scrutiny of international agreements: lessons learned* HL 387 (2017-19), para 58; Smith, Lang and Bjorge, above n 50 at 521.
[88] HM Government, above n 6 at 9.
[89] Constitutional Reform and Governance Act 2010, s 25.
[90] House of Lords European Union Committee, above n 8 at para 105.
[91] House of Lords European Union Committee, above n 87 at para 75.

That gap is of particular importance for treaty amendments, which may make substantial and significant changes. The IAC has recently set out a full range of concerns but, to date, the government has been vague as to parliamentary consultation on amendments.[92] However, some progress is being made. In 2019, the House of Lords European Union Committee called for explanatory memoranda to 'be clear when the full CRAG procedure will apply, to ensure that changes are made in a proportionate, clear and transparent fashion, and that resources are deployed appropriately'.[93] The government has now accepted this proposition.[94]

Consulting the Devolved Administrations

In a statement on post-Brexit trade treaties in July 2018, the UK government announced its intention to consult 'Parliament, the devolved administrations, local government, business, trade unions, civil society and the public from every part of the UK.'[95] However, the devolved administrations have complained that they have not been sufficiently consulted.[96] The current arrangements for consultation are largely set out in a 2013 Memorandum of Understanding.[97]

Brexit has prompted greater interest in treaty-making from the devolved administrations and legislatures. In particular, the conflict between the pro-Brexit UK government and the anti-Brexit Scottish government has involved considerable acrimony. In 2018, the Scottish Parliament attempted to legislate to require the consent of Scottish ministers to the application of subordinate legislation by UK ministers on matters of retained EU law.[98] The provision was found to be outside the lawful competence of the Scottish Parliament.[99]

This is not the place to explore the full range of possible responses to this problem. However, we make three observations. First, the 2013 Memorandum predates subsequent developments in devolution. In particular, Scotland and Wales have in the interim been the subjects of new Acts of Parliament that have significantly extended the competencies – both legal and institutional – of their devolved

[92] House of Lords International Agreements Committee, above n 39 at paras 62-72.

[93] Twenty-ninth Report from the House of Lords European Union Committee, *Treaties considered on 12 February 2019* HL 287 (2017-19), para 3.

[94] Foreign, Commonwealth and Development Office, *Treaties and Memoranda of Understanding (MOUs): Guidance on practice and procedures* (November 2021), 13.

[95] *Hansard*, HC Deb Vol 645, col 41 (16 July 2018).

[96] Welsh Assembly External Affairs and Additional Legislation Committee, *International agreements: a suggested approach to engagement and scrutiny* (October 2019); Scottish Government, *Scotland's Role in the Development of Future UK Trade Arrangements* (August 2018).

[97] *Memorandum of Understanding and Supplementary Agreements Between the United Kingdom Government, the Scottish Ministers, the Welsh Ministers, and the Northern Ireland Executive Committee* (October 2013), Concordat D; *cf* House of Lords International Agreements Committee, above n 39 at paras 56-61.

[98] UK Withdrawal from the European Union (Legal Continuity) (Scotland) Bill 2018, s 17.

[99] *Reference on the Continuity Bill*, above n 6.

administrations. Second, closer involvement of the devolved administrations may strengthen the UK's negotiating hand by further reinforcing the democratic consensus behind any mandate. Furthermore, sometimes the other negotiating party – for example the EU during CETA negotiations with Canada in the 2010s – requires the involvement of provincial administrations. Third, however, caution should be exercised in any comparison between UK devolution and federalism in Canada and Australia. Indeed, even in those countries, it is the federal Parliament that scrutinises treaties, despite challenges to the federal Parliament's legal authority to enact all the consequent legislation (resolved in favour of the provinces in Canada).[100]

Conclusion

It is now high time for Parliament to resume the vigorous approach to the scrutiny of treaty-making that it once had. In doing so, it will of course have to make robust decisions about how best to employ its limited resources, because the volume of treaties now signed could easily overwhelm an indiscriminate system of parliamentary review. However, the practical challenges should not be allowed to veil the basic principle that Parliament should be presented with a real choice when considering a treaty. At least until very recently and even now only in some cases, Parliament has not had that real choice under the Ponsonby Rule codified (imperfectly) in CRAG. It is too often presented with the very thing that Arthur Ponsonby found so objectionable: a fait accompli.

Progress has been made, particularly with the renewed focus on treaty-making following Brexit. However, it is important that Parliament's institutional structures and the government's approach continue to evolve to reflect the principled justifications for greater and more effective parliamentary input into the treaty-making process. This chapter has been far from a comprehensive review of those possible reforms, but we suggest that the focus of reform should be the cooperation between government and parliamentary actors *during negotiations*. That not only enables Parliament to have a real opportunity to shape policy (or reject it), but also helps to secure a democratic consensus that will in many cases strengthen the UK's negotiating position.

When it comes to pre-ratification scrutiny (under the CRAG processes), the Commons and Lords have a chance now to work together to close the gaps in the previously rather fragmented coverage of new treaties. It is to be hoped that

[100] See C Côté, 'Federalism and Foreign Affairs in Canada', in C Bradley (ed), *The Oxford Handbook of Comparative Foreign Relations Law* (Oxford, Oxford University Press, 2019). In Australia, a series of High Court decisions that the federal Parliament could legislate to enact treaties even in areas otherwise reserved to states provoked the 1996 reforms that produced the Joint Standing Committee on Treaties: see chapter fifteen.

the government will join in that cooperation by giving time for proper reporting to be carried out. Such cooperation may be aided by the expertise of a joint treaties committee, but current arrangements – a cross-hatching of subject specialism in the Commons and overall oversight in the Lords – deserve a fair trial. However, there is one other important reform to be made here: Parliament's scrutiny committees and/or parliamentarians generally should be given power to raise particular treaties for debate and a vote. The current government dominance of parliamentary time weakens even further the powers Parliament has under CRAG.

Finally, we recommend that the power of the Commons under CRAG be revisited. When Ponsonby stood at the despatch box in 1924, he envisaged the House having the final word on treaty-making. CRAG does not give them that power – only a power to delay ratification. That watering-down has (in part) been at the root of the Commons' inability to stimulate governmental cooperation in its scrutiny processes. Were the House of Commons' power to be fortified – given 'teeth', with a power of veto – it would act as an incentive to government not only to take democratically justifiable decisions, but also to explain those decisions to Parliament at an early stage, at which Parliament can still make a useful contribution.

9

Regulating the Civil Service

> It may safely be asserted that, as matters now stand, the government of the country could not be carried on without the aid of an efficient body of permanent officers, occupying a position duly subordinate to that of the ministers who are directly responsible to the Crown and to Parliament, yet possessing sufficient independence, character, ability, and experience to be able to advise, assist, and, to some extent, influence, those who are from time to time set over them.
>
> Stafford Northcote and Charles Trevelyan (1854)[1]

Introduction

In this, the third of our chapters about prerogative powers exercised by the executive, the argument is similar to that about treaties: transferring a power from the prerogative to statute can make little difference to how the power is exercised in practice. In brief, the main argument in this chapter can be summarised as follows. The civil service had traditionally been regulated by Orders in Council made under the prerogative. In the late twentieth century, concerns about politicisation and the need to protect the core values of the civil service led to increasing demands that it be placed upon a statutory footing. This was eventually achieved in the Constitutional Reform and Governance Act 2010 (CRAG). But, since then, concerns about politicisation have continued, and if anything, have increased: the statutory basis has done little to protect the position of senior civil servants.

There is, however, one important exception to this argument: when the intelligence agencies were put on a statutory basis in the 1980s and 1990s, it transformed their operations. So, we start briefly with MI5, MI6 and GCHQ, before turning to the civil service more generally.

The Spies Come in from the Cold

For a remarkably long time, the intelligence agencies remained protected from public and parliamentary scrutiny by a bipartisan consensus that intelligence could

[1] SH Northcote and CE Trevelyan, *Report on the Organisation of the Permanent Civil Service* (London, 1854), 2.

not be discussed in public. So far as official government policy was concerned, the British security and intelligence services did not exist. They operated under the prerogative, but since they did not have any legal personality, their activities did not fall under the normal rule of law. They did not have powers such as those that the police possessed to arrest, search property, and compel disclosure of bank records for example. If caught breaking and entering or tapping telephones, they had to rely on blind eyes being turned. The aggrieved citizen had no recourse to law in respect of an organisation that did not exist.

That began to break down with a series of court cases in the 1980s. In 1984, the European Court of Human Rights (ECtHR) upheld a complaint about the tapping of his phone by a British antiques dealer, James Malone, since it was not authorised by law.[2] That judgment led directly to the Interception of Communications Act 1985, which provided for a commissioner to monitor warrants for telephone tapping and a tribunal to investigate complaints. The next ECtHR case involved Torsten Leander, a Swedish Marxist who had been dismissed from the Karlskrona Naval Museum: in consequence of that judgment, all security services were held to require a statutory basis.[3] This judgment came in the same year as *Attorney General v Guardian Newspapers Ltd (No 1)*, sparking a series of cases (the *Spycatcher* litigation) in which the UK government unsuccessfully sought to suppress publication of the memoirs of former MI5 employee Peter Wright.[4] This made it hard to deny the existence of the Security Service, leading Sir John Donaldson to comment 'it may be that the time has come that Parliament should regularise the position of the [Security] Service'.[5] The Security Service agreed. Its annual report for 1987–8 concluded that 'There is complete acceptance among staff of the desirability of legislation for the Security Service.'[6]

The consequence was the Security Service Act 1989, which at last put the Security Service on a statutory footing. Section 1 of the Act defined its functions as the protection of national security, in particular against threats from espionage, terrorism and sabotage, and from actions intended to undermine parliamentary democracy; and to safeguard the economic well-being of the UK against threats from overseas. The Act created a tribunal to investigate complaints, as well as a Security Service Commissioner. MI6 and GCHQ were envious, and both agencies supported the move to their own legislation in the Intelligence Services Act 1994 (ISA), complete with the creation of a tribunal and Commissioner. The 1994 Act also fostered parliamentary oversight by way of the creation of a new Intelligence and Security Committee (ISC) which was composed of nine parliamentarians from both Houses appointed by the Prime Minister.

Subsequent legislation includes the Regulation of Investigatory Powers Act 2000; Justice and Security Act 2013; and Investigatory Powers Act 2016 (IPA).

[2] *Malone v UK* (1984) 7 EHRR 14.
[3] *Leander v Sweden* (1987) 9 EHRR 433.
[4] *Attorney General v Guardian Newspapers Ltd* (No 1) [1987] 3 All ER 316.
[5] *General v Guardian Newspapers Ltd (No 2) (CA)* [1990] 1 AC 109, 190.
[6] C Andrew, *The Defence of the Realm: The Authorised History of MI5* (London, Penguin, 2010), 766.

This legislation introduced new Judicial Commissioners to approve the issue of warrants, together with an overarching Investigatory Powers Commissioner, and expanded the remit, resources and independence of the Intelligence and Security Committee. In consequence, the intelligence and security agencies are subject to surveillance and scrutiny by a network of supervisory bodies, which has greatly strengthened their accountability. Before embarking on any operation, they have to engage in detailed legal analysis of whether the operation meets tests of proportionality and necessity, in pursuit of their objectives of national security, economic wellbeing or the prevention and detection of serious crime. Contrasting the position with the civil service, a former head of GCHQ has pithily explained:

> If you start in MI5, MI6 or GCHQ today as a young graduate, you absolutely need to know your ISA 1994 and IPA 2016 to do your job properly and lawfully. You don't need to understand the CRAG 2010 to do a job in the Treasury or DHSC.[7]

Regulation by Orders in Council

The Constitutional Reform and Governance Act 2020 (CRAG) placed the civil service on a statutory basis. To understand the background of this reform, we need to go all the way back to the origins of the modern civil service in the Northcote-Trevelyan *Report on the Organisation of the Permanent Civil Service*, published in 1854.[8] Central to the philosophy of the report was that the civil service was to be impartial, and civil servants were to be selected on merit, on the basis of fair and open competition. A limited number of political appointments were consistent with Northcote-Trevelyan principles, but the goal was to end the days of recruitment based on patronage and nepotism. On the basis of the report, the Civil Service Commission was established in 1855 by Order in Council in order to oversee examinations and recruitment procedures.[9] Subsequent debates about the role of the Commission, recruitment, special advisers, the Civil Service Code, and the need for a Civil Service Act can all be traced back to Northcote-Trevelyan. In fact, the report was alive to the possibility that a government might, through the prerogative, make radical changes to the structure of the civil service, and recommended at the end that its principles be enshrined in legislation:

> It remains for us to express our conviction that if any change of the importance of those that we have recommended is to be carried into effect, it can only be successfully done through the medium of an Act of Parliament … A few clauses would accomplish all that is proposed in this paper.[10]

[7] Personal communication from Ciaran Martin.
[8] Northcote and Trevelyan, above n 1.
[9] WL Bathurst, 'At the Court at Buckingham Palace, the 21st day of May' *The London Gazette* (London, 1855).
[10] Northcote and Trevelyan, above n 1 at 23.

But it took over 150 years before that legislation came to pass. The next major milestone was the Haldane *Report on the Machinery of Government*, published in 1918.[11] It established the conceptual basis for the relationship between civil servants and ministers. The report came at a time of rapid growth in the size of government departments in the aftermath of the First World War. Policy could not be made on the basis of the expertise of ministers and MPs alone: more detailed support was required, including on research capacity, and scientific (and social science) analysis. The Haldane model provided that civil servants have a relationship of mutual interdependence with ministers. Ministers rely on civil servants for their expertise, and civil servants on ministers for their authority.[12] The civil service has no distinct legal identity or personality, and must serve the government of the day. The corollary of this relationship is that civil servants are accountable to ministers, who are in turn accountable to Parliament. The Haldane model has underpinned our understanding of the constitutional role of the civil service ever since.

The next milestone, which led to development of the Civil Service Code and helped to re-ignite demands for a Civil Service Act, came in the 1980s. In 1985, Clive Ponting, a senior civil servant in the Ministry of Defence, was prosecuted for breach of the Official Secrets Act 1911 by leaking information on the Belgrano, an Argentinian cruiser that had been sunk in the Falklands War. Ponting was sensationally acquitted, the jury finding that his actions had been in the interests of the state.[13] To remind officials where their duty and their loyalty lay, the Cabinet Secretary and Head of the Civil Service Sir Robert Armstrong issued a note, now known as the *Armstrong Memorandum*, which reaffirmed the Haldane framework:

> In general the executive powers of the Crown are exercised by and on the advice of Her Majesty's Ministers, who are in turn answerable to Parliament. The Civil Service as such has no constitutional personality or responsibility separate from the duly constituted Government of the day.[14]

The memorandum went on to state that if a civil servant felt an issue of conscience was involved in any departmental affairs, they must consult a superior officer or the Permanent Secretary. Subsequently, the trade union for senior civil servants, the FDA, argued for a civil service code of ethics. Building on this, the Commons Treasury and Civil Service Committee in 1994 published a huge report which proposed three further changes: a Civil Service Code, an independent appeals procedure, and a Civil Service Act.[15]

[11] Ministry of Reconstruction, *Report of the Machinery of Government Committee* (London, 1918).

[12] M Stanley, 'The Westminster Model – Summary' (*Understanding the Civil Service*) www.civilservant.org.uk/wm-summary.html.

[13] C Ponting, The Right to Know: The Inside Story of the Belgrano Affair (London, Sphere Books, 1985).

[14] R Armstrong, The Duties and Responsibilities of Civil Servants in relation to Ministers (1985).

[15] Fifth Report from the House of Commons Treasury and Civil Service Committee, *The Role of the Civil Service* HC 27-I (1993–94).

The Campaign for a Civil Service Act

The arguments for a Civil Service Act included criticism of using the prerogative and Orders in Council, which represented 'primary legislation … without parliamentary consent', and offered 'extremely flimsy protection if there is any reason to be worried about the self-righting mechanisms of the system'.[16] A Civil Service Act would have psychological significance, embedding the key principles of the civil service, and reinforcing the interest of Parliament in them, as well as fostering wider debate: it was 'time to complete the unfinished business of Mr Gladstone in the 1860s'.[17] Against this, the government argued that a Civil Service Act risked being purely declaratory legislation, which was superfluous; it might lead to inflexibility in managing the service; or it might 'foster the notion that the Civil Service constituted a separate estate of the realm, with an authority of its own and responsibilities transcending its duties to Ministers'.[18]

The Treasury and Civil Service Committee identified different ideas amongst the advocates of a Civil Service Act, from a brief encapsulation of the essential values of the civil service, to a measure which would enshrine 'the organization and management of the Civil Service, and the rights of civil servants and the rights of Parliament'.[19] The committee was not convinced of the case for a wide ranging Act, but believed there would be 'considerable value in a much narrower statute, principally designed to give statutory backing for the new mechanisms for maintaining the essential values of the Civil Service':

> The passage of such an Act would reflect the interest of Parliament, as the representative of the electorate, in the preservation of the values of the Civil Service; it would set the terms of the custodial responsibility of the Government of the day for the Civil Service. Such an Act would require the Government to consult on a new Civil Service Code and lay such a Code before Parliament …[20]

In its response to the committee, the government was cautious about statutory backing, but accepted the case for a Civil Service Code and a direct line of appeal.[21] A code, based on the four principles of honesty, integrity, impartiality, and objectivity was introduced in 1996, together with an independent appeals procedure to the Civil Service Commission.[22]

Five years later the Committee on Standards in Public Life (CSPL) raised again the case for a Civil Service Act. Publishing a wide ranging report in 2000, CSPL queried the sustainability of the Civil Service Commission being based solely upon

[16] ibid at para 113, quoting John Garrett and Peter Hennessy.
[17] ibid at para 114, quoting Peter Hennessy.
[18] ibid at para 115, quoting Sir Brian Hayes.
[19] ibid at para 116, quoting John Garrett.
[20] ibid.
[21] Cabinet Office, *The Civil Service: Taking forward Continuity and Change* (Cm 2748, 1995).
[22] HM Government, *Civil Service Code* (2015).

the prerogative, because this meant that formal changes to the civil service were not subject to parliamentary debate.[23] A growing number of voices were calling for the values of the civil service to be placed on a statutory footing, and government resistance was beginning to falter; but it was to be another ten years and a succession of draft Bills before one finally became an Act.

Draft Legislation for a Civil Service Act

The first indication of a governmental shift towards a Civil Service Act was in their response to a report from the House of Lords Select Committee on the Public Service in July 1998, when the New Labour government stated that they intended to introduce a statute.[24] In 2002, the Cabinet Secretary Sir Richard Wilson re-affirmed the government's commitment in his valedictory lecture.[25] But nothing materialised. In 2003, CSPL expressed concern about the lack of progress,[26] and in order to urge the government on, the House of Commons Public Administration Select Committee (PASC) took the unusual step in 2004 of publishing a draft Civil Service Bill, saying that legislation was long overdue.[27]

PASC made a number of points about their proposed Bill. First, an Act must ensure that the core civil service values are not subject to 'the whim of any Government without prior Parliamentary debate and scrutiny'.[28] Second, PASC noted the increased reliance on special advisers, and called for a clearer outline of their roles and responsibilities. Third, in the subsequent publication of their *Taming the Prerogative* report, PASC added that an Act should address the growing problem of 'politicisation' of the civil service. As PASC explained, civil servants 'enjoy no statutory rights (or indeed existence), owe no allegiance to the public and answer solely to the government of the day. It is therefore very hard for them to resist Ministerial instructions to perform essentially political acts.'[29]

In response, the government published their own *Draft Civil Service Bill Consultation Document*, together with a more restricted draft Bill.[30] The government were 'not convinced of the case for a wide-ranging Civil Service Act as a

[23] Sixth Report from the Committee on Standards in Public Life, *Reinforcing Standards: Review of the First Report of the Committee and Standards in Public Life* (Cm 4557-I, 2000).

[24] Chancellor of the Duchy of Lancaster, *Government's Response to the Report from the House of Lords Select Committee on the Public Service* (Cm 4000, 1998).

[25] R Wilson, 'Portrait of a Profession Revisited' (2003) 81 *Public Administration* 365.

[26] Ninth Report from the House of Commons Committee on Standards in Public Life, *Defining the Boundaries within the Executive: Ministers, Special Advisers and the permanent Civil Service* (Cm 5775, 2003).

[27] First Report from the House of Commons Public Administration Select Committee, *A Draft Civil Service Bill: Completing the Reform* HC 128-I (2003–04).

[28] ibid at para 5.

[29] D Gladstone, *Memorandum to the House of Commons Public Administration Select Committee* HC 422 MPP04 (May 2003).

[30] Cabinet Office, A Draft Civil Service Bill: Consultation Document (Cm 6373, 2004).

mechanism for either furthering or delimiting reforms of the Civil Service'. Instead they favoured 'a much narrower statute' designed to 'maintain the essential values of the civil service'. A statute, the government argued, should not change the Haldane model; should not diminish the flexibility and responsiveness of the civil service; nor make it immune to reform.

The author of those words was probably Sir Andrew Turnbull, Cabinet Secretary and Head of the Civil Service from 2002–05. In his valedictory lecture, Turnbull voiced his scepticism about a Civil Service Act:

> I have always thought that the proponents of a Civil Service Act had completely unrealistic expectations of what it would achieve. Most of the problems that concern people would not in my view have been addressed by such an Act while some new problems would be created. When things have gone wrong at the interface between the civil service and politicians they have nearly always been around values and behaviour, not rules and enforcement.[31]

Turnbull suggested that significant progress was being made to improve the workings of the civil service without using statute or prerogative. For instance, during his tenure the civil service became 'much more open to ideas from think tanks, consultancies, governments abroad, special advisers, and frontline practitioners'.[32] Even though legislation could certainly effect change, it would only do so in an abstract way. There were specific issues that needed to be addressed, rather than the overarching philosophy.

The Constitutional Reform and Governance Act 2010

Pace picked up when Gordon Brown became Prime Minister in June 2007. In his first week in office, he published *The Governance of Britain*, featuring wide ranging plans to reform the prerogative including proposals for civil service legislation (see chapter three). The Civil Service Commission would be placed on a statutory footing, and the historic principle of appointment on merit would be made a legal reality.[33] In March 2008, the government published detailed legislative proposals as Part 5 of the Draft Constitutional Renewal Bill, which were then scrutinised by PASC and a Joint Committee. Both parliamentary committees welcomed the proposals, but wanted to see them strengthened. The draft Bill did not do enough to guarantee the financial and operational independence of the Civil Service Commission; nor did it provide the Commissioners with a mechanism that would allow them to carry out investigations into the operation of the Civil Service Code without the consent of the government.[34]

[31] A Turnbull, 'Valedictory Lecture' *The Guardian* (London, 27 July 2005).
[32] ibid.
[33] Ministry of Justice, *The Governance of Britain* (Cm 7170, 2007), paras 40–8.
[34] *Report of the Joint Committee on the draft Constitutional Renewal Bill* HL 166-I HC 551-I (2007–08), paras 254, 263.

The government was then hit by the financial crisis of 2008–9, and it was not until July 2009 that the Constitutional Reform and Governance Bill was introduced into Parliament, with Part 1 designated to the regulation of the civil service. It was only in October that it had its second reading in the House of Commons, and not until March 2010 that the Bill reached the Lords. The House of Lords Constitution Committee brought out a rushed report, with a useful summary of the provisions on the civil service:

> The Bill puts the Civil Service Commission on a statutory footing, confers on the Minister for the Civil Service the power to manage the civil service, requires the Minister to publish a code of conduct for the civil service and sets out some minimum requirements for the code (including obligations of political impartiality, integrity, honesty, etc). The Bill provides for the principle of appointment on merit on the basis of fair and open competition, and sets out some exceptions where this principle will not apply. Separate provision is made for special advisers. The Bill does not extend to MI5, MI6, GCHQ or the Northern Ireland Civil Service. Subject to these exceptions, the Bill removes prerogative powers governing the management of the civil service, but prerogative powers will be retained in relation to security vetting.[35]

The committee lamented that these important reforms would not receive the attention they required so long as they formed part of a wider Bill, and noted that almost no changes had been made in response to earlier criticisms.[36] In the event, there was no time for further scrutiny: debate was foreclosed by the ensuing dissolution, the Bill went into the wash up, and the only parts which survived in the Constitutional Reform and Governance Act 2010 (CRAG) were Part 1 on the civil service and Part 2 on the ratification of treaties. One objective of civil service legislation, that it would stimulate parliamentary interest and wider debate, had certainly not been realised: by this time, all eyes were on the forthcoming election.

A brief summary of Part 1 of CRAG is as follows. Section 2(1) establishes the Civil Service Commission as a statutory body, with details of its composition contained in Schedule 1. The Commissioners must all be appointed following a process of fair and open competition; to buttress their independence, they cannot be re-appointed. Commissioners cannot be appointed without the agreement of the First Commissioner; and the First Commissioner is to be appointed following consultation with leaders of the two largest opposition parties.[37]

The Commission's duties are twofold. First, under section 9(5), they must hear appeals brought by civil servants under the Civil Service Code and make recommendations as to how the matter should be resolved. Second, in accordance with section 11, the commission, in consultation with the Minister for the Civil Service, must publish recruitment principles with which civil service

[35] Eleventh Report from the House of Lords Constitution Committee, *Constitutional Reform and Governance Bill* HL 98 (2009–10), para 10.

[36] ibid at paras 12–3.

[37] Constitutional Reform and Governance Act 2010, sch 1, para 2.

management must comply. These principles must be based on the requirement, now statutorily enshrined in section 10(2), that selection 'must be on merit on the basis of fair and open competition'. Only short-term appointments are exempt from this requirement, as well as special advisers. The Commission may participate in recruitment exercises, and typically do so for the most senior positions.

Section 5 requires that the Minister for the Civil Service publish a Civil Service Code and lay the code before Parliament. The code forms part of the terms and conditions of service of all civil servants. The minimum requirements for the code are that civil servants must carry out their duties with integrity, honesty, objectivity and impartiality.

Special advisers have their own code.[38] They are exempt from the impartiality and objectivity requirements under section 7(5), and from the requirement to be appointed on merit and on the basis of fair and open competition under section 10(3). Special advisers must be appointed by a minister in order to assist that minister personally, with the appointment agreed by the Prime Minister. The Minister for the Civil Service must prepare an annual report about serving special advisers and lay the report before Parliament. This has proved a useful exercise in transparency, with a list of all special advisers, their departments, and their salaries being published in December of each year by the Cabinet Office.

The most important power in CRAG is deceptively the most simply worded. Section 3(1) presents the Minister for the Civil Service (by convention the Prime Minister) with a statutory power similar to the old prerogative power – the 'power to manage the civil service'.[39] The explanatory notes to the Act explain that this includes the powers of appointment or dismissal. But it goes much wider, including the powers to restructure Whitehall by creating or abolishing departments, to change the governance of departments, and to have a stronger say in the appointment and dismissal of senior civil servants. All of these things have accelerated in the last ten years, as we explain in the concluding sections of this chapter. Putting the power to manage the civil service on a statutory basis has in no way hampered the government's willingness or capacity for civil service reform.

Effect of CRAG: (1) The Civil Service Commission

The role of the Civil Service Commission remained essentially unchanged by CRAG. In their annual report from 2010–11, the first after the Act was passed, the Commission stated that 'the Act did not make any significant changes to

[38] Cabinet Office, *Code of Conduct for Special Advisors* (2016).

[39] In their comment on the government's draft Bill, PASC highlighted some concerns with this section but the government later noted that they were merely codifying existing practice. See House of Commons Public Administration Select Committee, above n 27 at para 22; J Harris, *Legislating for a Civil Service* (Institute for Government, 2013), 7.

the activities of the Civil Service Commissioners'.[40] All the duties and functions prescribed by CRAG had been present in the Civil Service Order in Council 1995. The same number of complaints were brought and heard in 2010–11 as in 2009–10 before the Act was passed.[41] The passing of CRAG had encouraged the Commission to review their recruitment principles, leading to some minor changes.[42] According to the commission's survey, the period from 2009–11 saw a modest increase of 11 per cent in awareness of the Civil Service Code amongst civil servants.[43]

None of the commission's more recent annual reports mention the effect of the Act in any significant way. In evidence to PASC for their 2013 report *Truth to Power: how Civil Service reform can succeed*, the commission confirmed that the purpose of the Act was not necessarily to alter the day-to-day workings of the civil service, nor to bring about fundamental reform, but to place the values of open recruitment and impartiality on a statutory footing in order to ensure their preservation.[44]

Nevertheless, the statutory backing of CRAG proved important when the Civil Service Commission came under pressure. In particular, it was able to resist attempts by Francis Maude to appoint Commissioners that were more supportive of his agenda because of the requirement in CRAG that such appointments should be agreed by the First Commissioner.[45] Maude was infuriated, but the commission was able to hold the line; without the statutory safeguard, it would have been much harder to do so.[46] It remains to be seen whether the new First Civil Service Commissioner, Gisela Stuart, is willing to hold a similar line: it is not the job of the Civil Service Commission to lead the charge on civil service reform.[47]

Impact of CRAG: (2) Civil Service Reform

Ironically, the years immediately after the passage of CRAG saw three intensive bouts of reform and restructuring in Whitehall, disproving any fears that statutory codification might ossify the civil service or prove a brake upon reform. The first wave was led by Francis Maude as Minister for the Cabinet Office; the second was triggered by Brexit; the third was led by Michael Gove in the Cabinet Office and Dominic Cummings in No 10.

[40] Civil Service Commission, *Annual Report and Accounts 2010–11* HC 1180 (2011), para 2.1.

[41] ibid at para 5.

[42] The Commission decided to limit the length of absence for reappointed civil servants from the Civil Service to five years, and to prevent return on promotion without fair and open competition.

[43] In 2009, 75 per cent of civil servants were aware of the Civil Service Code. This figure increased to 81 per cent in 2010, and to 86 per cent in 2011.

[44] Civil Service Commission, *Written evidence to the House of Commons Public Administration Select Committee* (CSR 24) HC 74 (2012–13).

[45] Constitutional Reform and Governance Act 2010, sch 1, para 3(5).

[46] Personal communication.

[47] A Thomas, 'It is not right to appoint a politician to lead the Civil Service Commission' (*Institute for Government*, 9 December 2021) www.instituteforgovernment.org.uk/blog/civil-service-commissioner.

In the 2010–15 government, the Prime Minister David Cameron effectively delegated his responsibilities as Minister for the Civil Service to Francis Maude, Minister for the Cabinet Office and Paymaster General. Maude initiated a sweeping reform programme aimed at improving Whitehall efficiency and giving ministers greater say in the running of their departments. This included giving the Prime Minister greater choice when appointing a new Permanent Secretary, putting Permanent Secretaries on fixed-term contracts, and allowing ministers to appoint more political advisers.

Maude set out his ambitious agenda to improve efficiency in his *Civil Service Reform Plan*, published in June 2012. His initial attempt to give ministers greater choice in the appointment of Permanent Secretaries was blocked by the Civil Service Commission, whose practice was to put forward a single name. Maude wanted to require the commission to present the Prime Minister with a choice of appointable candidates, as happened for other public appointments (see chapter ten). Maude's progress report in 2013 recorded: 'The recent Civil Service Commission guidance strengthens ministerial involvement in the different stages of the appointment process, but does not go as far as the Government would have liked.'[48] The commission found itself out on a limb, with few supporters outside Whitehall: the Institute for Government and the Institute for Public Policy Research (IPPR) both published reports recommending that ministers should be given a choice of candidates when appointing a new Permanent Secretary.[49] Threatened with legislation, the commission backed down and, in 2014, amended its policy to allow ministers a choice.[50] The commission insist that the Prime Minister is presented with a list only of those candidates deemed appointable, and occasionally this still means a single name when the competition throws up only one appointable candidate.[51]

The IPPR report, based on experience of the civil services in Australia and New Zealand, also recommended fixed term contracts for Permanent Secretaries. In 2014, Maude introduced fixed-term five-year contracts, and the government has periodically published the tenure end dates of all the Permanent Secretaries in post. The Cabinet Office adds:

> There is no automatic presumption in favour of renewal, but short renewals may be possible at the discretion of the Prime Minister in cases where performance has been strong and an extension is supported by the relevant Minister.[52]

[48] Cabinet Office, *Civil Service Reform Plan: One Year On* (2013), 21.

[49] A Paun, J Harris and I Magee, *Permanent Secretary Appointments and the Role of Ministers* (Institute for Government, 2013); G Lodge, S Kalitowski, N Pearce and R Muir, *Accountability and Responsiveness in the Senior Civil Service: Lessons from Overseas* (London, Institute for Public Policy Research, 2013).

[50] Civil Service Commission, *Annual Report and Accounts 2014–15* HC 251 (2015), 6–7 and 17–18; P Riddell, 'By Prime Ministerial Appointment: the PM and Permanent Secretaries' (*Institute for Government*, 17 October 2014) www.instituteforgovernment.org.uk/blog/prime-ministerial-appointment-pm-and-permanent-secretaries.

[51] I Watmore, 'Foreword' in Civil Service Commission, *Annual Report and Accounts 2019–20* HC 455 (2020), 9–10.

[52] *Hansard*, HC Deb cW (21 October 2019) (Simon Hart).

Maude's reform agenda also involved bringing more outsiders into Whitehall. He doubled the numbers of non-executive directors on the boards of Whitehall departments, and boosted their role; but performance remained patchy, with few Secretaries of State showing much interest or competence in chairing the revamped departmental boards.[53] There was also minimal interest from his Cabinet colleagues in another of his initiatives, extended ministerial offices (EMOs), intended to boost recruitment of external appointees to work alongside officials in a ministerial policy unit.[54] The Civil Service Commission created a new exception to allow recruitment without competition of chosen individuals as temporary civil servants for up to five years, but without a right to transfer into the civil service unless they underwent fair and open competition. It was not until the 2015 government that a small number of ministers experimented with this Whitehall version of ministerial *cabinets*, but the experiment was soon killed off by Theresa May.[55]

The second wave of civil service reform can be dealt with more briefly, since it involved restructuring rather than reform, and was a by-product of Brexit. When Theresa May became Prime Minister in July 2016 following David Cameron's resignation after his defeat in the Brexit referendum, she announced the creation of two new Whitehall departments. The Department for Exiting the European Union (DExEU) was formed to negotiate the terms of the UK's withdrawal from the European Union, and the Department for International Trade was established to negotiate new trade agreements with other countries. In neither case was there any need for parliamentary approval, or even debate: the new departments were created under the statutory power to manage the civil service in section 3(1) CRAG. This was another illustration that CRAG presented no obstacle to fundamental changes in the organisation of Whitehall. Yet another instance came with Boris Johnson's decision to close DExEU in January 2020, and six months later to merge the Department for International Development with the Foreign and Commonwealth Office.

The third wave of civil service reform saw a resurrection of the radical ideas espoused by Francis Maude, this time from two new leaders appointed by Boris Johnson in 2019: Michael Gove as Chancellor of the Duchy of Lancaster in the Cabinet Office, and Dominic Cummings as Johnson's senior adviser in No 10. It can also be dealt with briefly, since it is a work in progress, which initially lacked a clear and coherent strategy. There was no equivalent to Maude's *Civil Service Reform Plan*, or his systematic follow up; instead there was Michael Gove's Ditchley speech of June 2020, and occasional sniping by Cummings on his blog.[56]

[53] R Hazell, A Cogbill, D Owen, H Webber and L Chebib, *Critical Friends: the Role of Non-Executives on Whitehall Boards* (London, Constitution Unit, 2018).

[54] B Yong and R Hazell, *Special Advisers: Who They Are, What They Do and Why They Matter* (Oxford, Hart Publishing, 2014), 197–9.

[55] A Gouglas and M Brans, 'UK Extended Ministerial Offices: On the Road to Cabinetisation' (*Constitution Unit Blog*, 9 February 2016) www.constitution-unit.com/2016/02/09/uk-extended-ministerial-offices-on-the-road-to-cabinetisation/.

[56] M Gove, 'The Privilege of Public Service' (Ditchley Annual Lecture, Oxford, 27 June 2020); For a critique, see B Maddox, *Reform at the Centre of Government* (Institute for Government, 2020).

But Gove's criticisms of Whitehall for its weaknesses in digital services, high turnover, poor evaluation, and need for greater diversity of thought crystallised a year later in the *Declaration on Government Reform* issued by the Cabinet Office in June 2021. It contained a 30-point improvement plan grouped under the headings of people, performance and partnership, with the promise of regular progress reports.[57] Following Cummings' departure in November 2020, and Gove's reshuffle in September 2021, it is hard to know how much of this reform agenda will survive. In November 2021, Policy Exchange advocated for greater powers for the Civil Service Commission to supervise all internal promotions in the civil service, and to open all senior positions to external competition.[58] But standing back from such suggestions, and Gove and Cummings' plans, once again the fundamental point to make is that CRAG presented few obstacles to what at times looked like a set of radical, even revolutionary, reforms: the statutory power to manage the civil service gives the Prime Minister immense capacity to reshape Whitehall and to change its ways of working.

Impact of CRAG: (3) Continuing Concerns about Politicisation

Since the passage of CRAG, concerns about politicisation have continued, and if anything, have increased. Concerns about politicisation of the civil service are not new, and go back at least to the premiership of Margaret Thatcher. But her concern was to appoint officials who got things done, rather than people who necessarily shared her ideology. Concerns surfaced again when Tony Blair became Prime Minister and strengthened the role of No 10 and his senior advisers. Politicisation is seldom sharply defined, but it comprises a range of different concerns about the weakening or undermining of the civil service: the main ones are addressed below.[59]

Greater Ministerial Involvement in Civil Service Appointments and Dismissals

In recent years, Prime Ministers have shown growing interest in senior civil service appointments. We related above how Francis Maude introduced a change in policy in 2014 to allow ministers greater choice when appointing Permanent Secretaries. The choice remains that of the Prime Minister, not the Secretary of

[57] Cabinet Office, *Declaration on Government Reform* (2021), 9–10.

[58] B Barnard, *Open, Meritocratic and Transparent: Reforming Civil Service Appointments* (Policy Exchange, 2021).

[59] For a characteristically thoughtful analysis, see R Mountfield, 'Politicisation and the Civil Service' (2002) www.civilservant.org.uk/library/2002_mountfield_politicisation.pdf.

State; and the choice is from amongst candidates deemed appointable by the Civil Service Commission.[60] Occasionally, the Prime Minister will veto an appointment, as happened when David Cameron vetoed David Kennedy, Chief Executive of the Climate Change Committee, who had been selected to be the Permanent Secretary of the Department of Energy and Climate Change.[61] But, when Boris Johnson became Prime Minister, there was an unprecedented wave of departures of six Permanent Secretaries, including the Cabinet Secretary, Sir Mark Sedwill, who resigned after weeks of hostile press briefing from No 10.[62] Whilst individual Permanent Secretaries have occasionally had to leave, this was the first time a whole cohort of senior Permanent Secretaries has been removed.

Even more controversially, Dominic Cummings claimed in evidence to a parliamentary committee that it was he who had selected Simon Case to be Permanent Secretary in No 10;[63] despite the Cabinet Manual providing that 'the Cabinet Secretary is appointed by the Prime Minister on the advice of the retiring Cabinet Secretary and the First Civil Service Commissioner'.[64] The 2021 *Declaration on Government Reform* states that

> We will ensure that ministers have visibility of Senior Civil Service appointments in the departments they lead, and provide the Prime Minister and Cabinet Secretary with the broadest possible choice of new Permanent Secretaries and Directors General.[65]

It remains to be seen whether this portends a fresh attempt to extend ministerial choice over senior civil service appointments, or heralds a truce after the initial cull of six Permanent Secretaries.

Undermining Recruitment on Merit, and Fair and Open Competition

The principle of recruitment on merit on the basis of fair and open competition is enshrined in section 10(2) of CRAG, and the Civil Service Commission are the

[60] For details of this process, see Civil Service Commission, above n 51 at 6–8.

[61] Civil Service World, 'PM in rare veto of permanent secretary job' (*Civil Service World*, 5 December 2012) www.civilserviceworld.com/professions/article/pm-in-rare-veto-of-permanent-secretary-job.

[62] Constitution Unit, *Monitor 76* (London, Constitution Unit, 2020), 11–2; P Murphy 'Why it matters that so many senior civil servants are quitting under Boris Johnson' (*The Conversation*, 2 September 2020) www.theconversation.com/why-it-matters-that-so-many-senior-civil-servants-are-quitting-under-boris-johnson-145257.

[63] S Payne and G Parker, 'Relations between Johnson and cabinet secretary fray over Cummings ties' *Financial Times* (London, 28 May 2021).

[64] Cabinet Office, *The Cabinet Manual*, 1st edn (2011), para 4.53; For details of this process, see I Watmore, *Oral evidence to the House of Commons Public Administration and Constitutional Affairs Committee* HC 1314 (16 March 2021), QQ29-31.

[65] Cabinet Office, above n 57 at 4.

guardians of the principle through their recruitment principles. Special advisers are an exception, discussed below. But the cap of two advisers per Cabinet minister has been avoided by the appointment of additional advisers as temporary civil servants. Under the 1997–2010 Labour government, there were reported to be as many as 20 temporary civil servants (usually called political advisers or 'pads') who acted like special advisers. Similar appointments happened under the coalition, where a minister like Michael Gove recruited three or four policy advisers in addition to his quota of special advisers.[66] Gove has shown similar disregard for recruitment on merit in his choice of trusted non-executives to serve on departmental boards. When he became Justice Secretary in 2015, he dismissed all of the relevant non-executives in order to appoint his own; and at the Cabinet Office in 2020, he brought in a group of non-executives who had been longstanding allies.[67] The CSPL has identified 'an increasing trend amongst ministers to appoint supporters or political allies as [non-executive directors]',[68] and it has been estimated that around 20 per cent of departmental non-executives were appointed more for their political support than for their commercial or professional experience.[69] One of the non-executives brought in by Gove, his close ally as chair of the Vote Leave campaign Gisela Stuart, was later appointed as First Civil Service Commissioner.

Growth of Special Advisers

Special advisers are the single greatest driver of politicisation in Whitehall. After a small start under Harold Wilson, their numbers have grown and grown: from around 25 under Harold Wilson and James Callaghan, dipping to 14 at the start of the Thatcher government, then rising to 34 under Major. There was a step change under Blair, who doubled the numbers in 1997 to 73, in particular to strengthen the government's media and communications capacity. The large increase in numbers led to increased fears of patronage, and renewed calls for regulation.[70] Both Conservatives and Liberal Democrats pledged a reduction but by the end of their coalition government the number had risen to just over 100. Under Johnson the numbers have risen again, to 114, of whom almost half (51) worked in No 10.[71]

The Blair government also saw a step change in the power and influence of special advisers. Blair's Chief of Staff, Jonathan Powell, and his press secretary, Alastair Campbell, were both given formal powers to instruct civil servants.

[66] Yong and Hazell, above n 54 at 197.

[67] Thomas, above n 47.

[68] Committee on Standards in Public Life, *Standards Matter 2: The Committee's Findings* (2021), 24.

[69] M Gill, R Clyne and G Dalton, *Ten Questions the proposed Commissioner for Public Appointments must answer* (Institute for Government, 2021), 5–6.

[70] Fourth Report from the Public Administration Select Committee, *Special Advisers: Boon or Bane* HC 293 (2000–01); Joint Committee on the draft Constitutional Renewal Bill, above n 34 at paras 289–300.

[71] Cabinet Office, *Annual Report on Special Advisers 2020* (2020).

They wielded more power than most ministers. The same was true of Dominic Cummings, Johnson's senior adviser, even though he never took the title of Chief of Staff.

Marginalisation of the Civil Service

The rise of special advisers, and growing reliance on think tanks and other external sources, has ended the civil service's monopoly of advice to ministers, and of expertise. Special advisers can operate as a barrier between the department and the minister. The Ministerial Code reminds them that 'Ministers have a duty to give fair consideration and due weight to informed and impartial advice from civil servants';[72] but there is a lot of evidence of civil service advice being marginalised or ignored, and of senior officials being increasingly reluctant to speak truth to power.[73]

Growing Centralisation and the End of Collective Cabinet Government

Like the growth of special advisers, centralisation underwent a step change under Blair, who preferred sofa government to collective Cabinet decision-making. It can be measured by the increase in the staff at No 10. Under Thatcher and Major, the staff serving the Prime Minister had numbered around 90 people; by 1998 they had risen to 120; and by 2005 had peaked at over 200. Among this group, there has been a large increase in the number of special advisers advising the Prime Minister. Whilst Major had eight special advisers, Blair in 1998 had 16, later rising to 28 in 2004.[74] Ten years later, Cameron had a similar number, 26 in 2014; but under Johnson the number has doubled, to 51.

Centralisation took a further twist under Johnson, with Dominic Cummings' insistence that departmental special advisers report to him as well as to their Secretary of State.[75] An extreme example was No 10's insistence that the Chancellor of the Exchequer Sajid Javid sack all his special advisers, which prompted his resignation; his successor Rishi Sunak is served by a team of special advisers shared with No 10.[76] Centralisation has also extended to the Cabinet Office, with Cummings'

[72] Cabinet Office, *Ministerial Code* (2019), para 5.2.

[73] Eighth Report from the House of Commons Public Administration Committee, *Truth to Power: How Civil Service reform can succeed* HC 74 (2013–14).

[74] G Jones and A Blick, 'The PM and the centre of government from Blair to Cameron' (*LSE Blog*, 21 May 2010) www.blogs.lse.ac.uk/politicsandpolicy/the-pm-and-the-centre-of-uk-government-from-tony-blair-to-david-cameron-how-much-will-change-in-the-transition-from-single-party-to-coalition-government/.

[75] T Durrant, 'No 10 should give up its control of special advisers' (*Institute for Government*, 18 November 2020) www.instituteforgovernment.org.uk/blog/no10-should-give-its-control-special-advisers.

[76] K Balls, 'Sajid Javid quits as No 10 takes control' *The Spectator* (London, 13 February 2020); Cabinet Office, *Annual Report on Special Advisers 2021* (2021).

plans to establish a NASA-style control centre there realised in September 2021 with the creation of the National Situation Centre and seen by commentators as a power grab by No 10 with officials working under closer political direction than ever before.[77]

Breach of Civil Service Values and the Rule of Law

The Ministerial Code requires that ministers should 'not ask civil servants to act in any way which would conflict with the Civil Service Code'.[78] Under the core value of integrity, the Civil Service Code requires officials to comply with the law and uphold the administration of justice. The pressures first of Brexit, and then the Covid crisis, have put these values and the officials who uphold them under intense strain. The parliamentary wrangles over Brexit saw multiple examples, with the government losing high-profile court cases (see chapter five), and the Prime Minister threatening to ignore a clear statutory duty to extend the Article 50 period.[79] The last straw came when the Johnson government introduced the Internal Market Bill which would, if enacted, have authorised breaches of the UK's international law obligations. This led to the resignation of Sir Jonathan Jones, Treasury Solicitor and head of the Government Legal Service.[80] The Covid crisis has also seen the government taking several legal shortcuts which have undermined of the rule of law.[81] This includes losing court cases over cronyism in the award of contracts during the Covid crisis; contracts which must have sorely tested civil service values of integrity and impartiality.[82]

Conclusion

The preceding section has extended back to the premiership of Tony Blair, and before that to Margaret Thatcher, to show that politicisation is not a new concern.

[77] P Maguire, 'Dominic Cummings moves No 10 staff to heart of Whitehall' *The Times* (London, 13 August 2020). www.thetimes.co.uk/article/dominic-cummings-moves-no-10-staff-to-heart-of-whitehall-in-latest-move-in-war-on-civil-service-j8wr8k6cr; G Corera, 'Inside the government's secret data room' (*BBC News*, 15 December 2021) www.bbc.co.uk/news/technology-59651706.

[78] Cabinet Office, above n 72 at para 5.1.

[79] A Mohdin, 'Boris Johnson sabotage letter to EU would break law' *The Guardian* (London, 9 September 2019) www.theguardian.com/politics/2019/sep/09/boris-johnson-sabotage-letter-to-eu-would-break-law.

[80] R Hogarth, 'Jonathan Jones' resignation points to wider questions about breaking international law' (*Institute for Government*, 8 September 2020) www.instituteforgovernment.org.uk/blog/treasury-solicitor-resignation-rule-law.

[81] M Russell, R Fox, R Cormacain and J Tomlinson, 'The marginalisation of the House of Commons under Covid has been shocking; a year on, Parliament's role must urgently be restored' (*Constitution Unit*, 21 April 2021) www.constitution-unit.com/2021/04/21/covid-and-parliament-one-year-on/.

[82] Public Law Project, 'High Court rules: Gove broke the law' (*Public Law Project*, 9 June 2021) www.goodlawproject.org/update/gove-broke-the-law/.

Indeed, it was concerns about politicisation in the 1980s and 1990s which led to growing calls for a Civil Service Act. The hope was that embedding the core civil service values in primary legislation and putting the Civil Service Commission on a statutory basis would restore the authority of the civil service and strengthen the hands of officials in speaking truth to power. But the legislation eventually passed in CRAG was essentially conservative, codifying what had previously been in Orders in Council: it provided a statutory foundation for the civil service, but said almost nothing about the superstructure. In particular, CRAG was silent about the relationship between ministers and civil servants, whereas arrangements in other Westminster systems specify more clearly who is accountable for what.[83]

Nevertheless, CRAG represents an important backstop, establishing the powers and tenure of the Civil Service Commissioners and putting in law the absolute requirement of appointment on merit. The statutory foundation has been particularly important for the Civil Service Commission, whose role and powers could more easily have been diminished under the prerogative. The only level at which choice is permitted is the Prime Minister's choice of Permanent Secretaries. The commission regard that practice as acceptable so long as only appointable candidates are the subject of choice, and independent panels make the judgement of who is and is not appointable. That may start to change following the appointment of Gisela Stuart as First Civil Service Commissioner. Suggestions that ministerial choice should be extended to lower levels of the civil service, starting with Directors General and with the choice exercised by the Secretary of State rather than the Prime Minister, have up to now been resisted. But the commission has no power to stop dismissals; nor the steady growth of special advisers; nor the marginalisation of the civil service and of expert advice in key decisions. The wave of dismissals and departures in 2019–20 is of particular concern, lest it set an expectation of similar culls by incoming Prime Ministers in the future.

The decade since CRAG has seen further politicisation, intensifying under the Johnson government. CRAG has provided little defence against that. Dominic Cummings and other senior advisers in No 10 would appear to have breached the spirit if not the letter of section 8(5) CRAG, which prohibits special advisers from authorising the expenditure of public funds or exercising power in relation to civil servants. The Civil Service Commission has remained silent, mindful of its narrow remit, and of the government's previous willingness to clip its wings. Parliament has also been largely silent, save for occasional reports from PASC which the government has easily brushed aside.[84] The government has swept all before it, making full use of the Prime Minister's comprehensive statutory power to manage the civil service; and when trouble strikes, it can suit the government to

[83] Harris, above n 39.

[84] Fifth Special Report from the House of Commons Public Administration Select Committee, *Truth to Power: How Civil Service reform can succeed: Government Response to the Committee's Eighth Report of Session 2013–14* HC 955 (2013–14).

leave lines of accountability blurred – it makes blame shifting easier. In a lecture entitled *Tomorrow's Government*, Sir Richard Wilson presciently observed:

> When push comes to shove it is Ministers of the Crown who are entitled to carry the day. If strong Prime Ministers want to change the constitutional running of the Government or the Civil Service or the country, they can do so, provided only that they can carry their colleagues and their backbenchers with them.[85]

He wrote that before the civil service was put on a statutory basis. But it is a measure of the limited impact of CRAG that it could equally have been written afterwards.

[85] R Wilson, *Tomorrow's Government (RSA Lecture)* (London, Constitution Unit, 2007), 14.

10

Public Appointments

> ... patronage runs especially deep in Britain because of our history as a constitutional monarchy, with the royal prerogative allowing Ministers to exercise wide, diverse and often ancient powers of patronage.
>
> House of Commons Public Administration Select Committee (2003)[1]

Introduction

Large numbers of public appointments are made under the prerogative. No one knows how many, and there is no official list. Whenever the government wishes to appoint someone to a role for which there is no statutory authority, they do so using the prerogative. Examples include appointments to the House of Lords; to permanent non-statutory bodies such as the chair and board members of the BBC, or the Committee on Standards in Public Life; or ad hoc positions such as the appointment of Kate Bingham as head of the UK Vaccine Taskforce, or Louise Casey as Homelessness Tsar. Non-statutory inquiries have been established under the prerogative, such as the Iraq Inquiry chaired by Sir John Chilcot (see chapter fourteen). And important constitutional watchdogs operate under the prerogative, including two which regulate public appointments: the Commissioner for Public Appointments, and the House of Lords Appointments Commission.

Until recently, the use of prerogative powers conferred a wide discretion on ministers to appoint whoever they liked. There was no requirement to advertise or run a competition – ministers could reach out and appoint someone well known to them, and often did. Or if they did not know anyone who they could appoint, they would select someone from a list provided by the whips. But, in the last 25 years, that discretion has become significantly restricted. The Commissioner for Public Appointments, established in 1995, ensures that almost all public appointments to arm's length public bodies are made following fair and open competition. Since 2007, the top 50 or so public appointments have been subject to a further safeguard: pre-appointment scrutiny hearings by parliamentary committees.

[1] Fourth Report from the House of Commons Public Administration Select Committee, *Opening up the Patronage State* HC 165 (2002–03), para 1.

Judicial appointments are now regulated by the statutory Judicial Appointments Commission (JAC), established in 2006. And, since 2000, appointments to the House of Lords have been regulated by the House of Lords Appointments Commission (HoLAC), which nominates some of the crossbench peers and scrutinises political nominees for propriety. As a result of the work of these different bodies, the patronage wielded by ministers has become circumscribed: lightly in the case of HoLAC; severely in the case of the JAC; significantly in the case of the Commissioner for Public Appointments, but less so recently as the Commissioner's powers have been curtailed.

House of Lords Appointments

After the power to appoint ministers, the most important patronage in the hands of the Prime Minister is the power to grant peerages that confer a seat in the House of Lords. The prerogative power to appoint peers officially rests with the monarch, but is in practice exercised only on the advice of the Prime Minister. The power has been overlain by statute, in a series of recent Acts. First, the Life Peerages Act 1958 enabled the monarch to confer life peerages, with the right to sit and vote in the House of Lords; though following passage of the 1958 Act, it is arguable that the creation of a life peerage is a statutory and not a prerogative power.[2] Then the House of Lords Act 1999 removed the right of most hereditary peers to sit and vote in the Lords; and the House of Lords Reform Act 2014 allowed members to retire or resign permanently from the Lords, actions which were previously impossible because their peerages were conferred for life.

Legislation imposes no constraint on the numbers or the individuals whom the Prime Minister may choose to appoint and the practice of rewarding party donors with peerages goes back at least to the premiership of Lloyd George.[3] There has been a broad understanding that Prime Ministers should not simply pack their own side in the Lords, but there is no enforcement mechanism over this understanding other than self-restraint. However, in the last 20 years, the power to award peerages has become slightly more restricted in two ways. First, by the creation of the House of Lords Appointments Commission. And second, by initial commitments from the main political parties about the need for proportionality to regulate party balance in the House of Lords. Though both developments appeared to offer constraints upon the power to award peerages, they have been weakened under the premiership of David Cameron, and further weakened under Boris Johnson.

[2] T Foot, 'A Note on the Creation of Peers' (*Constitution Unit*, 30 January 2021) www.ucl.ac.uk/constitution-unit/sites/constitution_unit/files/a_note_on_the_creation_of_peers.pdf.

[3] J Calvert, G Abuthnott and T Calver, 'New Tory sleaze row as donors who pay £3m get seats in House of Lords' *Sunday Times* (London, 6 November 2021).

The most important thing which remains completely unconstrained is the size of the House of Lords. There is no overall cap on its size, and with patronage being irresistible to most party leaders, its size has crept gradually upwards. Profligate appointments by David Cameron sent the size of the House spiralling up to over 800 members. Following the House of Lords Reform Act 2014, there was cross-party discussion in the Lords to encourage peers to retire. The Lord Speaker, Lord Fowler, set up the Committee on the Size of the House, chaired by Lord Burns, to implement a scheme of voluntary retirement; this was based on the principle of 'two out, one in', shared across the parties with the aim of gradually bringing the House back down to 600. The hope was that, if the House showed restraint in persuading members to retire after 15 years, the Prime Minister might exercise similar restraint in making new appointments. Theresa May showed more restraint than her predecessor, and the annual monitoring reports of the Lord Speaker's Committee showed that the size of the House was slowly coming down.[4] But Boris Johnson defied convention by appointing 79 new peers in his first 18 months in office: almost double the 43 peers created by Theresa May during her three years as Prime Minister.[5] In consequence, the size of the House of Lords has started rising again, as has the Conservative group which was already the largest group in the Lords.

Related to the size of the Lords is the issue of party balance: a key factor in driving up the size of the House has been the wish of successive Prime Ministers to top up their own side. Prime Ministers do not simply appoint from their own party, but invite smaller numbers of nominations from other party leaders. As a result, Prime Ministers effectively control the party balance as well as the overall size of the House. The Labour Party recognised the need for a clearer convention about party balance in the Lords following their 1997 manifesto commitment to remove the hereditary peers. The party stated

> Our objective will be to ensure that over time party appointees as life peers more accurately reflect the proportion of votes cast at the previous general election … No one political party should seek a majority in the House of Lords.[6]

Tony Blair made large numbers of Labour and Liberal Democrat appointments, which greatly increased proportionality, but this principle was never rigidly adhered to.[7] The coalition government, formed in 2010, adopted a similar

[4] *Third Report from the Lord Speaker's Committee on the Size of the House* (2019), para 2.

[5] J Goddard, 'New Lords Appointments: December 2020' (*House of Lords Library*, 19 January 2021) www.lordslibrary.parliament.uk/new-lords-appointments-december-2020/; M Russell, 'Boris Johnson's 36 new peerages make the need to constrain prime ministerial appointments to the House of Lords clearer than ever' (*Constitution Unit Blog*, 31 July 2020) www.constitution-unit.com/2020/07/31/boris-johnsons-36-new-peerages-make-the-need-to-constrain-prime-ministerial-appointments-to-the-house-of-lords-clearer-than-ever/.

[6] Labour Party, *New Labour: Because Britain Deserves Better* (1997), 32–3.

[7] For details of party balance across appointments per Prime Minister since 1958, see M Russell and T Semlyen, *Enough is Enough: Regulating Prime Ministerial Appointments to the Lords*

commitment, that 'Lords appointments will be made with the objective of creating a second chamber reflective of the share of the vote secured by the political parties in the last general election'.[8] The hope was that this might lead to a convention, respected by both main parties, that new appointments should observe a proportionality principle. But any such hope was torpedoed by David Cameron, and then completely sunk by Boris Johnson.

The only small constraint on prime ministerial appointments is the House of Lords Appointments Commission (HoLAC), created in 2000. It is an advisory, non-departmental public body which was created under the prerogative. Its first function is to make nominations to the independent crossbenches. Successive Prime Ministers have undertaken to approve without amendment the commission's recommendations for new crossbenchers, and during its first ten years the commission nominated 53 people to the crossbenches. But the Prime Minister still controls the numbers to be appointed. After David Cameron became Prime Minister, those numbers have been greatly reduced: in 2012, he asked the commission in future to nominate only two individuals per year, and the 2010–15 Parliament saw only eight nominations. At the same time, Cameron expanded his power to nominate in each Parliament up to ten distinguished public servants to the crossbenches on their retirement, by broadening the range of people who could be nominated, and by removing the requirement of retirement from the nomination process.[9] Under Boris Johnson, the number nominated by the commission has shrunk even further: he invited no nominations from the commission for almost three years, between June 2018 and February 2021, when two more crossbenchers were appointed.[10] At the same time, Johnson appointed eight non-affiliated peers, four times the number HoLAC had appointed to the crossbenches.[11]

The commission's second function is to vet for propriety all nominations to the House, including nominees from the political parties. The commission plays no part in assessing the suitability of those nominated, which is a matter for the parties themselves. Its role is strictly limited to assessing propriety.[12] The commission's website states that 'the making of a donation or loan to a political party cannot of itself be a reason for a peerage'. The commission does not have a right of veto and

(London, Constitution Unit, 2015); For details of party balance across the chamber and in appointments per year since 1999, see M Russell, *The Contemporary House of Lords: Westminster Bicameralism Revived* (Oxford, Oxford University Press, 2013), 75.

[8] HM Government, *The Coalition: our programme for government* (2010), 27.

[9] *Hansard*, HC Deb Vol 583, col 37W (26 June 2014).

[10] House of Lords Appointment Commission, 'Two new non-party-political peers' (24 February 2021).

[11] T Burns, 'The House of Lords is too large: party leaders must put aside short-term interests and agree plans to reduce its numbers' (*Constitution Unit Blog*, 25 June 2021) www.constitution-unit.com/2021/06/25/the-house-of-lords-is-too-large-party-leaders-must-put-aside-short-term-interests-and-agree-plans-to-reduce-its-numbers/.

[12] This has been interpreted by the Commission as meaning that the nominee should be in good standing in the community and with the public regulatory authorities, and that their past conduct will not bring the House of Lords into disrepute.

can merely draw its concerns to the Prime Minister's attention. Nevertheless, the commission's vetting function has proved effective in screening out some of the candidates put forward. During its first 15 years, it is said that ten peerages were screened out in this way.[13] HoLAC's 2013–15 report disclosed that it successfully queried a further seven nominations in 2015.[14] But, in 2020, Boris Johnson went against the advice of HoLAC in appointing Peter Cruddas, a former Conservative Party Treasurer who had donated over £3 million to the party. This was the first time a Prime Minister has ignored the advice of HoLAC.[15]

Prime ministerial use of the prerogative to make appointments to the Lords thus remains essentially unregulated, save for the limited control by HoLAC. Under Cameron, May, and Johnson, there have been occasional suggestions that they might 'pack' the Lords with Conservative peers in order to get government legislation through.[16] This could place the monarch in a very awkward position. The last time any such move was attempted explicitly was immediately before the passage of the Parliament Act 1911, when the monarch was still considered to have some discretion on the matter and the request from Prime Minister Asquith to create additional peers was refused by King George V – at least until a general election had been held to test public opinion on the policy matter under dispute. Should such a request be made today, it is not clear whether the monarch would be able to resist it. For this and other reasons, the House of Commons Public Administration Select Committee (PASC), and its successor the Public Administration and Constitutional Affairs Committee (PACAC), have proposed tighter regulation of this prerogative power.[17]

Given the backsliding in recent years, effective regulation can come about only through statute. The original intention, shared by Labour and the Conservatives, was that HoLAC should be a statutory body, as recommended by the Wakeham Royal Commission on reform of the House of Lords.[18] In 2021, Lord Norton introduced his House of Lords (Peerage Nominations) Bill, the fourth such attempt

[13] P Dominiczak, S Swinford and C Hope, 'Revealed: seven peerages blocked after failing vetting process' *Daily Telegraph* (London, 6 August 2015) www.telegraph.co.uk/news/politics/11826722/Revealed-Seven-peerages-blocked-after-failing-vetting-process.html.

[14] House of Lords Appointment Commission, *Annual Report 2013–2015* (2015), para 36.

[15] Letter from Boris Johnson to Lord Bew (21 December 2020).

[16] J Watts, 'Speaker of House of Lords warns Theresa May against appointing new peers to get Brexit bills passed' *The Independent* (London, 6 January 2017) www.independent.co.uk/news/uk/politics/speaker-house-of-lords-theresa-may-lord-fowler-create-new-tory-peers-brexit-legislation-lloyd-george-a7512496.html; N Morris, 'Boris Johnson intends to pack House of Lords with Brexiteers to correct pro-Remain bias' (*iNews*, 26 August 2019) www.inews.co.uk/news/brexit/boris-johnson-brexit-latest-house-of-lords-brexiteers-pro-remain-bias-330739.

[17] Second Report from the House of Commons Public Administration Select Committee, *Propriety and peerages* HC 153 (2007–08), para 135; Eighth Report from the House of Commons Public Administration and Constitutional Affairs Committee, *The Strathclyde Review: Statutory Instruments and the power of the House of Lords* HC 752 (2015–16), paras 36–8.

[18] *Hansard*, HL Deb Vol 612, cols 1131-1132 (4 May 2000) (Lord Strathclyde and Baroness Jay); Royal Commission on Reform of the House of Lords, *A House for the Future* (Cm 4534, 2000).

in 20 years to give HoLAC a statutory basis.[19] If it were a statutory body, its role and responsibilities would be clearer, for example in relation to the number of crossbenchers who could be appointed, and whether nomination by HoLAC was the sole route to the crossbenches. A much bigger question is whether the size of the House of Lords should also be limited by statute, given the failure of voluntary efforts to do so. The chair of the Lord Speaker's Committee on the Size of the House, Lord Burns, has said that 'Prime Ministerial patronage and the ability to appoint an unlimited number of members, who are entitled to a seat for life, is the root cause of the persistent increase in the size of the House.'[20] The unrestraint of recent Prime Ministers, coupled with their undermining of HoLAC, has led Meg Russell to conclude that:

> … in an environment where those at the heart of the government machine have become dismissive of constitutional convention and constraint, the only sure way to control the size of the Lords is to legislate to remove the Prime Minister's unfettered power.[21]

The Commissioner for Public Appointments

The Office of the Commissioner for Public Appointments (OCPA) owes its origins to the very first report of the Committee on Standards in Public Life (CSPL), chaired by Lord Nolan. Nolan was concerned at 'the lack of checks and balances on the exercise of Ministers' considerable powers of patronage', and recommended that 'an independent Public Appointments Commissioner should be appointed to regulate, monitor and report on the public appointment process'.[22] The Prime Minister John Major acted swiftly to implement all of Nolan's recommendations, and within months the government had introduced a Public Appointments Order in Council and had appointed the First Commissioner, Sir Len Peach. This swift action illustrates the advantages of operating under the prerogative: the Commissioner has never been a creature of statute, and subsequent changes to OCPA's powers and functions have been made by issuing fresh Orders in Council.

The Commissioner's prime task is to ensure that the selection of candidates assessed as appointable is made on merit following a process of open and fair competition. Appointments are still made by ministers who make the final decision, but the Commissioner helps to ensure that they select from a short list of appointable candidates, chosen from a strong and diverse field. In addition to

[19] For examples of previous attempts, and additional information on the work of the House of Lords Appointment Commission, see E Scott, 'Reforming the House of Lords Appointment Commission' (*House of Lords Library*, 20 August 2021) www.lordslibrary.parliament.uk/reforming-the-house-of-lords-appointments-commission/.

[20] Burns, above n 11.

[21] Russell, above n 5.

[22] First Report from the Committee on Standards in Public Life, *Standards in Public Life* (Cm 2850-I, 1995).

publishing a Code of Practice, the Commissioner regulates public appointments by issuing additional guidance, investigating complaints, conducting regular audits, and recruiting and accrediting independent assessors to chair selection panels.

The system has been subject to occasional reviews. In 2003, PASC found that the system still smacked of cronyism:

> Ministers now find themselves in a half-way house: they can no longer determine appointments … as their predecessors once could; yet they retain enough direct involvement in the process to leave them open to allegations of cronyism. This state of affairs harms public confidence in government …[23]

PASC's suggestion that a Public Appointments Commission should take over the actual process of appointment from ministers proved a step too far, as did the recommendation that all independent assessors should come within the Commissioner's remit.[24] When Sir David Normington became Commissioner in 2011, he found the appointments system had become too process-oriented, slow and burdensome, and subsequently instituted a more proportionate principles and risk-based system.[25] But such streamlining was not enough for David Cameron, a Prime Minister who enjoyed exercising patronage, especially to arts and cultural bodies. In 2015, Cameron asked Sir Gerry Grimstone to conduct a review of the system of public appointments, with a view to further streamline the system, but also to reassert ministerial control. Grimstone obliged, reminding people that 'Ministers are at the heart of the public appointments system', and proposing a new set of Public Appointment Principles to be backed by a Governance Code that was agreed by ministers. This would replace OCPA's Code of Practice, and OCPA's independent assessors would be replaced by advisory assessment panels set up by the department. Having been a central player in helping to organise appointment competitions, the Commissioner was reduced to being a referee:

> The Commissioner's role is to provide an independent check and balance in order to help maintain integrity, including conducting spot checks, responding to any concerns raised by panel members, and considering complaints.[26]

The government warmly welcomed the Grimstone report, but the outgoing Commissioner, Sir David Normington, protested at the diminution of the Commissioner's role. The government would now be setting the rules, rather than OCPA, and the government would be appointing the selection panels, removing the Commissioner's power to choose independent assessors:

> Taken together, Grimstone's proposals would enable ministers to set their own rules; override those rules whenever they want; appoint their own selection panels; get

[23] House of Commons Public Administration Select Committee, above n 1 at para 67.

[24] Baroness Fritchie, *Memorandum to the House of Commons Public Administration Select Committee* HC 122-I (2005).

[25] Commissioner for Public Appointments, *Annual Report 2011–12* (2012), 9.

[26] G Grimstone, 'Executive Summary' in *Better Public Appointments: A Review of the Public Appointments Process* (Cabinet Office, 2016), para 32.

> preferential treatment for favoured candidates; ignore the panel's advice if they don't like it; and appoint someone considered by the panel as not up to the job.[27]

The CSPL and PACAC shared Sir David Normington's concerns, with PACAC warning that the changes 'may be leading to an increasing politicisation of senior public appointments'.[28]

The new system was introduced under the Public Appointments Order in Council 2016. As under the previous Code, ministers should be engaged early on in the planning process and at every stage of the competition. This includes agreeing on the job description, the duration of the appointment, the process for appointment and the selection criteria. What is different in the new Code is that the relevant minister should agree the composition of the Advisory Assessment Panel, which should include an independent member and a departmental official. The departmental official is responsible for representing and making other members aware of the minister's views throughout the process. Finally, the minister should be able to meet the appointable candidates before deciding on the appointment.

The Code requires a list of 'significant appointments' to be agreed by ministers and the Commissioner. Agreed lists for both England and Wales are published on the Commissioner's website. In order to provide additional reassurance that these appointments are being made solely on merit, a Senior Independent Panel Member (SIPM) is required to sit on the Advisory Assessment Panels. The Commissioner should be consulted about the selection of SIPMs by the relevant minister, but has no veto on the choice.

The newly appointed commissioner, Peter Riddell, was consulted by the Cabinet Office about the new Public Appointment Principles contained in the Governance Code on Public Appointments as they were being drafted.[29] In a lengthy debate between May and November 2016, he made a number of suggestions which were accepted:

- First, SIPMs should not be politically active or connected with the sponsoring department. (Though he also pressed for Independent Panel Members not to be politically active, this was not agreed).
- Second, if ministers want to dispense with a competition or appoint someone who has been judged unappointable by an interview panel, they must consult the Commissioner in advance.

[27] D Normington, 'The five reasons I'm concerned about plans to overhaul the public appointments process' (*Civil Service World*, 21 March 2016) www.civilserviceworld.com/news/article/sir-david-normington-the-five-reasons-im-concerned-about-plans-to-overhaul-the-public-appointments-process.

[28] Committee on Standards in Public Life, 'CSPL statement on PACAC's report on public appointment process' (2016); Seventh Report from the House of Commons Public Administration and Constitutional Affairs Committee, *Appointment of the Commissioner for Public Appointments* HC 869 (2015–16), para 3.

[29] Cabinet Office, *Governance Code on Public Appointments* (2016).

- Third, the Nolan principle of fairness, on which the Commissioner can rely when assessing competitions and exemptions from competitions, should be retained.

In his last year in office, Peter Riddell reported that the central question remained the balance between ministerial involvement and appointment on merit. That depended on restraint and good sense. Ministers had not sought to appoint a candidate deemed by the panel to be unappointable. But they had rejected some strong candidates, and there were other worrying signs that the balance was under threat. Ministers had attempted to appoint people as SIPMs with clear party affiliations, but had backed down after consulting the Commissioner. In a few cases, they had sought to pack the interview panel with their allies. A parallel concern was the growth of unregulated appointments, such as non-executive members of departmental boards, where people with business expertise had been partly replaced by political allies of ministers.[30]

Similar concerns were expressed by CSPL:

> Ministers should not appoint unqualified or inexperienced candidates to important public roles. Such appointments feed public perceptions of cronyism and corruption and undermine public trust … In order to guarantee that the assessment of merit is fair and nonpartisan, it should be undertaken by a panel which includes a credible independent element.[31]

In September 2021, William Shawcross was appointed as the new Commissioner for Public Appointments. Concerns were expressed about his unfamiliarity with senior recruitment processes and his independence and willingness to challenge the government where necessary. Both concerns were tested at his pre-appointment scrutiny hearing, but in the event, PACAC endorsed his appointment.[32] It remains to be seen whether he will be as robust as his predecessor. Looking over his shoulder will be PACAC and the CSPL, who commented in June that the system 'is highly dependent on both the willingness of ministers to act with restraint and the preparedness of the Commissioner to speak out against breaches of the letter or the spirit of the Code'.[33]

In the final report of their *Standards Matter 2* inquiry, CSPL went further, recommending that the Commissioner needed to be put on a statutory basis: 'regulators which exist solely as the creation of the executive are potentially liable to be abolished or compromised with ease'.[34] The committee cited evidence from

[30] Letter from Peter Riddell to Lord Evans (7 October 2020).

[31] Committee on Standards in Public Life, *Standards Matter 2: Committee Findings* (2021), para 71.

[32] Fourth Report from the House of Commons Public Administration and Constitutional Affairs Committee, *Appointment of William Shawcross as Commissioner for Public Appointments* HC 662 (2021–22); See also M Gill and G Dalton, *Ten Questions the proposed Commissioner for Public Appointments must answer* (Institute for Government, 2021).

[33] Committee on Standards in Public Life, above n 31 at para 83.

[34] Committee on Standards in Public Life, *Upholding Standards in Public Life* (2021), para 2.26.

Sir David Normington, who spoke from his experience as First Civil Service Commissioner as well as Commissioner for Public Appointments:

> … the Civil Service legislation, that gave me absolute clarity of my powers, and I knew that those powers and the Commission's powers could not be changed, except by going back to Parliament. In contrast, my powers as Public Appointments Commissioner were in an Order in Council which I knew could be changed by a stroke of the pen and a nod of the Privy Council. And that did mean I suddenly felt very vulnerable to an argument with government … I knew it was perfectly within the government's power, with very little public debate and accountability to Parliament, to change the rules.[35]

Pre-Appointment Scrutiny Hearings for Senior Public Appointments

A further safeguard against appointment on the basis of patronage rather than merit is the system of pre-appointment scrutiny hearings by select committees. This originated under Gordon Brown, as part of his wider ambitions to reform the prerogative (see chapter three). Brown's 2007 White Paper *The Governance of Britain* announced that in future the most senior public appointments would be submitted to parliamentary scrutiny:

> … the Government nominee for key positions … should be subject to a pre-appointment hearing with the relevant select committee. The hearing would be non-binding, but in the light of the report from the committee, Ministers would decide whether to proceed. The hearings would cover issues such as the candidate's suitability for the role, his or her key priorities, and the process used in selection.[36]

The Cabinet Office and the House of Commons Liaison Committee (consisting of all the select committee chairs) subsequently agreed a list of just over 50 key positions which would be subject to the new procedure. Since then, there have been over 100 pre-appointment scrutiny hearings held by 20 different select committees. Although the committees have no formal power of veto, they can require the government to think again if they raise serious questions about a candidate, or issue a negative report. Since 2007, there have been ten pre-appointment hearings which have called appointments into question. In only four cases out of the ten did the appointment continue.[37] In three cases, the candidate decided to withdraw; in

[35] ibid.

[36] Ministry of Justice, *The Governance of Britain* (Cm 7170, 2007), para 76.

[37] For details of nine of these hearings, see R Hazell 'Improving Parliamentary Scrutiny of Public Appointments' (2019) 72 *Parliamentary Affairs* 223, 233; The tenth hearing concerned the appointment of Baroness (Tina) Stowell to the Chair of the Charity Commission in February 2018. In that case, the Digital, Culture, Media and Sport Committee issued a negative report, but the appointment nevertheless went ahead.

one case, the government withdrew the candidate; and two candidates were forced to resign after appointment because of statements made at the pre-appointment hearing.[38]

More often than not, when a committee gives a candidate a hard time or issues a negative report, the appointment does not go ahead. Committee screening for conflicts of interest has also proved, in some cases, more stringent than the government's recruitment processes. And evaluation studies suggest there is a wider deterrent effect: because pre-appointment scrutiny is rigorous, testing, and public, ministers will be reluctant to put forward weak candidates who will not pass muster before the select committee.[39]

Two suggestions have been advanced for increasing the effectiveness of pre-appointment scrutiny. The first came from a review initiated by the Commons Liaison Committee, which reminded committees that they need not feel confined by the list prepared by the Cabinet Office, but should feel free to scrutinise any ministerial appointment they felt necessary. It encouraged committees to be more strategic, with periodic reviews of the public appointments in their subject area to decide which merit a scrutiny hearing. It also advised committees to be more systematic in preparing for hearings, with a written questionnaire issued to candidates inviting them to disclose any conflicts of interest, to demonstrate their experience and expertise, their independence, and to indicate their initial priorities once in post.[40]

The second suggestion for strengthening pre-appointment hearings has come from CSPL, who proposed a more independent process for appointing constitutional watchdogs:

> The appointments process for these roles, including the Chair of CSPL, ACOBA, the House of Lords Appointments Commission, the Commissioner for Public Appointments, and the Independent Adviser on Ministers' Interests, require a greater element of independence. The Commissioner has suggested that assessment panels for these roles could have a majority of lay members, or the relevant Parliamentary Select Committee could have the power of veto.[41]

In their final report, CSPL dropped mention of a potential parliamentary veto and proposed only that assessment panels should have a majority of independent members.[42] The idea of a veto goes back to an earlier proposal from the Commons Liaison Committee, who in 2011 proposed that the list of key appointments be divided into three categories. First tier posts should require a joint appointment by government and Parliament, second tier posts should be subject to an effective veto, and for the remainder of posts, holding a pre-appointment hearing should be at

[38] ibid at 232–4.
[39] ibid at 235.
[40] Third Report from the House of Commons Liaison Committee, *Pre-Appointment Hearings* HC 2307 (2017–19), para 34.
[41] Committee on Standards in Public Life, above n 31 at para 90.
[42] Committee on Standards in Public Life, above n 34 at para 5.21.

the discretion of the committee.[43] The government rejected the committee's three-tier approach, but in recent years Parliament has gradually assumed a stronger role: accumulating a veto over the appointment of the Comptroller and Auditor General, the Parliamentary Ombudsman, Office for Budgetary Responsibility, Chair of the UK Statistics Authority, and the Information Commissioner.[44]

Judicial Appointments

The appointment of judges is the sphere in which the prerogative power of appointment has most effectively been curbed. A once cosy and informal system presided over by the Lord Chancellor, with few checks and balances, has been transformed into a statutory system where the Lord Chancellor is left with no discretion. Formally, High Court judges and above are still appointed by the Queen, acting under the prerogative. In selecting judges for appointment, old-style Lord Chancellors exercised considerable discretion, aided by a handful of officials, and limited chiefly by a requirement to consult the senior judges via secret soundings. The Lord Chancellor decided all appointments up to the High Court, with more senior appointments formally decided by the Prime Minister, but invariably acting on the advice of the Lord Chancellor.

Old-style Lord Chancellors with legal backgrounds were often well placed to assess individual candidates, many of whom might be known to them. In the first half of the twentieth century, candidates might be known as much through politics as the law: many MPs became judges.[45] By the middle of the century, the practice of appointing MPs had largely ceased and by the late twentieth century, the system for appointing judges began to be criticised for its informality, secrecy and dependence on old-boy networks. Appointment was by a tap on the shoulder. There were no advertisements, application forms, job interviews or selection criteria: the Permanent Secretary canvassed opinions from judges and barristers, and at monthly meetings the Lord Chancellor consulted the senior judges. These secret soundings gave the senior judges considerable sway; the high level of judicial influence translated into judicial self-replication, with those appointed being almost invariably successful male barristers, with private school and Oxbridge backgrounds.[46]

[43] First Report from the House of Commons Liaison Committee, *Select Committees and Public Appointments* HC 1230 (2010–12).

[44] House of Commons Liaison Committee, above n 40 at paras 31–33; Hazell, above n 37 at 238–9; In 2021, the government declined to honour the Select Committee's advice on the appointment of the Information Commissioner. See Fifth Report from the House of Commons Digital, Culture, Media and Sport Committee, *Pre-appointment hearing for Information Commissioner* HC 260 (2021–22), para 15.

[45] R Cranston, 'Lawyers, MPs and Judges' in D Feldman (ed), *Law in Politics, Politics in Law* (Oxford, Hart Publishing, 2015).

[46] G Gee, R Hazell, K Malleson and P O'Brien, *The Politics of Judicial Independence in the UK's Changing Constitution* (Cambridge, Cambridge University Press, 2015), 161.

The lack of diversity – and not just in terms of women, minorities and less privileged backgrounds, but also the need to appoint more solicitors and lawyers from non-commercial practice – was one of the main driving forces for change. Following an independent review by the First Commissioner for Public Appointments, Sir Len Peach (see page 143), a new scrutinising body was established in 2001, the Commission for Judicial Appointments (CJA). The body was established under the prerogative, and the first Commissioner Sir Colin Campbell was appointed by Order in Council, with a remit to audit the appointments process, recommend improvements and handle complaints. The CJA was not charged with running the appointments process, which remained in the hands of the Lord Chancellor. But Campbell quickly identified serious and chronic problems, criticising the self-replicating nature of the process and consequent failure to increase diversity. He recommended creating a new process centred around an independent appointments body.

The then Lord Chancellor, Lord Irvine, was reluctant to cede power to an appointments body – which was one of the reasons for his abrupt dismissal by Tony Blair in 2003. Following intense negotiations between the new Lord Chancellor, Lord Falconer, and the Lord Chief Justice Lord Woolf, the framework was laid for a wholly new system of judicial appointments built around an independent Judicial Appointments Commission (JAC).[47] Created by Part 4 of the Constitutional Reform Act 2005, the JAC completely changed the appointment process. In place of secret soundings and taps on the shoulder, all judicial vacancies are now advertised, from the highest to the lowest, and there is then a highly formalised selection process involving short listing by tests or paper sifts, interviews, and for some posts, presentations or role-playing. The JAC was created as a recommending body, but in identifying a single name for each vacancy, it effectively functions as an appointing body. The Lord Chancellor could accept or reject this recommendation, or request its reconsideration. In practice, Lord Chancellors nearly always accepted the recommendation, with only five occasions from nearly 3,500 recommendations between 2006–13 when this was not so.[48]

Under the Crime and Courts Act 2013, the role of the Lord Chancellor was reduced even further with power to make all lower-level judicial appointments being transferred to senior judges. After selection by the JAC, most tribunal judges are appointed by the Senior President of Tribunals, and Circuit judges and District judges are appointed by the Lord Chief Justice. The Lord Chancellor is still involved in appointments to the High Court and above, but the scope for ministerial discretion is extremely limited. By the time Jack Straw was appointed Lord Chancellor in 2007, frustration was growing that the Lord Chancellor no longer had a real choice. Straw was also frustrated at the JAC's failure to increase diversity, and the

[47] Department for Constitutional Affairs, *The Lord Chancellor's Judiciary Related Functions: Proposals (the Concordat)* (2004).

[48] Gee, Hazell, Malleson and O'Brien, above n 46 at 163. Note that the rejections of appointments on these five occasions were on relatively minor procedural grounds, rather than substantive disagreement.

Ministry of Justice was frustrated at the slow and cumbersome nature of the JAC's processes. So great was the friction that the JAC was subjected to seven different reviews in the first seven years of its existence.[49] Confidence reached such a low point that in 2009–10, the Ministry considered abolishing the JAC and bringing appointments back in-house. But they concluded that the politics of doing so would be too difficult.[50]

Straw's frustration that the Lord Chancellor had no real choice reached its apogee when he tried to question the proposed appointment of Sir Nicholas Wall as President of the Family Division in 2010, but the panel re-submitted the same name; Straw's doubts were subsequently confirmed when Sir Nicholas was forced to retire early on health grounds.[51] Kenneth Clarke concluded that the Lord Chancellor's power to refuse the JAC's recommendations was in effect unusable, which is why he was relaxed about passing the final say over lower level appointments to the senior judges. In terms of numbers, the Lord Chief Justice and Senior President of Tribunals are now the primary decision makers, making 97 per cent of all judicial appointments. And senior judges continue to exert significant influence over the JAC, which helps explain the shift in their attitudes from initial suspicion, and even outright hostility, when the JAC was first established, to a determination to fight for its survival when it was threatened with abolition in 2009–10.

The dilution of the Lord Chancellor's role represents a fundamental shift from the old ministerial model of appointments. The Lord Chancellor still remains responsible for the appointments system as a whole, accounting to Parliament for its effectiveness. It remains to be seen for how long governments will tolerate being responsible for a system from which the Lord Chancellor is largely excluded. Two forces might drive change. One is the slow progress in diversifying the judiciary: experience in other common law countries has shown it requires ministerial involvement in senior appointments to create a more diverse judiciary. The second driver is concern at the lack of democratic legitimacy in the face of growing judicial power: increasingly when judges hand down an unwelcome decision, politicians are starting to ask how the judges were appointed. This concern crystallised in 2021 with a Policy Exchange pamphlet that argued:

> Ministerial input into the appointments system provides one of the few channels for ensuring that senior judges enjoy an appropriate measure of democratic legitimacy … a wrong turn was taken in 2005 when the judicial appointments system was overhauled, with the Lord Chancellor marginalised from senior selection decisions. There is a strong case to make for enlarging the role of the Lord Chancellor.[52]

[49] For details of the seven reviews, see ibid at 167.

[50] ibid at 168.

[51] J Straw, *Aspects of Law Reform: An Insider's Perspective (The Hamlyn Lectures)* (Cambridge, Cambridge University Press, 2013), 58–9.

[52] R Ekins and G Gee, *Reforming the Lord Chancellor's Role in Senior Judicial Appointments* (Policy Exchange, 2021), 10.

Robert Buckland indicated his wish to review the role of the Lord Chancellor, but this may not be shared by his successor Dominic Raab, who was appointed in September 2021. If the Lord Chancellor seeks greater discretion over senior judicial appointments, the judges can be expected to protest that this will undermine judicial independence. But, so long as the Lord Chancellor is invited to choose from a list of those deemed appointable by the selection panel, there is no real threat, because all the short-listed candidates will have been independently judged to be capable of holding high judicial office.

Conclusion

In the last 25 years, the patronage wielded by ministers in making public appointments has become significantly circumscribed thanks to the creation of three new regulatory bodies (OCPA, JAC, and HoLAC), and pre-appointment scrutiny hearings by select committees. But, the power of these bodies varies greatly, and in recent years Prime Ministers have loosened the controls over public appointments generally, and in particular, over the power to appoint new peers. For regulation to be effective, and not subject to backsliding, the regulatory bodies discussed in this chapter would be better protected if they were enshrined in statute, with clear statutory powers and functions

The difference can be illustrated by the history of the JAC, which operates on a secure statutory foundation. If it were not a creature of statute, the Ministry of Justice might have been more tempted to try to abolish it in 2009–10. By contrast, it was not difficult for David Cameron to reduce the role of OCPA, and for both Cameron and Johnson to side-line HoLAC in order to extend their powers of patronage. OCPA's role was easily changed by Order in Council and HoLAC's role was easily undermined because its powers and functions were only loosely defined, and successive Prime Ministers had never truly fettered the right to appoint unlimited numbers of peers themselves.

Conventions have proved insufficient to check the temptation for Prime Ministers to pack their own side in the House of Lords, leading to an upwards spiral in its size. Given the failure of voluntary restraint, the only effective remedy would appear to be statutory controls; including putting HoLAC on a statutory basis. The CSPL felt unable to make such a recommendation, because 'a statutory HOLAC should be considered as part of a broader House of Lords reform agenda'.[53] But it did recommend that the Commissioner for Public Appointments should be given a statutory foundation (along with the Independent Adviser on Ministerial Interests, and the Advisory Committee on Business Appointments).[54]

[53] Committee on Standards in Public Life, above n 34 at para 2.37.
[54] ibid at para 2.32.

A statutory foundation would help to guard against eroding the Commissioner's powers, as happened in 2016 with the publication of the Public Appointment Principles in the Governance Code; or in extremis, to protect the office from abolition. There is also the psychological factor which applies to all non-statutory bodies, to CSPL and HoLAC as much as to OCPA, that without the security of a statutory foundation they may be inclined to pull their punches; although there was no sign of that from Peter Riddell during his time as Commissioner, even with one hand tied behind his back.

For the JAC, our critique is the reverse: that it has too much power, leaving ministers effectively with no discretion. Although nominally advisory, it has become de facto an appointing body, and one controlled by the judges. To restore to ministers some real choice, the JAC and selection panels for the most senior appointments should be required to submit a short list of appointable candidates rather than a single name. That should not be a threat to judicial independence, because the candidates will have been judged appointable; and it should enable faster progress on diversity.

Finally, though pre-appointment scrutiny hearings can never substitute for more effective regulatory checks at an earlier stage, the House of Commons has more power than it realises. Committee chairs express frustration because they have no power of veto, but they do have considerable influence. Candidates have withdrawn when faced with a negative report; others have resigned as a result of statements made at the pre-appointment hearing. The Commons Liaison Committee has shown how committees could make pre-appointment hearings more effective if they develop a more strategic and selective approach. Following the precedent of the Comptroller and Auditor General and the Parliamentary Ombudsman, the independence of the main constitutional watchdogs could be strengthened if Parliament had a power of veto over their appointment.

11

The Prerogative of Mercy

Introduction

Upon her coronation, the Queen swore an oath to 'cause Law and Justice in Mercy to be Executed in all [Her] Judgements'.[1] This oath is one of the oldest parts of the coronation ceremony, with a pedigree reaching back at least to the tenth century,[2] and the quality of mercy being an important aspect of medieval kingship in both England and Scotland.[3] The royal prerogative of mercy (RPM) forms part of this enterprise. Although 'mercy' and 'justice' have often been closely entwined – conceptually and institutionally – it is clear that in the present day the prerogative of justice (if it can still be said to exist) is exercised solely through the courts,[4] while the prerogative of mercy is exercised by the government, by means of letters patent under the Great Seal or the royal sign manual upon ministerial advice.[5] More commonly, we refer to these letters patent as 'pardons'. Mercy, unlike justice, 'begins where legal rights end'.[6]

There is a great deal that could – and has – been written on the use of the RPM and the concept of mercy. However, we restrict ourselves to five key questions:

- What is a pardon and who can grant one?
- How have pardons been used historically?
- What uses of the RPM survive to the present day?
- How do the courts supervise the use of the RPM?
- Where do we go from here? Are reforms to the RPM necessary or desirable?

[1] Coronation Oath Act 1689, s 3.

[2] M Clayton, 'The Old English *Promissio regis*' (2008) 37 *Anglo-Saxon England* 91. For the medieval and Tudor oaths, see G Watt, 'The Coronation Oath' (2017) 19 *Ecclesiastical Law Journal* 325.

[3] K Lewis, *Kingship and Masculinity in Medieval England* (London, Routledge, 2013), 17-30; C Neville, 'The beginnings of royal pardon in Scotland' (2016) 42 *Journal of Medieval History* 559, 581-2.

[4] *Prohibitions del Roy* (1607) 77 ER 1342; *R v Foster* [1985] QB 115, 130.

[5] Criminal Law Act 1967, s 9; Before the Criminal Law Act 1827, s 13 (which permitted warrants under the sign manual for conditional pardons granted to convicted felons), all pardons were required to be made by letters patent under the great seal: *R v Beaton* (1763) 1 Black. W. 479, 96 Eng. Rep. 277; J Chitty, *A practical treatise on the Criminal Law* (London, Butterworth & Sons, 1819), 381.

[6] *De Freitas v Benny* [1976] AC 234, 247 (Lord Diplock).

What is a Pardon and Who can Grant One?

The RPM is the power to grant pardons. A pardon is a relief from the punishment due under the law, often (at least in the modern era) on the basis of reasons that are outside a judge's purview. The RPM is exercised by the Queen on the advice of ministers. In England and Wales, the responsible minister is now the Secretary of State for Justice (following the transfer of responsibilities from the Home Office to the new Ministry of Justice in 2007).[7] In Scotland, the use of pardons is not a reserved matter and therefore falls within devolved competence, so that Scottish ministers have the exercise of the RPM.[8] In Northern Ireland, the RPM is only exercisable in transferred matters and then only by the Northern Irish Justice Minister.[9] Pardons in relation to terrorism, for example, are outside devolved competence in Northern Ireland.[10] Should the responsible minister wish to obtain the advice of the Criminal Cases Review Commission (CCRC) on a matter relating to the exercise of the prerogative, he or she may make a reference, but the CCRC's advice will be conclusive of the matter referred.[11] The first ever reference was made in February 2020, followed by two further cases in 2020-21.[12]

As well as pardons granted under the RPM, there are also statutory pardons. In recent years, statutory pardons have been granted largely out of remorse for the state of the law in former times. For example, following the (prerogative) pardon granted to Alan Turing in 2013, others convicted of buggery and certain other abolished sexual offences have been granted statutory pardons.[13] The Scottish government is currently considering statutory pardons for those convicted of offences relating to the miners' strike in 1984-85.[14] In centuries past, statutory pardons have been used for other purposes, such as creating incentives for smugglers, burglars, clippers of coins and others to become informants on their fellow criminals.[15] These statutory pardons do not fall within the ambit of this chapter, since the RPM is unaffected by additional pardons created by Parliament, and statutory pardons do not raise the same concerns about arbitrary executive power and lack of scrutiny.

[7] Reply to written question HL2637 (18 November 2014). The RPM is a 'reserved matter' under the Wales Act 2006, sch 7A, para 8(1) (as amended by the Wales Act 2017).

[8] Scotland Act 1998, s 53.

[9] Northern Ireland Act 1998, s 23 (as amended in 2010). Should there be no NI Justice Minister (as during 2017-2020), this power may not be exercised: *Re Buick's Application for Judicial Review* [2018] NICA 26, [35]; *Re JR80's application for judicial review* [2019] NICA 58, [68]-[74].

[10] Northern Ireland Act 1998, sch 3, para 9(1)(d).

[11] Criminal Appeals Act 1995, s 16(1), (2A). There appears to be no similar provision for the equivalent Scottish Commission.

[12] Criminal Cases Review Commission, *Annual Report and Accounts 2020/21* (HC 404, July 2021), 34.

[13] Policing and Crime Act 2017, ss 164-72; Historical Sexual Offences (Pardons and Disregards) (Scotland) Act 2018.

[14] Scottish Government, *A Fairer, Greener Scotland: Programme for Government 2021-22* (September 2021), 103.

[15] W Hawkins, *A Treatise of the Pleas of the Crown*, vol 2 (John Curwood ed, London, S Sweet, 1824), 531.

The legal effect of a prerogative pardon is not to overturn a conviction, but to spare the pardoned from a penalty.[16] However, a pardon under the prerogative to forestall any criminal proceedings may be pleaded in bar, so long as a plea to the general issue ('guilty' or 'not guilty') has not yet been entered.[17] This second rule is consistent with the first, since it is founded on the reasoning that the pardon destroys 'the end and purpose of the indictment, by remitting that punishment which the prosecution is calculated to inflict'.[18]

This may be contrasted with the apparent position in the US, where:

> A pardon reaches both the punishment prescribed for the offence and the guilt of the offender; and when the pardon is full, it releases the punishment and blots out of existence the guilt, so that in the eye of the law the offender is as innocent as if he had never committed the offence.[19]

However, even in the UK, it is sometimes possible to obtain compensation when a pardon has been granted for a 'miscarriage of justice' or where there has been 'serious default' in the investigation.[20] Further, a pardon must in some circumstances prescribed by statute be treated by a court *as if* it had wiped out the original conviction.[21] On the other hand, this latter statutory provision in particular reinforces the general rule: a pardon does not in law remove the conviction.

It is sometimes said that there are three or four 'forms' of pardon.[22] However, while pardons have in recent times chiefly been granted in three *situations* – 'as a special remission granted after a prisoner has been released early by mistake, as a conditional pardon to commute a sentence (such as the death penalty to life imprisonment) or as a free pardon to address a miscarriage of justice'[23] – there are only two *forms* of pardon: free and conditional.[24] Either a pardon is granted free and absolute, or it is conditional on the performance of some (lesser or different) punishment. If the condition is unfulfilled, the pardon is void. The form of a particular pardon will depend on the precise words used in the grant.[25]

[16] *R v Foster* [1985] QB 115, [130].

[17] M Lucraft (ed), *Archbold: Criminal Pleading, Evidence and Practice* (Sweet & Maxwell, 2021), 4-225 to 4-227. A pardon may not be pleaded to an impeachment by the Commons in Parliament (though the Crown may pardon after impeachment): Act of Settlement 1700, s 3.

[18] W Blackstone, *Commentaries on the Laws of England*, vol 4 (London, 1769), 26.

[19] *Ex parte Garland* 71 US 333, 380.

[20] Criminal Justice Act 1988, s 133 (as amended by the Criminal Justice and Immigration Act 2014, s 61); Armed Forces Act 2006, s 276; Terrorism Act 2000, sch 4, para 9; Proceeds of Crime Act 2002, s 72. Although the legislation is ambiguous, it is assumed that a 'pardon' here refers to a free pardon, as in the Forfeiture Act 1870, s 2 and the Clergy Discipline Measure 2003, s 28.

[21] Prevention of Oil Pollution Act 1971, s 19A(8)(b), (9)(b); Merchant Shipping Act 1995, s 145(2)(b), (3)(b), (5)(b); Serious Crime Act 2007, s 4(1).

[22] Eg, Lord Faulks in reply to written question HL2637 (18 November 2014). The constitutions of several British Overseas Territories also list four specific powers of pardon: eg, Constitution of the Falkland Islands, s 71.

[23] A Bradley, K Ewing and C Knight, *Constitutional and Administrative Law*, 17th edn (Harlow, Pearson, 2018), 260.

[24] E Coke, *The Third Part of the Institutes of the Laws of England* (London, M Flesher, 1644), 233.

[25] ATH Smith, 'The Prerogative of Mercy, the Power of Pardon and Criminal Justice' [1983] *Public Law* 398, 417.

Further, as will be shown below, pardons are also available in a wide variety of situations, such as where there has been a miscarriage of justice that cannot be remedied by the courts.

Finally, a power to grant a pardon should be distinguished from a power to grant a dispensation. The latter is no longer within the Crown's power, following the enactment of Article 2 of the Bill of Rights 1689.[26] Pardons are retrospective, while a dispensation is prospective. A pardon cannot be granted before an offence has actually occurred.[27] Furthermore, it is most likely not within the Crown's power to issue a general pardon.[28] These restrictions not only help prevent the Crown licensing agents to operate outside the ordinary law; they also mean that the pardon power is exercised at a point when the pardoner is able to take stock of the particular offence committed and its context.

How Have Pardons Been Used Historically?

The RPM used to play a major role, closely connected to the exercise of justice. However, one by one, the uses to which the RPM has been put have dwindled. Those of greatest importance historically were five in number:

1. In *homicide cases*, where culpability was lessened by excuse or justification, to relieve killers of the otherwise mandatory death penalty. Alongside other techniques, such as benefit of clergy and the wide discretion of the jury, the courts used pardons to give effect to the distinction in culpability between what we now know as murder and manslaughter.[29] Notably, the recommendations for these pardons usually came from the judge, and the pardons came to be granted as a matter of course upon the judge's request.[30] Some vestige of this use of the prerogative remains elsewhere in the Commonwealth. For example, in *Pitman v Trinidad and Tobago*, the Privy Council held that a convicted murderer who had not been able to make out the (limited) partial defence of diminished responsibility but who suffered from 'significant mental abnormality' could pray in aid the RPM, since carrying out a death penalty on such convicts 'cannot now be constitutionally justified'.[31]
2. To provide *relief from wrongful conviction*. Before the Criminal Appeal Act 1907, which established the Court of Criminal Appeal, rights and methods of

[26] It was resisted by judges even before this: J Baker, *The Oxford History of the Laws of England: Volume XI 1483-1558* (Oxford, Oxford University Press, 2003), 65.

[27] *Attorney General of Trinidad and Tobago v Phillip* [1995] 1 AC 396.

[28] Blackstone, above n 18 at 400.

[29] ND Hunard, *King's Pardon for Homicide Before AD 1307* (Oxford, Clarendon Press, 1969); H Lacey, *The Royal Pardon: Access to Mercy in the Fourteenth-Century* (York, York Medieval Press, 2009); JM Beattie, 'The Royal Pardon and Criminal Procedure in Early Modern England' (1987) 22 *Historical Papers* 9, 10-1.

[30] Beattie, ibid at 13.

[31] *Pitman v Trinidad and Tobago* [2017] UKPC 6, [50].

appeal in criminal cases were very limited. For example, even if the Court for Crown Cases Reserved (established in 1848) decided that a conviction was unsafe, its only remedy was to recommend the use of the RPM.[32]

3. To encourage some offenders to turn '*King's (or Queen's) evidence*'. Offenders who had assisted the authorities to bring their fellow miscreants to justice, 'though … not entitled as of right to pardon, yet the usage, lenity and the practice of the courts [was] to stop the prosecution against them and they [had] an equitable title to a recommendation for the King's mercy'.[33] Such incentives are now generally provided by sentencing powers.[34]
4. To *commute a death penalty* to a more appropriate punishment. In the seventeenth and eighteenth centuries, the number of capital offences dramatically increased. This was matched by a widespread use of pardons (on judicial recommendation). Conditional pardons were almost always offered (except for particularly heinous crimes) to give offenders the option of transportation to Virginia, the West Indies or (later) Botany Bay, Australia.[35] However, although great numbers of offenders were pardoned in this way, some – generally murderers, other very serious wrongdoers and people of local notability – were executed, both to punish the particular wrongdoing and to act as a deterrent against committing one of the (very numerous) capital offences.[36] Commutation of sentence was an extremely common practice right up to the final years of the death penalty in the UK. Between 1900 and 1949, 45.7 per cent of the 1,210 people sentenced to death were not in fact executed, thanks to the RPM.[37]
5. Where *politically expedient*, such as to a friend or ally of the King or one of his advisers. Parliament felt sufficiently worried by these to pass a statute attempting (rather unsuccessfully) to limit the use of pardons in 1328.[38]

One important observation may be made about these historical uses of the RPM: very few of them involved a true exercise of mercy. The first two are part of criminal justice itself, whether as a matter of the law's content or as an important part of the justice system. The third and fourth uses are largely driven by public policy. As to the fifth, there were of course times when pardons were granted out of the personal exercise of mercy by the King or an adviser, but other motivations were doubtless also present. The traditional grant of pardons to those who had supported a successful usurper to the throne is particularly multifaceted.[39]

[32] A useful sketch of the history of criminal appeals was given by Lord Sales JSC in *Re McGuinness's Application for Judicial Review* [2020] UKSC 6, [25], [37].

[33] *R v Rudd* (1775) 1 Cowper 331, [334] (Lord Mansfield).

[34] Eg, Sentencing Act 2020, s 388.

[35] J Baker, *Introduction to English Legal History*, 5th edn (Oxford, Oxford University Press, 2019), 557-8.

[36] Beattie, above n 29 at 19-22.

[37] *Report from the Royal Commission on Capital Punishment* (Cmd 8932, September 1953), para 42.

[38] The Statute of Northampton 2 Edw III, c 2 (1328); *cf* Baker, above n 35 at 557.

[39] Lacey, above n 29 at 98-100.

What Uses of the RPM Survive to the Present Day?

Although Parliament has never tried to abolish the RPM, it has by steady increments removed many of its most important historical uses.[40] The growth in new institutions to accommodate criminal appeals, the demise of the death penalty and the new robustness of criminal law since the late nineteenth century have all contributed to this tightening restriction. As the Northern Irish Court of Appeal recognised in *McGeough v Secretary of State for Northern Ireland*, the RPM is now generally restricted to three situations.[41]

1. 'Special Remissions'

The RPM is used for the early termination of a custodial sentence when the prisoner has been mistakenly led to expect an earlier release date than that prescribed by law. This is the source of much of the modern UK litigation on the RPM,[42] and is in essence an administrative correction governed by guidance issued by Her Majesty's Prison and Probation Service.[43] However, the number of special remissions has varied considerably: between 1992-96, 192 were granted, while only five were granted between 1997-2008.[44]

2. Pardon for Especially Good Conduct

As the 2009 *Governance of Britain* report noted, 'The Royal Prerogative remains the only way of terminating a sentence early in recognition of remarkably good conduct in custody and is still occasionally applied in such cases.'[45] Such pardons may be granted for assistance to the prison authorities in preventing escape, injury or death.

The most recent example of a pardon granted for exemplary conduct was in 2020, when Steven Gallant, following his famous use of a narwhal horn to waylay a terrorist on London Bridge in November 2019, had his 17-year minimum term for murder reduced by 10 months.[46] However, apart from a press statement to the BBC, no official announcement of this pardon was made.

[40] Ministry of Justice, *The Governance of Britain: Review of the Executive Royal Prerogative Powers: Final Report (2009)*, para 60.

[41] *McGeough v Secretary of State for Northern Ireland* [2012] NICA 28, [13].

[42] Eg, *R (Page) v Lord Chancellor* [2007] EWHC 2026 (Admin); *R (Shields-McKinley) v Lord Chancellor* [2019] EWCA Civ 1954.

[43] National Offender Management Service, *Sentence Calculation – Determinate Sentenced Prisoners* (2015), ch 13.

[44] *Hansard*, HC Deb Vol 483, col 701 (25 November 2008).

[45] Ministry of Justice, above n 40 at para 64(c).

[46] BBC, 'London Bridge attack: Steven Gallant up for early release after confronting knifeman' (*BBC News*, 18 October 2020), www.bbc.co.uk/news/uk-54588407.

3. Miscarriages of Justice

The RPM's use to provide an appeals process has disappeared with the advent of the statutory criminal appeal courts. The Criminal Appeal Act 1907 provided a right of appeal from the Crown Court, and this has since been supplemented by a right of appeal from the Magistrates' Courts.[47] The Criminal Appeal Act 1995 ushered in the Criminal Cases Review Commission (CCRC), which has powers to review convictions and refer them as an appeal to the courts.[48] It is likely that an attempt to use the RPM to subvert the statutory appeals process would fall foul of the dictum of Lord Reid in *Burmah Oil Co v Lord Advocate*: 'The prerogative is really a relic of a past age, not lost by disuse, but only available for a case not covered by statute.'[49]

However, the CCRC also has a statutory power under section 16(2) of the 1995 Act to recommend a case to the Secretary of State for a pardon.[50] It follows that Parliament foresaw the RPM retaining a role in remedying miscarriages of justice (or some similar category of cases). This conclusion is supported by the frequent references to pardons in recent legislation providing for compensation upon a miscarriage of justice.[51] Two questions arise from this. First, what legitimate role does the RPM retain to set aside a punishment imposed by the courts where the courts will not do so on appeal? And second, when should the CCRC exercise its section 16(2) power to recommend such a pardon?

The RPM retains a residual role to correct miscarriages of justice where the courts are unable to do so. The Crown's long-standing policy on the use of free pardons reflects this:

> A decision by the Secretary of State for Justice to recommend the use of the royal prerogative of mercy to grant a free pardon is restricted to cases where it is impractical for the case to be referred to an appellate court and, secondly, where new evidence has arisen that has not been before the courts, demonstrating beyond any doubt either that no offence was committed or that the defendant did not commit the crime. The applicant must be technically and morally innocent. These criteria have proper regard to the constitutional position that the courts decide whether a person is guilty of an offence, not the Government.[52]

This approach recognises that there will be rare cases in which a miscarriage of justice is prevented from being remedied by the courts, perhaps because of rules about the admissibility of evidence.[53] In this way, the RPM remains, as Lord Justice

[47] Magistrates' Courts Act 1980, s 108.
[48] Criminal Appeal Act 1995, ss 9-10.
[49] *Burmah Oil Co v Lord Advocate* [1965] AC 75, 101; *cf Shields-McKinley*, above n 42 at [56].
[50] Criminal Appeal Act 1995, s 16(2).
[51] See above n 20.
[52] *Hansard*, HC Deb Vol 483, col 701 (25 November 2008).
[53] See *R (Shields) v Justice Secretary* [2008] EWHC 3102 (Admin), [33]; *Report from the Royal Commission on Criminal Justice* (Cm 2263, 1993), ch 11, paras 17–18.

Watkins put it in *R v Secretary of State for the Home Department, ex parte Bentley*, 'a constitutional safeguard against mistakes'.[54]

However, it is a limited remedy, since it does not overturn the wrongful conviction itself. In 2015, some queried whether it would be appropriate for the CCRC to use the section 16(2) power to mitigate the perceived harshness of the test of a 'real possibility' of wrongful conviction when considering referral of a case to the appeal courts. The House of Commons Justice Committee firmly rejected this, arguing that this would erode the constitutional separation between executive and judicial powers and that a pardon could only ever be a sticking-plaster solution, to be reserved for extraordinary cases in which no judicial remedy could be obtained.[55] On that basis, the CCRC restricts its use of the section 16(2) power and usually refers cases to the appeal courts. It has only recommended the use of a pardon on one occasion.[56]

The institution of the CCRC lessens the constitutional tension between the executive and judicial branches when such rare cases arise. An example of the difficulties that could be caused before this can be found in the cases of David Cooper and Michael McMahon, who were convicted of murdering Reginald Stevens in a post office in Luton in September 1969. The cases came to the Court of Appeal five times in the 1970s, four of which were on a reference by the Home Secretary. None of the appeals, several of which sought (unsuccessfully) to adduce new evidence, were upheld. The Home Office, however, repeatedly stated that 'the independence of the judiciary means that it is not for the Home Secretary to substitute his own view for that of the Court of Appeal'.[57] Yet eventually public confidence in the criminal justice system was being eroded by the case, and the publication of a well-received book on the subject by Ludovic Kennedy precipitated the immediate release of both prisoners by the then Home Secretary, William Whitelaw:

> The case is wholly exceptional and I judge that there is a widely felt sense of unease about it. I share that unease. … in the unique circumstances of this case, I believe that we have reached the point where I must say 'enough is enough'.[58]

Cooper and McMahon's convictions were later quashed in July 2003 upon a reference by the CCRC, although both had died in the meantime.

The challenge to normal constitutional conventions in this case demonstrates the utility of an independent and expert body like the CCRC. Not only is the CCRC a more suitable body than a politician to consider the use of a pardon for a miscarriage of justice, its very existence should provide a better safeguard against

[54] *R v Secretary of State for the Home Department, ex parte Bentley* [1994] QB 349, 365.

[55] Twelfth Report from the House of Commons Justice Committee, *Criminal Cases Review Commission* HC 850 (2014-15), para 29.

[56] Criminal Cases Review Commission, *Annual Report and Accounts 2010/11* (HC 1225, July 2011), 22.

[57] *Hansard*, HC Deb Vol 941, col 874 (14 December 1977).

[58] *Hansard*, HC Deb Vol 988, cols 719-720 (18 July 1980); L Kennedy, *Wicked Beyond Belief: The Luton Murder Case* (London, Granada, 1980).

such exceptional cases arising in future, being better able to pick up miscarriages of justice at an early stage and being better resourced and equipped than defendants to bring appeals based upon difficult new evidence.

However, some cases fall outside these three conventional categories, and merit brief attention. As Lord Justice Watkins noted in *ex parte Bentley*, 'it is an error to regard the prerogative of mercy as a prerogative right which is only exercisable in cases which fall into specific categories. The prerogative is a flexible power and its exercise can and should be adapted to meet the circumstances of the particular case.'[59]

4. Special Posthumous Pardons

In December 2013, Alan Turing was granted a posthumous pardon for his conviction for homosexual activity. This fell outside the Crown's long-standing policy on the use of free pardons, since Turing was not 'technically innocent'. However, the Justice Secretary at the time justified the use of the RPM by the fact that the conviction would today be considered 'unjust and discriminatory'.[60] As noted above, this personal (prerogative) pardon was shortly followed by a general (statutory) pardon for those convicted of similar offences.

5. Release on Compassionate Grounds

There remains a discretion to exercise the RPM on compassionate grounds. Although statutory powers of early release now also exist,[61] these are 'not the same as, or coterminous with' the prerogative, such that both may coexist.[62] The courts have repeatedly recognised that the exercise of the RPM in such a situation is a matter for ministers and not the Court of Appeal in reviewing sentence.[63]

6. Informers

Although now generally provided for by sentencing powers,[64] incentives for criminals to provide information may still be provided by the RPM in certain situations.

[59] *ex parte Bentley*, above n 54 at 365.

[60] Ministry of Justice, 'Royal pardon for WW2 code-breaker Dr Alan Turing' (*HM Government*, 24 December 2013) www.gov.uk/government/news/royal-pardon-for-ww2-code-breaker-dr-alan-turing.

[61] Criminal Justice Act 2003, s 248; Crime (Sentences) Act 1997, s 30.

[62] *Shields-McKinley*, above n 42 at [87]-[88].

[63] *R v Bernard* [1997] 1 CrAppR (S) 135; *R v Stephenson* [2018] EWCA Crim 318; *R v DM* [2021] EWCA Crim 203.

[64] Eg, Sentencing Act 2020, s 388.

For example, in July 1996, the Home Secretary Michael Howard granted conditional pardons to offenders John Haase and Paul Bennett (following information they had given after being sentenced). Both were later convicted of perverting the course of justice when the information turned out to be false.[65]

7. Northern Ireland

Part of the Good Friday Agreement included an Early Release Scheme for certain prisoners. This operated under statute in the Northern Ireland (Sentences) Act 1998. However, it has since become clear that the RPM was used to grant pardons to certain individuals who 'for technical reasons fell outside the letter of the Early Release Scheme'.[66] Furthermore, ministers issued to other individuals letters of assurance and even pardons, as part of an 'On the Run' (OTR) scheme. The OTR scheme was operated largely in secret, for which – alongside administrative failings – it was robustly criticised by a review led by Lady Justice Hallett in 2014 as well as by the House of Commons Northern Ireland Affairs Committee in 2015.[67]

How do the Courts Supervise the Use of the RPM?

There has been a definite trend towards the justiciability of the RPM over the past 30 years. As recently as the 1970s, Lord Diplock could confidently hold that 'Mercy is not the subject of legal rights. It begins where legal rights end'.[68] In his Lordship's view,

> In tendering his advice to the sovereign, the Home Secretary is doing something that is often cited as the exemplar of a purely discretionary act as contrasted with the exercise of a quasi-judicial function.

This echoed a similar approach taken by Lord Denning a few years earlier, that

> The law would not inquire into the manner in which that prerogative was exercised. The reason was plain – to enable the Home Secretary to exercise his great responsibility without fear of influence from any quarter or of actions brought thereafter complaining that he did not do it aright.[69]

[65] M Bright, 'Why did Howard release two dangerous gangsters?' *The Observer* (London, 13 February 2005).

[66] BBC, '16 Irish republicans received royal pardons since 2000' (*BBC News*, 25 March 2015) www.bbc.co.uk/news/uk-northern-ireland-32053605.

[67] H Hallett, *The Report of the Hallett Review: An Independent Review into the On the Runs Administrative Scheme* (HC 380, July 2014); Second Report from the House of Commons Northern Ireland Affairs Committee, *The administrative scheme for "on-the-runs"* HC 177 (2014-15).

[68] *De Freitas*, above n 6 at 247-8.

[69] *Hanratty v Lord Butler* (1971) SJ 382, 386.

Indeed, even in Lord Roskill's famous discussion of the justiciability of prerogatives in *Council of Civil Service Unions v Minister for the Civil Service* (*GCHQ*), the RPM was considered non-justiciable along with treaty powers, war powers and others.[70]

However, there has been a marked shift away from this position and towards justiciability, both in the UK and abroad.[71] In the UK, the major shift occurred in *ex parte Bentley*,[72] in which Bentley's sister sought judicial review of the Home Secretary's decision not to grant a posthumous free pardon to Bentley, who had previously been hanged for murder despite the jury's recommendation of mercy. On the one hand, the court rejected Bentley's challenge to the Home Office policy on granting pardons, holding that 'the formulation of criteria for the exercise of the prerogative by the grant of a free pardon [is] entirely a matter of policy which is not justiciable'.[73] On the other hand, the court held that the Home Secretary's decision had been improperly made because he had failed to take into account that a different form of pardon (a conditional pardon) might be granted. Furthermore, Lord Justice Watkins noted (obiter) that refusal of a pardon 'solely on the grounds of sex, race or religion' would be justiciable.

Despite some initial uncertainty,[74] the *Bentley* line of authority has now certainly overtaken the older approach. In *Lewis v Attorney-General of Jamaica*, the majority of the Privy Council thought that the 'personal nature' of the power weighed less than the fact that 'the act of clemency is to be seen as part of the whole constitutional process of conviction, sentence and the carrying out of the sentence'.[75] Although the merits of the decision were for the Crown (the Governor General in that case), the court would ensure that 'proper procedural standards are maintained'.[76] The High Court appeared to go further in *R (B) v Home Secretary*, when asked to determine whether the Home Secretary was required to take into account any assistance the prisoner had rendered to the authorities before (as well as after) sentence.[77] For Lord Justice Keane, the dividing line really came between exercises of prerogative in the realm of 'high policy' and those outside it. Such a use of the pardon power was something the courts were 'well qualified to deal with' given their similar considerations in sentencing.[78]

[70] *Council of Civil Service Unions v Minister for the Civil Service* [1985] AC 374, 418.

[71] A Novak, *Comparative Executive Clemency: The Constitutional Pardon Power and the Prerogative of Mercy in Global Perspective* (Abingdon, Routledge, 2016), ch 8. The exception is France; *cf* R Levy, 'Pardons and Amnesties as Policy Instruments in Contemporary France' (2007) 36 *Crime & Justice* 551, 557.

[72] *ex parte Bentley*, above n 54.

[73] ibid at 363.

[74] *Reckley v Minister of Public Safety and Immigration (No. 2)* [1996] AC 527.

[75] *Lewis v Attorney-General of Jamaica* [2001] 2 AC 50, [54].

[76] ibid at [47] and [50].

[77] *R (B) v Home Secretary* [2002] EWHC 587 (Admin).

[78] ibid at [22]-[23].

Another important ground of review is upon errors of law. In *R (Shields) v Justice Secretary*, the Divisional Court had to consider an unusual situation.[79] Shields had been convicted for attempted murder in Bulgaria and his appeals there had been unsuccessful. Furthermore, the Bulgarian authorities refused to re-investigate the case when Shields brought forward new evidence. Instead, they suggested that a pardon could be granted by the UK (under Article 12 of the Convention on the Transfer of Sentenced Persons 1983). The Lord Chancellor believed that Article 13 of the Convention prevented the UK from doing so. However, that was an error of law and so the refusal of a pardon was overturned.

It therefore appears that judicial review will now extend to most exercises of the RPM, notwithstanding the facts that the intensity of that review will usually allow the decision maker a 'wide degree of latitude'[80] and that the formulation of the criteria for its exercise is generally a non-justiciable matter of policy.[81] The courts of Australia seem ready to reach a similar conclusion, again despite older, apparently categorical authority.[82] In some contexts the court will go further. In *Lendore v Trinidad and Tobago* and *Pitman*, the Privy Council has held that the RPM can be prayed in aid in order to avoid a breach of constitutional rights (for convicts sentenced to death).[83] (It should be noted, however, that section 14 of the Constitution of Trinidad and Tobago gives the courts wide powers to prevent such infringement, which may make these cases non-comparable with the UK jurisprudence on justiciability.)

However, although the courts have extended the reach of judicial review of pardons in the last three decades, they have also made clear that the RPM remains outside the usual process of conviction and sentencing. Indeed, they have been cautious about recognising a duty to exercise the RPM in certain cases because it would undermine that usual process.[84] They are also resistant to the notion that there could be a legitimate expectation of a pardon being granted because of pardons in similar circumstances.[85] Restricted as its uses have become, particularly following the passage of statutory appeal procedures, pardons are perhaps more than ever highly individual remedies or favours granted in very special circumstances. That does not mean that they need be rare, or that ministers can act improperly, but the courts will require a high threshold to be crossed before intruding on that 'wide degree of latitude'.

[79] *Shields*, above n 53.
[80] *McGeough*, above n 41 at [14].
[81] *ex parte Bentley*, above n 54 at 363; *Page*, above n 42 at [16]-[17].
[82] A Twomey, 'The Prerogative and the Courts in Australia' (2021) 3 *Journal of Commonwealth Law* 55, 96-9.
[83] *Lendore v Trinidad and Tobago* [2017] UKPC 25, [20]; *Pitman*, above n 31.
[84] Eg, *Shields-McKinley*, above n 42 at [55]-[56], where the applicant had neglected to apply to the Court of Appeal.
[85] *Re Rodger's Application for Judicial Review* [2014] NIQB 79, [78]-[88].

The Future: Are Reforms to the RPM Necessary or Desirable?

Although the RPM is now largely restricted to a few, special cases, it remains an extraordinary executive power. In the US, in the last month of his time in the White House, President Trump pardoned 116 people as president and was said actively to be considering a pardon for himself.[86] Even if matters in the UK do not reach such a fever pitch, the fallout from the OTR scheme in relation to Northern Ireland shows that pardons can be of great public interest and importance.[87] Given the extraordinary nature of pardons, it is unsurprising that they have attracted several calls for reform already. We shall first consider two of them, and why they present flawed critiques of the status quo, before turning to some suggestions of our own.

First, the then Lord Chancellor Jack Straw proposed in 2009 that the power to grant pardons should be transferred to the courts.[88] This proposal overlooks three important points. First, the exercise of mercy must be distinguished from the exercise of justice. Only the latter is the proper domain of the courts. As Lord Bingham put it,

> Mercy, in its first meaning given by the Oxford English Dictionary, means forbearance and compassion shown by one person to another who is in his power and who has no claim to receive kindness. Both in language and literature mercy and justice are contrasted. The administration of justice involves the determination of what punishment a transgressor deserves, the fixing of the appropriate sentence for the crime. The grant of mercy involves the determination that a transgressor need not suffer the punishment he deserves, that the appropriate sentence may for some reason be remitted. The former is a judicial, the latter an executive, responsibility.[89]

To this, it may be added that it would simply be incoherent for a court to punish with one hand and pardon with the other. If a consideration of which the court may properly have cognisance means that punishment should be stayed, lifted or varied, then the court (whether at first instance or on appeal) should refrain from imposing that punishment using its existing powers.[90] Furthermore, the uses of the RPM that might properly be called part of the criminal justice system –

[86] US Department of Justice, 'Clemency Statistics' (*US Department of Justice*, 2 February 2022) www.justice.gov/pardon/clemency-statistics#DonaldJTrump. See also BBC, 'Donald Trump: Could the US president pardon himself?' (*BBC News*, 18 January 2021) www.bbc.co.uk/news/world-us-canada-40693249.

[87] C Buckler, 'Secret royal pardons granted to NI paramilitaries' (*BBC News*, 10 June 2014) www.bbc.co.uk/news/uk-northern-ireland-27760311.

[88] J Straw, 'Michael Shields: press release by the Justice Secretary' *The Times* (London, 9 September 2009).

[89] *Reyes v The Queen* [2002] UKPC 11, [44].

[90] The possibility of incoherence was noted in Blackstone, above n 18 at 31.

considerations of culpability, relief from wrongful conviction, and even the commutation of death sentences – have already been transferred to the courts. The residual uses of the RPM (except perhaps special remissions) fall outside the realms of criminal justice: pardons for good behaviour are highly discretionary and using the RPM to correct for miscarriages of justice is predicated on the *inability* of the courts to act.

A second flawed proposal for reform is simply to codify the RPM by statute or to recreate it as a statutory power. Proponents of such a reform argue that 'Where a person has been wrongly convicted, he seeks justice and not mercy, and this should be given as a statutory right and not as an executive prerogative.'[91] However, this fails for the same reason as Straw's proposal: appeals are already accommodated by the courts, and the CCRC has eliminated many of the previous concerns about executive interference in criminal justice. In fact, as we have seen, the RPM is now particularly useful *beyond* the justice system. Its chief residual use within standard processes is in 'special remissions', and codification could be usefully targeted there.

Most importantly, these options would do very little to improve the *mechanisms of accountability* around the RPM. For example, conversion of the power into statute would not make it more amenable to judicial review, particularly given the developments of the last three decades. What is more, judicial review by itself is not enough. Instead, those seeking reform should look to other, non-legal routes to enhanced scrutiny. We suggest that three reforms may be appropriate.

First, the ability to exercise the RPM in secret should be restricted. As the Hallett Review noted, 'There is no requirement in law to publish the use of the RPM. By convention, the use of the RPM to grant a free pardon is published in *The London Gazette*, but its use in other cases is not.'[92] This caused particular difficulties for that review, which was considering the use of 'letters of assurance' to suspected members of the IRA who were OTR. The review identified some individuals who had received post-conviction pardons as well as their letters of assurance, but the lack of a central register or regular official publication made these enquiries an uncertain exercise. In their report on the scheme, the House of Commons Northern Ireland Affairs Committee report concluded that the Secretary of State's refusal to name which of those recipients of pardons were OTRs was wholly unacceptable.[93]

There is an important public policy point here – one that cannot be addressed via expanding judicial review. Using powers secretly, particularly pardon powers in highly politically charged contexts, risks abuse of those powers. Furthermore, a lack of basic transparency as to the numbers of pardons granted (and the reasons behind them) hinders those seeking to assess the importance and relevance of the RPM in modern practice.

[91] Smith, above n 25 at 421.

[92] Hallett, above n 66 at para 8.13; *cf* Written answer to HC 221302 (20 January 2015).

[93] House of Commons Northern Ireland Affairs Committee, above n 67 at para 58.

The lack of transparency is particularly peculiar when a pardon is granted for exemplary conduct, which might be thought to provide incentives to other convicts and to constitute a symbol of public praise for the recipient. For example, not even the partial remission granted to Steven Gallant in 2020 was published, with the only official source being a press statement to the BBC.

Luckily the remedy here is quite simple. There should be a statutory duty to publish the grant of a free pardon. Conditional pardons or remissions granted for exemplary conduct should also be published. It would be impracticable to require the publication of all other uses of the RPM, such as special remissions, which are in any case more administrative exercises of the power. Furthermore, there are particular concerns for confidentiality where a pardon is granted to an informer and in a select number of other cases (for example, involving national security). However, it would be desirable to maintain registers of all uses of the RPM within each jurisdiction. Statistics derived from this register could be reported each year to the Commons Justice Select Committee.

A second reform which might easily be made is to impose a statutory duty upon the Secretary of State to seek advice as to the exercise of the RPM. One difficulty with this reform is that the RPM is used in a variety of situations. This suggests that a variety of advisory bodies would be needed. For example, the CCRC would be an inappropriate adviser for the granting of pardon or remission on the grounds of exemplary behaviour. A more appropriate advisory body for this would be the Parole Board. This problem is solved in some countries, including several African nations, British Overseas Territories and Commonwealth states, by having a special advisory body which must be consulted before the use of the prerogative of mercy (although the advice is not binding).[94] However, instituting such a body in the UK would undermine the established role of the CCRC in cases concerning miscarriages of justice.

The two uses of the RPM that most clearly call for controls are: (a) in remedying miscarriages of justice; and (b) early release (excluding special remissions). It is in these two uses that the RPM challenges the division of constitutional responsibility between the courts and the executive and presents an open door to abuse of power. We propose, therefore, that separate statutory duties should exist for each of these two uses, to refer the exercise of the RPM in the first case to the CCRC and in the second to the Parole Board. This may require some developments to the Parole Board's structure, but the Board has proved itself capable of adaptation to other challenges and further reform is already in discussion (at least in England and Wales).[95]

[94] Eg, Constitution of Kenya, s 133; Falklands Islands Constitution Order 2008, art 70; Cayman Islands Constitution Order 2009, art 40. The Constitution of Jamaica, art 90 requires the Governor General to act on the recommendation of the Privy Council.

[95] Ministry of Justice, *Root and branch review of the parole system* (2020). Recent reforms include the formation of 'assessment panels' as part of the new, internal 'reconsideration' procedure: Ministry of Justice, *Review of the Parole Board Rules and Reconsideration Mechanism* (CP 29, February 2019).

Our third suggestion for reform also concerns institutions, but in this case institutions of investigation rather than advice. At present, the exercise of the RPM is not a matter that can be reviewed by the Parliamentary Ombudsman.[96] While we recognise that the Ombudsman has no particular expertise in these matters, unlike the courts, it does seem in principle beneficial for the use of (or failure to use) the RPM to be capable of review by a body that is more closely acquainted with the processes and priorities of government than the courts. It would likely be necessary to provide for a carve-out in highly confidential cases, but we note that oversight is provided in a comparable context by the Independent Reviewer of Terrorism Legislation. Had such a body had oversight of the OTR scheme in Northern Ireland, for example, it is possible that the administrative failings would not have been quite so grave.

Conclusion

While in past centuries the RPM was a central part of the criminal justice system itself – allowing for the commutation of the death penalty in capital offences, the distinguishing between murder and manslaughter, and even the overturning of unsafe convictions – those functions have been replaced by statutory and other legal developments. With one exception (administrative 'special remissions'), pardons now act *outside* the criminal justice system.

Therefore, although intertwined in the coronation oath and now defunct practice, justice and mercy have separated out, with two distinct mechanisms. The first, justice, is enhanced by non-arbitrariness and a robust, systematised set of institutions – the courts. The second, mercy, is a more slippery fish. It is both governed by moral codes and necessarily (largely) free of legal rules. There is an inherent degree of arbitrariness.[97] Perhaps that is what lies behind the courts' 'wide degree of latitude' afforded to ministers exercising the RPM, and their resistance to allowing the doctrine of legitimate expectations to encompass pardons.

That distinction between justice and mercy tells us something about reform too. While it may be appropriate to make (administrative) special remissions subject to a statutory scheme, as part of the system of justice, we must resist the temptation immediately to apply codification to the RPM as a one-size-fits-all solution. For mercy resists easy categories. The courts have repeatedly emphasised – and history has demonstrated – the flexibility of the RPM and the constantly evolving field of its uses.

However, even if we are to allow a degree of arbitrariness or 'latitude', that does not mean that there should be no accountability. We have highlighted three

[96] Parliamentary Commissioner Act 1967, sch 3, para 7.

[97] See A Perry, 'Pardons' in D Sobel and S Wall (eds), *Oxford Studies in Political Philosophy*, vol 8 (Oxford, Oxford University Press, 2021), 215.

possible areas for reform: more transparent reporting; mandatory advice; and enhanced institutional supervision. None of these detract from the essentially merciful nature of the remaining uses of the RPM, nor would they impede the flexibility of the power. Rather, they would balance those important aspects of the prerogative against the need to ensure that it is not abused.

12

Passports

Introduction

A passport is an administrative document, issued by a state to its citizens to facilitate their travel to other states by proving their citizenship. It is important to distinguish passports from citizenship. Whilst one must be a British national to obtain a British passport, it is not necessary that all British nationals should have a British passport. Similarly, British citizenship brings certain rights; but the right to a passport is not one of them. In this book we are concerned with the Crown's non-statutory powers, including the power of issuing (and, more importantly, of cancelling) passports. However, while not the primary focus of this chapter, it is important to recall that the passport power operates alongside a wide range of statutory powers, including powers to deprive British nationals of citizenship.

In the modern era, and at least since the First World War, the 'ready issue of a passport is a normal expectation of every citizen'.[1] Unlike in many other countries, passports in the UK are issued by the Crown under the royal prerogative and the policy criteria for their withdrawal under the prerogative are not governed by any piece of legislation.[2] Rather, the responsible minister (since 2011, the Home Secretary) sets out the policy to Parliament from time to time, most recently in 2013.[3] This is highly unusual. Even in Canada, where passports are also issued under the prerogative, the criteria have been codified in prerogative legislation (the Canadian Passports Order 1981).

In recent years, particular focus has been placed on the use of the prerogative to withdraw passports for national security reasons. In the six years between 2013–18, a total of 86 passports were withdrawn or refused on the grounds of national security, of which 13 were returned after internal review.[4] In this field, the prerogative operates alongside legislative powers introduced by the Terrorism Prevention and

[1] *R v Secretary of State for Foreign and Commonwealth Affairs, ex parte Everett* [1989] QB 811, 820 (Taylor LJ). For the history of the modern passport, see: K Diplock, 'Passports and Protection in International Law' (1946) 32 *Transactions of the Grotius Society* 42; NW Sibley, 'The Passport System' (1906) 7 *Journal of the Society of Comparative Legislation* 32; and DW Williams, 'British Passports and the Right to Travel' [1974] *International & Comparative Law Quarterly* 642.

[2] P Scott, 'Passports, the Right to Travel, and National Security in the Commonwealth' (2020) 69 *International & Comparative Law Quarterly* 365.

[3] *Hansard*, HC Deb Vol 561, cols 68WS–70WS (25 April 2013).

[4] HM Government, *Transparency Report: Disruptive Powers 2018/19* (CP 212, March 2020), 19.

Investigation Measures Act 2011 (TPIM), under which the Secretary of State may apply to the High Court for a TPIM notice, which may impose a selection of a range of requirements, including the surrender of a passport.[5] In addition, police officers at ports have statutory powers to seize travel documents temporarily, which gives an opportunity to consider the use of the prerogative or TPIM powers to withdraw the passport.[6]

This chapter sets out the current practice in the use of the passport powers, considers the nature of those powers and their amenability to judicial review, and finally turns to proposals for reform.

The Prerogative in Practice

Although the criteria for the issue and withdrawal of a passport are not addressed in any piece of legislation, the Crown has from time to time published its policy. This practice began with Viscount Palmerston, then Foreign Secretary, who ordered in 1846 that regulations be published as to the criteria for the issuing of a passport, including the central criterion that the recipient must be a British subject.[7] At that stage, passports were still something of a sporadic requirement, although the need for identification documents for travel became more widespread in the later nineteenth century.[8] However, at the end of the First World War, 'temporary' requirements across Europe for aliens to hold passports became permanent.[9] By the middle of the twentieth century, therefore, the policy focus had turned to the withdrawal of a passport rather than its issue. In 1958, the Earl of Gosford set out as a minister the outline of the government's policy on the matter:

> The Foreign Secretary has the power to withhold or withdraw a passport at his discretion, although in practice such power is exercised only very rarely and in very exceptional cases. First, in the case of minors suspected of being taken illegally out of the jurisdiction; secondly, persons believed on good evidence to be fleeing the country to avoid prosecution for a criminal offence; thirdly, persons whose activities are so notoriously undesirable or dangerous that Parliament would be expected to support the action of the Foreign Secretary in refusing them a passport or withdrawing a passport already issued in order to prevent their leaving the United Kingdom; and fourthly, persons who have been repatriated to the United Kingdom at public expense and have not repaid the expenditure incurred on their behalf.[10]

[5] Terrorism Prevention and Investigation Measures Act 2011, sch 1, paras 2(3)(c), (d), 2(4)-(5).

[6] Counter-Terrorism and Security Act 2015, sch 1.

[7] P Scott, 'Citizenship' in *The National Security Constitution* (Oxford, Hart Publishing, 2018), 172.

[8] J Torpey, *The Invention of the Passport: Surveillance, Citizenship and the State* (Cambridge, Cambridge University Press, 2000), 93–111.

[9] ibid at 116–7.

[10] *Hansard*, HL Deb Vol 209, cols 860-1 (16 June 1968).

The practice came to the fore at various times through the 1960s and 1970s. For instance, during the Congo Crisis in the early 1960s, the Lord Privy Seal, Ted Heath, announced that the passport of any UK national taking up military engagement in the Congo other than under the UN Command would be invalidated or withdrawn.[11] A slightly more liberal attitude was taken to British mercenaries returning from Angola in the mid-1970s. Their passports were withdrawn but reissued if the mercenaries signed undertakings not to return to Angola.[12] The action was carried out because the mercenaries were passport-holders 'whose past or proposed activities are so demonstrably undesirable that the grant or continued enjoyment of passport facilities would be contrary to the public interest', a criterion set out in the Foreign Office's restatement of the withdrawal policy in 1974.[13]

A more complex scenario was presented by the Unilateral Declaration of Independence (UDI) in Southern Rhodesia by Prime Minister Ian Smith in November 1965. The UDI and ensuing regime were deemed illegal by the UK and the UN, and the UN imposed sanctions in a Security Council Resolution on 29 May 1968. Among other measures, the UK withdrew the passports of those undermining (or likely to undermine) the sanctions and of those actively supporting (or likely to encourage) the illegal regime, as well as removing rights of entry to the UK from Commonwealth and UK citizens using passports issued by the regime or who had encouraged the 'unconstitutional action in Southern Rhodesia'. Southern Rhodesian passports issued before the UDI were still regarded as valid, being issued by the Governor under Her Majesty's name.[14]

There are three relevant points of interest in this episode. First, while passports could be withdrawn under the prerogative, rights of entry had to be removed by statutory instrument.[15] This is a prime example of the interplay between prerogative and statutory powers, and the careful, highly technical legal drafting that is required to protect the prerogative power from being elided with statute. Second, the exercise of these interconnected powers was to be monitored by an advisory committee, whose members were: Mr Justice Cairns, Sir William Oliver (former Vice Chief of the Imperial General Staff), Sir William Murrie (a retired civil servant), and Frederick Pedler (later Sir Frederick, a colonial official and businessman). The committee was to scrutinise all cases of passport withdrawal relating to Southern Rhodesia, and to perform 'special re-examination' of any case referred to it by the Commonwealth Secretary.[16] Third, this category of passport withdrawals

[11] *Hansard*, HC Deb Vol 638, cols 27-8 (12 April 1961).

[12] *Hansard*, HL Deb Vol 368, cols 1201-7 (9 March 1976); *Scott*, above n 7 at 176.

[13] *Hansard*, HC Deb Vol 881, col 265W (15 November 1974).

[14] *Hansard*, HC Deb Vol 723, cols 4-5 (25 January 1966).

[15] The Southern Rhodesia (United Nations Sanctions) Order 1968, art 12, made under the sweeping powers of the Southern Rhodesia Act 1965. This Order was, in fact, rejected by the House of Lords. This was the last serious challenge to the convention that the Lords do not vote down a statutory instrument and precipitated the collapse of ongoing cross-party talks on Lords reform. The Lords agreed to a virtually identical order, The Southern Rhodesia (United Nations Sanctions) (No. 2) Order 1968, just a few weeks later.

[16] *Hansard*, HL Deb Vol 293, cols 1549-52 (27 June 1968).

fell outside the criteria set out in 1958. In the Foreign Office policy statement of 1974, the Southern Rhodesian policy was recognised as separate from the general public interest category.[17]

Indeed, the scope of the government's policy on passport withdrawal has expanded over time. The present policy was set out by Theresa May, then Home Secretary, in 2013. In a written statement to the House of Commons, she set out that a passport would be withdrawn for:

1. A minor whose journey was known to be contrary to a court order, to the wishes of a parent or other person or authority in whose favour a residence or care order had been made or who had been awarded custody; or care and control.
2. A person for whose arrest a warrant had been issued in the United Kingdom, or a person who was wanted by the United Kingdom police on suspicion of a serious crime.
3. A person who is the subject of:
    a. a court order, made by a court in the United Kingdom, or any other order made pursuant to a statutory power, which imposes travel restrictions or restrictions on the possession of a valid United Kingdom passport;
    b. bail conditions, imposed by a police officer or a court in the United Kingdom, which include travel restrictions or restrictions on the possession of a valid United Kingdom passport;
    c. an order issued by the European Union or the United Nations which prevents a person travelling or entering a country other than the country in which they hold citizenship;
    d. a declaration made under section 15 of the Mental Capacity Act 2005.
4. A person may be prevented from benefitting from the possession of a passport if the Home Secretary is satisfied that it is in the public interest to do so. This may be the case where:
    a. a person has been repatriated from abroad at public expense and their debt has not yet been repaid. This is because the passport fee supports the provision of consular services for British citizens overseas; or
    b. a person whose past, present or proposed activities, actual or suspected, are believed by the Home Secretary to be so undesirable that the grant or continued enjoyment of passport facilities is contrary to the public interest.[18]

The careful reader will note that the public interest category (4b in particular) has gradually widened.[19] Long gone is the high threshold of 1958 – 'activities … so notoriously undesirable or dangerous that Parliament would be expected to support the action of the Foreign Secretary' – and even the 1974 formulation of 'so *demonstrably* undesirable' (emphasis added) has been replaced by the perception of the Home Secretary.

[17] *Hansard*, HC Deb Vol 881, col 265W (15 November 1974).

[18] *Hansard*, HC Deb Vol 561, cols 69WS-70WS (25 April 2013).

[19] *Scott*, above n 7 at 175–6; The phenomenon was first noted by Lord Orr-Ewing in 1976: *Hansard*, HL Deb Vol 370, cols 699-700 (6 May 1976).

A Prerogative Power?

The Court of Appeal in *R v Secretary of State for Foreign and Commonwealth Affairs, ex parte Everett* had 'no doubt that passports are issued under the Royal prerogative in the discretion of the Secretary of State'.[20] However, the court did not address a challenge to this assumption made a few years previously by Sir William Wade. For Wade, a prerogative power was the 'ability to alter people's rights, duties, or status under the laws of this country which the courts of this country enforce'.[21] A passport did not, in his view, meet this definition, since it was 'simply an administrative document' that did 'not have the slightest effect upon [the bearer's] legal rights … [since] [t]hose rights are a matter of common and statute law, which the Crown has no power to alter'.[22] He suggested that the powers to issue and withdraw a passport were non-legal powers, and not of the prerogative at all (see chapter two).

A similar conclusion has been reached by Adam Perry. However, for Perry, even Wade's narrow definition of a prerogative power is too broad. In *Everett*, he points out, the court found that the Secretary of State owed a legal duty to give reasons for refusing the passport application.[23] The refusal therefore gave rise to a legal duty and so would be classed as a *legal* power under Wade's definition.[24] Perry argues that a further element is required for a power to be 'prerogative' rather than administrative: the choice or intention to effect legal change. He argues that duties of fairness (including the duty to give reasons) apply to the Crown without any such intention, in a manner analogous to individuals' duties in tort (eg not to assault another person). Just as the duty not to assault someone does not make an assault an exercise of a legal power, so the duties of fairness do not make certain administrative powers of the Crown 'legal' (and therefore 'prerogative') either.

This is not the book for a detailed examination of such an academic question. However, the debate is important for our survey because it highlights a way in which passport powers are different to some of the other prerogatives we look at in this book. A passport is, at heart, an administrative document. It does not grant rights or status, but it does perform a function. That function is to enable the *utilisation* of rights. Unlike the power to sign treaties, on the one hand, an exercise of passport powers is fundamentally connected to an individual; unlike the granting of a pardon, on the other, it does not change the legal status of that individual. Passport powers are rarely used on their own, however. As will be evident from the government's stated criteria, they are most used in conjunction with statutory powers to maintain law and order or to protect national security.

[20] *ex parte Everett*, above n 1 at 817 (O'Connor LJ).
[21] HWR Wade, *Constitutional Fundamentals* (London, Stevens & Sons, 1980), 46.
[22] ibid at 51.
[23] *ex parte Everett*, above n 1 at 818.
[24] A Perry, 'The Crown's Administrative Powers' (2015) 131 *Law Quarterly Review* 652, 662.

Quite separately from the question of whether the passport power is a *prerogative*, some have challenged the continued *existence* of the passport prerogative, given the availability of other powers to achieve similar ends. In *R (XH) v Home Secretary*, the appellants argued that TPIM had replaced the prerogative by a complete statutory scheme for the withdrawal of a passport.[25] TPIM empowers the Home Secretary to impose travel restrictions on individuals (TPIMs), such as requiring them to surrender or not seek to obtain travel documents, on grounds including suspected involvement in terrorism-related activity. A key difference in practice between the TPIM power and the passport prerogative is that the TPIM power can only be exercised under the procedural and substantive limits set out in the Act. For example, a TPIM can generally only be imposed for a year. The appellants' argument in *XH* rested on the principle advanced in *Attorney General v De Keyser's Royal Hotel* (see chapter seventeen): Parliament had legislated in this area, and the existence of the statutory power precluded the use of the prerogative. The Court of Appeal disagreed. In their view, use of the *De Keyser* principle 'depends upon establishing a necessary implication in the TPIM Act that the prerogative powers of refusal to issue and cancellation were abridged or put into abeyance by the statutory scheme,' and that 'The test for such a necessary implication is a strict one.'[26]

Paul Scott has recently advanced a further challenge to the continued existence of the passport prerogative.[27] He argues that the right to travel (ie to enter and exit the UK) is 'the key adjunct of the statutory right of abode which a British passport holder (who must be a British citizen) by definition enjoys' under section 2(1) of the Immigration Act 1971. As the removal of a passport under the prerogative would interfere with this statutory right, it cannot be permitted. For a court to approve such reasoning would involve a considerable departure from the narrow test applied in *XH*. A 'right to travel' is not explicitly granted by the 1971 Act and has not (yet) been recognised by the courts. It is true that in section 33(5) of the 1971 Act, the prerogative is only explicitly preserved as regards aliens, but there is no explicit curb on the prerogative as it applies to British citizens, nor that 'necessary implication' required by *XH*. Nevertheless, this argument demonstrates the fragility of the prerogative and the danger to the executive in relying on purely prerogative powers. Were the UK to ratify Protocol 4 of the European Convention on Human Rights (ECHR), for example, which by Article 2 sets out a (qualified) right of freedom to leave any country (including one's own), then an argument like Scott's would begin to have real bite and threaten the government's ability to take action, even where that action is necessary and desirable.

[25] *R (XH) v Home Secretary* [2017] EWCA Civ 41.
[26] ibid at [89].
[27] *Scott*, above n 2 at 184–5.

Justiciability and Judicial Review

Since *Everett*, it has been clear that decisions to withdraw a passport are subject to the standard tools of judicial review.[28] The Court of Appeal in that case applied what the court saw as the reasoning of the majority of their lordships in *Council of Civil Service Unions v Minister for the Civil Service* (*GCHQ*),[29] namely that the justiciability of a prerogative power depended on whether or not its subject matter was 'high policy' (as Lord Justice Taylor put it in *Everett*).[30] The Lords Justices saw it as 'common sense' that the Crown's powers over passports 'fell into an entirely different category' to foreign affairs and other non-justiciable areas.[31] Although this blunt method of reasoning might be said to be somewhat skeletal, it must be said that the court's conclusion was unsurprising. In his case-note on *GCHQ*, Ewing had stated some years previously that 'the issuing of passports is one of only a few such [justiciable] powers which leap from the pages of the textbooks with arms extended'.[32] Unlike issues of 'high policy', the withdrawal of a passport was 'a matter of administrative decision'.[33]

One further potential route for judicial control lies in Protocol 4, Article 2 of the ECHR, which protects the right of everyone in the state to liberty of movement and the freedom 'to leave any country, including his own', save as provided by restrictions

> such as are in accordance with law and are necessary in a democratic society in the interests of national security or public safety, for the maintenance of public order, for the prevention of crime, for the protection of health or morals, or for the protection of the rights and freedoms of others.[34]

However, the UK – alongside only Greece, Switzerland and Turkey of the Members of the Council of Europe – has not ratified Protocol 4. This reluctance is chiefly caused by concern that the UK law on the rights of residence of certain British nationals (for example, British National (Overseas)) would be incompatible with Articles 2 and 3 of the Protocol.[35] However, in response to a question by the

[28] *ex parte Everett*, above n 1.
[29] *Council of Civil Service Unions v Minister for the Civil Service* [1985] AC 374.
[30] *ex parte Everett*, above n 1 at 820.
[31] ibid at 817 (O'Connor LJ).
[32] KD Ewing, 'Prerogative, Judicial Review and National Security' (1985) 44 *Cambridge Law Journal* 1, 2.
[33] *ex parte Everett*, above n 1 at 820 (Taylor LJ).
[34] This echoes the provisions of Article 27 of the Citizen's Directive (2004/38/EC), by which the UK was bound from 2004.
[35] Department for Constitutional Affairs, *Report on the UK Government's Inter-Departmental Review of the UK's Position under various International Human Rights Instruments* (July 2004) quoted in Seventeenth Report from the Joint Committee on Human Rights, *Review of International Human Rights Instruments* HL 99 HC 264 (2004–05), para 37; *cf Hansard*, HL Deb Vol 706, col 170WA (15 January 2009); *Hansard*, HL Deb Vol 707, cols 56WA-57WA (28 January 2009); *Hansard*, HL Deb Vol 708, col 50WA (24 February 2009); *Hansard*, HL Deb Vol 707, col 46WA (18 March 2009).

late Lord Lester of Herne Hill, Baroness Symons of Vernham Dean stated at the despatch box that 'certain other provisions of the protocol may be incompatible with our arrangements for issuing passports and with Armed Forces discipline'. As a British national may – in effect – only leave the UK with a passport, it is clear that ratification of Protocol 4 would introduce an external standard against which could be measured not only the Crown's policy of withdrawing passports but also particular instances of such an exercise.

Reform

The time for imposing controls on the passport powers is long overdue. It is now almost half a century since Sir William Wade and Bernard Schwartz described this prerogative as 'the only really objectionable arbitrary power which the Crown still claims',[36] and JUSTICE described the legal right to a passport as 'a basic constitutional necessity'.[37] In 2009, the government accepted in principle the need for 'comprehensive legislation on the procedures for issuing passports'.[38] No such legislation has yet been forthcoming.

The discussion above has identified two main problems with the current state of the law and practice in this area. First, the policy criteria according to which the passport powers are exercised are entirely within the control of the government. This has led to a steady expansion of the criteria, bringing with it an increasing vagueness as to their definition. Second, extra-curial scrutiny of the use of these powers is minimal. Beyond the inclusion of basic statistics in the annual Transparency Report and occasional questions in Parliament (seldom on specific cases), there is no systematic independent review of the passport powers and no effective means of redress for individuals besides the courts.

Three broad avenues lie open for reform. The first is the ratification of Protocol 4 of the ECHR, with appropriate reservations to overcome the specific issues identified by the government, as recommended by the Joint Committee on Human Rights in 2005.[39] The terms of the reservations would have to be drawn up with some care, but the government accepted in 2009 that this course of action 'would in theory be possible'.[40] This would give an additional tool to the courts in assessing the use of the passport powers by placing proportionality at the forefront of the inquiry. However, the scope of and policy for use of the prerogative would remain within the control of the government, and expanding the courts' capacity to review

[36] B Schwartz and HWR Wade, *Legal Control of Government: Administrative Law in Britain and the United States* (Oxford, Clarendon Press, 1972), 63.

[37] JUSTICE, *Going Abroad: A Report on Passports* (London, Brown & Son, 1974), para 48.

[38] Ministry of Justice, *Governance of Britain: Review of the Executive Royal Prerogative Powers: Final Report* (2009), para 38.

[39] *Joint Committee on Human Rights*, above n 35 at para 38.

[40] *Hansard*, HL Deb Vol 708, col 50WA (24 February 2009).

its exercise on human rights grounds would not prevent future Home Secretaries expanding their stated criteria even further.

The second avenue is the implementation of a statutory right to a passport. The UK is something of an outsider in its casual approach to the right to a passport. In many countries, the right to a passport and the processes of issuance and cancellation are set out in law.[41] New Zealanders have had a statutory right to a passport since the Passports Act 1980.[42] Even before this, the power to grant passports had been rendered statutory (although with an apparently wide discretion) by the Passports Act 1946. In Australia, the right to a passport is relatively recent,[43] but the power to cancel a passport appears to have been made statutory by the wide-ranging section 6 of the Passports Act 1920. As for Canada, although passports are still managed under the prerogative, the Canadian Passports Order 1981 governs the criteria for cancellation. There have been occasional calls for a statutory right to a passport in the UK, including Private Members' Bills in the House of Commons, but these have been largely sidelined.[44]

A statutory right to a passport would most naturally be accompanied by codification of the criteria for cancelling a passport. Codification brings a degree of stability, predictability and transparency. We have traced above the ways in which the government's policy on the cancellation of passports has shifted over the past half-century. Some flexibility brings benefits, of course. It is not always possible to anticipate novel situations in this area. However, at least in the realm of national security, the government has wide-ranging statutory powers such as TPIMs, which mitigate against this risk. In our view, the desire for flexibility has for too long been privileged over the benefits of a codified set of criteria. As we have outlined, and as Lord Justice Taylor noted in *Everett*, passport powers may be a 'matter of administrative decision' but it is one 'affecting the rights of individuals and their freedom of travel'.[45] We no longer live in a world where passports are purely a matter of foreign affairs, of guarantees of safe passage and reciprocal freedoms. They are now fundamental to the utilisation of the full rights of a British citizen, necessary for travel and the most widely recognised certificate of citizenship. The government has impliedly recognised this in the transfer of passport administration from the Foreign and Commonwealth Office to the Home Office in 2011.

Codification would still be possible without statute, but statute is by far the preferable route. Countries around the world have framed similar powers in statute and it is therefore evidently possible to preserve a necessary degree of flexibility whilst promoting predictability in the majority of cases through statutory

[41] Eg, Passgesetz 1986 (Germany), ss 6-8; Passport Act 1856, Passport Act 1926 (USA); *cf* P Lansing, 'Freedom to Travel: Is the Issuance of a Passport an Individual Right or a Governmental Prerogative' (1981) 11 *Denver Journal of International Law & Policy* 15.

[42] Passports Act 1980 (NZ), ss 3-4. Now Passports Act 1992 (NZ), ss 3-4.

[43] Australian Passports Act 2005, s 7.

[44] HC Bill 177 (1967–68); HC Bill 78 (1975–76).

[45] *ex parte Everett*, above n 1 at 820.

codification. A passport is no less important to a UK citizen than to an Australian, New Zealander or German, but it is only in the UK that the government has sole power to determine the criteria for cancelling that passport. Furthermore, passport powers are already subject to judicial review: changing the basis of the power to statute would not change this position.[46] On the other hand, we recognise that a statutory right to a passport would be a large step, and note that Canada's solution of using prerogative legislation goes some way towards codifying the use of passport powers while preserving the executive's ability to change the criteria for cancellation with relative ease. Even that small step would, in our opinion, be in the right direction.

The third route for reform lies in additional extra-curial scrutiny. The Home Affairs Select Committee recommended in 2015 that the Independent Reviewer of Terrorism Legislation (IRTL) should be allowed to review the exercise of the prerogative passport powers alongside TPIMs, and that the Home Secretary should report to the House of Commons quarterly (again, alongside TPIMs).[47] This reflected the Independent Reviewer's own suggestion from 2014, which he repeated in 2016.[48] Not only, he stressed, does this omission from the scope of independent review create a patchy coverage of counter-terrorism measures, but also gives rise to an impression that the unreviewed powers (such as the passport prerogative) will be used for the purposes of doing the government's 'dirty work'. The Home Secretary flatly rejected this recommendation in July 2017:

> I consider that including non-statutory powers within the Independent Reviewer's remit would again risk diluting the clarity of that remit, and may set an unhelpful precedent given that Prerogative powers are also used in a range of other contexts across Government. Furthermore, not all refusals of passports under these criteria may necessarily be on the grounds of terrorism-related activity, risking uncertainty as to which cases should be considered by the Independent Reviewer and which should not.[49]

However, a judicious reader might be left disappointed by these three reasons. First, there is no reason why including a clearly defined power within the IRTL's remit would dilute clarity just because the source of that power was not statute. Second, there are ample precedents for independent review of the exercise of prerogative powers, such as the House of Lords Appointments Commission, or the Commissioner for Public Appointments (see chapter ten). There is even a precedent in relation to the passport power: the advisory committee established

[46] Save that the government may not narrow a discretion granted by statute, which may contrast with the prerogative: *R (on the application of Sandiford) v The Secretary of State for Foreign and Commonwealth Affairs* [2014] UKSC 44; *cf Scott*, above n 2 at 184.

[47] Nineteenth Report from the House of Commons Home Affairs Select Committee, *Counter-terrorism: Foreign Fighters* HC 993 (2014–15), para 8.

[48] Independent Reviewer of Terrorism Legislation, *The Terrorism Acts in 2013* (2014), 103–4; Independent Reviewer of Terrorism Legislation, *The Terrorism Acts in 2015* (2016), 7–8.

[49] HM Government, *The Government Response to the Annual Report on the Operation of the Terrorism Acts in 2015 by the Independent Reviewer of Terrorism Legislation* (Cm 9489, 2017), 4.

during the Southern Rhodesia episode in the 1960s (see above). Third, the Crown exercises the prerogative according to a set of policy criteria. In doing so, it should determine which criterion for disqualification applies in each case. Those connected to national security could be overseen by the IRTL, while others might better be policed by bringing them under the jurisdiction of another body, such as the Parliamentary Ombudsman.[50]

Conclusion

At first glance, passport powers may seem like a niche, technical and unimportant topic in a book discussing much more wide-ranging prerogatives. Indeed, as we have touched upon, there are some who would argue they are not prerogative powers at all. Yet passports have become, and (particularly in the absence of national identity cards) will continue to be, of central importance to individual citizens. Furthermore, as we have seen in recent years, they may be the focus of political debate. The colour, design and wording of a passport has an undeniable emotional pull. Upon opening a UK passport, the reader is greeted by the traditional formula: 'Her Britannic Majesty's Secretary of State Requests and requires in the Name of Her Majesty …'. It is a tangible symbol of the monarch and her ministers interceding on behalf of the individual citizen.

Perhaps for some, that intercession is more valuable as a voluntary act and to place too many controls on it would detract from the passport's worth. It is important not to scorn such emotional connections to the state. Yet such an emotional response must be balanced against the reality of the modern world. We no longer live in the eighteenth century; passports are not personal intercessions made by the monarch. As the importance of international travel and of being able to prove one's citizenship has increased, passports have at the same time become more routine, administrative documents and more fundamental to the individual citizen. While the passport itself may not confer rights or status, a decision to cancel it has profound effects on the freedom of the citizen concerned.

Predictability, stability and non-arbitrariness in the application of rules are central pillars of the rule of law and the freedom of the individual. For too long, the criteria for cancelling passports have expanded entirely at the behest of the executive. Although judicial review mitigates some of the impact of the status quo, it is insufficient to provide stability and predictability in the rules themselves. It is time to codify those criteria with greater firmness, whether by statute or prerogative legislation, and it would also be desirable to impose greater institutional scrutiny on the use of the passport powers, to avoid the government using the prerogative power for its 'dirty work' and avoiding the rigours of the controls that Parliament has already sought to impose.

[50] This would require amendment of the Parliamentary Commissioner Act 1967, sch 3, para 5.

13

Honours

> Our evidence suggested that the perception that honours are linked to donations to political parties is prevalent. It is a serious concern that many members of the public do not view the honours system as open or fair.
>
> House of Commons Public Administration Select Committee (2012)[1]

Introduction

The Queen is the *fons honorum*, the 'fount of all honours', and may create and bestow such dignities as she sees fit.[2] This power of the monarch is exhibited in the appointment of peers as well as the bestowal of lesser honours.[3] The modern 'system' of honours is generally considered to have come into existence in 1917, with the foundation of the Order of the British Empire (although it includes other orders). It is this 'honours system' with which we are concerned in this chapter, rather than any hereditary or royal honours, or life peerages (for the latter, see chapter ten).

In the modern era, honours are generally granted upon advice from the Prime Minister, except for certain orders which remain at the personal disposal of the Queen (namely, the Order of Merit, the Order of the Garter, the Order of the Thistle, and the Royal Victorian Order). There has been a long-standing tension between the Prime Minister's political and constitutional roles, brought to a head in repeated 'cash for honours' scandals over the course of the past century and more. As a result, the Prime Minister is advised on the bestowal of honours by governmental committees. This chapter examines these current arrangements, considers existing means of scrutiny (judicial and extra-curial), and makes modest proposals for reform.

[1] Second Report from the House of Commons Public Administration Select Committee, *The Honours System* HC 19 (2012–13), para 22.

[2] *The Prince's Case* (1606) 8 Co Rep 1a, 18b; J Comyns, *A Digest of the Laws of England*, vol 7, 5th edn (Anthony Hammond ed, London, Strachan, 1822), 62; House of Lords, 'The Third Report on the Dignity of a Peer' in *Reports from the Lords Committees touching The Dignity of a Peer of the Realm*, vol 2 (London), 37; *Sanatan Dharma Maha Sabha of Trinidad and Tobago v Attorney General of Trinidad and Tobago* [2009] UKPC 17, [30].

[3] *Black v Chrétien* 2001 CanLII 8537 (ON CA), [23]. Note, however, that the peerage in question was in fact to be created under the Life Peerages Act 1958, not the prerogative.

Current Practice

Lists of honours appear biannually, issued at New Year and on the Queen's official birthday in June. The general civilian list, which includes 'political honours' (honours given to politicians), is supplemented by lists of honours given to members of the military, diplomatic corps and royal household. Lists have also been issued upon special occasions, such as coronations or jubilees, and it is common practice for shorter lists of political honours to appear upon the resignation of a Prime Minister or the dissolution of a Parliament.[4] The political honours awarded on these latter occasions are predominantly appointments of life peers, and only constitute a small number of the awards of other honours. In October 2020, the (delayed) Queen's birthday honours list was supplemented by an additional list of awards in recognition of contributions during the Covid-19 pandemic.

Since 1993, nominations for civilian honours come from members of the public and also directly from government departments. Around one third of all nominations are now submitted via a public online form.[5] Major reforms to the honours system were put in place in 2005. The government rejected a proposal by the House of Commons Public Administration Select Committee (PASC) to set up an independent Honours Commission,[6] but accepted the proposals set out in a Cabinet Office review by Sir Hayden Phillips.[7] Under this system, nominations are examined by ten subject-specialist committees, whose chairs (together with the Cabinet Secretary, the Permanent Under Secretary of the Foreign, Commonwealth and Development Office and the Chief of the Defence Staff) collectively form the Cabinet Office's Main Honours Committee. These committees are made up of official members (usually senior civil servants) and other members independent of government, the latter forming a majority. The chair of each committee is an independent member. The only committee on which no current civil servant sits is the Parliamentary and Political Service Committee, established unilaterally by David Cameron in 2012, whose official members are the chief whips of the government and official opposition.[8]

Recommendations from the specialist committees are sent to the Main Honours Committee, which reviews the proposals before sending a list to the Prime Minister's Office. It is for the Prime Minister to recommend the list to the Queen, and names may be added or removed by the Prime Minister from the list recommended by the committee. Prime Ministers Tony Blair in March 2006 and Gordon Brown in July 2007 made commitments not to make any alterations

[4] Honours lists have appeared regularly following every dissolution since 1959, apart from 2017. The first Resignation Honours list followed the resignation of Lord Rosebery in 1895.

[5] Cabinet Office, *The Fourth Report on the Operation of the Honours System 2015–2019* (2019), 16.

[6] Fifth Report from the House of Commons Public Administration Select Committee, *A Matter of Honour: Reforming the Honours System* HC 212-I (2003–04), para 161.

[7] Cabinet Office, *Review of the honours system* (2004).

[8] *Hansard*, HC Deb Vol 545, cols 42WS-43WS (17 May 2012).

to the committee's list.[9] However, in 2012 David Cameron recommended four last-minute knighthoods for ministers who had been shuffled out of post, as well as a Companion of Honour for Sir George Young Bt. PASC noted with surprise that Cameron had effectively by-passed the Parliamentary and Political Service Committee which he had himself set up only months earlier.[10]

In addition to making the formal recommendation of the honours lists, the Prime Minister plays a further role, in setting the 'strategic direction' of the honours system, to be used as a guide for nominators and for the honours committees.[11] For example, Gordon Brown wished to prioritise 'unsung heroes' who volunteered in their communities, and launched a 'Good Neighbour MBE' campaign to promote awareness of his intention to recognise such service.[12] David Cameron had a similar theme, although explicitly linked to his 'Big Society' political slogan.[13] Theresa May (followed now by Boris Johnson) moved away from such a singular focus and introduced a range of categories, including those who 'aid social mobility, enhancing life opportunities and removing barriers to success', and who 'work to tackle discrimination in all its forms'.[14]

Opportunities for post-award scrutiny are limited. It is not permitted for MPs to raise questions to the Prime Minister about a particular exercise of the honours prerogative at Question Time or in a Debate on Supply, although the matter may be raised on a motion.[15] Further, information relating to the conferring of any honour or dignity is exempt from the statutory freedom of information request framework.[16]

Forfeiture

Honours may be forfeited for bringing the honours system into disrepute. Upon forfeiture, the honour is cancelled and annulled under the prerogative, either by letters patent (for knights bachelor) or by direction of the Queen and erasure from the register of the relevant order (for other honours). A notice of forfeiture is placed

[9] Ministry of Justice, *The Governance of Britain* (Cm 7170, 2007), para 85.

[10] Seventh Report from the House of Commons Public Administration Select Committee, *The Honours System: Further Report with the Government Response to the Committee's Second Report of Session 2012–13* HC 728 (2012–13), para 7.

[11] For Boris Johnson's guidelines, see Cabinet Office, 'Governance' (*The Honours System of the United Kingdom*) www.honours.cabinetoffice.gov.uk/about/governance/#main.

[12] Cabinet Office, *Three Years of Operation of the Reformed Honours System* (2008), 27–8.

[13] Cabinet Office, *The Second Report on the Operation of the Honours System* (2011), 3.

[14] Cabinet Office, above n 5 at 5.

[15] *Hansard*, HC Deb Vol 155, cols 1843-4 (27 June 1922); M Hutton, D Natzler, M Hamlyn, C Lee, C Mawson, C Poyser, E Samson and K Lawrence, *Erskine May: Parliamentary Practice*, 25th edn (LexisNexis Butterworths, 2019), para 22.16; *cf Hansard*, HC Deb Vol 183, cols 150-51 (18 December 1990).

[16] Freedom of Information Act 2000, s 37.

in the *London Gazette*. Although the guidelines for forfeiture continue to develop, currently the four 'hard triggers' are: professional disbarment, criminal conviction (with a sentence of over three months), conviction for a sexual offence (with a sentence of any length), and having been found to have committed a sexual offence after a 'trial of the facts'.[17] Forfeiture is considered by the Forfeiture Committee, which is formed of three permanent independent members, the Treasury Solicitor, and its chair (a senior civil servant).[18] Although forfeiture is relatively unusual, a total of 50 honours were annulled between 2011 and 2019.[19] Since 1980, notifications have appeared in the *London Gazette* for the forfeiture of seven knighthoods (of which one was surrendered voluntarily) and one damehood. In a 2019 report, the Cabinet Office noted that the number of historic child sexual abuse cases being raised had increased over its reporting period, and that ACRO criminal record checks are now completed on all nominees.[20]

The forfeiture arrangements have come under attack on three fronts. First, following posthumous revelations of child sexual abuse carried out by Sir Jimmy Savile, there was a widespread desire to annul his knighthood (and other honours).[21] However, just as an honour (unlike a military medal) cannot be awarded posthumously, so 'There is no posthumous forfeiture of honours.'[22] In September 2021, new forfeiture guidance was adopted which allows the Forfeiture Committee to publish a formal statement that forfeiture proceedings would have been commenced against a deceased recipient, had they been alive and convicted, where allegations of criminal behaviour are made within ten years of death and the police consider the allegations so serious as to warrant taking a full witness statement from the accuser.[23] Such statements were immediately published in the *London Gazette* in respect of Jimmy Savile and Cyril Smith.[24]

Second, PASC criticised the vagueness of the criteria for forfeiture, following the annulment of Fred Goodwin's knighthood on 1 February 2012.[25] Mr Goodwin had been the CEO of the Royal Bank of Scotland Group (RBS) until its collapse and bail-out by the government in 2008. Neither of the two 'hard triggers' then in place applied to Fred Goodwin, but the committee felt that 'the scale and severity of the impact of his actions as CEO of RBS made this an exceptional case'.[26]

[17] Cabinet Office, above n 5 at 19; *cf* PQ 38694 (6 June 2016). The policy was updated on 30 September 2021 to add the third and fourth 'triggers': Cabinet Office, 'Having honours taken away (forfeiture)' (27 December 2017) www.gov.uk/guidance/having-honours-taken-away-forfeiture.

[18] Cabinet Office, *The Third Report on the Operation of the Reformed Honours System* (2014), 12.

[19] ibid at 11; Cabinet Office, above n 5 at 42.

[20] Cabinet Office, *The Fourth Report on the Operation of the Honours System* (2019), 18.

[21] T Rowley and S Marsden, 'Jimmy Savile could be stripped of knighthood, says David Cameron' *The Times* (London, 9 October 2012).

[22] PQ HL5633 (11 March 2015).

[23] Cabinet Office, 'Having honours taken away (forfeiture)', above n 17.

[24] *London Gazette* (30 September 2021, 63488), 17304.

[25] House of Commons Public Administration Select Committee, above n 1 at para 106.

[26] Cabinet Office, *Goodwin Knighthood Decision* (HM Government, 31 January 2012).

The third criticism of the current forfeiture system is that it is not sufficiently reflexive to parliamentary scrutiny. The House of Commons passed a motion on 20 October 2016 recommending to the Forfeiture Committee that Sir Philip Green's knighthood should be annulled, following the publication of the joint report into BHS Ltd by the Work and Pensions and Business, Innovation and Skills Select Committees.[27] Sir Philip had sold BHS (formerly British Home Stores) for £1 in 2015, with company debts estimated at £1.3 billion in April 2016, including a pension fund deficit of £571 million. Eventually, Sir Philip agreed to pay £363 million into the pension scheme.[28] Unlike in the case of Fred Goodwin, who himself had been the subject of an Early Day Motion in 2009,[29] in this case the chair of the Forfeiture Committee appeared to require one of the 'hard triggers' to be met before annulment would be recommended. In a letter to the Work and Pensions Select Committee in January 2017, he pointed to the ongoing inquiries of the independent regulator.[30] These inquiries are now long concluded, and Sir Philip retains his knighthood.

Justiciability

It has long been held that the honours prerogative is non-justiciable. It was included in Lord Roskill's list of non-justiciable prerogatives in *Council of Civil Service Unions v Minister for the Civil Service* (*GCHQ*), and the question has been resolved in direct litigation on the point in Australia, Canada and Scotland.[31] In the Scottish case of *Senior-Milne v Advocate General for Scotland*, Lord Drummond Young set out the basis of the courts' reluctance to review the exercise of the honours prerogative in the UK. He compared the decision to make a gift, which is 'entirely discretionary in nature' and does not involve legal rights or any legitimate expectation.[32] The language of gift-giving is well chosen. The Queen can be under no obligation to bestow an honour, nor her ministers to advise her to do so. A citizen may expect to receive one, but has no right to have that expectation enforced by the courts, just as he has no recourse to the courts for his expectation

[27] *Hansard*, HC Deb Vol 615, cols 981-1022 (20 October 2016); *cf* First Report from the House of Commons Work and Pensions and Business Innovation and Skills Committees, *BHS* HC 54 (2016–17).

[28] G Ruddick and S Butler, 'Philip Green agrees to pay £363m into BHS pension fund' *The Guardian* (London, 28 February 2017) www.theguardian.com/business/2017/feb/28/philip-green-agrees-pay-363m-bhs-pension-fund.

[29] EDM (Early Day Motion) 1068 (11 March 2009).

[30] Letter from Jonathan Stephens to Frank Field (17 January 2017) www.parliament.uk/globalassets/documents/commons-committees/work-and-pensions/Correspondence/Sir-Jonathan-Stephens-to-Chair-regarding-Sir-Philip-Green-knighthood-24-01-17.pdf.

[31] *Council of Civil Service Unions v Minister for the Civil Service* [1985] AC 374, 417-8; *Kline v Official Secretary to the Governor-General* [2013] HCA 52, (2013) 249 CLR 645, [11], [38]-[39]; *Black v Chrétien* 2001 CanLII 8537 (ON CA); *Senior-Milne v Advocate General for Scotland* [2020] CSIH 39, [18]-[20].

[32] *Senior-Milne v Advocate General for Scotland* [2020] CSIH 39, [19].

that a political party will deliver on its manifesto pledges.[33] Such questions are fundamentally ill-suited to curial adjudication.[34]

However, it is possible that an honour may be conferred on the basis of advice motivated by corruption or bribery. A case brought on those grounds would not rely on individual legal rights or legitimate expectations but rather on the misconduct of the official or minister in their public office. In a powerful extra-judicial article, Lord Mance considered this point and advocated for a 'more refined approach' to the question of the justiciability of the honours prerogative, 'rather than the blanket approach of excluding all possibility of judicial review because of the subject matter'.[35] In obiter comments in a 2007 case, Lord Justice Sedley also questioned the inclusion of some exercises of the prerogative on Lord Roskill's list, including 'the grant of honours for reward'.[36] This question awaits determination, but a change from the status quo, to recognise a limited scope for judicial review, may encourage 'a level of procedural robustness which self-regulation has so far failed to achieve'.[37] It would certainly be peculiar if procuring honours for bribes, an act that constitutes a crime under the Honours (Prevention of Abuses) Act 1925, were not also judicially reviewable.

No case has yet raised the forfeiture of an honour. While sharing a distinctly political element with the power to award an honour, the courts generally apply stricter demands of 'natural justice' to processes of forfeiture in other contexts, and it might be expected that similar standards would apply to honours.[38] These standards usually require an unbiased tribunal and the opportunity to make representations. It is perhaps notable in this regard that the Forfeiture Committee has recently reformed its procedures, to give all prospective recipients notice of the possibility of future forfeiture and to give recipients the opportunity to make representations to the Forfeiture Committee in all cases not involving a 'hard trigger'.[39]

Reform

A frequent companion to the biannual honours lists is the demand for reform to the honours system. From time to time, since the foundation of the Order of the British Empire in 1917, there has been a flurry of formal inquiries into that

[33] *R v Secretary of State for Education and Employment, ex parte Begbie* [2000] 1 WLR 1115, [1129].

[34] B Hadfield, 'Judicial Review and the Prerogative Powers of the Crown' in M Sunkin and S Payne (eds), *The Nature of the Crown: A Legal and Political Analysis* (Oxford, Oxford University Press, 1999), 216–7; N Cox, 'The Royal Prerogative in the Realms' (2007) 33 *Commonwealth Law Bulletin* 611, 633.

[35] J Mance, 'Justiciability' (2018) 67 *International & Comparative Law Quarterly* 739, 753–4.

[36] *R (Bancoult) v Secretary of State for Foreign and Commonwealth Affairs* [2007] EWCA Civ 498, [46]. The Court of Appeal decision on the main case was overturned in the House of Lords.

[37] M McKeown and S Thomson, 'Sources of Law and the UK Honours System' (2012) 14 *Scots Law Times* 81.

[38] *McInnes v Onslow-Fane* [1978] 1 WLR 1520.

[39] Cabinet Office, above n 5 at 18–9.

prospect.[40] Most recently, the House of Commons Public Administration Select Committee (PASC) issued a full report in 2012.[41] However, many of the controversies regarding the honours system are outside the scope of this chapter. For example, this is not the place to discuss proposals to replace the Order of the British Empire with an Order of British Excellence.[42] Furthermore, our survey does not attempt to tackle the question of the balance of honours between the civilian, military and diplomatic lists or the common concern that honours may be awarded to some public servants almost automatically, rather than on the basis of any further merit.[43] Rather, we shall focus our comments on procedural reforms: reforms that will improve the accountability, independence and transparency of the honours system itself.

Accountability

Since the 2005 reforms following the Phillips review, there has been a notable shift in the way that nominations for the honours system are scrutinised. The Honours Scrutiny Committee, first established as the Political Honours Scrutiny Committee in 1923, has been abolished, and its role in assessing whether a recipient was a fit and proper person has been subsumed into the honours committee structure. Since 2001, party political donations have needed to be registered with the Electoral Commission, and this register is available to the honours committees in making their assessments.

This transformation has brought considerable benefits. The system for awarding honours is now much more rigorous than it was 20 years ago and there are fewer opportunities for awards of dubious motivation. However, one way to improve post-grant scrutiny yet further would be to include the details of honours awarded to political party donors in the triennial report on honours prepared by the Cabinet Office. Those reports could also usefully include the numbers of honourees nominated by the government and by the public respectively.

Yet, post-Phillips, there is now *less* pre-award scrutiny of last-minute additions to the honours list by the Prime Minister. The Phillips review anticipated that this scrutiny – previously provided by the Honours Scrutiny Committee – would be taken on by the House of Lords Appointments Commission (HoLAC).[44] Although this was initially the case, HoLAC's terms of reference ceased to include this function from April 2010.[45] As David Cameron's last-minute nomination of

[40] See H Armstrong, *Honours: History and reviews* (House of Commons Library Briefing Paper 02832, February 2017), 19–22.

[41] House of Commons Public Administration Select Committee, above n 1.

[42] Fifth Report from the House of Commons Public Administration Select Committee, *A Matter of Honour: Reforming the Honours System* HC 212 (2003–04), paras 149–153.

[43] House of Commons Public Administration Select Committee, above n 1 at paras 20–40.

[44] Cabinet Office, above n 5 at paras 25 and 168–9.

[45] Armstrong, above n 40 at 27.

five honourees in 2012 shows (see above), Prime Ministers retain a considerable ability to bypass the honours committees. At least in the case of last-minute nominations, then, there is a serious scrutiny gap.

Independence

The post-Phillips reforms have brought pre-award scrutiny almost entirely in-house within the Cabinet Office. Parliament now has no role in pre-award scrutiny. A system of honours committees that is essentially a part of the Cabinet Office – no matter how many independent members sit on those committees – is open to political interference. To be clear, this risk is not of corruption, but rather manifests in the Prime Minister playing an overly powerful role in designing the structure of the system itself. That was amply demonstrated by David Cameron's unilateral decision to set up the Parliamentary and Political Service Committee (again in 2012).[46]

These challenges to accountability and independence might be addressed by the formation of an independent Honours Commission. Initially proposed by PASC in 2004, this idea was vociferously resurrected in their 2012 report.[47] Again, the proposal was rejected by the government for reasons PASC did 'not find … convincing'.[48] In 2004, Sir Hayden Phillips thought that the costs – both in bureaucracy and in loss of expertise – would be too great.[49] However, that should not preclude a re-examination of the merits. Recruitment of staff for the Commission could bring over the expertise of the Ceremonial Branch of the Cabinet Office, which itself was previously based in the Treasury (1937–68) and Civil Service Department (1968–81).

Furthermore, an independent Commission could take its lead from the Advisory Council on the Order of Canada, which consists of six *ex officio* members and up to seven others (usually members of the Order) appointed by the Governor General.[50] It 'took non-partisanship to a whole new level, by totally removing the prime minister and Cabinet from the nomination and approval process'.[51] Nominations are made (as is also possible in the UK) by the public, rather than solely by the government.[52] A similar Council advises on nominations

[46] *Hansard*, HC Deb Vol 545, cols 42WS-43WS (17 May 2012).

[47] House of Commons Public Administration Select Committee, above n 1 at para 68.

[48] House of Commons Public Administration Select Committee, above n 10 at para 4.

[49] Cabinet Office, above n 5 at para 20.

[50] Constitution of the Order of Canada, art 7. The six *ex officio* members are: the Chief Justice of Canada (Chair), the Clerk of the Privy Council, the Deputy Minister for Canadian Heritage, the Chairperson of the Canada Council, the President of the Royal Society of Canada, and the Chairperson of the Board of Directors of Universities Canada.

[51] C McCreery, *The Order of Canada: Genesis of an Honours System*, 2nd edn (Toronto, University of Toronto Press, 2018), 153.

[52] ibid at 297.

for the Order of Australia, although the Australian Prime Minister appoints eight of the 19 members (the others largely being representatives of the states).[53] The Australian Council has a similar nominations process too, although the Prime Minister may act as a referee for a nomination; but honours are not awarded to serving politicians.

Placing a new, independent Honours Commission on a statutory footing would give its recommendations greater stature and its members a firmer footing in insisting upon those recommendations, as well as preventing Prime Ministers from introducing new categories of nominees unilaterally. It would also be able to incorporate an independent Honours Forfeiture Committee, as proposed by PASC in 2012.[54] Indeed, there may even be considerable merit in combining such a new Commission with a reformed HoLAC (see chapter ten). Admittedly, there are also considerable challenges that must be met, including the question of appointment to the Commission and the role of the Prime Minister: should he or she become (as with the appointment of bishops) little more than a 'constitutional post-box', relaying the Commission's recommendations to the monarch? Nevertheless, in our view the case for an independent Commission is sufficiently strong that it should now seriously be considered, taking into account the experiences of reform in Australia and Canada.

Transparency

In its 2012 report, PASC recommended that the Prime Minister should cease to give 'strategic direction' to the honours system.[55] This is a question both of independence and of transparency: by what criteria are honours to be awarded? While on the face of it the Prime Minister's direction of the system smacks of political interference, the guidelines actually play an important role in enhancing the transparency of the system.

While honours cannot be mere gifts of the Prime Minister, they are (at least analogous to) gifts from the Crown.[56] Although there is broad consensus that merit must be the predominant factor behind individual awards, honours remain what they have always been: indications of outstanding achievement by individuals in sectors deemed of particular importance to the state. The government of the day has a legitimate role in determining what those sectors are. Such decisions should not be made behind closed doors but rather declared in the open. That is not to say that honours should be refused to all those who disagree with the government. The current Prime Minister's seven categories include a mixture of

[53] Constitution of the Order of Australia, art 4.
[54] House of Commons Public Administration Select Committee, above n 1 at para 117.
[55] ibid at para 68.
[56] See *Senior-Milne*, above n 32 at [19].

broad headings such as 'individuals who are unleashing our potential in emerging sectors' and more targeted groups such as 'those working to support the Union'.[57] There is room enough for political dissent. However, the exercise of the prerogative power of awarding honours is one of the ways in which the state flies the flag for values which it deems worthy of praise and by which it should itself be judged. That essential quality of honours requires strategic direction from the Prime Minister, given in a transparent and public way.

Indeed, it is for that reason that post-grant scrutiny of honours should be enhanced. A step forward was taken following PASC's 2012 reports, when the Cabinet Office agreed to post longer citations for major honourees (although only at the knighthood, damehood and Companion of Honour levels).[58] As we have set out, opportunities for questioning an award in Parliament are presently limited, and parliamentarians have been frustrated at the lack of responsiveness of the Forfeiture Committee to motions of censure in the Commons. We do not propose that forfeitures should be reduced to a vote on the floor of the Commons. However, just as the government has a legitimate role in 'flying the flag' via the honours system, so Parliament should not feel inhibited in challenging the values the government has thereby chosen to exhibit.

Conclusion

The modern honours system has been contentious for most of its lifetime, since the foundation of the Order of the British Empire in 1917. Significant improvements in the system have been made, and the merits of the post-Phillips reforms in 2005 should not be downplayed. There are further developments that can and should take place, balancing the need to eliminate corrupt practices, the importance of public confidence in the honours system and the legitimate role of democratically elected governments in shaping a system of public honours. Those reforms include enhancements to transparency and the revisiting of the argument for an independent Honours Commission. These are all essentially political (and highly contentious) questions – that is one reason why the courts have been loath to intervene, save perhaps in cases of corruption. The honours system is a dangerous voyage between the Scylla of political cronyism and the Charybdis of rigid bureaucracy. Perhaps the best that any system of scrutiny can do is to ensure that the ship is seaworthy, the seamen able and the captain ready to be held to account for any deviations from the charted course.

[57] Cabinet Office, above n 11.

[58] House of Commons Public Administration Select Committee, above n 1 at para 49; House of Commons Public Administration Select Committee, above n 10 at 7.

14

Public Inquiries

I saw an old man in the Park;
I asked the old man why
He watched the couples after dark;
He made this strange reply:—
'I am the Royal Commission on Kissing,
Appointed by Gladstone in' 74;
The rest of my colleagues are buried or missing;
Our Minutes were lost in the last Great War.
But still I'm a Royal Commission
Which never has made a Report,
And acutely I feel my position,
For it must be a crime (or a tort)
To be such a Royal Commission.
My task I intend to see through,
Though I know, as an old politician,
Not a thing will be done if I do.'

Punch (1934)[1]

Introduction

The primary purpose of most public inquiries is to establish facts, particularly where substantial concerns have arisen regarding the conduct of a public body.[2] However, inquiries are employed in a wide variety of contexts and serve a broad range of secondary purposes. They may be set up to draw a line under a crisis or to do political damage, to apportion blame or deflect criticism, to sweep a scandal under the carpet or draw out lessons to be learned. Such variety has two consequences. First, public understanding of the different types of inquiry is limited. For example, campaigners often claim that nothing but a 'full', judge-led inquiry will suffice. Yet a judge-led inquiry may be held in private and nonetheless be tightly

[1] AP Herbert, 'Pageant of Parliament' *Punch* (vol 186, 27 June 1934), 708. Extract printed with kind permission of United Agents LLP on behalf of the Executors of the Estate of Jocelyn Herbert, MY Perkins and Polly MVR Perkins.

[2] *Hansard*, HC Deb Vol 583, col 50WS (30 June 2014).

constrained by terms of reference set by the government. Second, the types of public inquiry are numerous: there is no one 'right way' to conduct an inquiry, although this has not stopped such an assertion arising. In the 1920s, the emphasis was on independence from party politics, after the disastrous Marconi scandal (where the inquiry divided along party lines).[3] In the 1960s, a more court-like procedure was recommended by Lord Salmon's Royal Commission on Tribunals of Inquiry. From the 1990s, it has been recognised that less 'legalism' might be preferable, although *legal* conceptions of 'fairness' pervade the statutory procedural rules.[4]

In 2005, a new statutory framework was created for public inquiries set up by ministers. The vast majority of public inquiries now conducted are statutory, under the Inquiries Act 2005.[5] Previously, inquiries were customarily set up under non-statutory powers (although occasionally under specific statutes),[6] with separate statutory powers providing the necessary 'teeth': the ability to summon witnesses, to compel the production of evidence and to administer oaths.[7] The 2005 Act repealed much of this earlier legislation but explicitly

> does not affect any power of Her Majesty to establish a Royal Commission, or … any power of a Minister or other person (whether under a statutory provision or otherwise) to cause an inquiry to be held otherwise than under this Act.[8]

As a result, statutory inquiries are available as an alternative, but not mandatory, regime. In this chapter, we use the term 'statutory inquiry' in relation to inquiries under the 2005 Act. There are a range of other, important forms of statutory inquiry, such as inquiries by the Children's Commissioner,[9] but these only arise in specific circumstances and therefore do not directly stand in contrast to the non-statutory powers we examine in this book, unlike the more generic 2005 Act.

There have been over 70 public inquiries since 1990,[10] and their processes continue to evolve. Questions of the purpose, effectiveness and cost of inquiries and the detailed structure of their procedures deserve greater consideration than there is space for in this volume. We are chiefly concerned in this chapter, therefore, with the question of why non-statutory inquiries continue to exist despite the Inquiries Act 2005, and whether they should finally be subsumed into the Act.

[3] L Blom-Cooper, *Public Inquiries: Wrong Route on Bloody Sunday* (Oxford, Hart Publishing, 2017), 5.

[4] Inquiry Rules 2006, SI 2006/1838, rr 13-5.

[5] National Audit Office, *Investigation into government-funded inquiries* (HC 836, May 2018), 34-6. This chapter is not concerned with statutory inquiries carried out by government departments.

[6] Eg, Inquiry into Historical Institutional Abuse Act (Northern Ireland) 2013.

[7] Chiefly provided by the Tribunals of Inquiry (Evidence) Act 1921, among other statutes.

[8] Inquiries Act 2005, s 44(4). Some prior legislation remains: First Report from the House of Lords Committee on the Inquiries Act 2005, *The Inquiries Act 2005: post-legislative scrutiny* HL 143 (2013-14), para 39.

[9] Children Act 2004, s 3.

[10] Institute for Government, 'Public Inquiries' (*Institute for Government*, 21 May 2018) www.instituteforgovernment.org.uk/explainers/public-inquiries.

Statutory Inquiries

Central to the 2005 Act is a quid pro quo: only statutory inquiries, bound by the procedural and other rules of the Act, are granted statutory 'teeth' (the powers to compel witnesses and the production of documents and to take evidence on oath).[11] Two requirements stand out. First, there are the Inquiry Rules 2006, which contain a plethora of detailed regulations for the conduct of hearings and payments for legal representation. For example, an inquiry's chairman must send a 'warning letter' to anyone explicitly or significantly criticised in a report.[12] Although there is some flexibility afforded to the chairman,[13] the style of a statutory inquiry is to a large extent predetermined. Second, section 18 of the 2005 Act creates a presumption that the inquiry will sit in public, although this may be displaced to the extent the responsible minister or the chairman thinks it conducive to the inquiry's task or in the public interest.[14]

Sometimes, a statutory inquiry arises by 'converting' a non-statutory inquiry.[15] Recent examples of such conversions include the Independent Inquiry into Child Sexual Abuse and the Post Office Horizon IT Inquiry.[16] The main reason for such conversions is to take the benefit of the statutory 'teeth' that only the Act can grant. Similarly, inquests can be converted into statutory inquiries. Although inquests do have some ability to sit in private and use 'closed material procedures' to hear certain confidential evidence (relating to national security),[17] they are stymied when faced with confidential police reports that cannot be put to the jury. For example, in 2015 the inquest into the police shooting of Anthony Grainger was converted into a statutory inquiry at the request of the judge, HHJ Teague.[18]

Under section 1 of the 2005 Act, a minister may commence an inquiry under the Act where: '(a) particular events have caused, or are capable of causing, public concern, or (b) there is public concern that particular events may have occurred'. Whether or not to launch an inquiry is in many cases a sensitive issue. The courts have been at pains to stress the breadth of the Secretary of State's discretion under section 1: 'The decision whether to order an inquiry, and if so its nature, is one for the Secretary of State. No one is entitled to a public inquiry.'[19] However, the

[11] Inquiries Act 2005, ss 17(2), 21, 35.

[12] Inquiry Rules 2006 (SI 2006/1838), r 13(3).

[13] Inquiries Act 2005, s 17.

[14] ibid at s 19(3).

[15] ibid at s 15.

[16] Blom-Cooper, above n 3 at 133-4; T Jarrett, *The Independent Inquiry into Child Sexual Abuse and background* (House of Commons Library Briefing Paper 07040, August 2016); Department for Business, Energy and Industrial Strategy, *Post Office Horizon IT inquiry 2020: terms of reference* (22 September 2021).

[17] Coroners (Inquest) Rules 2013 (SI 2013/1616), r 11; Justice and Security Act 2013, ss 6-11.

[18] The Anthony Grainer Inquiry, *Report into the Death of Anthony Grainger* (HC 2353, 2019), paras 1.23-26.

[19] *R (Persey) v Secretary of State for Environment, Food and Rural Affairs* [2002] EWHC 371 (Admin), 69.

discretion is not so wide that the court will never intervene. In *R (Litvinenko) v Home Secretary*, the widow of a murdered ex-Soviet agent and defector sought a declaration that the Home Secretary's refusal to set up a statutory inquiry (following the failure of the inquest into the death) was irrational.[20] The High Court agreed and quashed the decision, although Lord Justice Richards refused to grant a mandatory order that a statutory inquiry should be set up: the Home Secretary's 'discretion under section 1(1) of the 2005 Act is a very broad one and the question of an inquiry is … difficult and nuanced. I do not think that this court is in a position to say that the Secretary of State has no rational option but to set up a statutory inquiry now.'[21] (However, the Home Secretary subsequently set up a statutory inquiry.) Furthermore, in *In the matter of an application by Geraldine Finucane for Judicial Review*, the Supreme Court held that a promise to hold a public inquiry into a death did not give rise to a 'legitimate expectation' enforceable by the deceased's widow, but was a statement of policy and susceptible to change.[22]

Non-Statutory Inquiries

When an 'inquiry' is undertaken outside of the terms of the Inquiries Act 2005, it is not always clear whether it is a public inquiry or some other investigatory exercise or consultation. Furthermore, a non-statutory public inquiry can appear under different guises, such as a 'panel' or 'review'. However, it is possible to identify three main types of non-statutory public inquiries:

1. *Ad hoc inquiries.* A non-statutory inquiry is not bound by the requirements of the 2005 Act as to procedure or public hearings, but neither does it have the 'teeth' of a statutory inquiry that allow it to compel witnesses or the production of evidence.[23] Such inquiries are therefore highly reliant on the voluntary involvement of those being investigated.[24] One of the most common uses of non-statutory inquiries is therefore the investigation of government departments. They are capable of being governed by bespoke rules of procedure, which often creates 'a more inquisitorial and less formal approach'.[25] Furthermore, not being subject to the statutory presumption of

[20] *R (Litvinenko) v Home Secretary* [2014] EWHC 194 (Admin). The failure of the inquest because of evidence excluded on national security grounds would now be less likely following the Coroners (Inquest) Rules 2013 (SI 2013/1616).

[21] *Litvinenko*, ibid at 74-75.

[22] *In the matter of an application by Geraldine Finucane for Judicial Review (Northern Ireland)* [2019] UKSC 7.

[23] *Attorney-General of Australia v Colonial Sugar Refinery Co. Ltd* [1914] AC 237, 257.

[24] N Bamforth, 'Political Accountability in play: the Budd Inquiry and David Blunkett's resignation' [2005] *Public Law* 229, 235.

[25] G Cowie, *Non-statutory public inquiries* (House of Commons Library Briefing Paper SN02599, November 2021), 12.

public hearings, ad hoc non-statutory inquiries have greater flexibility to hear evidence in private. It is sometimes also said that a non-statutory inquiry can report more quickly.[26] However, it is arguable that sometimes the need to create a bespoke, non-statutory set of procedural rules can actually slow down such inquiries.[27] High profile examples include the Hutton Inquiry into the death of Dr David Kelly (2003-04), the Hillsborough Independent Panel (2009-12) and the Harris Review into suicides in custody by 18-24 year olds (2014-15).

2. *Inquiries by a committee of the Privy Council.* Such inquiries are merely 'a variation of variation on the non-statutory ad hoc form of inquiry', where the members are all (or are all made) Privy Counsellors.[28] They hold their meetings in private and all members are bound by their oaths or affirmations, such that confidential information relating to national security may more easily be examined. Recent examples include the Chilcot Inquiry (2009-16) into the UK's involvement in the Iraq War, and the Detainee Inquiry (2010-13) into whether the UK government was involved in the improper treatment of detainees in the aftermath of the '9/11' terrorist attacks. Notably, the Chilcot Inquiry – although it examined the evidence in private – agreed a disclosure protocol with the government before publication, which (extraordinarily) permitted release of otherwise highly classified information in the public interest.[29]
3. *Royal Commissions.* Frequently used in Australia, these are now employed rarely in the UK.[30] Royal Commissions are distinguished by their greater formality, being constituted under Royal Warrants, and by their broad subject-matter. They have a long history, their origins 'lost in hazy mists of the incompletely recorded past',[31] and have been employed for some of the most significant moments in our history, such as the compilation of the Domesday Book. They reached their modern apogee in the nineteenth century, used as a major tool for deliberating widespread legal, governmental and societal reforms.[32] The last Royal Commission to report in the UK was on reform

[26] Eg, the Home Office, announcing an inquiry into policing following the conviction of the murderer of Sarah Everard, said that 'Given the need to provide assurance as swiftly as possible, this will be established as a non-statutory inquiry' (5 October 2021): Home Office, 'Inquiry launched into issues raised by Couzens conviction' (5 October 2021) www.gov.uk/government/news/inquiry-launched-into-issues-raised-by-couzens-conviction.

[27] Cowie, above n 25 at 10.

[28] ibid at 26. Members not already Privy Counsellors may be made such: Cabinet Office, *The Report of the Detainee Inquiry* (December 2013), para 1.6.

[29] Iraq Inquiry, *The Report of the Iraq Inquiry*, vol 1 (HC265-I, 2016), 10-15.

[30] J Beer, *Public Inquiries* (Oxford, Oxford University Press, 2020), para 1.45, fn 66.

[31] HM Clokie and JW Robinson, *Royal Commissions of Inquiry; The Significance of Investigations in British Politics* (Stanford, Stanford University Press 1937), 24.

[32] B Lauriat, '"The Examination of Everything" – Royal Commissions in British Legal History' (2010) 31 *Statute Law Review* 24; TJ Lockwood, 'A History of Royal Commissions' (1967) 5 *Osgoode Hall Law Journal* 172, 182.

of the House of Lords (1999-2000).[33] In recent years, there has been some renewed interest in Royal Commissions, including in the Conservative Party's 2019 manifesto, but the promised Royal Commission on Criminal Justice has still not been set up.[34]

A Prerogative Power?

As we set out in chapter two, a prerogative power has been defined in several different ways. If Sir William Wade's relatively narrow definition is adopted, a 'prerogative' power must be a legal power peculiar to the Crown. Apart from Royal Commissions (which are established under royal warrants, issued under the prerogative), non-statutory ad hoc inquiries could be established by anyone, although there might be some difficulty in calling these 'public'. As Jason Beer points out,

> There is no statutory impediment to prevent any person or body from setting up a non-statutory inquiry into any issue or subject that they wish, provided they can convince people to participate in the inquiry, can fund the inquiry, and can persuade the public of the authority of its conclusions.[35]

One example is the Gulf War Illnesses Inquiry headed by Lord Lloyd of Berwick (2004).[36] That is why in this chapter we speak of 'non-statutory inquiries' rather than 'inquiries under the prerogative'.[37] On the other hand, non-statutory inquiries are heavily reliant on voluntary evidence. It is therefore highly likely that a non-statutory inquiry will be set up by the government.

Parliamentary Commissions

A third type of inquiry is a parliamentary inquiry. Inquiries are frequently conducted by Select Committees, but also by specially constituted parliamentary commissions. In its 2005 report, preceding the 2005 Act, the House of Commons Public Administration Select Committee (PASC) recommended that such commissions should be preferred to 'exercise of the prerogative power of the Executive'.[38]

[33] Royal Commission on the Reform of the House of Lords, *A House for the Future* (Cm 4534, January 2000).

[34] Conservative Party, *Get Brexit Done: Unleash Britain's Potential* (2019), 19. The Labour Party manifesto also promised Royal Commissions, on 'a public health approach to substance abuse' and health and safety legislation: Labour Party, *It's Time for Real Change* (2019), 44, 62.

[35] Beer, above n 30 at para 2.08.

[36] T Lloyd, N Jones and M Davies, *The Lloyd Inquiry: independent public inquiry on Gulf War Illnesses* (London, 2004).

[37] This distinction may affect the interpretation of the exclusions for 'investigations … by virtue of Her Majesty's prerogative' in the Freedom of Information Act 2000, ss 30(2)(a)(iii), 31(1)(h), (i).

[38] First Report from the House of Commons Public Administration Select Committee, *Government by Inquiry* HC 51-I (2004-05), para 215.

This was rejected by the Brown government's wholesale review of prerogative powers in 2009,[39] and has not resurfaced. Although parliamentary commissions can play an important role, like the recent Parliamentary Commission on Banking Standards (2012-13) set up following the LIBOR-rigging scandal, and might help build cross-party consensus on policy,[40] it is unclear how they would replicate the protection for national security provided by (eg) a Privy Council committee.

Reform

In many other chapters in this book, we have described how a statutory regime has replaced functions that previously were conducted under the prerogative. Inquiries form an exception to that general rule. Although most inquiries take place under the 2005 Act, there is no presumption that an inquiry will be statutory: Cabinet Office guidance requires government departments to consult with the Cabinet Office Propriety and Ethics Team on the merits of the different types of inquiry in any individual case.[41]

In its 2014 post-legislative scrutiny report into the 2005 Act, a House of Lords Select Committee could 'see no good reason why the Act should not be used as a matter of course when establishing an Inquiry'. Otherwise, 'there is a question as to why we have the statute at all'.[42] The government rejected this recommendation, wary of fettering the broad ministerial discretion under section 1 of the Act to set up a statutory inquiry, particularly since (it was claimed) a non-statutory inquiry might in some cases be 'preferable in the interests of justice and in dealing with the matter in a cost effective and timely way'.[43] In this last section of our chapter, we examine those competing claims.

Cost

Inquiries are famously expensive. The Chilcot Inquiry into the Iraq War (2009-16) cost over £13 million[44] and the Bloody Sunday Inquiry (1998-2010) ran to around £200 million.[45] The costs of smaller inquiries still run into the millions of pounds.

[39] Ministry of Justice, *The Governance of Britain: Review of the Executive Royal Prerogative Powers: Final Report* (2009), para 97.

[40] G Atkins, 'A cross-party parliamentary commission is the best way to build lasting social care reform' (*Institute for Government*, 25 November 2019) www.instituteforgovernment.org.uk/blog/cross-party-parliamentary-commission-build-lasting-social-care-reform.

[41] Cabinet Office, *Inquiries Guidance* (2012), 3.

[42] House of Lords Select Committee on the Inquiries Act 2005, above n 8 at para 61.

[43] Ministry of Justice, *Government Response to the Report of the House of Lords Select Committee on the Inquiries Act 2005* (Cm 8903, 2014), paras 14-15, 31, 92.

[44] The Iraq Inquiry, 'Inquiry Costs' (*National Archives*) www.iraqinquiry.org.uk/the-inquiry/inquiry-costs.

[45] Blom-Cooper, above n 3 at 3.

However, as the House of Lords Select Committee on the Inquiries Act pointed out, high costs are not a distinction of statutory inquiries: the Chilcot Inquiry, for example, was non-statutory.[46] It may be that the costs of some otherwise mandatory procedures can be saved, but in practice cost is not a strong reason for preferring a non-statutory inquiry.

Time

As noted above, there is also no particular reason why a non-statutory inquiry should be quicker than a statutory one. Appropriate flexibility is built into the 2005 Act to create a slimmed down inquiry (if needed), and using the Act gives a head-start in determining the applicable procedural rules, even if the burden of those rules cannot be lifted beyond an irreducible minimum.

Private vs Public

The most significant difference between statutory and non-statutory inquiries is that the former are conducted under the presumption that they will be held in public. While there are often legitimate reasons for initiating an inquiry in private, such as national security or sensitive economic concerns, the fact that there is no (published) process or set of criteria for determining whether an inquiry is to be statutory or not means that 'Serious questions have been raised about the motivation behind [such] decisions.'[47] Indeed, in the *Litvinenko* case, the High Court found that the Home Secretary's stated reasons for refusing a statutory inquiry were irrational.[48] So long as ministers have the ability to side-step the provisions of the 2005 Act, there will be a perception that – at least in some cases – they are doing so in order to avoid awkward public scrutiny of government decisions and actions. To mitigate this perception, the House of Lords Select Committee recommended that ministers should be required to give reasons for any decision to hold a non-statutory inquiry.[49]

Another solution would be to incorporate greater scope for private hearings and secret evidence under the 2005 Act, beyond the current provisions to restrict public hearings.[50] Indeed, statutory inquiries have been very useful where an inquest has failed because it lacks those very powers. However, as Emma Ireton has argued, 'each time a concession is made against openness, there is a real risk that public confidence in the public inquiry process, and thereby the effectiveness

[46] House of Lords Select Committee on the Inquiries Act 2005, above n 8 at paras 77 and 192-3.
[47] E Ireton, 'The Ministerial Power to Set Up a Public Inquiry: Issues of Transparency and Accountability' (2016) 67(2) *Northern Ireland Legal Quarterly* 209, 217.
[48] *Litvinenko*, above n 20.
[49] House of Lords Select Committee on the Inquiries Act 2005, above n 8 at para 93.
[50] Inquiries Act 2005, s 19.

of that process, is diminished'.[51] Were the 2005 Act to be amended, it might not only become bloated and unwieldy but also might command a lesser degree of public confidence.

Compulsion vs Cooperation

A statutory inquiry may have some flexibility, but its procedures are still to some extent based around an adversarial model. The standard rules envisage heavy legal representation of participants, although (for example) the Leveson Inquiry into press standards forbade press core participants from questioning complainants directly, that role falling instead to Counsel to the Inquiry. Sometimes, the more naturally inquisitorial style of a non-statutory inquiry, based on cooperation rather than compulsion, is 'more conducive for evidence gathering'.[52] In some situations, however, the compellability of evidence is not only desirable but necessary. In some cases, in which Article 2 of the European Convention on Human Rights (the right to life) is engaged, such as where the state may be implicated in an unnatural death, the European Court of Human Rights has held that a non-statutory inquiry does not comply with Article 2 because its effectiveness is undermined by the non-compellability of key witnesses.[53]

Furthermore, a public inquiry must command public confidence: sometimes, it is only statutory 'teeth' that can give confidence that the inquiry is fully empowered to get at the truth.[54] As a result, the Lords Select Committee recommended that inquiries should usually be conducted under the Act and that 'No inquiry should be set up without the power to compel the attendance of witnesses unless ministers are confident that all potential witnesses will attend.'[55]

Authority and Independence

Hand in hand with public confidence is the question of authority and independence. It might be thought that only a statutory inquiry could be a 'full' inquiry, in the sense often demanded by campaigners. Yet 'the practical authority of an inquiry turns more upon the political circumstances than on its formal status'.[56] The identity of the chairman and the conduct of the process matter too. The Chilcot

[51] E Ireton, 'How Public is a Public Inquiry?' [2018] *Public Law* 277, 278.

[52] Fifth Report from the House of Commons Public Administration and Constitutional Affairs Committee, *A Public Inquiry into the Government's response to the Covid-19 pandemic* HC 541 (2019-21), para 18.

[53] *Edwards v UK* (2002) 35 EHRR 19. See also *Re Finucane's Application for Judicial Review* [2019] UKSC 7, [134].

[54] J Thomas, 'The Future of Public Inquiries' [2015] *Public Law* 225, 233.

[55] House of Lords Select Committee on the Inquiries Act 2005, above n 8 at para 82.

[56] Bamforth, above n 24 at 236.

Inquiry's findings were widely respected because of their thoroughness, despite that inquiry being non-statutory. That perception was helped by the disclosure protocol the Inquiry had agreed with the government. That is not to say that form does not matter: the forthcoming Covid-19 inquiry under Baroness Hallett is statutory, in part to give it greater independence and authority,[57] and Royal Commissions were doubtless *à la mode* in 2019 manifestos because of their impressive titles.

Conclusion

Public inquiries are a constant presence in our public life, and there is little chance of them vanishing any time soon. Questions of their cost, their purpose, their independence and procedures will continue to arise. In this chapter we have not attempted to tackle those important concerns. Instead, our purpose has been to explore the competing claims and uses of parallel statutory and non-statutory regimes. Unlike in several other cases explored in this book, inquiries stand as an example where there is little appetite to replace surviving non-statutory powers with legislation. However, some reform may be desirable. In particular, although the Inquiries Act 2005 should not be made a comprehensive regime, parliamentary committees have made a strong case that a statutory inquiry should be the default, and that the government should give reasons to depart from that presumption. In practice, this is to a large extent already the case, but it will require continued monitoring by both the courts and Parliament to ensure that the appropriate balance between statutory and non-statutory inquiries is maintained.

[57] House of Commons Public Administration and Constitutional Affairs Committee, above n 52 at paras 18-22.

PART 4

The Prerogative in Comparative Context

15

Reform of the Prerogative in Australia, Canada and New Zealand

Introduction

Part four of this book looks at the prerogative in a comparative context, with two chapters. This chapter looks at the prerogative in Australia, Canada and New Zealand, and the similar debates which have taken place there about the reform of the prerogative. Chapter sixteen then studies reserve powers in six other countries with written constitutions in order to explore the parallels between the prerogative and reserve powers as a form of executive veto.

This chapter does not attempt to describe all of the prerogative powers in Australia, Canada and New Zealand, but focuses on a few of the most important: dissolution and prorogation; the war-making power; ratification of treaties; and judicial appointments. Between the three countries and with the UK, the similarities are much greater than the differences. As part of their constitutional settlements, Australia, Canada and New Zealand all inherited the Crown and the royal prerogative. The Queen is represented by a Governor General who has a similar role to the monarch in the UK, including exercising the reserve powers inherent in the prerogative.

With Australia and Canada being federations, the Queen is also represented by a Governor in each of Australia's six states, and by a Lieutenant Governor in each of Canada's ten provinces. Although their experience has created a wealth of interesting constitutional precedents, the summary below is mainly confined to that at the national level. It is inevitably brief and impressionistic, intended to give a sense of how the same issues in relation to the prerogative have arisen in all three countries, and how they have faced many of the same difficulties and dilemmas as the UK. With dissolution and prorogation, the key issue is whether the Crown retains a reserve power to refuse a request. With the war-making power and treaties, the question is the balance of power between the executive and parliament; while with judicial appointments, the question is how much discretion the executive should continue to enjoy.

Dissolution and Prorogation

The Reserve Power to Refuse Dissolution

In this first section, on dissolution, we address two questions which have been prominent in the UK: whether a Prime Minister can advise the dissolution of Parliament, or merely request it; and the impact on dissolution of fixed-term Parliament legislation. In Australia, Canada and New Zealand the power to dissolve, prorogue and summon Parliament is exercised by the Governor General, acting on the advice of the Prime Minister; but it is heavily overlaid with convention.

Precedents from all three countries show that dissolution is a discretionary reserve power which the Governor General has the right to refuse. The New Zealand Prime Minister Sir George Gray was refused a dissolution twice in 1877, when the Parliament was only in its second session. There are numerous examples of Australian Governors exercising their reserve power to refuse a dissolution, notably from the time when party discipline was more fluid and Parliaments less stable. This enabled Stanley De Smith to write in 1964:

> That a Prime Minister does not have an absolute right to demand a dissolution is a generally accepted proposition in Britain, Canada, Australia and New Zealand; the difficulty arises when one attempts to define the circumstances in which the Queen or the Governor-General will be constitutionally entitled to reject his request.[1]

The circumstances in which a Governor General might refuse a request for dissolution are similar to those under the Lascelles principles; which should not be surprising, since the principles were largely based upon experience in the Dominions rather than in the UK (see page 51). One of the main precedents, referred to in Alan Lascelles' letter to *The Times*, was the King-Byng affair in Canada in 1926, which illustrated two of the Lascelles principles: that dissolution should not necessarily be granted soon after a previous election, or if an alternative government was available. The brief facts were as follows. The Prime Minister Mackenzie King, having called an election in October 1925, saw his numbers greatly reduced in the new Parliament, but struggled on with support of the Progressives. In June 1926, after a scandal in the Customs Department, and facing a formal motion of no confidence, King asked the Governor General Lord Byng for a dissolution. Byng refused, the Parliament being only eight months old, and on the understanding that the Progressives were now willing to support the Conservative opposition led by Arthur Meighen. King resigned, and Meighen was commissioned to form a government, but it was soon defeated when the Progressives withdrew their support. Meighen then sought a dissolution, and when King won the ensuing election, Byng had to re-appoint King as Prime Minister.

[1] SA De Smith, *The New Commonwealth and its Constitutions* (London, Stevens & Sons, 1964), 98–9.

At the time, the political outcome seemed to vindicate King; but history has since been kinder to Byng.[2] It has nevertheless led subsequent Canadian Governors General to be wary about refusing controversial requests for dissolution. On several occasions, in 1963, 1974, 1979 and 2008, dissolutions were granted to a minority government despite the possibility of a differently composed government being formed instead.[3] Governors General may also indicate their reluctance informally: when, in 1979, the Prime Minister Joe Clark sought an early dissolution just seven months after the previous election, the Governor General kept him waiting for two hours before granting his request.

The Impact of Fixed Term Parliament Legislation

The Fixed-term Parliaments Act 2011 was judged a failure in the UK, with both the Conservative and Labour parties committed to its repeal in the 2019 election. It had failed to deliver fixed terms, and was deemed incompatible with Westminster traditions. Repeal of the Act would 'return to the tried and tested position of the past over many centuries'.[4] The Westminster debate ignored the fact that in recent years fixed-term legislation has been introduced in Australia (at state level) and Canada (in Ottawa as well as the provinces). The Australian legislation has been more effective in ensuring that Parliaments run for the fixed four-year parliamentary term. Typical is New South Wales, which in 1995 amended the state Constitution Act to provide that the Governor may dissolve the Legislative Assembly 'only in the circumstances authorised by this section'.[5] These circumstances include where the Assembly passes a motion of no confidence, or blocks supply. The Governor may then dissolve the Assembly, but retains the option of appointing an alternative government instead.

Due to the entrenched nature of the Crown in Canada's constitutional framework, it was not possible to restrict the vice-regal power of dissolution without a constitutional amendment. The fixed-term legislation passed by the federal Parliament in 2007 provided for four-year terms, with the next election to be held in October 2009, but with this proviso: 'Nothing in this section affects the powers of the Governor General, including the power to dissolve Parliament at the Governor General's discretion.'[6] In October 2008, the Prime Minister Stephen Harper exploited the proviso to seek an early election to improve the position of his minority government. There was discussion as to whether the Governor General could refuse his request on the basis that early dissolution should only follow a

[2] For a full account and summary of the academic commentary, see A Twomey, *The Veiled Sceptre: Reserve Powers of Heads of State in Westminster Systems* (Cambridge, Cambridge University Press, 2018), 388–402.

[3] DM Jackson, *The Crown and Canadian Federalism* (Toronto, Dundurn, 2013), 64.

[4] *Hansard*, HL Deb Vol 816, col 1278 (30 November 2021) (Lord True).

[5] Constitution Act 1902 (NSW), s 24B.

[6] Canada Elections Act 2000, s 56.1 (as amended in 2007).

parliamentary vote of no confidence; but a court challenge firmly dismissed the idea.[7] At the provincial level, fixed term legislation has similarly preserved the discretionary power of the Lieutenant Governor in order to avoid the need for constitutional amendment. As Premiers can still ask for an early dissolution where expedient, the consequence is that fixed terms have been less effective in Canada than in Australia.

Nevertheless, the norm is observed more often than not: since passing fixed-term legislation, most Canadian Parliaments have run to full term. All the provincial legislatures except Nova Scotia have introduced fixed terms, from British Columbia in 2001 to Quebec in 2013. The federal Parliament has experienced early dissolution twice, and each of the provincial Parliaments once, save for Saskatchewan.[8] Even so, more parliamentary sessions have run the full term: by January 2021 there had been 24 sessions running the full fixed term, and ten early dissolutions.[9]

In Australia, all the state Parliaments except Tasmania have introduced fixed terms, starting with New South Wales in 1995 and the latest being Queensland, which legislated to do so in 2015.[10] State Governors retain the power of early dissolution in limited and prescribed circumstances, such as where the government loses confidence or there is deadlock between the two chambers; but so far there have been no early dissolutions. By January 2021, the aggregate score in the Australian states had been 17 sessions running the full fixed term, with no early dissolutions.[11]

So, if a future government at Westminster ever feels brave enough to re-introduce fixed terms, it could learn from the experience in Australia and Canada. Fixed-term legislation does not establish a rigid rule that all Parliaments must run for the fixed term. But it does establish a new norm, that they will normally do so; and in most of the Australian states, they must do so, unless one of the conditions permitting early dissolution is met.[12]

The Reserve Power to Refuse Prorogation

In the UK, anyone who supposed that prorogation was automatically granted on the advice of the Prime Minister should have been disabused by *R (Miller) v The*

[7] *Conacher v Canada* [2101] FCA 131.

[8] G Chezenko, 'Fixing What Ain't Broke: The New Norm of Fixed-Date Elections in Canada' (2017) 8(3) *Mapping Politics* 83.

[9] R Hazell, *Written evidence to the Joint Committee on the Fixed-Term Parliaments Act* HC 1046 HL 253 FTP0013 (January 2021), para 7.

[10] S Bennett, *House of Representatives Fixed Terms: Barriers to Implementation* (Australian Parliamentary Library Research Paper 15 2008–09, November 2008); P Congdon, 'In a Fix: Fixed-Term Parliaments in the Australian States' (2013) 41 *Federal Law Review* 265.

[11] Hazell, above n 9 at para 6.

[12] The exceptions being Tasmania (see ibid) and Western Australia. In Western Australia, the fixed-term legislation is similar to that in Canada, preserving an open-ended prerogative power for the Governor to dissolve Parliament early upon request.

Prime Minister, which clearly established that the power to prorogue was limited by the constitutional principle of parliamentary accountability (see chapter 5).[13] In Canada and New Zealand, some of the older authorities suggest there is no reserve power to refuse prorogation.[14] But following the controversial prorogation in Canada in 2008, a growing number of scholars recognise that it is a reserve power.[15] The early election called by Stephen Harper in October 2008 saw the return of another minority government. Harper survived the debate on his government's throne speech, but the announcement of fierce budget cuts on 27 November provoked the three opposition parties into tabling a motion of no confidence against his government. The Liberals and New Democratic Party agreed to form a coalition, supported by the Bloc Québecois. Before Parliament could resume to debate the confidence motion, Harper asked the Governor General Michaëlle Jean for a prorogation. The Governor General consulted constitutional experts and agreed to only a short prorogation, during which the government revised its budget proposals and the opposition coalition fell apart. The decision to grant prorogation when the government was facing a no confidence motion remains controversial, but Anne Twomey concludes:

> In circumstances where a dissolution is inappropriate and an alternative government is unlikely to last for long, the better path might be to allow a relatively short prorogation to see whether confidence can be restored rather than exercising a reserve power.[16]

Doubt about whether prorogation was a discretionary reserve power may have stemmed from the shortage of hard examples of prorogation being refused. But there are a few instances of prorogation being refused in Australia. In New South Wales in 1899, Earl Beauchamp refused prorogation to the Premier George Reid who wished to avoid an imminent vote of no confidence (which Reid subsequently lost). In 1909, the Governor of Western Australia refused prorogation to the Premier Newton Moore until he had secured supply.[17] More common are instances of the Governor using the right to encourage and to warn to suggest a shorter period of prorogation: as Michaëlle Jean did in Canada in 2008, her predecessor Lord Dufferin did in 1873 (two to three months rather than six), and Sir Stanley Burbury did in Tasmania in 1981 (three months not six).[18]

[13] The Supreme Court ducked the question whether prorogation is a discretionary reserve power, saying that the parties had conducted the proceedings on the basis that the Queen was obliged by constitutional convention to accept ministerial advice to prorogue Parliament, and adding 'In the circumstances, we express no view on that matter': *R (Miller) v The Prime Minister; Cherry v Advocate General* [2019] UKSC 41, [30].

[14] Privy Council Office, *Manual of Official Procedure of the Government of Canada* (Ottawa, Government of Canada, 1968), 150; A Quentin-Baxter, *Review of the Letters Patent 1917 Constituting the Office of Governor-General of New Zealand* (Cabinet Office, Wellington, 1980) 20 [66], 115 [142].

[15] J Wheeldon, 'Constitutional Peace, Political Order or Good Government? Organizing Scholarly Views on the 2008 Prorogation' (2014) 8 *Canadian Political Science Review* 102.

[16] Twomey, above n 2 at 602.

[17] ibid at 594 and 596.

[18] ibid at 591 and 598–603.

As with Boris Johnson's prorogation of Parliament to avoid scrutiny of his Brexit plans in 2019, prorogation has been sought elsewhere to shut down parliamentary scrutiny, with the main examples being in Canada. In 1873, the Prime Minister Sir John Macdonald asked the Governor General Lord Dufferin to prorogue Parliament, which prevented the committee inquiring into the Pacific Railway scandal from tabling its report. In 2003, the Prime Minister Jean Chrétien sought prorogation during the transition to his successor Paul Martin, which conveniently delayed publication of a damning report by the Auditor General into a sponsorship scandal. In 2009, Stephen Harper obtained a prorogation which terminated a parliamentary inquiry into the treatment of Afghan detainees. In all three cases prorogation was granted, but in 1873, Dufferin did insist on establishing a Royal Commission to inquire into the Pacific Railway scandal. Some commentators have concluded that the Governor General has no discretion to refuse prorogation.[19] But the better view is that it depends on the seriousness of the corruption or illegality being inquired into: if it would give grounds for dismissal of the government, then termination of an inquiry through prorogation might be sufficiently serious to justify refusal.[20]

The War-Making Power: The Balance between the Executive and Parliament

As in the UK, there has been growing debate in Australia, Canada and New Zealand in the last 20 years over whether Parliament should have a greater say over military deployment overseas. The issues are broadly the same: whether there should be a vote as well as a debate; whether the debate should take place before or after the commencement of military action; and whether parliamentary control should be recognised in a convention, or formalised in statute. In the country-by-country analysis which follows, Canada is the country where debate is the most advanced, and New Zealand the least.

Canada

As in the UK, the power to deploy troops vests in the Crown under section 15 of the Constitution Act 1867, not in Parliament. There is a long, although unsteady, tradition in Canada of the idea of consulting Parliament over war. As long ago as 1910, in the debate on establishing a Canadian navy, Prime Minister Wilfrid Laurier insisted that deployment was 'a matter that must be determined by

[19] NA Macdonald and JWJ Bowden, 'No Discretion: On Prorogation and the Governor General' (2011) 34 *Canadian Parliamentary Review* 7.

[20] Twomey, above n 2 at 610.

circumstances, upon which the Canadian Parliament will have to pronounce and will have to decide in its own best judgment'.[21]

According to the then-orthodox theory of the indivisible Imperial Crown, if the UK was at war, then the Dominions were also at war. While declarations of war bound Canada (as a matter for the Imperial Crown), it was for Parliament to commit to active deployment of troops.[22] However, modern warfare is seldom conducted with declarations of war (see chapter seven), the relationship between the UK and her former Dominions has fundamentally changed, and the concept of the indivisible Imperial Crown is long gone. National independence, modern military deployments, and the Cold War led to a more patchwork approach to parliamentary consultation in Canada from the 1950s to the 1990s.[23] Prime Ministers Jean Chrétien and Paul Martin refused to hold parliamentary votes on deployments in Kosovo in 1999 and Afghanistan in 2001 and 2002 and on a combat mission in Kandahar, Afghanistan in 2005. This approach was opposed by the Bloc Québécois, the Reform Party, and the new Conservative Party (from 2003).

The victorious Conservative Party's 2006 election manifesto contained a commitment to 'Make Parliament responsible for exercising oversight over the conduct of Canadian foreign policy and the commitment of Canadian Forces to foreign operations'.[24] Conservative Prime Minister Stephen Harper appeared to fulfil this promise, holding votes on deployments in Kandahar in 2006, Libya in 2011, and Iraq in 2014 and 2015. This approach was initially followed by Liberal Prime Minister Justin Trudeau, who held a vote on a training and assistance mission in Iraq in 2016, but not when deploying an air taskforce to Mali that same year. Whilst the Standing Committee on National Defence in 2019 recommended that the government should continue to assist UN efforts in Mali,[25] the Conservative Party criticised the Committee for '[identifying] the dangers of modern peacekeeping without recommending an oversight role for Parliament' and recommended that Canada should only commit troops to peacekeeping missions following a debate and vote in the Commons.[26]

However, while the practice of parliamentary votes appears to be building into a convention, it is important to understand the political circumstances surrounding these votes. Stephen Harper's real motivation in asking Parliament to extend the Kandahar mission in 2006 may have been to 'increase the perceived legitimacy of his government's decision' and 'launder controversial policies through

[21] Parliament of Canada, *House of Commons Debates*, 11th Parliament, 2nd Session, Vol 2 (3 February 1910), 2965.

[22] N Hillmer and P Lagassé, 'Parliament will decide: an interplay of politics and principle' (2016) 71 *International Journal* 328, 332–3.

[23] ibid at 333.

[24] Conservative Party of Canada, *Stand Up for Canada: Federal Election Platform* (2006), 45.

[25] Canadian House of Commons Standing Committee on National Defence, *Canada's Role in International Peace Operations and Conflict Resolution* (May 2019), 86.

[26] ibid at 129.

the Commons'.[27] This tactic of pre-emptively sharing blame for potentially dangerous missions is not an isolated example.[28] It is often politics rather than principled belief that is a key motivation for the government to subject its decision to a vote. When politics changes, so may practice.

There is a growing debate over the need to formalise control of the war prerogative in Canada, with comparisons drawn to arrangements in the UK and the US.[29] An important question is the mode of control – convention or statute. Legislation could require a constitutional amendment, as it would otherwise risk infringing section 15 of the Constitution Act 1867.[30] If that were the case, establishing a convention would be the easier course. A codified convention would also allow greater latitude in terms of drafting: previous attempts to legislate by the Reform Party in the 1990s produced a Bill that was too prescriptive and impractical.[31]

Australia

Section 51(vi) of the Australian Constitution empowers the federal Parliament to pass laws in relation to 'naval and military defence'. However, under section 61, executive powers (including the prerogative) are exercisable by the Governor General, who is also Commander-in-Chief of the Defence Force under section 68. This is, of course, tempered by the convention that the Governor General acts on the advice of the Prime Minister and Cabinet. Under section 8 of the Defence Act 1903 (as amended), it is ministers who have 'general control and administration of the Defence Force'.[32]

Although there is no statutory rule that Parliament must be consulted on troop deployments, a belief that Parliament ought to be consulted was expressed as early as 1950 during a Senate debate on the Korean War.[33] However, this idea failed to take root. Debates and votes have taken place about most deployments for the last 70 years (though always after the decision has been taken by the Cabinet), and these have sometimes met with opposition (Malaya in 1955, Vietnam in 1965 and Iraq in 2003).[34] But Prime Ministers have repeatedly reminded Parliament that

[27] Hillmer and Lagassé, above n 22 at 335.

[28] P Lagassé, *Accountability for national defence: Ministerial responsibility, military command and parliamentary oversight* (Institute for Research on Public Policy, 2010), 14–8; ibid at 336.

[29] Most recently, see PJ Lim, 'Reforming Canada's war prerogative' (2020) 26 *Canadian Foreign Policy Journal* 345.

[30] P Lagassé, 'The Crown's Powers of Command-in-Chief: Interpreting Section 15 of Canada's Constitution Act, 1867' (2013) 18 *Review of Constitutional Studies* 189; *cf* ibid at 351.

[31] Lim, above n 29 at 353.

[32] B Nelson, 'The Role of Government and Parliament in the Decision to Go to War' (2015) 63 *Papers on Parliament* 1, 4.

[33] W Ashley, *Commonwealth Parliament Debates*, Senate (6 July 1950), 4834.

[34] D McKeown and R Jordan, *Parliamentary involvement in declaring war and deploying forces overseas* (Parliament of Australia Parliamentary Library Background Note, March 2010).

'the decision to commit Australian armed forces to combat is of course one that constitutionally is the prerogative of the Executive'.[35]

Calls for greater parliamentary scrutiny have intensified in the past 20 years, since the instigation of the 'war on terror' and the Iraq War. Although the Australian Parliament had no explicit vote on troop deployments to Afghanistan in 2001, motions passed in the House and Senate affirmed Australia's commitment to support the United States-led action. Deployments followed in October, and were later renewed in 2005 without a parliamentary vote. The deployments to Afghanistan were the more remarkable because they were NATO-led, at a time when Australia did not have a formal relationship with NATO.[36] The Parliament did, however, have the opportunity to debate the 2003 Iraq War: in the House, the Labor Party opposition failed to defeat the government's motion, but in the Senate a motion of censure narrowly passed. When withdrawal came in 2008, no parliamentary approval was sought.

The most notable recent example of the absence of parliamentary control is the 2014 deployment to Iraq against ISIL. Prime Minister Tony Abbott promised that Cabinet and the opposition would be consulted, but there would be no further parliamentary involvement.[37] Australia deployed 600 personnel and began airstrikes. Senator Scott Ludlam of the Green Party put forward a Private Senator's Bill to introduce mandatory parliamentary approval, but this was defeated on second reading.[38]

Ludlam and the Green Party have been the major proponents of war powers reform since the demise of the Australian Democrats in 2007, introducing a series of similar Bills. Outside of Parliament, reform is supported by the Australians For War Powers Reform campaign group.[39] The campaign has garnered support from former Prime Minister Malcolm Fraser, former Defence Secretary Paul Barratt,[40] and former Chief of Army Peter Leahy.[41]

However, neither the Liberals nor Labor support reform due to the belief that requiring prior parliamentary approval for deployments is 'fraught with danger' and would harm 'flexibility'.[42] The Labor Party Conference resolved in 2018 that a future Labor government would refer the issue to an inquiry by the Joint Standing Committee on Foreign Affairs, Defence and Trade.[43] Some commentators have

[35] R Hawke, *Commonwealth Parliament Debates*, House of Representatives (21 January 1991), 3.

[36] Nelson, above n 32 at 17–8.

[37] T Abbott, *Parliament of Australia Hansard*, House of Representatives (26 August 2014), 8556.

[38] Defence Legislation Amendment (Parliamentary Approval of Overseas Service) Bill 2014 (Senate Bill 44, 2013–16); S Ludlam, 'The Australian parliament must have the power to decide if we go to war' *The Guardian* (17 July 2014).

[39] A Broinowski, *How does Australia go to War? A call for accountability and change* (Australians for War Powers Reform, 2015).

[40] M Fraser and P Barratt, 'Going to war is a matter for Parliament' *The Australian* (8 September 2014).

[41] 'MPs must debate troop deployments: Leahy' *The Sydney Morning Herald* (17 June 2010).

[42] S Conroy, *Parliament of Australia Hansard*, Senate (30 September 2014), 7274.

[43] A Remeikis, 'Labor vows to restore penalty rates and address gender pay gap – as it happened' *The Guardian* (18 December 2018) www.theguardian.com/australia-news/live/2018/dec/18/labor-national-conference-day-three-politics-live.

turned their attention to the possibility of establishing a convention, analogous with the practice in the UK.[44] Yet there is a long road still to travel for reform of the war powers in Australia.

New Zealand

Conventions surrounding the war-making power are much less developed in New Zealand, with the Parliament seldom holding a vote before the deployment of troops abroad. It has become customary for the House to hold a debate, but this generally occurs after the commitment has been announced by the government. This was the case for deployments in Kuwait in 1990 and 1991, Bosnia-Herzegovina in 1994, Timor-Leste in 1999, Iraq and Afghanistan in June 2003, Afghanistan in 2009 and Iraq in 2015.

Where New Zealand has joined international coalitions at an early stage, with commitments in principle rather than a definite plan, Parliament has been granted a greater voice. In 2001, the government announced promptly that it was responding to the US's and UN's call for action following the 9/11 bombings. A special motion to support the offer of SAS troops and other assistance was passed by 112 votes to 7. In March 2003, the government chose not to join the allied invasion of Iraq. Parliament did hold a debate, but on an opposition motion against the government's decision, which was defeated.

After New Zealand joined the global coalition to counter ISIL, Prime Minister John Key announced the deployment of 143 personnel on a training mission to Iraq in February 2015.[45] Although there was a debate, opposition parties objected to the absence of a vote.[46] They pressed the point partly because there was a split in the governing National Party, and partly because of the success of parliamentary opponents to UK airstrikes in Syria in 2013, referred to in the debate.[47]

In New Zealand, then, there is an expectation that at least a debate should be held, but this almost always takes place after deployment. There is some limited support among parliamentarians for prospective votes, but little willingness by governments to deliver that. In Australia, there have been Private Member's Bills to require mandatory parliamentary approval of military action, but both major parties remain opposed. Practice in Canada is the most advanced, having held a series of parliamentary votes which may amount to a nascent convention, and growing debate about whether to formalise the convention, or even to entrench it in statute.

[44] PE Mulherin, 'War-Power Reform in Australia: (Re)considering the Options' (2020) 66 *Australian Journal of Politics and History* 633.

[45] US Department of State, *Joint Statement Issued by Partners at the Counter-ISIL Coalition Ministerial Meeting* (3 December 2014).

[46] *New Zealand Hansard*, Vol 703, 1815-6 (24 February 2015) (Andrew Little), 1817 (Russel Norman), 1819 (Winston Peters).

[47] *New Zealand Hansard*, Vol 703, 1830 (24 February 2015).

Treaty Scrutiny: The Balance between Parliament and the Executive

As in the UK, the majority of parliamentary treaty scrutiny in Canada, Australia and New Zealand takes place after signature but before ratification. The efficacy of parliamentary scrutiny varies considerably between the three countries. In Australia, the role of the Joint Standing Committee on Treaties (JSCOT) is well established. There are various committees of the New Zealand Parliament that conduct some treaty scrutiny, while in Canada the federal Parliament lacks a central treaty scrutiny committee. None of them require the parliamentary approval of any treaties.

Canada

In Canada, the power to 'conduct all diplomatic and consular relations on behalf of Canada' belongs to the minister for the Department of Foreign Affairs, Trade and Development.[48] However, this has not displaced the prerogative power to make treaties on behalf of Canada.[49] The prerogative is exercised formally by the Governor General, on the advice of ministers.

After a long period with a relatively high level of treaty scrutiny, from the mid 1920s to the mid 1960s, parliamentary scrutiny of international agreements waned in Canada for the next four decades.[50] That started to change when the new Conservative government under the leadership of Stephen Harper came to power in 2006 with a manifesto pledge to 'Place international treaties before Parliament for ratification.'[51] In 2008, the government published a *Policy on Tabling of Treaties in Parliament*.[52] It will table all treaties – not just those requiring ratification – with an explanatory memorandum, and then usually wait at least 21 sitting days before taking legal steps to bring the treaty into force, or before introducing any necessary implementing legislation. In 2020, the policy was updated with additional requirements for Free Trade Agreements. For these, the Minister of Foreign Affairs will table a notice of intent to enter into negotiations and the objectives for negotiations, as well as an economic impact assessment.

However, the policy does not include any special mechanism to enable scrutiny by committees, or for Parliament to debate on a treaty. In the first five years,

[48] Department of Foreign Affairs, Trade and Development Act 2013, s 10.

[49] *Canada (Prime Minister) v Khadr*, 2010 SCC 3; [2010] 1 SCR 44.

[50] J Harrington, 'Redressing the Democratic Deficit in Treaty Law Making: (Re)Establishing a Role for Parliament' (2005) 50 *McGill Law Review* 465.

[51] Conservative Party of Canada, above n 24 at 45.

[52] Government of Canada, 'Policy on Tabling of Treaties in Parliament' (*Department of Foreign Affairs and International Trade Treaty Law Division*, November 2020) www.treaty-accord.gc.ca/procedures.aspx.

only 21 of the 173 treaties laid before Parliament were scrutinised, and only one was debated within the specified 21 days.[53] Furthermore, the government has not always followed Parliament's negative view of a treaty. In 2009, the Committee on Fisheries and Oceans recommended against ratification of the revised Convention on Future Multilateral Cooperation in the Northwest Atlantic Fisheries, and their report was passed in the House 147 votes to 142 (against the minority government). However, the Convention was still ratified on 11 December 2009.[54]

With Canada's dualist approach to international law, treaties do not have direct effect in Canadian domestic law without legislation to implement them (as in the UK). However, unlike in the UK, the federal Parliament cannot legislate on matters of provincial competence.[55] Many treaties deal with matters that fall under provincial jurisdiction. While provincial consent is not required for ratification, the federal government may consult with the provinces before signing treaties that touch on matters of provincial jurisdiction. The provinces were involved in negotiating the EU-Canada Comprehensive Economic and Trade Agreement (CETA) in the 2010s, but that was only at the EU's insistence. The negotiations for the contemporaneous Trans-Pacific Partnership (TPP) were conducted by Ottawa alone.[56] The 2008 treaty policy has been criticised for allowing the federal Parliament to scrutinise treaties that it lacks the jurisdiction to implement, 'while provincial parliaments are totally left aside'.[57]

Australia

Parliamentary scrutiny of treaties in Australia was changed radically with reforms in 1996. Criticism had grown of the federal government's lack of consultation with the states in negotiating treaties and legislating to implement them. Calls for greater scrutiny were provoked by a series of High Court cases which upheld the federal Parliament's power to legislate in areas that were constitutionally reserved to the states.[58] In a report issued in 1995, the Senate's Legal and Constitutional References Committee recommended:

- all treaties should be tabled at least 15 sitting days prior to ratification or signature, along with a treaty impact statement;

[53] SL Danesi, 'Tabling and waiting: a preliminary assessment of Canada's treaty-tabling policy' (2014) 20 *Canadian Foreign Policy Journal* 189, 193, 204.

[54] ibid at 202.

[55] Constitution Act 1867 (CA), s 92.

[56] CE Côté, 'Federalism and Foreign Affairs in Canada' in C Bradley (ed), *The Oxford Handbook of Comparative Foreign Relations Law* (Oxford, Oxford University Press, 2019), 289.

[57] ibid at 292.

[58] Parliament of Australia Joint Standing Committee on Treaties, *A history of the Joint Standing Committee on Treaties: 20 years* (Report 160, March 2016), 10; D Mason, 'Deliberative democratising of Australian treaty making: putting into context the significance of online access to the treaty process' (2016) 24 *Journal of Law, Information and Science* 1, 17; The High Court cases were

- a Joint Standing Committee on Treaties (JSCOT) should be formed; and
- the question of mandatory prior parliamentary approval of treaties should be referred to JSCOT.[59]

These recommendations were implemented by the government in 1996, save for the last, which was postponed to a review after two years and has not been fully resolved.[60] The states are no longer pressing for a veto on treaty-making. More important issues for them are the level of consultation, and involvement in negotiations – state officials may be included in the negotiating team where the subject of the treaty falls within state expertise.

JSCOT is composed of nine members from the House of Representatives and seven Senators. Its level of assessment conventionally falls into three categories:

- Category 1 treaties are the most important, tabled at least 20 joint sitting days before ratification (which may equate to several calendar months). The majority of treaties fall under this category.
- Category 2 treaties are uncontroversial or standard form, tabled at least 15 joint sitting days before ratification.
- Category 3 treaties are minor, usually technical amendments to treaties of which Australia is already a party. JSCOT is informed, given a brief explanatory statement, and can elevate the treaty to Category 1 or 2.

Unlike the New Zealand Foreign Affairs, Defence and Trade Committee (FADTC) (see below), JSCOT usually conducts inquiries itself rather than farming out the task of scrutiny; although other committees may conduct their own inquiries too. Scrutiny is informed by the government's national interest analysis of each treaty, and the government is expected to respond to committee reports within three months.[61]

As in the UK, the focus of treaty scrutiny reform in recent years has been on trade agreements. Similarly, too, there is an awareness that the most meaningful impact on trade policy can be made before or during negotiations.[62] Although the Australian Parliament has done some pre-signature treaty scrutiny,[63] it is hampered by a lack of information. In order to address this shortfall, JSCOT in 2021 recommended that the government should publish its negotiating aims and objectives for all future trade treaties, and brief the committee biannually on the

Koowarta v Bjelke-Peterson (1982) 153 CLR 168, *Commonwealth v Tasmania* (1983) 158 CLR 1 and *Richardson v Forestry Commission of Tasmania* (1988) 164 CLR 261.

[59] Parliament of Australia Senate Legal and Constitutional References Committee, *Trick or Treaty? Commonwealth Power to Make and Implement Treaties* (November 1995).

[60] Parliament of Australia Joint Standing Committee on Treaties, above n 58 at 14–5.

[61] Senate Standing Order C42(1) requires a response within 3 months. House of Representatives Resolution 29 September 2010 requires a response within 6 months.

[62] Parliament of Australia Senate Foreign Affairs, Defence and Trade References Committee, *Blind Agreement: Reforming Australia's Treaty-making Process* (2015).

[63] Parliament of Australia Joint Standing Committee on Treaties, *Strengthening the Trade Agreement and Treaty-Making Process in Australia* (Report 193, August 2021), 4, 23.

status of upcoming and current negotiations.[64] As for improving consultation and transparency, some progress has been made with the formation in 2020 of a Ministerial Advisory Council, which brings together business, industry and community representatives with trade expertise.[65]

New Zealand

Until 1998, there was little formal parliamentary scrutiny of treaties in New Zealand. Calls for parliamentary control intensified following the 1993 referendum to introduce a mixed-member proportional voting system, and the consequent concern that a minority government would have exclusive control of treaty-making.[66] From 1998, the government committed to table some international agreements before the House.[67] This was adopted into Standing Orders in 1999 (now Standing Order 405(1)), affirmed by the government in 2000, and subsequently included in the Cabinet Manual.[68] The categories of treaties covered are slightly wider than in the UK:

- treaties that are to be binding on ratification (Standing Order 405(1)(a));
- multilateral treaties from which the government wishes to withdraw (Standing Order 405(1)(c)); and
- major bilateral treaties 'of particular significance' (Standing Order 405(1)(d)).

Once a treaty has been tabled, it is referred to the FADTC, which assigns scrutiny to an appropriate select committee rather than conducting scrutiny itself.[69] All treaties tabled must be accompanied by a national interest analysis,[70] which must include an explanation of its advantages and disadvantages,[71] though these NIAs have been widely criticised for their lack of objectivity.[72]

The scrutiny performed by the select committees is patchy. Analysis of their reports suggests that they add little value, and rely heavily on the government-produced NIAs.[73] But, unlike in Canada, there is a mechanism to enable debate

[64] ibid at 28.

[65] ibid at 21–3 and 27.

[66] M Chen, 'A Constitutional Revolution? The Role of the New Zealand Parliament in Treaty-Making' (2001) 19 *New Zealand Universities Law Review* 448, 451.

[67] D McGee, *Parliamentary Practice in New Zealand*, 4th edn (Mary Harris and David Wilson ed, Auckland, Oratia, 2017), 685–6.

[68] Most recently in New Zealand Cabinet Office, *Cabinet Manual*, 6th edn (2017), para 7.123–7.133.

[69] McGee, above n 67 at 689.

[70] New Zealand Standing Order 405(2).

[71] New Zealand Standing Order 406.

[72] New Zealand Parliament Regulations Review Committee, *Inquiry into regulation-making powers that authorise international treaties to override provisions of New Zealand enactments* (12 March 2002); McGee, above n 67; T Riley, 'Something Weird: An Examination of Parliamentary Involvement in New Zealand's Treaty-making Process' (2018) 5 *Public Interest Law Journal of New Zealand* 11.

[73] Riley, ibid; T Dunworth, 'The Influence of International Law in New Zealand: Some Reflections' in C Morris, J Boston and P Butler (eds), *Reconstituting the Constitution* (Heidelberg, Springer, 2011), 325.

on these reports. If the treaty is to be implemented via primary legislation, the committee report on the treaty will be debated in government time, before or as part of the first reading debate on the implementing legislation.[74] If legislation is not required, the committee report may be set down as a member's order of the day.[75] However, such members' orders are rarely selected by the Business Committee for debate.[76] The government does occasionally choose to initiate debate on particular treaties, as it did on a New Zealand-Singapore economic partnership in 2000, and members can also petition the Business Committee for a debate to be held.[77]

The patchy scrutiny in New Zealand may in part be the result of its small, single-chamber Parliament of only 120 members. But smaller size cannot explain the difference in approach between Australia and Canada: the Parliament in Canberra is half the size of that in Ottawa, and yet Australia has the stronger system of scrutiny. The drive in Australia came originally from the Senate, concerned about human rights treaties, and subsequently from JSCOT: without a similar dedicated committee Canada may continue to lag behind. But all of these Parliaments have started doing more to try and scrutinise free trade agreements during negotiations, and both Canada and Australia have had some commitments from government to increase transparency. Nevertheless, difficulties continue with finding time to debate committee reports; with involving the states in Australia and the provinces in Canada; and finding a meaningful way to scrutinise treaties during the negotiating stage.

Judicial Appointments: Fettering Executive Discretion

In 2005, the UK made a huge change to judicial appointments, overhauling a system which gave the Lord Chancellor a lot of discretion in the appointment process and introducing a tightly regulated system run by a statutory Judicial Appointments Commission who nominate a single name for appointment (see chapter ten). At around the same time, Canada started to experiment with parliamentary hearings for Supreme Court Justices, and it had earlier introduced Judicial Advisory Committees for lower-level federal appointments. Australia also introduced advisory panels for federal judicial appointments, except for the top court. But, in Australia and Canada, judicial appointments have become a political football, with these reforms subsequently being reversed by Conservative governments restoring greater discretion. New Zealand has never had advisory appointment panels, but

[74] New Zealand Standing Orders 250(2)(a), 285(4)(c).

[75] New Zealand Standing Order 254(2).

[76] McGee, above n 67 at 691.

[77] New Zealand Parliament Senate Foreign Affairs, Defence and Trade Committee, *Report on the agreement between New Zealand and Singapore on a closer economic partnership* (588 NZPD 6329–6357, 2000); McGee, ibid.

with a much smaller pool, eligible candidates are well known to the law officers who control the system.

Canada

Judicial appointments in Canada operate on three levels: those to the Supreme Court of Canada; other federal courts and provincial and territorial superior courts; and the provincial and territorial lower courts. The federal government is responsible for appointments to the first two of these, and we confine ourselves to the federal level of appointment.[78]

Appointments to the Supreme Court are made formally by the Governor General.[79] Section 4(1) of the Supreme Court Act 1985 sets out that there shall be nine judges, of whom three must be from Quebec. Of the remainder, by convention selection is strongly determined by region. Ontario usually provides three justices; the western provinces two; and the Atlantic provinces one.[80]

Historically, the Prime Minister alone was responsible for advising the Governor General, with lesser or greater input from the Minister for Justice.[81] But the last 20 years have seen three distinct approaches to Supreme Court appointments. The first reform was under Prime Minister Paul Martin in 2004. Martin's system saw a government-created long list vetted by a panel of MPs to form a short list, from which the Prime Minister would select his nominee, who would then be put before an ad hoc committee of parliamentarians. Five judges were appointed under this method until 2013, by both Martin and Stephen Harper, his successor. However, in 2013, the Supreme Court invalidated Harper's appointment of Marc Nadon from Quebec.[82] After this, Harper abandoned the process and appointed three judges in 2014–15 without parliamentary input. He even publicly questioned the Chief Justice's integrity in the Nadon case.[83]

In his 2015 election manifesto, Liberal leader Justin Trudeau promised to restore the all-party approach to Supreme Court appointments. As Prime Minister, he set out a new process involving four key elements:

- an official and open application process;
- an advisory board of seven members;

[78] Except that the federal government is responsible for judicial appointments in Nunavut.

[79] Supreme Court Act 1985, s 4(2).

[80] A Dodek and R Cairns Way, 'The Supreme Court of Canada and Appointment of Judges in Canada' in P Oliver, P Macklem and N Des Rosier (eds), *The Oxford Handbook of the Canadian Constitution* (Oxford, Oxford University Press, 2017), 212.

[81] Privy Council Minute 3374 (25 October 1935); ibid at 217.

[82] *Reference re Supreme Court Act, ss 5 and 6* 2014 SCC 21; see R Devlin and A Dodek, 'The Achilles heel of the Canadian judiciary: the ethics of judicial appointments in Canada' (2017) 20 *Legal Ethics* 43, 50–3.

[83] S Fine, 'Chief Justice hits back at Prime Minister over claim of improper call' *The Globe and Mail* (2 May 2014).

- published assessment criteria and application questionnaire; and
- additional eligibility requirements and guidance to the panel to seek judges who are functionally bilingual as well as diverse.[84]

There has also been recent reform to the system of federal appointments to other courts. The roots of the current system stretch back to changes made in 1989 to combat criticisms of political patronage. Advice on appointments is given by Judicial Advisory Committees (JACs), which receive and screen applications for vacancies.

Two main changes have taken place since 1989. First, the composition of JACs has been hotly contested, with Prime Minister Harper adding a representative of local law enforcement as part of a 'tough on crime' initiative in 2004.[85] Justin Trudeau removed this additional representative in 2016, as well as restoring the voting power of the nominee of the provincial Chief Justice that had been removed by Harper.[86]

The second change to the process since 1989 has been the strength of the JACs' recommendations. In 1991, they were asked to say whether a candidate was recommended, highly recommended, or not recommended. In 2007, Stephen Harper removed the 'highly recommended' category, thus expanding the government's discretion when making appointments. It has since been restored by Justin Trudeau in 2016.[87]

Ted Morton and Dave Snow suggest the Trudeau reforms were in some ways as 'political' as Harper's. By weakening the force of JACs' recommendations, Harper's system opened possibilities for political patronage and recruitment for ideological compatibility. Trudeau has made increased diversity a central aim of judicial recruitment.[88] In April 2016, only 35 per cent of the federal bench were female.[89] Since the 2016 reforms, 57 per cent of some 300 new appointments have been female, 3 per cent from indigenous populations and 10 per cent BAME.[90] The first judge of colour on the Supreme Court, Mahmud Jamal, was appointed in June 2021. Trudeau's 'political' aims therefore seem to have been met; but their connection to the politics of a single Prime Minister may threaten their longevity. That instability will remain part of the JAC system for as long as it remains politically contested, and a locus for political point-scoring.

[84] FL Morton and D Snow (eds), 'Judicial Recruitment and Selection' in *Law, Politics and the Judicial Process in Canada* (Calgary, University of Calgary Press, 2018), 127–8.

[85] Dodek and Cairns Way, above n 80 at 223.

[86] Office of the Commissioner for Federal Judicial Affairs Canada, 'Judicial Advisory Committees – Guidance for Judicial Advisory Committee Members' (*Government of Canada*, October 2016) www.fja.gc.ca/appointments-nominations/committees-comites/guidelines-lignes-eng.html.

[87] Dodek and Cairns Way, above n 80 at 222 and 228.

[88] Morton and Snow, above n 84 at 120 and 124.

[89] Dodek and Cairns Way, above n 80 at 225.

[90] Excluding additional appointments and elevations of existing judges within the judicial system. Office of the Commissioner for Federal Judicial Affairs Canada, 'Statistics regarding Judicial Applicants and Appointees' (*Government of Canada*, 28 October 2020) www.fja.gc.ca/appointments-nominations/StatisticsCandidate-StatistiquesCandidat-2020-eng.html.

Australia

With its federal system, Australia also has Commonwealth (federal) and state courts. As with Canada, we restrict our overview to the former. Formally, Australian federal judges are appointed by the Governor General on advice of the Attorney General. Appointees must generally be existing judges or legal practitioners of at least five years' standing.[91] In appointing judges to the High Court (Australia's top court), the federal Attorney General must consult state Attorneys General.[92] Beyond this, there is little statutory control over the process.[93]

Interest in judicial appointments increased in the 1980s and 1990s, as a result of some important High Court decisions, and also because of corruption scandals, including allegations against High Court Justice (and former Attorney General) Lionel Murphy.[94] However, no structural reforms were made to the process of appointment. Political accountability was thought to suffice.[95]

Limited reform came during the Labor governments of 2007–13, when Attorney General Robert McClelland announced the creation of advisory panels for federal appointments (except the High Court). The chief features were advertisement of vacancies, publicly available selection criteria, and an advisory panel consisting of two judges and a senior member of the Attorney General's Department.[96] Notably, McClelland did not take up the UK model of a Judicial Appointments Commission, as proposed by some Australian academics;[97] he said such a model was 'overly bureaucratic and … unreasonably intrusive as well as taking too long'.[98] His approach was endorsed by the Senate Legal and Constitutional Affairs References Committee in 2009.[99]

However, even the moderate reforms proposed by McClelland were abandoned by the Liberal-National coalition government in 2014.[100] This reversal has

[91] Federal Court Act 1976, s 6(2); High Court of Australia Act 1979, s 7; Federal Circuit and Family Court of Australia Act 2021, ss 11(2), 111(2).

[92] High Court of Australia Act 1979, s 6.

[93] E Handsley, '"The judicial whisper goes around": Appointment of Judicial Officers in Australia' in K Malleson and P Russell (eds), *Appointing Judges in an Age of Judicial Power: Critical Perspectives from Around the World* (Toronto, University of Toronto Press, 2006), 124.

[94] ibid at 124–6; J Bai and H Hobbs, 'Appointing Attorneys-General to the High Court: A Case for Reform' (2017) 42 *Alternative Law Journal* 286, 291. Murphy J died before a full inquiry could be completed.

[95] Australian Judicial System Advisory Committee, *Report to the Constitutional Commission* (1987), para 5.27.

[96] R McClelland, 'Judicial Appointments Forum' (Bar Association of Queensland Annual Conference, Gold Coast, 17 February 2008); Australian Government Attorney-General's Department, *Judicial Appointments: Ensuring a strong, independent and diverse judiciary through a transparent process* (2010); E Handsley and A Lynch, 'Facing up to Diversity? Transparency and the Reform of Commonwealth Judicial Appointments 2008–13' (2015) 37 *Sydney Law Review* 187.

[97] G Williams, 'High Court Appointments: the need for reform' (2008) 30 *Sydney Law Review* 30 161.

[98] McClelland, above n 96 at para 66.

[99] Parliament of Australia Senate Legal and Constitutional Affairs References Committee, *Australia's Judicial System and the Role of Judges* (December 2009), para 3.89.

[100] A Lynch, 'Judicial Appointments in Australia – Reform in Retreat' (*UK Constitutional Law Association Blog*, 26 May 2014) www.ukconstitutionallaw.org/2014/05/26/andrew-lynch-judicial-appointments-in-australia-reform-in-retreat.

persisted throughout the coalition government's time in office, with opposition from the Labor Party.[101] It goes against advice from the Australasian Institute of Judicial Administration, which published *Suggested Criteria for Judicial Appointments* in 2015,[102] and from the Law Council of Australia, which in 2021 recommended advisory panels appointed by an independent impartial body or by the Attorney General.[103]

In September 2020, the Attorney General Christian Porter made a reference to the Australian Law Reform Commission (ALRC), requesting a report on potential reforms to ensure judicial impartiality and lack of bias.[104] This followed a series of scandals involving allegations of sexual harassment, corruption and bullying by judges.[105] In its consultation paper, the ALRC suggested that the federal government should commit to a more transparent process, including publication of vacancies and criteria for appointment, as well as aiming for 'candidates who reflect the diversity of the community'.[106] It cited the 2008 protocol for appointments under Attorney General Robert McClelland as 'an appropriate model for such reform', as well as noting the AIJA's *Suggested Criteria*.[107] The ALRC handed their report to the Attorney General in December 2021.

New Zealand

Judicial appointments in New Zealand are made by the Governor General, acting on advice, given in most cases by the Attorney General.[108] Apart from basic eligibility requirements (judges must have been barristers or solicitors for at least seven years) there are no statutory controls on the appointment process.[109]

Since 2016, the Attorney General has been required to publish information on the process and how applications are sought.[110] The nine-page *Judicial Protocol*, published by the Crown Law Office in 2014, sets out four broad selection criteria: legal ability, qualities of character, 'personal technical skills', and 'reflection of society'.[111] In addition, at least for the appellate courts, the Attorney General

[101] M Whitbourn, 'Review considers shake-up of federal judicial appointments' *The Sydney Morning Herald* (3 May 2021).
[102] Australasian Institute of Judicial Administration, *Suggested Criteria for Judicial Appointments* (2015).
[103] Law Council of Australia, *Policy on the Process of Judicial Appointments* (June 2021), 4.
[104] Australian Law Reform Commission, 'Review of Judicial Impartiality – Terms of Reference' (*Australian Government*, 11 September 2020) www.alrc.gov.au/inquiry/review-of-judicial-impartiality/terms-of-reference/.
[105] G Williams, 'Integrity must rule process of judging conduct of judges' *The Australian* (14 February 2021).
[106] Australian Law Reform Commission, *Judicial Impartiality: Consultation Paper* (CP 1, April 2021), 26.
[107] ibid at 27.
[108] Supreme Court Act 2003, s 17; Senior Courts Act 2016, s 100.
[109] Senior Courts Act 2016, s 94.
[110] ibid, s 93.
[111] Crown Law Office, *Judicial Protocol* (April 2014), 3–4.

'will consider the overall make-up of the court, including the diversity of the bench and the range of experience and expertise of the current judges'.[112]

For the High Court, expressions of interest are called for by public advertisement every three years. The list of candidates is compiled by the Solicitor General, who may invite the Attorney General and senior judges to suggest further names. Then the Solicitor General asks senior judges to give the candidates a rating. This long list is presented to the Attorney General, who determines a short list with the agreement of the Chief Justice. Further interviews and checks are then carried out by the two law officers, before appointment by the Attorney General of a preferred candidate.[113]

For the appellate courts there is no public advertisement, as potential candidates (usually serving judges) will be known to the Attorney General.[114] A short list of three is settled, again with the agreement of the Chief Justice. It is then for the Attorney General to select the final appointee, notify Cabinet, and advise the Governor General.

The system in New Zealand, therefore, is built on the 'tap-on-the-shoulder' model. The two law officers play a central role – one that has not gone uncriticised.[115] Some safeguard is provided by the role of the Chief Justice, but former Attorneys General have been unabashed about trying 'hard to put a stamp on the judiciary'.[116] Furthermore, despite the 'commitment to actively promoting diversity in the judiciary' heralded in the foreword to the *Judicial Protocol*, little detail has been given about how this is to be achieved.[117] The system remains opaque, and the Crown Law Office's approach is perhaps exemplified by the fact that the *Protocol* has not been updated to take account of the legislative overhaul of the courts in 2016.

Conclusion

It is difficult to draw firm conclusions from this brief account of four different prerogative powers, but some general points can be made. First, it is notable how much has changed in the last 20 years, and is still changing. As in the UK, prerogative powers are becoming more tightly regulated, but with some ebb and flow. Fixed-term Parliament legislation in Canada is a product of the last 20 years, in Australia the last 25. Calls for greater parliamentary scrutiny of war powers have intensified in all Parliaments in the last 20 years, particularly since the allied

[112] ibid at 8.
[113] ibid at 4-5.
[114] ibid at 8.
[115] BV Harris, 'A Judicial Commission for New Zealand: a good idea that must not be allowed to go away' [2014] *New Zealand Law Review* 383, 395.
[116] G Palmer, 'Judicial Selection and Accountability: Can the New Zealand System Survive?' in BD Gray and RB McClintock (eds), *Courts and Policy: Checking the Balance* (Wellington, Brookers, 1995), 45.
[117] Crown Law Office, above n 111 at 1.

occupation of Iraq and Afghanistan. New procedures for scrutinising treaties were initiated in the Australian Parliament in 1996, in New Zealand in 2000, and in Canada in 2008. And the system of judicial appointments has been tightened in all three countries in the last 20 years.

Second, the direction of travel is largely one way, towards tighter regulation; the main exception being judicial appointments in Australia and Canada, where Liberal and Conservative governments have undone or weakened the reforms of their Labor and Liberal predecessors. But if there is a left-right split on regulation of judicial appointments, that does not carry over into regulation of war-making powers or treaties. In Canada, it is Conservative governments which have allowed more parliamentary debate on military deployments, and Conservative governments which have introduced procedures for parliamentary scrutiny of treaties.

Third, as with all the prerogative powers, there are genuine difficulties in getting the balance right. The decision to refuse dissolution or prorogation is particularly finely balanced, and context specific: the brief account at the start of this chapter does not begin to do justice to all the considerations involved. With military deployment, and parliamentary scrutiny of treaties, the difficulties are of a different kind: difficulties of proportionality, requiring a system of triage to distinguish between major and minor treaties, and different levels of military engagement; but also difficulties of institutional competence and information sharing – all governments have struggled with sharing some military intelligence, and with disclosing their full hand when negotiating treaties.

Fourth, a point worth repeating about parliamentary capacity is differences of size. New Zealand has a single-chamber Parliament with 120 members; Australia has 151 members in the House of Representatives and 75 members of the Senate; Canada has 338 members of the House of Commons, and 105 Senators; while Westminster has 650 MPs and over 800 members of the House of Lords. It is not surprising that New Zealand struggles to maintain the same level of scrutiny as much larger bicameral Parliaments. What is impressive is the effort the Australian Parliament has made to scrutinise treaties through a dedicated joint committee (JSCOT). Canada with a larger Parliament lags far behind. Westminster is catching up, but very late in the day, with the creation of the House of Lords International Agreements Committee in 2021.

16

Reserve Powers in Countries with Written Constitutions

Introduction

This chapter explores parallels between the prerogative and reserve powers in countries with written constitutions. By reserve powers we mean not emergency powers, but reserve powers as an arena of executive autonomy, unconstrained by the legislature: are there equivalent powers in other constitutions, and to what extent are they constrained by the legislature, or the courts?

To explore this question, we have taken four prerogative powers: dissolving Parliament, assent to legislation, the war making power, and entering into treaties. We have sought out and analysed the equivalent power in six democracies with written constitutions: Denmark, France, Germany, Japan, Norway, and the US. We have chosen these six countries because they are all advanced democracies. They all have written constitutions, but of varying dates: the US Constitution is the oldest, from 1787, and the Norwegian is the next oldest, from 1815. The constitutions of the other four countries date from after the Second World War: Japan from 1947, Germany 1949, Denmark 1953, France 1958 (though the Danish Constitution goes back to 1849). Three of the six countries are monarchies like the UK, which might therefore be expected to feature powers similar to the prerogative.

To test whether these reserve powers are the equivalent of prerogative powers, we ask in each case:

- Is this power exercisable by the executive without reference to the legislature?
- What are the constitutional and legal provisions regulating exercise of the power?
- What are the conventions and expectations regulating exercise of the power?
- What are the main instances illustrating how the power is exercised in practice?

And in each case, we set out the relevant provisions of the constitution, with a commentary explaining how the power has been interpreted by the courts, modified by legislation, or regulated by convention. Power is defined in the formal sense as the executive's ability to prevail in decision-making where there is a conflict of preferences between different constitutional actors.[1] In many cases, the executive

[1] S Lukes, *Power: A Radical View*, 2nd edn (Hampshire, Palgrave Macmillan, 2005).

is able to derive legitimacy for this power from the text of the written constitution. Take for instance the decision to go to war. In France, the Constitution allows for the legislature to have a debate within three days of military intervention. Parliament may express its preference, but it is the President who retains the final say.

But in many other cases the position is less clear cut. The constitution may be silent (as the Japanese Constitution is about treaties); it may be Delphic in its brevity (as are many of the provisions under review); it may be completely misleading (as is the case with many of the powers vested in the King in Denmark and Norway). As we shall see, written constitutions can be just as ambiguous as unwritten ones; just as reliant on convention; and continually evolving to reflect changes in political context and practice. These are all points which we develop further in the conclusion.

Table 1 Summary of executive and parliamentary systems in analysed countries

Country	Constitution	Executive System	Parliamentary System
United States	Constitution of the United States 1787	Presidential system featuring an executive President.	The United States Congress is a bicameral legislature composed of the Senate (Upper Chamber) and the House of Representatives (Lower Chamber).
Norway	The Constitution of the Kingdom of Norway 1814	Constitutional monarchy featuring a non-executive monarch and Prime Minister.	The Storting is a unicameral legislature.
Japan	Constitution of Japan 1947	Constitutional monarchy featuring a non-executive Emperor and Prime Minister.	The National Diet is a bicameral legislature composed of the House of Councillors (Upper Chamber) and the House of Representatives (Lower Chamber).
Germany	Basic Law for the Federal Republic of Germany 1949	Federal parliamentary republic featuring a President and Federal Chancellor.	The German Parliament is a bicameral legislature composed of the Bundesrat (Upper Chamber) and the Bundestag (Lower Chamber).
Denmark	The Constitutional Act of Denmark 1953	Constitutional monarchy featuring a non-executive monarch and Prime Minister.	The Folketing is a unicameral legislature.

(continued)

Table 1 ***(Continued)***

Country	Constitution	Executive System	Parliamentary System
France	Constitution of France 1958	Semi-presidential system featuring a President and Prime Minister.	The French Parliament is a bicameral legislature composed of the Senate (Upper Chamber) and the National Assembly (Lower Chamber).

Dissolution

The written constitutions of two out of the six countries analysed in this chapter do not provide for the dissolution of Parliament. In Norway, the Constitution requires the Storting to serve for rigid four-year terms. In the US, the House of Representatives and the Senate are prescribed to serve for two- and six-year terms respectively. In these countries, there exists no reserve power to bring a legislative session to an end and call for an early general election, nor does there exist any executive influence in this sphere.

> The members of the Storting function as such for four successive years.
>
> Article 71, Constitution of Norway

> The House of Representatives shall be composed of Members chosen every second Year by the People of the several States.
>
> Article 1(2), Constitution of the United States

> The Senate of the United States shall be composed of two Senators from each State, chosen by the Legislature thereof for six Years.
>
> Article 1(3), Constitution of the United States[2]

In the remaining four countries, the power of dissolution ranges from being tightly controlled by the legislative body to being at the complete discretion of the executive. The Constitution of Germany sits at the controlled end of this spectrum. Influenced by a post war aversion to political instability, the German Basic Law provides for no general power to dissolve Parliament.[3] Instead, the Basic Law accords for tightly circumscribed conditions in which a dissolution may be sought. Under the first condition, contained in Article 63, where the proposed Chancellor fails to secure a majority in the Bundestag, the President must choose

[2] In 1913, the Seventeenth Amendment to the US Constitution replaced 'chosen by the Legislature thereof' with 'elected by the people thereof', thus providing for direct election to the Senate.

[3] S Theil, 'An Aversion to Weimar: German Constitutional Hesitance on Dissolving the Bundestag' (*UK Constitutional Law Association Blog*, 23 November 2017) www.ukconstitutionallaw.org/2017/11/23/stefan-theil-an-aversion-to-weimar-german-constitutional-hesitance-on-dissolving-the-bundestag/.

between a dissolution or a governing minority. Under the second, contained in Article 68, the President may grant a dissolution on the request of the Chancellor where a motion of no confidence has been passed by the Bundestag. Responsibility over dissolution is thus dispersed between all three constitutional actors; the Chancellor, the Bundestag, and the President. It is not a reserve power controlled solely by the executive.

But this has not prevented the mechanism of dissolution from being abused. On three occasions, Chancellors have exploited the Article 68 provision to initiate a vote of no confidence, seek a mid-term dissolution, and gain a majority: Willy Brandt in 1972, Helmut Kohl in 1982, and Gerhard Schröder in 2005. The President has not once refused a request from the Chancellor. In an attempt to limit further abuse, the Federal Constitutional Court added a proviso to Article 68, that the Chancellor must only seek a dissolution where instability would prevent the ruling government from continuing to govern effectively. The President's affirmative judgement on what is essentially a political question has subsequently been supported by the Federal Constitutional Court.[4]

> The Federal Chancellor shall be elected by the Bundestag without debate on the proposal of the Federal President.
>
> If the person elected does not receive such a majority [of votes from Members of the Bundestag], then within seven days the Federal President shall either appoint him or dissolve the Bundestag.
>
> Article 63, German Basic Law

> If a motion of the Federal Chancellor for a vote of confidence is not supported by the majority of the Members of the Bundestag, the Federal President, upon the proposal of the Federal Chancellor, may dissolve the Bundestag within twenty-one days.
>
> Article 68, German Basic Law

Contrary to Weimar Germany's experience, the Constitution of the Third Republic of France, in force from 1870 to 1940, brought about a different kind of political instability. The power to dissolve the Lower House was exercisable by the President only with the consent of the Senate and was used on two occasions in 1870 and 1877. Viewed as antithetical to the system of parliamentarism fostered in this period, the power of dissolution fell into disuse.[5] In the Fourth Republic, dissolution was permitted to be exercised by the Council of Ministers under limited circumstances of no confidence, and when the Constitution of the Fifth

[4] BVerfG BvE 4/05; BVerfG 1983 EuGRZ 57; M Lovik, 'The Constitutional Court Reviews the Early Dissolution of the West German Parliament' (1983) 7 *Hastings International and Comparative Law Review* 79.

[5] In 1934, President Gaston Doumergue proposed that dissolution should be exercisable by the President on the advice of the Prime Minister, but this amendment was opposed on the 'fear that some future Prime Minister may hold the threat of dissolution over the Chamber as a lever to force through measures which he could never get through by other means': 'M. Doumergue's Problems' *The Spectator* (London, 26 October 1934), 606.

Republic was later drafted in 1958, Article 12 was designed to vest the broad and discretionary reserve power of dissolution in the hands of the President.[6] Today, the President may dissolve the National Assembly at will, although he cannot do so again within a year of this exercise, or when employing the exceptional powers contained in Article 16 in a time of emergency.

The President has utilised Article 12 on five occasions. In 1962 and 1968, Charles de Gaulle dissolved the National Assembly and appealed to the electorate to settle political and national crises. In 1981 and 1988, François Mitterrand dissolved the National Assembly in order to seek a parliamentary majority to implement his political programme. The need to dissolve Parliament in these circumstances was enhanced by the inequality of presidential and prime ministerial terms, although this has since been resolved by the constitutional amendments of 2001 that created equal five-year terms for both offices. Dissolution may still be sought at a moment of personal convenience, as happened the last time the National Assembly was dissolved in 1997 by Jacques Chirac.

> The President of the Republic may, after consulting the Prime Minister and the Presidents of the Houses of Parliament, declare the National Assembly dissolved.
>
> A general election shall take place no fewer than twenty days and no more than forty days after the dissolution.
>
> No further dissolution shall take place within a year following the said election.
>
> Article 12, Constitution of France

In Germany and France, early dissolutions have been the exception: the Bundestag and National Assembly have normally run for their prescribed four- and five-year terms. In Japan, however, the House of Representatives has run a full four-year term on only one occasion since the Constitution came into effect over 70 years ago. The Constitution provides for two mechanisms of dissolution. Under Article 69, the House of Representatives may be dissolved when a motion of no confidence is passed. This has been used on four occasions. Yet the instrument that has been routinely engaged is Article 7, which grants the Prime Minister unfettered reserve power to advise the Emperor on the matter of dissolution.

The Supreme Court of Japan has provided guidance as to when Article 7 may be employed: where a government Bill is rejected in Parliament, where the cabinet needs to ask for the views of the people, or new issues of importance arise.[7] Prime Ministers therefore use the reserve power to time dissolution around policy issues. This was the case for the 'postal dissolution' of 2005 when Junichiro Koizumi

[6] See M Debré, 'Speech before the Council of State' (Paris, 27 August 1958): 'Is there a need to insist on what a dissolution represents? It is the instrument of governmental stability. It can be the reward of a government which appears to have succeeded, the sanction of a government which appears to have failed. It allows a brief dialogue between the Head of State and the nation which can settle a conflict or make the voice of the people heard at a decisive hour.'

[7] Saiko Saibansho, Action for Recognition of the Status as a Member of the House of Representatives and a Claim for Remuneration 1955 (O) 96 (Minshu Vol 14 No 7), 1206.

sought a renewed mandate after the House of Councillors rejected a Bill to privatise the postal services.[8] After Koizumi won a majority of 296 seats, the House of Councillors agreed to pass the Bill.

> The Emperor, with the advice and approval of the Cabinet, shall perform the following acts in matters of state on behalf of the people: Dissolution of the House of Representatives; Proclamation of general election of members of the Diet.
>
> Article 7, Japan Constitution

> If the House of Representatives passes a no-confidence resolution, or rejects a confidence resolution, the Cabinet shall resign en masse, unless the House of Representatives is dissolved within ten days.
>
> Article 69, Japan Constitution

The Constitution of Denmark makes no explicit mention of the reserve power of dissolution. The Folketing is not formally dissolved before a general election and instead sits until a new Parliament is convened. But the Prime Minister does possess the ability to cut short the Folketing's prescribed four-year term and call for an early general election under Article 33(3) of the Danish Constitution. This is akin to the reserve power of dissolution,[9] exercisable by the Prime Minister alone who may do so in pursuit of a renewed mandate, in defiance of blocked legislation, or at a convenient time where he is likely to retain office.[10] In 2007, Anders Fogh Rasmussen utilised the Article 33 power to secure a slim majority and renew his bargaining position. Regardless of political incentive, the design of Article 33 has meant that it is customary for early elections to be called by the Prime Minister.[11]

> The Prime Minister shall cause a general election to be held before the expiration of the period for which the Folketing has been elected.
>
> Article 33(3) Constitution of Denmark

In France, Japan, and Denmark, the existence of a reserve power to dissolve a Parliament similar to the prerogative has resulted in Parliaments being dissolved at the discretion of the executive. Even in Germany, where power has been designed to be split between the executive, head of state and legislature, constitutional

[8] See J Koizumi, 'Press Conference' (8 August 2005): 'The conclusion reached by the Diet is that there is no need for privatization of the postal services. For my part, I would like to ask the people if there really is no need to privatise the postal services. You could even say that my dissolution of the Diet is a postal services dissolution.'; In October 2021, Prime Minister Fumio Kishida dissolved the House of Representatives on the issue of Covid recovery and retained a comfortable majority following the ensuing election.

[9] The Folketing itself recognises this right as one to dissolve the parliament. See Folketinget, *Folketinget – The Danish Parliament* (Christiansborg Palace, October 2013), 8: 'The Prime Minister can dissolve the Parliament, at any time, in the hope of obtaining a more stable majority.'

[10] H Helboe Pederson, 'The Parliament (FOLKETINGET): Powerful, Professional, and Trusted?' in P Christiansen, J Elklit and P Nedergaard (eds), *The Oxford Handbook of Danish Politics* (Oxford, Oxford University Press, 2020), 93.

[11] ME Hansen, 'The Government and the Prime Minister More than Primus Inter Pares' in ibid at 112.

constraints have not prevented the Chancellor from occasionally engineering a mid-term dissolution.

Executive Veto of Legislation

Two of the countries with more modern constitutions, namely Japan and France, used to have veto provisions in their prior settlements. In Japan, the Meiji Constitution (1889–1947) was enacted on the premise of the sovereignty of the Emperor, and thus conferred upon him the legislative power to promulgate and execute laws under Articles 5 and 6.[12] The Diet was only required to comment on legislation that had been initiated by the Emperor or Cabinet. Although the Emperor did not use his Article 6 power to veto legislation,[13] a shift in constitutional thought meant that the Constitution of 1947 eradicated this power and placed sole legislative authority in the Diet. There is thus no executive veto over legislation in Japan.

> A bill becomes a law on passage by both Houses, except as otherwise provided by the Constitution.
>
> Article 59, Constitution of Japan

> The Diet shall be the highest organ of state power, and shall be the sole law-making organ of the State.
>
> Article 41, Constitution of Japan

The Constitution of France 1791 granted the King a suspensive veto over legislation, that could be overridden by the efforts of three successive Parliaments to re-introduce the Bill. It was the use of this veto that helped to trigger the overthrow of the French monarchy and the establishment of the First Republic. Since the Constitution of the Second Republic was enacted in 1842, its text and all subsequent constitutions have included a provision to allow the President before promulgation to return a Bill to Parliament for reconsideration.[14] This provision is now manifested in Article 10, but is seldom used as the National Assembly may insist on promulgation with a simple majority. If (exceptionally) used, it is done to allow Parliament to amend any legislative faults or to evaluate the judgement

[12] I Hirobumi, *Commentaries on the Constitution of the Empire of Japan*, (Tokyo, Igirisu-Hōritsu Gakko, 1889), 12: 'In our Constitution, a positive principle is adopted, that is to say, the laws must necessarily emanate at the command of the Emperor. Hence it is sanction that makes a law. As the laws must necessarily emanate at the command of the Emperor, it naturally follows that he has power to withhold sanction to the same.'

[13] J Banno, *The Establishment of the Japanese Constitutional System* (London, Routledge, 1992), 3.

[14] Under the Third Republic, no President requested the reconsideration of a Bill. Under the Fourth Republic, twelve Bills were reconsidered, and only one of these was considered a Bill of notable importance: RK Gooch, *Governments of Continental Europe*, 1st edn (New York, Macmillan, 1940), 123; PM Williams, *Crisis and Compromise: Politics in the Fourth Republic*, 3rd edn, (London, Longman, 1958), 200.

of the Conseil Constitutionnel.[15] Although Article 10 allows for some degree of behavioural input from the President, it is often recognised that his role is one of *notaire* and he wields no executive veto.[16] On the other hand, the President does not really need a veto given his power to control the agenda of the Assembly on all important matters, and the effective end of *cohabitation* after the constitutional amendments of 2001 (see page 230).

> The President of the Republic shall promulgate Acts of Parliament within fifteen days following the final passage of an Act and its transmission to the Government.
>
> He may, before the expiry of this time limit, ask Parliament to reopen debate on the Act or any sections thereof. Such reopening of debate shall not be refused.
>
> Article 10, Constitution of France

We now move to those countries in which legislation is certified through the process of royal assent. In Denmark, Article 14 of the Constitution provides that legislation is only valid once signed by the King with the countersignature of one of his ministers. This raises the question whether the King is able to veto legislation by not granting assent. No monarch has ever exploited this uncertainty and, in practice, assent is always awarded to legislation that has completed its passage through the Folketing.[17] This is deemed to be due to the textual interpretation of Article 13, which declares the King as above politics. To refuse assent would thus violate the monarch's solemn declaration to adhere to the Constitution Act.[18]

> The signature of the King to resolutions relating to legislation and government shall make such resolutions valid, provided that the signature of the King is accompanied by the signature or signatures of one or more Ministers.
>
> Article 14, Constitution of Denmark

> A Bill passed by the Folketing shall become law if it receives the Royal Assent not later than thirty days after it was finally passed. The King shall order the promulgation of Statutes and shall see to it that they are carried into effect.
>
> Article 22, Constitution of Denmark

> The King shall not be answerable for his actions; his person shall be sacrosanct. The Ministers shall be responsible for the conduct of the government; their responsibility shall be determined by Statute.
>
> Article 13, Constitution of Denmark

[15] A Knapp and V Wright, *The Government and Politics of France*, 5th edn (London, Routledge, 2006), 89.

[16] F Mitterand, 'L'entrietien télévisé du president de la République' *Le Monde* (Paris, 16 July 1993).

[17] H Krunke, 'The Monarch's Constitutional Functions in Denmark' in R Hazell and B Morris (eds), *The Role of Monarchy in Modern Democracy: European Monarchies Compared* (Oxford, Hart Publishing, 2020), 28.

[18] It is debated whether the King's refusal to sign a Bill that he believed to violate the constitution would also violate his solemn declaration. See ibid.

Under Article 78 of the Constitution of Norway, the monarch may veto legislation by way of withholding royal assent to a Bill presented to him as the King in Council. Historically, Kings have made varying use of this power. King Karl III Johan withheld assent to 19 per cent of Bills presented to him between 1815–37. King Oscar II vetoed 2 per cent of Bills presented to him between 1884–1905 and, as with France, it was the use of the veto that triggered the end of his reign.[19] But, since the dissolution of Norway and Sweden in 1905, no King has vetoed legislation passed by the Storting. Of course, in accordance with the constitutional amendment of 1911, the Prime Minister must attach his countersignature to all decisions taken by the King in Council. As a consequence of this amendment, the monarch is unable to veto legislation at his own discretion, but may do so with the support of the Prime Minister. Should any attempt to veto legislation be made in the future, the Storting may override this decision so long as it passes the Bill again following a subsequent election. In this sense, just as the written Constitution provides the monarch of Norway with the reserve power to veto legislation, it also appoints the Storting as the final arbiter in the decision-making process.

> When a Bill has been approved by the Storting in two consecutive sittings, it is sent to the King with a request that it may receive the Royal Assent.
>
> Article 77, Constitution of Norway

> If the King assents to the Bill, he appends his signature, whereby it becomes law.
>
> If he does not assent to it, he returns it to the Storting with a statement that he does not for the time being find it expedient to give his assent. In that case the Bill must not be submitted to the King by the Storting then assembled.
>
> Article 78, Constitution of Norway

So far, analysis of the executive veto of legislation has been largely historical in that more can be said about the past than of any modern practical significance. The reserve power to veto legislation that once applied in Japan and France now no longer exists. The uncertainty of whether a reserve power exists in Denmark is mitigated by the monarch's long-standing obedience to political abstinence. The continuation of the reserve power in Norway is tempered by the political efforts of the last century to curtail the role of the monarch, and can in any event be countered by the next Storting. However, in the last of the two countries addressed in this chapter, the use of the executive veto remains an essential part of their constitutional arrangements.

Under the German Basic Law, the President must certify laws before they are promulgated. The concept of certification is often debated but this is today construed to mean that the President may refuse to sign Bills for procedural error and constitutional invalidity.[20] In 1976, Walter Scheel refused assent to a Bill that

[19] R Smith, 'Political Functions of the Monarch in Norway' in Hazell and Morris, above n 17 at 83–4.

[20] G Taylor, 'Refusals of Assent to Bills passed by Parliament in Germany and Australia' (2008) 36 *Federal Law Review* 83.

had not received the necessary consent of the Bundesrat. In 2006, Horst Köhler rejected a Bill on the basis that the division of responsibilities under Article 84(1) of the Basic Law had been infringed. There have been eight similar incidents since 1949, most recently in 2020 over a Bill on hate speech.[21] There is no requirement for the President's decision to be externally certified, and the procedure that allowed the President to seek an advisory opinion from the Federal Constitutional Court before refusing a Bill in 1951 has since been abolished. In most cases, the substantial examination of legislation is undertaken independently by the President.[22] Under Article 93(1) of the Basic Law and section 13(5) Federal Constitutional Court Act, the Bundestag, Bundesrat, or federal government may bring legal action against the President on the basis that refusal of assent constitutes a breach of his legal duties, although no party has yet done so.

> Laws enacted in accordance with the provisions of this Basic Law shall, after countersignature, be certified by the Federal President and promulgated in the Federal Law Gazette. Statutory instruments shall be certified by the authority that issues them and, unless a law otherwise provides, shall be promulgated in the Federal Law Gazette.
>
> Article 82(1) German Basic Law

In the US, the President's ability to veto legislation under Article 1(7) of the Constitution is viewed to be an inherent element of his role as leader of the executive. The veto was used sparingly until the presidency of Andrew Johnson (1865–69), and mainly on constitutional grounds; but, in the past 100 years, this reserve power has been used to veto 924 pieces of legislation.[23] In recent times, Donald Trump vetoed 10 Bills during his one term presidency, and both Barack Obama and George W Bush vetoed 12 Bills over the course of two terms. Unlike the Norwegian Storting who need only find a simple majority to override the executive's veto, a presidential veto can be overridden by a two-thirds majority of each House. Congress has found this majority in response to 69 presidential vetoes, although in a time of divided partisan alignment, it is becoming increasingly uncommon. Ronald Reagan suffered nine veto overrides while Obama and Trump experienced only one each. In December 2020, the House of Representatives voted 322 to 87 to overturn Donald Trump's veto of the National Defense Authorisation Act and in January 2021 this vote was replicated in the Senate by 81 to 13 votes. The US Constitution thus confers upon the President the reserve power to veto

[21] ibid at 90–5. The law on hate speech was subsequently narrowed and passed in 2021: J Bayer, 'Germany: New law against right-wing extremism and hate crime' (*Inforrm*, 24 April 2021) www.inforrm.org/2021/04/24/germany-new-law-against-right-wing-extremism-and-hate-crime-judit-bayer/.

[22] In another instance in 2006, Horst Köhler sought legal advice from Professor Friedrich Schoch. On one occasion in 1953, the government refused to provide a countersignature to legislation on the opinion that it violated the principle of equality and it was therefore not presented to the President. See Taylor, ibid at 93.

[23] G Copeland, 'When Congress and the President collide' (1983) 45 *Journal of Politics* 696; For a useful list of all presidential vetoes and congressional overrides, see 'List of United States presidential vetoes' (*Wikipedia*, 20 December 2021) www.en.wikipedia.org/wiki/List_of_United_States_presidential_vetoes.

legislation, whilst providing Congress with a power to override; but less than one in ten vetoes have been overridden.

The President may also prevent legislation from coming into force through the 'pocket veto', and previous incumbents have done so on 619 occasions in the last 100 years. After the President has withheld signature from a Bill, it is not returned to Congress and may not be overturned. Congress may seek to repass it, but this often requires significant concessions.[24] Concessions of a similar kind are made when the President uses the threat of vetoing legislation to bargain with the legislature. The larger the concession, the less likely a threatened Bill is to be vetoed.[25]

> Every Bill which shall have passed the House of Representatives and the Senate, shall, before it become a Law, be presented to the President of the United States: If he approve he shall sign it, but if not he shall return it, with his Objections to that House in which it shall have originated, who shall enter the Objections at large on their Journal, and proceed to reconsider it. If after such Reconsideration two thirds of that House shall agree to pass the Bill, it shall be sent, together with the Objections, to the other House, by which it shall likewise be reconsidered, and if approved by two thirds of that House, it shall become a Law.
>
> Article 1(7), Constitution of the United States

Of all the countries under review, the US thus has the strongest executive veto. The Japanese Constitution allows no executive veto; in Denmark and Norway the position is effectively the same because royal assent has become automatic; in France and Germany the President can return a Bill to Parliament on constitutional grounds, but this is rarely done. Only in the US is the executive veto regularly deployed or threatened. But, in shaping legislation, the President still has only a fraction of the power enjoyed by the executive in a parliamentary system, through its right to initiate legislation.

War-Making Power

There are few decisions more important than going to war. In some of the countries with written constitutions surveyed in this chapter, responsibility over the war-making power falls exclusively to the executive. In Japan, however, there is no reserve power to make war. On the contrary, Article 9 of the Constitution of Japan declares the country's dedication to pacifism. This is a significant departure from the Meiji Constitution that awarded command of the armed forces and authority to declare war to the Emperor. In the absence of constitutionally established armed forces, Japan established the National Police Reserve in 1950, to be exercised solely for self-defence purposes; though after the Diet reinterpreted

[24] CM Cameron, *Veto Bargaining: Presidents and the Politics of Negative Power* (Cambridge, Cambridge University Press, 2000), 61.

[25] ibid at 193.

Article 9 in 2014 and later passed the Legislation for Peace and Security 2015, the Self-Defence Forces may now participate in foreign conflict by coming to the defence of allies. As Article 9 is totemic for many Japanese, representing an unambiguous statement that Japan will never again be a belligerent nation, these changes sparked mass protests. Though the long serving Prime Minister Shinzo Abe pledged to amend Article 9 to allow Japan to establish a traditional armed force, the high threshold required for a constitutional amendment meant that he failed to do so before he left office in 2021.[26]

Since the Self-Defence Forces Act was passed in 1954, the Prime Minister, as Commander-in-Chief, can order the deployment of the Self-Defence Forces in times of clear, imminent attack. This is not akin to a reserve power as the Prime Minister must seek the prior approval of the Diet. The Diet has, however, legislated to reduce its oversight. In 1992, it passed the Peace Cooperation Law that established that their consent was not needed for UN operations.[27] In 2001, it passed the Anti-Terrorism Special Measures Law, enabling the Self-Defence Forces to assist with cooperation and support, search and rescue, and other anti-terrorism measures. The Prime Minister is only required to seek the Diet's ex post approval within 20 days of deployment. If the Diet disapproves, all operations are promptly terminated. In 2003, this measure was invoked to send non-combat troops to Iraq without the prior approval of the Diet.

> Aspiring sincerely to an international peace based on justice and order, the Japanese people forever renounce war as a sovereign right of the nation and the threat or use of force as a means of settling international disputes.
>
> In order to accomplish the aim of the preceding paragraph, land, sea, and air forces, as well as other war potential, will never be maintained.
>
> Article 9, Constitution of Japan

Bearing similarities to Japan, the German Basic Law provides for the establishment of armed forces for defence purposes. Aside from vesting command in the Federal Minister of Defence, the Basic Law is silent on the degree to which the President, Chancellor, or the Bundestag are involved in the decision to make war. This ambiguity may originally not have mattered, but as deployments became more frequent in the 1990s, the need for legal regulation became clear.[28] In 1994, the German Constitutional Court upheld the doctrine of 'combined power' to rule that military deployments abroad required prior parliamentary consent.[29] The government's decision to deploy German soldiers to Turkey for measures of aerial

[26] Under Article 96 of the Constitution of Japan, amendments to the Constitution must be initiated by the Diet, agreed upon by a two-thirds vote of each House, and receive a simple majority of votes cast at a referendum.

[27] RD Eldridge and M Katsuhiro, *The Japan Self-Defense Forces Law* (Cambridge Scholars Publishing, 2019), 6.

[28] W Wagner, D Peters and C Glahn, *Parliamentary War Powers Around the World, 1989–2004: A New Dataset* (Geneva, Geneva Centre for the Democratic Control of Armed Forces, 2010), 53.

[29] BVerfGE 2 BvE 3/92; BVerfGE 2 BvE 5/93; BVerfGE 2 BvE 7/93; BVerfGE 2 BvE 8/93.

surveillance in 2003 without parliamentary approval was later deemed to have violated the right of the Bundestag to conclude the decision-making process.[30]

The court's 1994 ruling was embodied in the Parliamentary Participation Act 2004, according to which the government must inform the Bundestag 'in good time' before any military deployment on the mandate, geographical and financial scope, legal basis, and the capabilities and use of troops. A simple majority is then required of the Bundestag in order to approve the operation. The 2004 Act also provides for a simplified procedure for deployments of low intensity that assumed approval has been awarded unless Parliament intervenes within seven days. Since then, the Bundestag has approved of over 70 military deployments. In fact, it has not yet refused a proposal to deploy troops abroad, thanks to informal conversations to settle any disagreements before proposals are introduced.[31] Although it is the Bundestag which makes the final decision, the executive has had a remarkable success rate, in what amounts almost to joint decision making.

> The Federation shall establish Armed Forces for purposes of defence.
>
> Apart from defence, the Armed Forces may be employed only to the extent expressly permitted by this Basic Law.
>
> Article 87a, German Basic Law

> Command of the Armed Forces shall be vested in the Federal Minister of Defence.
>
> Article 65a, German Basic Law

The Constitution of Denmark confers a similar responsibility upon the Folketing. Under Article 19(2) of the Constitution, the use of military force requires the consent of Parliament. In accordance with this provision, the Folketing approved a parliamentary resolution for the deployment of troops to Kosovo in 1998, Afghanistan in 2002, and Iraq in 2003 and 2014, and the Central African Republic in 2014. Consent was, however, not sought when sending special forces to Iraq and a submarine, corvette, and army unit to the Second Gulf War.[32] Central to Denmark's oversight is the need for broad political consensus. In the absence of broad support, Anders Fogh Rasmussen withdrew troops from Iraq before the 2007 election, even though he had 11 votes more than the required majority. Further strengthening the need for consensus, the simple majority required for parliamentary approval was replaced with a two-thirds majority in 2011.

Article 19(3) of the Danish Constitution requires the executive to consult with the Foreign Affairs Committee before making decisions on foreign policy, including the deployment of troops. The Foreign Affairs Committee will then advise the Folketing before a recommendation is introduced. The committee is a central part

[30] BVerfGE 2 BvE 1/03.

[31] Council of Europe Committee of Legal Advisers on Public International Law, *Expression of Consent by States to be Bound by a Treaty: Analytical Report and Country Reports* (Strasbourg, Council of Europe, 2001), 34.

[32] M Houben, *International Crisis Management: The approach of European states* (London, Routledge, 2005), 98.

of the decision-making process, often used to foster consensus.[33] But the executive has sometimes used its power to manipulate the committee. The committee was informed on a selective and delayed basis of deployments to Kosovo, Afghanistan, and Iraq. In 2001, the government engaged in discussion with the US on military contributions in Afghanistan two months before seeking the committee's support for such negotiations. As a result, the Folketing may be confronted with a fait accompli at a time when it would be damaging to renege on the government's private commitments.

> Except for purposes of defence against an armed attack upon the Realm or Danish forces the King shall not use military force against any foreign state without the consent of the Folketing. Any measure which the King may take in pursuance of this provision shall immediately be submitted to the Folketing. If the Folketing is not in session it shall be convoked immediately.
>
> Article 19(2) Constitution of Denmark

In Norway, Article 25 of the Constitution appoints the King as Commander-in-Chief of the armed forces and declares that the consent of the Storting is required for the deployment of the territorial army. In 1945, it was observed that 'the aim of [Article 25] was to prevent Norwegian troops from being used as mercenaries, and it was not supposed to be a legal obstacle against military disposition to strengthen the UN'[34] and similar organisations such as NATO. Requiring the consent of the Storting is thus not considered to be compulsory when UN and NATO obligations provide legitimacy for intervention, but the government has not been consistent in consulting the legislature; seeking consent before participating in the NATO air campaign of Kosovo in 1999, but failing to do so in the NATO endorsed bombing of Afghanistan in 2001. The executive retains the discretion as to when the legislature should be consulted, but does not possess a broad reserve power to engage in war.

> The King is Commander-in-Chief of the land and naval forces of the Realm.
>
> The territorial army and the other troops which cannot be classed as troops of the line must never, without the consent of the Storting, be employed outside the borders of the Realm.
>
> Article 25, Constitution of Norway

The US and France lie at the other end of the spectrum, with the executive having primacy over decisions to engage in armed conflict. In the US, Congress is empowered to declare war, and although it routinely did so prior to the Korean War in 1950, formal declarations of war are seldom issued in modern times. Today, Article 2(2) of the US Constitution, which makes the President Commander-in-Chief,

[33] ibid at 85.

[34] St prp nr 5, *Om Norges tiltredelse av De Forente Nasjoner* (Oslo, Utenriksdepartementet, 1945); C Ku and HK Jacobsen, *Democratic Accountability and the Use of Force in International Law*, (Cambridge, Cambridge University Press, 2009), 166.

is construed to grant a high degree of autonomy over military action that falls short of a formal declaration of war.[35] The War Powers Resolution, enacted in 1973 (via override of President Richard Nixon's veto), sought to curtail this autonomy by allowing Congress to adopt a concurrent resolution to terminate the use of armed forces that had been engaged without congressional approval.[36] Presidents have resisted acknowledging the constitutionality of the War Powers Resolution, but have usually acted consistently with it.

The Resolution also introduced other forms of ex post control, requiring the President to submit a report to Congress within 48 hours of the engagement of the armed forces into hostilities, and allowing Congress to terminate such engagement by withholding re-authorisation after 60 days. The Resolution encouraged the convention that the President should consult with Congress in 'every possible instance' before introducing the armed forces into hostilities, but consultation has often been evaded, by successive Presidents. In 2020, Donald Trump launched an airstrike in Iraq without congressional approval. After the Senate attempted to curtail the reserve power of the President by requiring him to seek congressional approval before launching any further military action in Iraq,[37] Trump vetoed the measure and claimed that Article 2 of the Constitution and the Authorisation for Use of Military Force Against Iraq Resolution provided adequate legitimacy for him to so do.[38]

> The Congress shall have Power to declare War.
>
> Article 1(8), Constitution of the United States
>
> The President shall be Commander in Chief of the Army and Navy of the United States.
>
> Article 2(2), Constitution of the United States

In France, there is no constitutional requirement for the President to consult Parliament before deploying the military, and the National Assembly has played no part in authorising deployments to the Gulf War, Yugoslavia, or Afghanistan. In 2007, the *Balladur Report*, commissioned by Nicolas Sarkozy, expressed dissatisfaction at the National Assembly's minimal role in military matters that could have potential consequences for France's reputation and future.[39] Following a narrow

[35] This role was not designed to grant the President this authority. See A Hamilton, 'The Federalist No 69' in A Hamilton, J Madison and J Jay, *The Federalist Papers* (Ian Shapiro ed, New Haven, Yale University Press, 2009), 349: 'The President is to be commander-in-chief of the army and navy of the United States. In this respect his authority would be nominally the same with that of the King of Great Britain, but in substance much inferior to it. It would amount to nothing more than the supreme command and directive of the military and naval forces, as first General and Admiral of the confederacy; while that of the British kings extends to the declaring of war and to the raising and regulating of fleets and armies, – all which, by the Constitution under consideration, would appertain to the Legislature.'

[36] 50 USC Ch 33.

[37] SJ Res 68.

[38] D Trump, 'Presidential Veto Message to the Senate for SJ Res 68' (White House, 6 May 2020).

[39] E Balladur, *Une Ve République plus démocratique – Comité de reflexion et de proposition sur la modernisation et le rééquilibrage des institutions de la Ve République* (Department of Legal and Administrative Information, 29 October 2007).

parliamentary vote on the matter, Article 35 was amended to require the executive to inform Parliament of its decision to engage in foreign hostilities within three days.[40] A debate may be held, but a vote is not required. The opportunity for debate may provide evidence of a conflict between the executive and legislature, but it is the executive which possesses the reserve power to conclude the decision. After four months of hostilities, the National Assembly is required to authorise continuation of the military mission. The Assembly has since exercised its ex post authority on several occasions, voting for the continuation of deployment in Kosovo in 2010, Libya in 2011, and Syria in 2017. Nevertheless, the *Balladur Report*'s aim to address the 'presidentialisation' of the French regime was unsuccessful as the ultimate war-making power continues to rest with the President.

> The President of the Republic shall be Commander-in-Chief of the Armed Forces. He shall preside over the higher national defence councils and committees.
>
> Article 15, Constitution of France

> A declaration of war shall be authorised by Parliament.
>
> The Government shall inform Parliament of its decision to have the armed forces intervene abroad, at the latest three days after the beginning of said intervention. It shall detail the objectives of the said intervention. This information may give rise to a debate, which shall not be followed by a vote.
>
> Where the said intervention shall exceed four months, the Government shall submit the extension to Parliament for authorization.
>
> Article 35, Constitution of France

There is thus a range of different practice in relation to the legislature's involvement in decisions to go to war. In Germany and Denmark, reflecting their consensual political culture, the legislature is closely involved: the Bundestag has approved over 70 military deployments, and the Folketing has almost always been consulted before Danish troops are deployed abroad. At the other end of the spectrum are France and the US, with no requirement of prior legislative approval. In France, the President is only required to inform Parliament after military deployment, and Parliament must authorise continuation of the mission after four months. Similarly, in the US, despite the Constitution giving Congress the power to declare war, in practice any control is generally ex post: the President must inform Congress within 48 hours, and Congress has the right to terminate engagement after 60 days.

The Ratification of Treaties

Certain constitutions very broadly lay out the circumstances in which parliamentary consent is required for ratification of treaties, but leave a considerable amount

[40] S Boyron, *The Constitution of France: A Contextual Analysis* (Oxford, Hart Publishing, 2012), 134.

of discretion as to when these circumstances are fulfilled. This is true of Denmark, and especially of Norway. In Denmark, parliamentary consent is required for agreements involving territorial changes and those requiring domestic legislative implementation. Treaties of this character may be consented to by a simple majority. Similarly, in Norway, parliamentary approval must be sought for treaties where implementation necessitates the enactment of legislation. Both constitutions provide that the Folketing and Storting must consent to treaties of 'major importance' and 'special importance', although as the exact scope of these expressions is unclear, the Prime Ministers of both countries retain a limited reserve power. One notable difference between the two countries is that whilst Article 19 of the Constitution of Denmark requires the consent of the Folketing in order to terminate an international agreement, no similar provision is included in the Constitution of Norway.

> Provided that without the consent of the Folketing the King shall not undertake any act whereby the territory of the Realm will be increased or decreased, nor shall he enter into any obligation which for fulfilment requires the concurrence of the Folketing, or which otherwise is of major importance; nor shall the King, except with the consent of the Folketing, terminate any international treaty entered into with the consent of the Folketing.
>
> Article 19, Constitution of Denmark

> Treaties on matters of special importance, and, in all cases, treaties whose implementation, according to the Constitution, necessitates a new law or a decision by the Storting, are not binding until the Storting has given its consent thereto.
>
> Article 26, Constitution of Norway

The reservation of certain treaties for parliamentary approval is also apparent in Germany, where Article 59(2) of the Basic Law provides that the Bundestag must approve of treaties that regulate political relations and treaties concerning federal legislation.[41] In 1952, the Federal Constitutional Court ruled that the regulation of political relations must directly affect the existence of the state, its integrity, or independence; and treaties concerning federal legislation must mean those which could only be carried out through new laws.[42] Under this approach, the government retained a large amount of discretion as to when it could use the reserve power to approve treaties as executive agreements. Since then, the court has adopted a broader position, arguing that Article 59(2) should be interpreted to include intergovernmental agreements that are of comparable weight and intensity to those requiring domestic legislation[43] and those that exceed existing legislation.[44] In its judgment on the Lisbon Treaty, the court placed a limit on integration of the European Union (EU) and required that parliamentary approval be

[41] Approval of the Bundesrat is only sought for treaties concerning certain legislative treaties.
[42] BVerfGE 2 BvE 2/51.
[43] BVerfGE 2 BvE 6/99.
[44] BVerfGE 2 BvE 2/07.

awarded to treaties that extend EU competencies.[45] These decisions have extended the circumstances in which the legislature is required to consent, but still leave the government with a wide measure of discretion.

> Treaties that regulate the political relations of the Federation or relate to subjects of federal legislation shall require the consent or participation, in the form of a federal law, of the bodies responsible in such a case for the enactment of federal law.
>
> Article 59(2) German Basic Law

Article 53 of the French Constitution requires parliamentary approval for the ratification of a wide range of treaties (see the text below). Such treaties are required to receive a simple majority in the National Assembly and the Senate. If a treaty appears to represent a challenge to the Constitution, the President must refer the matter to the Conseil Constitutionnel under Article 54, so that the court may advise whether the treaty requires a constitutional amendment.[46] In these cases, the President may summon the National Assembly and the Senate as one to reach a three-fifths majority in favour of amending the Constitution to make way for the treaty.

Where a treaty falls outside the scope of Article 53, the President has a reserve power to conclude negotiations through an executive agreement. Since 1998, the courts have upheld their responsibility under Article 55 to prioritise ratified treaties over Acts of Parliament in order to question whether executive agreements are made in violation of Article 53.[47] The court thus possesses the competence to deem the application of executive agreements invalid where they have not been duly ratified or approved. In 2001, the court declared the 1994 Franco-Senegalese accord as invalid on the basis that it had not obtained legislative authorisation and required the implementation of an Act of Parliament.[48] Here, the President's reserve power is regulated by the judiciary.

> Peace Treaties, Trade agreements, treaties or agreements relating to international organisation, those committing the finances of the State, those modifying provisions which are the preserve of statute law, those relating to the status of persons, and those involving the ceding, exchanging or acquiring of territory, may be ratified or approved only by an Act of Parliament.
>
> Article 53, Constitution of France

In contrast to France, the Constitution of Japan does not define what treaties might require the approval of the Diet.[49] Parliamentary consultation has thus relied

[45] BVerfGE 2 BvE 2/08.

[46] Certain treaties of constitutional importance, including the European Convention on Human Rights, were not referred to the French Constitutional Court and were not subject to parliamentary assent. Since the Treaty of Maastricht, the President has routinely referred EU treaties to the French Constitutional Court.

[47] CE Ass 18 December 1998 SARL Parc d'activités de Blotzheim et SCI Hasselaecker.

[48] Cass Civ 29 May 2001 Agence pour la sécurité de la navigation aérienne en Afrique.

[49] Under the former Meiji Constitution, the approval of the Diet was not required and the Emperor retained the reserve power to conclude treaties independently.

on the development of convention. In 1974, Foreign Minister Masayoshi Ohira announced in a statement that parliamentary approval was required in order to approve treaties that require legislation for their implementation; international agreements including budgetary issues; those which create fiscal obligations; and those which are politically important.[50] It is for the executive to decide whether a treaty falls under the Ohira principles and must be approved by a majority of votes in both Houses. If not, it may be concluded by the government alone as an executive agreement. To provide an example, the government has often used its existing authority under the Foreign Exchange and Foreign Trade Control Law 1949 to conclude both multilateral and bilateral trade agreements without parliamentary approval.[51]

> The Cabinet, in addition to other general administrative functions, shall … conclude treaties. However, it shall obtain prior or, depending on circumstances, subsequent approval of the Diet.
>
> Article 73, Constitution of Japan

Under Article 2 of the US Constitution, the Senate must provide consent to treaties before they are ratified. If two-thirds of the Senate vote in favour, the President may proceed to ratify the treaty. Since the Supreme Court declined to review Jimmy Carter's unilateral termination of the Sino-American Mutual Defense Treaty, the President has been able to withdraw from international agreements alone.[52] Congress has also legislated to reduce its role in relation to trade agreements, under the Commerce Clause of the Constitution which gives Congress the power to regulate commerce with foreign nations. Originating in the Trade Act of 1974, and renewed by the Trade Promotion Authority Act of 2015, the President was granted 'fast-track' authority to negotiate and conclude international trade agreements.[53] These agreements were then introduced to the Senate, automatically discharged from all committee scrutiny hearings, awarded limited opportunity for debate, and subject to a simple majority vote.[54] Under the limitations imposed by the Act, the fast-track authority expired in 2021 and has not since been renewed.

The President retains considerable flexibility when deciding how international agreements should be concluded, and what form they should take. The executive has developed three methods for doing so: agreements that require the authorisation of Congress prior to negotiation; those that require the approval of Congress after negotiation and before ratification; and sole executive agreements, ratified by

[50] *National Diet*, House of Representatives Foreign Affairs Committee 72d (20 February 1974).

[51] Y Iwasaw, *International Law, Human Rights, and Japanese Law: The Impact of International Law on Japanese Law* (Oxford, Oxford University Press, 1998), 24.

[52] HH Koh, 'Presidential Power to Terminate International Agreements' (2018) 128 *Yale Law Journal* 432, 434.

[53] Authorisation of this authority lapsed from 1994–2002 and 2007–15.

[54] US Congress, *Trade Promotion Authority Act (TPA)* (Congressional Research Service IF10038, December 2020), 1.

the President on his own constitutional authority. The President may be incentivised to limit the contents of executive agreements to that contained in domestic existing legislation;[55] but in practice, they have become the primary instrument by which international agreements are reached.[56]

> He shall have Power, by and with the Advice and Consent of the Senate, to make Treaties, provided two thirds of the Senators present concur.
>
> Article 2(2), Constitution of the United States

The constitutional provisions for the ratification of treaties are thus stricter than the requirements in the UK, in that they all require the approval of the legislature, rather than notification, which is what the codified Ponsonby Rule amounts to (see chapter eight). In France and Germany, the courts have also become involved in defining and tightening the circumstances where parliamentary approval is required. But all countries seek to distinguish between important treaties, especially those requiring legislation, or affecting the state's integrity or independence, which will require parliamentary approval; and lesser agreements which can be left to the executive – leaving the executive with some discretion as to what can be concluded by executive agreement.

Conclusion

A common critique of the royal prerogative is that it is too vague and uncertain; that it allows too much latitude to the executive; that it is too reliant on convention; and that it should be codified, and more tightly regulated by Parliament. What this chapter has shown is that these criticisms can also be levelled at the equivalent reserve powers in countries with written constitutions. All constitutions have gaps and silences, and we have included extracts from the constitutional texts to show how ambiguous and obscure many of them are.[57] That is not meant to be a criticism of written constitutions: it is inevitable, given that constitutions are high level texts leaving any detail to be provided in subsequent legislation. In many cases, as we have seen, subsequent legislation has been introduced to regulate more tightly the war-making power, or the executive's power to make treaties. But again, as we have seen, that still leaves a wide margin of uncertainty, and discretion for the executive: in all the countries under review, it is not completely clear which treaties require the approval of the legislature, and which can be ratified independently by

[55] Eg, the Paris Agreement, entered into through executive agreement by President Obama in 2016 and President Biden in 2021, did not exceed the scope of the Clean Air Act.

[56] O Hathaway, 'Presidential Power over International law: Restoring the Balance' (2009) 119 *Yale Law Journal* 140, 150.

[57] M Foley, *The Silence of Constitutions* (Oxford, Routledge, 1989); M Loughlin, 'The Silences of Constitutions' (2018) 16 *International Journal of Constitutional Law* 922.

the executive. Indeed, an element of discretion runs through all executive power: a conclusion we return to in chapter nineteen.[58]

It is difficult to generalise from the experience of six other countries, but they all provide examples of reserve powers which grant the executive a high degree of autonomy: indeed, in several cases more autonomy than that enjoyed by the British Crown or government under the prerogative. The French President and the Danish Prime Minister have open ended, and frequently exercised, powers to dissolve Parliament. The German President and the American President have power to veto legislation, which again they have exercised. The French President and the American President have considerable latitude to authorise military intervention without approval of the legislature. And in all six countries, the executive has discretion to ratify some international agreements without the approval of the legislature: unlike the UK, where all treaties must be laid before Parliament before ratification, even if Parliament then does little to scrutinise them (see chapter eight).

The third criticism of the prerogative, and of the UK's unwritten constitution, is that it is too reliant on convention: on self-restraint by constitutional actors not abusing their powers, or exercising them to the full. But written constitutions are also heavily reliant on convention. A good example of this is the Ohira principles in Japan, that regulate which treaties require parliamentary approval. Another example would be the granting of royal assent in Denmark and Norway which, over the years, has become automatic as it has in the UK and thus ceases to confer a power of veto.

A final observation from this brief comparative survey is how much all these reserve powers are still evolving. Written constitutions are fondly supposed to deliver certainty and stability; but in truth, they have to be fluid and capable of adapting to changing circumstances. They do so through court rulings, through new legislation, and through changing conventions. This chapter has given examples of all of these: it is striking how recent many of the examples are, and how all the constitutions are still evolving, just like that of the UK.

[58] H Mansfield, *Taming the Prince: The Ambivalence of Executive Power* (New York, Free Press, 1989); M Cohn, *A Theory of the Executive Branch: Tension and Legality* (Oxford, Oxford University Press, 2021).

PART 5

Reform of the Prerogative

17

The Role of the Courts

> This Court has … concluded that the Prime Minister's advice to Her Majesty was unlawful, void and of no effect. … This means that when the Royal Commissioners walked into the House of Lords it was as if they walked in with a blank sheet of paper. The prorogation was also void and of no effect. Parliament has not been prorogued.
>
> Baroness Hale (2019)[1]

Introduction

The role of the courts is sometimes misunderstood. Our task in this chapter is to outline that role as it stands but also to look at where it has come from and what challenges it faces going forward. The courts do not choose the cases which come before them. But in certain challenges to the prerogative they can in effect decline to adjudicate, by deciding that the case is non-justiciable. In recent years the courts have shown greater willingness to review prerogative powers previously regarded as non-justiciable. But the direction of travel is not all one way: there is ebb and flow, with some decisions where the courts appear to have expanded the scope of the prerogative, or upheld questionable exercises of prerogative power. Those cases attract far less attention from politicians than cases like *R (Miller) v The Prime Minister* (*Miller 2*), the source of the epigraph to this chapter.

It was in *Miller 2* that Baroness Hale, then President of the Supreme Court, announced in September 2019 the unanimous conclusion of all eleven justices that the Prime Minister had unlawfully advised the Queen to prorogue Parliament. The case was immediately controversial. However famous, *Miller 2* was an unusual case in the courts' role in monitoring use of the prerogative. Most such cases involve the rights of individuals. As a consequence, their subject-matter is dominated by those powers classed in this book as 'executive' (part three). *Miller 2*, by contrast, was a case about the use of a 'personal' prerogative (part two) and concerned the relationship between the Crown and Parliament, rather than between the Crown and individuals.

[1] *R (Miller) v The Prime Minister; Cherry v Advocate General*, UKSC Press Summary; *cf* [2019] UKSC 41, [69].

Thirty-five years before the judgment in *Miller 2*, the way in which the courts approach the prerogative was authoritatively set out in *Council of Civil Service Unions v Minister for the Civil Service* (*GCHQ*).[2] The Prime Minister (as Minister for the Civil Service) had banned employees of GCHQ from joining trades unions, by Order in Council issued under the prerogative. Although the House of Lords found that this was lawful, the Law Lords concurred that the royal prerogative was not immune from judicial review. Only those prerogative powers which fell into 'excluded categories' would be immune from its full scope.[3]

GCHQ was a turning-point in the courts' approach to the prerogative by establishing that the standard tools of judicial review apply.[4] Even the 'excluded categories' are subject to limited control by the courts. There are three stages of judicial consideration of a prerogative power:[5]

- Does the power exist?
- Is the extent of the power limited by the common law and statute?
- Was the exercise of the power lawful?

Only the last of these does not apply to the 'excluded categories'. In this chapter, we examine each of these three stages. Furthermore, we explore emerging challenges to the courts' approach, both from those seeking to limit executive autonomy and those seeking to preserve (and even expand) it.

Existence and Scope

The recognition of prerogative powers is a matter for the courts and the common law: as Sir Edward Coke famously said in the *Case of Proclamations*, 'the King has no prerogative but that which the law of the land allows him'.[6] The first task for the court, therefore, is to determine whether such a prerogative power exists, and whether its scope extends to include the action under review.

A Beginning

The modern law on the limits of the prerogative relies on principles derived from the *Case of Proclamations*. King James I had issued proclamations, including a

[2] *Council of Civil Service Unions and others v Minister for the Civil Service* [1985] AC 374.
[3] ibid at 418 (Lord Roskill).
[4] See *Belhaj v Straw* [2017] UKSC 3, [95]; *Al-Jedda v Secretary of State for Defence* [2010] EWCA Civ 758, [206]-[208].
[5] Sometimes, the second stage is split into two: J Williams, 'Prerogative Power after *Miller*: An Analysis in Four E's' in M Elliott, J Williams and A Young (eds), *The UK Constitution After Miller: Brexit and Beyond* (Oxford, Hart Publishing, 2018).
[6] *Case of Proclamations* (1610) 77 ER 1352; (1611) 12 Co Rep 74.

prohibition on new buildings in and about London. The prohibition could be lifted by payment of a fine – an attempt to bypass the Commons in introducing taxation. Sir Edward Coke, Chief Justice of the Common Pleas, stated that such a proclamation was not within the King's prerogative: the King could not by proclamation change 'any part of the common law, or statute law or customs of the realm'.[7]

Three significant points arise from *Proclamations*. First, that the prerogative is to be defined by the common law courts. Second, novel prerogative powers that affected legal rights could not be recognised, because (third) the proper place to create such powers was Parliament, with the assent of the House of Commons paramount in matters of taxation.

'Look in the Books'

The courts therefore approach the identification of prerogative powers by use of precedent. The method was made clear by Lord Bingham in *R (Bancoult) v Secretary of State for Foreign and Commonwealth Affairs*, adopting a famous dictum by Lord Camden in *Entick v Carrington*: 'If it is law, it will be found in our books. If it is not to be found there, it is not law.'[8] A consequence is that no new prerogatives can be created. As Lord Justice Diplock famously stated, 'It is 350 years and a civil war too late for the Queen's courts to broaden the prerogative.'[9]

However, in *R v Secretary of State for the Home Department, ex parte Northumbria Police Authority*, the Court of Appeal recognised (obiter) a power to keep the peace that was largely unsupported by precedent.[10] The Home Secretary had issued a circular authorising the Home Office to supply CS gas and plastic batons from a central store, even though the local police authority had refused to approve their use. The Divisional Court held that the Home Secretary could rely on the prerogative power of keeping the peace. The police authority argued that there was no such prerogative power because the authorities were silent on it. In the Court of Appeal, however, Lord Justice Nourse said that: 'I do not think that the scarcity [of authorities] is of any real significance. It has not at any stage in our history been practicable to identify all the prerogative powers of the Crown.'[11]

This approach seems at odds with the standard method set out in *Bancoult*. Although the Court of Appeal in *Northumbria* has found some defenders,[12] it has

[7] *Case of Proclamations* (1611) 12 Co Rep 74, 75; 77 ER 1352, 1353.

[8] *Entick v Carrington* (1765) 19 St Tr 1030, 1066; *R (Bancoult) v Secretary of State for Foreign and Commonwealth Affairs* [2000] 2 AC 115, 131.

[9] *BBC v Johns* [1965] Ch 32, 79; *cf Ruddock v Valaris* [2001] FCA 1329, [30].

[10] *R v Secretary of State for the Home Department, ex parte Northumbria Police Authority* [1989] QB 26.

[11] ibid at 56.

[12] S White, 'Keeping the Peace of the Realm' (2021) 42 *Adelaide Law Review* 101, 118-9.

more often been criticised.[13] Robert Ward has commented that the court deserves 'Full marks … for creative thinking.'[14] There are, however, three points of interest. First, the case did *not* concern the legal rights of individuals: it was a dispute between the Home Office and the police authority.[15] Courts may impose stricter limits on the prerogative where individuals' rights are concerned. Second, the court was reluctant to find against a power 'so valuable to the common good'.[16] Third, Lord Justice Purchas distinguished 'between the underlying prerogative power which indisputably resides in the Crown to "protect the realm," "keep the Queen's peace," "make treaties" etc. and the various ways in which that power is exercised and has been exercised over many centuries'.[17] Such a distinction highlights a difficulty in the precedent-based approach: prerogative powers derive from broad divisions of power between the monarch and other bodies; in novel situations, there will rarely be a direct precedent to prove a prerogative power, even if it would have been accepted as a royal power many centuries ago.

Although the approach taken in *Northumbria* has rarely been tested subsequently, it is likely to be confined to circumstances of necessity.[18] Even in emergencies, modern practice is usually to rely on broad statutory powers. For example, the government's response to the Covid-19 pandemic took the form of regulations under the Public Health Act 1984,[19] alongside a new Coronavirus Act 2020.

The First Limit: The Common Law

'[I]t is a fundamental principle of the UK constitution that, unless primary legislation permits it, the Royal Prerogative does not enable ministers to change statute law or common law.'[20] There are two important legal limits on the exercise of the prerogative: it must be consistent with (a) the common law and (b) statutes enacted by Parliament. However, the simple statement in *Proclamations* that the prerogative 'cannot change any part of the common law'[21] ignores a more complex reality.

[13] C Gearty, 'The Courts and Recent Exercises of the Prerogative' (1987) 46 *Cambridge Law Journal* 372, 374; S Payne, 'The Royal Prerogative' in M Sunkin and S Payne (eds), *The Nature of the Crown: A Legal and Political Analysis* (Oxford, Oxford University Press, 1999), 77; L Zines, 'The Inherent Executive Power of the Commonwealth' (2005) 16 *Public Law Review* 279, 287.

[14] R Ward, 'Baton Rounds and Circulars' (1988) 47 *Cambridge Law Journal* 155, 156.

[15] AW Bradley, 'Police powers and the prerogative' [1988] *Public Law* 298, 301-2.

[16] *ex parte Northumbria Police Authority*, above n 10 at [58].

[17] ibid at [45]-[46].

[18] See *Crown of Leon (Owners v Admiralty Commissioners)* [1921] 1 KB 590, 604; *Burmah Oil Co (Burma Trading) Ltd v Lord Advocate* [1965] AC 75, 115, 136.

[19] Public Health (Control of Disease) Act 1984, part 2A.

[20] *R (Miller) v Secretary of State for Exiting the European Union* [2017] UKSC 5, [50]; *cf Bancoult*, above n 8 at [44].

[21] *Case of Proclamations* (1611) 12 Co Rep 74, 75; 77 ER 1352, 1353.

As Sir William Wade recognised, one of the characteristics of a prerogative power is that it is '*legal* power – that is to say, the ability to alter people's rights, duties or status'.[22] For example, the granting of a pardon drastically alters the legal rights and status of a convict (see chapter eleven). However, even though prerogative powers *can* affect legal rights, that does not mean the prerogative can 'change any part of the common law'. This was judicially recognised in *Miller 1*: 'the important point is that [the prerogative] does not change the law, because the law has always authorised the exercise of the power'.[23]

The Supreme Court clarified that the prerogative could lawfully have legal consequences in two categories of case. First, the prerogative may change 'the facts to which the law applies'.[24] Most significantly, where war is declared, some otherwise lawful actions will be rendered treasonable, and the property of enemy aliens will be liable to confiscation. Second, sometimes 'it is inherent in the prerogative power that its exercise will affect the legal rights or duties of others'.[25] Thus, in *GCHQ* the government could alter the terms of service for civil servants, and in *Burmah Oil Co (Burma Trading) Ltd v Lord Advocate* it could destroy property in wartime (although with a duty to pay compensation).[26] In such cases, the 'better view' is that the common law *accommodates* the prerogative power and adjusts 'conflicting rights and interests'.[27]

Miller 1

In *R (Miller) v Secretary of State for Exiting the European Union* (*Miller 1*), the government sought to use the treaty-making power to withdraw from the treaties of the European Union (EU), following the 2016 referendum endorsing the UK's exit from the EU.[28] Gina Miller (and Deir dos Santos) claimed that the prerogative power could not do such a thing. Withdrawal would mean the loss of EU law rights that had direct effect in domestic law under the European Communities Act 1972.

In the Divisional Court, the claimants succeeded on the grounds that withdrawal would 'alter the domestic law of the UK and modify rights acquired in domestic law'[29] and because the prerogative had been abrogated by statute.[30] The Supreme Court found in their favour on slightly different and more novel grounds.

[22] HWR Wade, *Constitutional Fundamentals* (London, Stevens & Sons, 1980), 46.
[23] *Miller* [2017], above n 20 at [52].
[24] ibid at [53].
[25] ibid at [52].
[26] *Council of Civil Service Unions*, above n 2; *Burmah Oil Co*, above n 18.
[27] A Twomey, '*Miller* and the Prerogative' in Elliott, Williams and Young (eds), above n 5 at 74; *cf* S Sedley, 'The sound of silence: constitutional law without a constitution' (1994) 110 *Law Quarterly Review* 270, 290.
[28] The power of withdrawal was a logical corollary of the treaty-making power: *Miller* [2017], above n 20 at [54].
[29] *R (Miller) v Secretary of State for Exiting the European Union* [2016] EWHC 2768 (Admin), 95-96.
[30] ibid at 97-101.

The 1972 Act was a '"conduit pipe" by which EU law [was] introduced into UK domestic law'.[31] First, EU law was 'an entirely new, independent and overriding source of domestic law' and 'It would be inconsistent with long-standing and fundamental principle for such a far-reaching change to the UK constitutional arrangements [as withdrawal] to be brought about by ministerial decision … alone.'[32] It was for Parliament to effect or approve such a change.[33] Second, existing rights in EU law would also be interfered with, which the prerogative could not do (as the Divisional Court had said).[34] Third, the language of the 1972 Act demonstrated a 'clear implication' that only legislation could shut off the conduit pipe.[35]

This is not the place to debate the rights and wrongs of the judgments in *Miller 1*. However, we make two observations about the majority judgment. First, the second and third reasons given cohere with those in the Divisional Court. It is the first reason – that the prerogative could not make 'such a far-reaching change to the UK constitutional arrangements' – that is novel. On one view, it is evidence for a principle that the prerogative cannot frustrate such an important ('constitutional') statute, in this case by leaving the 'conduit pipe' standing empty.[36] On another, it is an assertion about the proper place of Parliament in determining the UK's constitutional order,[37] perhaps even a 'constitutional principle'.

Second, the majority's approach places a high value on individual rights. As we have seen, a concern for individual rights is a theme running through the cases. It has recently been clearly stated by the Supreme Court in another case:

> This court is required by long-established law to examine the nature and extent of the prerogative power and to determine whether the respondent has transgressed its limits *particularly* where the prerogative power may be being used to infringe upon an individual's rights.[38] (emphasis added)

The Security Services: Breaking the Law

Individual rights do not, however, always win the day. In *Privacy International v Secretary of State for Foreign and Commonwealth Affairs* (the *Third Direction* case),[39] the question arose whether the prerogative could ever authorise the

[31] *Miller* [2017], above n 20 at [65].
[32] ibid at [80]-[81].
[33] ibid at [82].
[34] ibid at [83].
[35] ibid at [84].
[36] P Craig, 'Epilogue: *Miller*, the Legislature and the Executive', in S Juss and M Sunkin (eds), *Landmark Cases in Public Law* (Oxford, Hart Publishing, 2017), 311.
[37] Twomey, above n 27 at 85-6.
[38] *Elgizouli v Secretary of State for the Home Department* [2020] UKSC 10; [2020] 2 WLR 857, [161].
[39] *Privacy International v Secretary of State for Foreign and Commonwealth Affairs* [2021] EWCA Civ 330.

commission of an unlawful act. Before the Security Service Act 1989, MI5 was constituted under the prerogative and required to conduct its operations in accordance with a Directive (the 'Third Direction') issued by the Home Secretary in 1952 (see chapter nine). Undercover agents might sometimes 'need to participate in conduct which may or would be criminal or tortious in order to maintain their cover'.[40] Although the *Third Direction* case was mainly concerned with the situation after 1989, the Court of Appeal also considered the position as it had been under the prerogative.

In the view of the court, it is possible for the prerogative to authorise the commission of an unlawful act.[41] In support of this proposition were adduced three cases. First, *De Keyser's Royal Hotel v Attorney-General* and *Burmah Oil* showed respectively that unlawful trespass and deliberate destruction of property could be carried out under the prerogative 'in the case of necessity, in circumstances of defence of the realm in time of war'.[42] Second, the court extended this principle to defence of the realm *outside* wartime, citing in support the 'broad approach' of *Northumbria Police Authority*, and quoting Lord Justice Nourse: 'There is no historical or other basis for denying to the war prerogative a sister prerogative of keeping the peace within the realm.'[43]

The court's remarks come as something of a surprise. The government thought the outcome sufficiently in doubt that it sought enactment of the Covert Human Intelligence Sources (Criminal Conduct) Act 2021.[44] The judgment was roundly criticised by Robert Craig and Gavin Phillipson, who found the reliance on the prerogative of keeping the peace (ie preventing crime) as authority to commit crime 'close to being a contradiction in terms'.[45] Furthermore, as Hayley Hooper has noted, the broad approach of the court in *Third Direction* raises a 'glimmer of doubt' as to whether Lord Justice Laws was right to say in another case that '*All* the functions of the Security Service are and have been since the coming into force of the Security Service Act 1989, statutory functions' (emphasis added).[46] If the Home Secretary in *Northumbria* was entitled to rely upon the dormant public order role of sheriffs, despite the establishment of the police 'for many years now', what other skeletal prerogative powers might be lurking in the closet?

[40] ibid at [8].

[41] ibid at [79].

[42] ibid at [80]-[81].

[43] *ex parte Northumbria Police Authority*, above n 10 at 58; *Privacy International*, above n 39 at [83].

[44] Previous, more limited provision was made in the Regulatory and Investigatory Powers Act 2000 and the Investigatory Powers Act 2016. See J Dawson, *Covert Human Intelligence Sources (Criminal Conduct) Bill 2019-2021* (House of Commons Library Briefing Paper 9012, October 2020).

[45] R Craig and G Phillipson, 'Protecting National Security by Breaking the Law? Prerogative, Statute and the Powers of MI5' [2021] *Modern Law Review* 1, 8-10.

[46] HJ Hooper, 'The Principle of Legality and Prerogative Power after the Third Direction Case' (*UK Constitutional Law Association Blog*, 26 April 2021) www.ukconstitutionallaw.org/2021/04/26/hayley-j-hooper-the-principle-of-legality-and-prerogative-power-after-the-third-direction-case; *R (A) v Director of Establishments of the Security Service* [2009] EWCA Civ 24, [28].

The Second Limit: Statute

The second limb of the 'fundamental principle' limiting the extent and existence of the prerogative is statute. The foundation of the principle is in the sovereignty of Parliament.[47] A prerogative power can be abolished or limited by statute explicitly[48] or by 'necessary implication'.[49] In some cases, a statute covers 'the whole ground' so that there is 'no room' for the operation of the prerogative.[50] Finally, a prerogative power 'cannot frustrate the purpose of a statute or a statutory provision, for example by emptying it of content or preventing its effectual operation'.[51]

These tests for the abrogation of the prerogative by statute vary greatly in their breadth. We shall examine the first three – abrogation by express words, 'necessary implication' and covering 'the whole ground' – before turning to what has been termed the 'frustration principle'.[52]

De Keyser's Royal Hotel

The leading modern authority on the relationship between the prerogative and statute is *De Keyser*.[53] In May 1916, the Crown seized a large hotel in London. This was purportedly done under regulations made under the Defence Acts, to house the headquarters of the Royal Flying Corps. However, the Crown denied that the hotel's owners were entitled to the compensation that would normally have been due under the regulations.

The House of Lords held that the statutory compensation was payable. The prerogative could not be relied upon because it had been abrogated by statute.[54] However, their lordships reached their conclusions in subtly different ways. For Lord Dunedin, 'if the whole ground of something which could be done by the prerogative is covered by the statute, it is the statute that rules'.[55] However, Lord Parmoor held that statute might abrogate the prerogative: (a) by express words; (b) by 'necessary implication'; or (c) where it is 'made for the public good'.[56] He thought that the Defence Acts came under category (c), but then appeared to blend this with the requirements of 'necessary implication' (b): 'where a matter has been

[47] See *Laker Airways Ltd v Department of Trade* [1997] QB 643, 719-21 (Roskill LJ); *R v Secretary of State for the Home Department, ex parte Fire Brigades Union* [1995] 2 AC 513, 552 (Lord Browne-Wilkinson); *Miller* [2017], above n 20 at [48]; Craig, above n 36 at 309.

[48] Bill of Rights 1689, arts 1, 2; Fixed-term Parliaments Act 2011, s 3(2).

[49] *De Keyser's Royal Hotel v Attorney-General* [1920] AC 508, 576 (Lord Parmoor).

[50] ibid at 526 (Lord Dunedin).

[51] *Miller* [2017], above n 20 at [51].

[52] R Craig, 'Casting Aside Clanking Medieval Chains: Prerogative, Statute and Article 50 after the EU Referendum' (2016) 79 *Modern Law Review* 1019.

[53] *De Keyser's Royal Hotel*, above n 49.

[54] *Pace* Lord Moulton: ibid at 554.

[55] ibid at 526.

[56] ibid at 576.

directly regulated by statute there is a necessary implication that the statutory regulation must be obeyed'.[57] Lord Atkinson, and Lord Sumner, used the language of statutory interpretation: 'in all this legislation there is not a trace of a suggestion that the Crown was left free to ignore these statutory provisions'.[58]

Lord Parmoor's 'implication' comes not from the language of the statute but from external principle: 'unless no other interpretation is possible, justice requires that statutes should not be construed to enable the land of a particular individual to be confiscated without payment'.[59] It is not dissimilar to Lord Moulton's view that there should be a 'presumption' that the Crown uses statutory rather than prerogative powers.[60]

The Legacy of *De Keyser*

From a distance, then, *De Keyser* presents a coherent picture, but upon closer inspection the fine details are murky. One of the consequences is some inconsistency in subsequent cases. However, a variety of approach is to be expected: the purpose and context of statutes varies, as do prerogative powers and their particular uses. In each case, the court can be expected to adopt an approach informed by principle. For example, the principled rationale behind *De Keyser* was stated by Lord Parmoor:

> The constitutional principle is that when the power of the Executive to interfere with the property or liberty of subjects has been placed under Parliamentary control, and directly regulated by statute, the Executive no longer derives its authority from the Royal Prerogative of the Crown but from Parliament, and that in exercising such authority the Executive is bound to observe the restrictions which Parliament has imposed in favour of the subject.[61]

The court was clearly concerned with executive interference with legal rights. However, an interference with rights does not mean that the court will favour abrogation in all cases. In *R (XH) v Home Secretary*, the Court of Appeal was invited to find that the prerogative power to withdraw passports had been replaced by statutory powers under counter-terrorism legislation. The court disagreed, favouring a test of necessary implication and holding that 'The test for such a necessary implication is a strict one.'[62]

Rights are not the only factor at play. In *ex parte Molyneaux*, Taylor J held that, although some treaty-making power was a 'transferred matter' under the Northern Ireland Constitution Act 1973, there was no implication that the prerogative

[57] ibid at 576.
[58] ibid at 508, 536 (Lord Atkinson) and 562 (Lord Sumner).
[59] ibid at 576.
[60] ibid at 554. Lord Moulton did not agree that the prerogative had been abrogated.
[61] ibid at 575.
[62] *R (XH) v Home Secretary* [2017] EWCA Civ 41, [89].

power had been abrogated.[63] Partly this was a pragmatic decision in the instant case (since the Northern Ireland Executive was suspended and unable to wield its statutory power), but it may also demonstrate a disinclination of the courts to bind the government's hands on the international plane. For example, in *R v Secretary of State for Foreign and Commonwealth Affairs, ex parte Rees-Mogg*, Lord Justice Lloyd appeared to conclude that a prerogative power (the treaty-making power used in an EU context) could be fettered by statute only in express terms.[64] In *R (McCord) v Prime Minister*, the court held that section 10 of the European Union (Withdrawal) Act 2018 (requiring action in accordance with the Northern Ireland Act 1998) did not constrain the exercise of the treaty-making prerogative in negotiating the UK's exit from the EU.[65]

Sometimes, the courts seem to recognise the 'public good' or importance of a prerogative power, and are resistant to its erosion by statute. In *Third Direction*, the court cited with approval Lord Justice Purchas in *Northumbria*, who required 'express and unequivocal terms' to abrogate 'executive action … directed towards the benefit or protection of the individual'.[66] The court quoted John Locke: 'prerogative is nothing but the power of doing public good without a rule'.[67] Relatedly, in Australia, there is a 'strong presumption' against the abrogation of 'important' prerogatives.[68]

While it is difficult to compare cases involving different statutes, whose interpretation is central to the question, this degree of uncertainty is undesirable. As Stephenson says, 'It is important that, in those areas where a prerogative power exists alongside equivalent executive powers conferred by statute, individuals know what the law is.'[69] It is to be hoped that the courts begin to explain their differing approaches in more detail.

The 'Frustration Principle'

A further element of the primacy of statute is that a prerogative 'cannot frustrate the purpose of a statute or a statutory provision, for example by emptying it of content or preventing its effectual operation'.[70] This principle, recognised in *Miller 1*, is said to derive from *R v Secretary of State for the Home Department, ex parte Fire Brigades Union (FBU)*.[71]

[63] *Ex parte Molyneaux and others* [1986] 1 WLR 331.

[64] *R v Secretary of State for Foreign and Commonwealth Affairs, ex parte Rees-Mogg* [1994] QB 552, 567.

[65] *R (McCord) v Prime Minister and others* [2019] NICA 49, [127].

[66] *ex parte Northumbria Police Authority*, above n 10 at 53; *Privacy International*, above n 39 at [84].

[67] J Locke, *Essay concerning the True Original, Extent and End of Civil Government*, 4th edn (London, 1713), 316.

[68] P Stephenson, 'The Relationship between the Royal Prerogative and Statute in Australia' (2021) 44 *Melbourne University Law Review* 1001, 1018, 1026.

[69] ibid at 1016.

[70] *Miller* [2017], above n 20 at [51].

[71] *ex parte Fire Brigades Union*, above n 47.

In *FBU*, the government had decided to replace a scheme of criminal injuries compensation made under prerogative power with a statutory scheme, which Parliament enacted.[72] The Home Secretary had the statutory power to commence the statutory scheme, but government policy changed and the decision was taken not to commence. The House of Lords held by a majority of three to two that this decision was unlawful: the Home Secretary had a discretion as to *when* to bring in the statute, but not *whether* to do so. At the heart of the majority's decision was the recognition of an implied statutory duty to consider commencement.[73] The 'prerogative power is curtailed so long as the statutory duty continues to exist'.[74] This was a development from *De Keyser*: Parliament had legislated for a new scheme, and the government – while it was not bound to commence the statute – could not simply *ignore* Parliament's wishes.[75] The distinction from *De Keyser* was that the statutory limit was not yet in force.

Constitutional Principles: *Miller 2*

In the Supreme Court's decision in *Miller 2*,[76] there emerged a new framing of the limits on the prerogative: constitutional principle. Building on the traditional limits, the Supreme Court unanimously held that the prerogative is limited by the 'constitutional principles' of parliamentary sovereignty and a newly recognised principle of parliamentary accountability.[77] The Prime Minister could not lawfully advise the Queen to prorogue Parliament if 'the prorogation has the effect of frustrating or preventing, without reasonable justification, the ability of Parliament to carry out its constitutional functions as a legislature and as the body responsible for the supervision of the executive'.[78]

One difficulty some have identified with understanding *Miller 2* lies in the wording of the test: although expressed as a test of the *extent* of the power, does 'without reasonable justification' not suggest some analysis of the *manner* of exercising the power?[79] Perhaps driven by a desire for judicial unanimity, the court may have used 'extent' as a proxy for the 'manner of exercise' stage of review, which would have required a determination of justiciability (see below). However, the Supreme Court distinguished the need for 'justification' from a review of 'motive', and were aided in formulating their test by the fact that the Prime Minister had

[72] Wade doubted whether the original scheme was truly a 'prerogative': Wade, above n 22 at 58-66.

[73] *ex parte Fire Brigades Union*, above n 47 at 554 and 575–576; see G Phillipson, 'A dive into deep constitutional waters: Article 50, the prerogative and parliament' (2016) 79 *Modern Law Review* 1064, 1081-2.

[74] *ex parte Fire Brigades Union*, above n 47 at 576 (Lord Nicholls).

[75] ibid at 551–552 (Lord Browne-Wilkinson).

[76] *R (Miller) v The Prime Minister; Cherry v Advocate General* [2019] UKSC 41.

[77] ibid at [44] and [46].

[78] ibid at [50].

[79] See J Finnis, *The Unconstitutionality of the Supreme Court's Prorogation Judgment* (Policy Exchange, 2019), 14-5.

provided *no* justification to the court.[80] They did not actually have to set out any test of reasonableness, except to say that 'the Government must be accorded a great deal of latitude in making decisions of this nature'.[81]

For the court, with 'constitutional principle' understood as a principle of the common law, this 'third' limit was no different to the first – the common law.[82] As we have seen, both the common law and statutory limits on the prerogative are usually concerned with the rights of individuals and the principle of parliamentary sovereignty. The Supreme Court in *Miller 2* recognised a constitutional principle beyond parliamentary sovereignty, approving the words of Lord Bingham in a 2006 case: 'the conduct of government by a Prime Minister and Cabinet collectively responsible and accountable to Parliament lies at the heart of Westminster democracy'.[83]

Limiting the prerogative by constitutional principle is not unknown elsewhere in the Commonwealth. In Australia, the prerogative is part of the executive power granted by section 61 of the Constitution. Alongside other grounds of review, the courts of Australia must ensure that the common law (including the prerogative) is applied in a manner consistent with constitutional principle.[84]

It will fall to later cases to determine the extent of the 'constitutional principle' approach in the UK. Are all common law 'fundamental principles' to apply to the prerogative? The difficulty here is unpredictability as new principles come to be recognised.[85] This is connected to a wider problem in 'common law constitutionalism': an intervention of the courts not based on incremental development can erode legal certainty and infringe on the proper role of Parliament.[86] The approach marks a departure from the 'look in the books' method of identifying the prerogative and its limits. While this might be justified, it comes with a concomitant risk of expanding prerogative power as well as limiting it: as *Northumbria* and *Third Direction* show, normative reasoning and constitutional principle can be employed to make the case for greater executive autonomy too.

The Third Stage: Manner of Exercise

The final stage of the courts' review of prerogative powers is to review the manner of the power's exercise. It is at this stage alone that the court may refrain from review because the particular prerogative power is non-justiciable.

[80] *Miller* [2019] above n 76 at [58].
[81] ibid at [58].
[82] ibid at [49].
[83] ibid at [46]; *cf Bobb v Manning* [2006] UKPC 22, [13].
[84] *Lange v Australian Broadcasting Corporation* (1997) 189 CLR 50; *John Pfeiffer Pty Ltd v Rogerson* (2000) 203 CLR 503; see A Twomey, 'The Prerogative and the Courts in Australia' (2021) 3 *Journal of Commonwealth Law* 55, 62-3.
[85] Eg, the recognition of 'open justice' in *Kennedy v Charity Commissioners* [2014] UKSC 20.
[86] *Elgizouli v Secretary of State for the Home Department* [2020] UKSC 10, [170]-[171] (Lord Reed).

Before the 1970s, the orthodoxy was that the courts did not have jurisdiction over the prerogative, except to determine its existence and extent.[87] As we have seen, even those tools of review have become potent. Yet one of the most important changes in the courts' approach to the prerogative came in the *GCHQ* case in 1984. There, the House of Lords set out that 'the controlling factor in determining whether the exercise of prerogative power is subject to judicial review is not its source but its subject matter'.[88] *GCHQ* was a watershed moment. The House of Lords held that only prerogative powers that fell into certain 'excluded categories', including 'high policy', were to be non-justiciable.[89] Lord Roskill gave a helpful list of non-justiciable powers: 'the making of treaties, the defence of the realm, the prerogative of mercy, the grant of honours, the dissolution of Parliament and the appointment of ministers as well as others'.[90]

The courts do not shrink from briskly dismissing claims of non-justiciability where the power falls 'into an entirely different category', as with passport powers (see chapter twelve).[91] In other cases, such as the royal prerogative of mercy (pardons), the standard tools of judicial review have been introduced over a longer period of time. In *GCHQ*, Lord Diplock had included pardon powers in his list of non-justiciable prerogatives. However, in *R v Secretary of State for the Home Department, ex parte Bentley*, the court made cautious first steps, holding that the Home Secretary had not considered all options open to him and (obiter) that a discriminatory refusal of a pardon would be unlawful.[92] It now appears that judicial review will now extend to most exercises of the pardon power (see chapter eleven).

However, judicial review of prerogative powers often affords the decision-maker a 'wide degree of latitude'.[93] In particular, there is considerable discretion given to the drawing up of criteria for exercising a prerogative power, which is sometimes viewed as a non-justiciable matter of policy.[94] That deference was affirmed by the Supreme Court in *R (Sandiford) v The Secretary of State for Foreign and Commonwealth Affairs*, holding that 'prerogative powers have to be approached on a different basis from statutory powers' and that 'There is no necessary implication, from their mere existence, that the State as their holder must keep open the possibility of their exercise in more than one sense': a blanket policy might be appropriate in the case of a prerogative where it is not in respect to a statutory power.[95]

[87] H Woolf, J Jowell, C Donnelly and I Hare, *De Smith's Judicial Review*, 8th edn (London, Sweet & Maxwell, 2018), para 3-038.

[88] *Council of Civil Service Unions*, above n 2 at 407 (Lord Scarman).

[89] ibid at 418 (Lord Roskill).

[90] ibid.

[91] *R v Secretary of State for Foreign and Commonwealth Affairs, ex parte Everett* [1989] QB 811, 817.

[92] *R v Secretary of State for the Home Department, ex parte Bentley* [1994] QB 349.

[93] *McGeough v Secretary of State for Northern Ireland* [2012] NICA 28, [14].

[94] *ex parte Bentley*, above n 92 at 363; *R (Page) v Secretary of State for Justice* [2007] EWHC 2026 (Admin), 16-17.

[95] *R (Sandiford) v The Secretary of State for Foreign and Commonwealth Affairs* [2014] UKSC 44, [62].

Challenging the *GCHQ* Approach

This chapter has been structured according to the current orthodoxy, confirmed in *Miller 2*, that it is for the courts to determine the existence and extent of all prerogative powers; but that some prerogative powers are not judicially reviewable when it comes to the manner of their exercise, based upon their subject-matter. That list-based approach has come under attack on two fronts.

First, the list of unreviewable prerogative powers is not fixed. For example, the courts have shifted their approach to pardon powers, discussed above. The courts are also willing to adjudicate on matters ancillary to the exercise of an (otherwise non-justiciable) prerogative power. In *R (FDA) v Prime Minister*, the court accepted that the question of whether the Prime Minister had misinterpreted the Ministerial Code was justiciable, even though the power to dismiss the minister was not.[96]

Second, there is a growing challenge to the idea that it is possible to draw up a universally applicable list of prerogative powers defined by their subject-matter. A variety of this attack came in *R v Secretary of State for Foreign and Commonwealth Affairs, ex parte Bancoult (No. 2)*, where Lord Justice Sedley suggested that 'the grant of honours for reward, the waging of a war of manifest aggression or a refusal to dissolve Parliament at all might well call in question an immunity based purely on subject-matter'.[97] In *R (Marchiori) v The Environment Agency*, Lord Justice Laws said that judicial review 'remains available to cure the theoretical possibility of actual bad faith on the part of ministers making decisions of high policy'.[98] Furthermore, some subject-matters are difficult to define: for example, Ewan Smith has recently argued that the category of 'foreign policy' is too unstable to be reliable in determining justiciability,[99] despite frequent judicial dicta that such matters are outside the 'constitutional limits of the court's competence'.[100] By comparison, in Australia, foreign policy is not treated as a forbidden area for the courts, because all executive power is subject to constitutional limits.[101]

Furthermore, in *GCHQ* itself Lord Diplock said that judicial review was available for decisions which had '*consequences* which affect some person (or body of persons) other than the decision-maker' (emphasis added), by altering their rights or obligations or by depriving them of some benefit or advantage.[102] This suggests that subject-matter alone is not the only factor that determines justiciability. One possible future direction for the courts is to analyse justiciability according to

[96] *R (FDA) v Prime Minister* [2021] EWHC 3279 (Admin).

[97] *R v Secretary of State for Foreign and Commonwealth Affairs, ex parte Bancoult (No. 2)* [2007] EWCA Civ 498, [46].

[98] *R (Marchiori) v The Environment Agency* [2002] EWCA Civ 3, [40].

[99] E Smith, 'Is Foreign Policy Special?' (2020) 41 *Oxford Journal of Legal Studies* 1040.

[100] *Shergill v Khaira* [2014] UKSC 33, [42]; *cf Miller* [2017], above n 20 at [160] (Lord Reed); *R (Abbasi) v Secretary of State for Foreign and Commonwealth Affairs* [2002] EWCA Civ 1598, [106].

[101] *Hicks v Ruddock* [2007] FCA 299, [85] (Tamberlin J).

[102] *Council of Civil Service Unions*, above n 2 at 408.

three factors: the subject-matter of the power; the effect of the decision; and the identity of the decision-maker.[103]

It is uncertain which way the courts will lean on this question. While in *Belhaj v Straw* (a case about the non-justiciability of foreign acts of state), it was said that a broader, case-by-case approach was preferable, with regard (in that context) to the separation of powers and the sovereign nature of the activities,[104] the court in *Miller 2* very noticeably steered away from the question of the non-justiciability of the manner of exercise of certain prerogative powers. The current President of the Supreme Court, Lord Reed, said in *Miller 1* that 'the legalisation of political issues is not always constitutionally appropriate, and may be fraught with risk, not least for the judiciary'.[105]

The Johnson government has clear concerns that the law on justiciability is intruding on the proper realm of executive autonomy, particularly after the *Miller* cases. In commissioning the Independent Review of Administrative Law in 2020, they asked the panel to consider 'Whether the legal principle of non-justiciability requires clarification.'[106] The panel noted that 'the remaining pockets of non-justiciability are likely to remain in place'; but also that 'in the past 40 years, no new instances of non-justiciable powers or issues have been recognised by the courts'.[107] Partly, this was because the justiciability issue was often not raised in cases where it might have been expected.[108] In the end, the panel favoured 'leaving questions of justiciability to the judges', noting that 'disappointment with the outcome of a case (or cases) is rarely sufficient reason to legislate more generally'.[109]

The Role of the Courts

It cannot be doubted that the years since *GCHQ* have seen tighter control of the use of the prerogative by the courts, which has reflected a generally expanded approach in judicial review more generally. We make two observations. First, although cases involving the prerogative are rare, there has been a shift in the way in which the courts approach the question of its limits. While it has been clear since *Proclamations* that the prerogative cannot override the common law, this control has long been intimately connected to individual liberty and private rights. In recent years 'constitutional principle' has come to the fore. In *Miller 1*, the Supreme Court asserted that it was for Parliament alone to make such a great

[103] A Sapienza, *Judicial Review of Non-Statutory Executive Action* (Alexandria NSW, The Federation Press, 2020), 74.

[104] *Belhaj*, above n 4 at [90]-[95].

[105] *Miller* [2017], above n 20 at [240].

[106] Independent Review of Administrative Law, *Terms of Reference* (2020), para 2.

[107] *Report from the Independent Review of Administrative Law* (CP 407, 2021), para 2.42.

[108] ibid at paras 2.44-45.

[109] ibid at paras 2.98, 2.100.

change in the UK's 'constitutional arrangement'; in *Miller 2*, the court found that the prerogative could not infringe constitutional principle, including parliamentary accountability.

Second, explicitly engaging constitutional principle in determining the limits of the prerogative opens the door to other changes in the courts' traditional approach. With the recognition of apparently novel constitutional principles may come calls to recognise new uses of prerogative power (as in *Northumbria* and *Third Direction*), founded on more open-ended constitutionalist reasoning rather than precedent. Furthermore, the more demanding the legal limits on prerogative power, the more controversial those limits will become. For an example, see the dissenting judgments in *FBU*, where Lord Keith called the majority judgment 'a most improper intrusion into a field which lies peculiarly within the province of Parliament'.[110]

As a result of cases like *Miller 2*, the battlefront that *GCHQ* opened up over justiciability at the third stage has spread to include the earlier stages of judicial review of the prerogative. We turn now, briefly, to outline the main issues in that debate.

Institutional Competence

One problem the courts face in reviewing several prerogative powers is that they are often unable to weigh up the full range of factors and evidence in the same way as the executive decision-maker. This is not a problem confined to the prerogative, and features across the whole spectrum of judicial review, particularly where 'macro-political' factors are at play or broad statutory powers are in issue.[111] However, one of the central problems with reviewing (certain) prerogative powers is that they frequently raise questions of 'high policy'. For example, in *GCHQ*, the central question was a balance between individual rights and national security.

There is a dual challenge here. First, the court simply does not always have access to the full range of materials that were necessary to make the decision. That position has changed somewhat with the courts' more open attitude to applying 'closed material procedures', which allow some sensitive material to be heard in private. Furthermore, 'interveners' (eg John Major in *Miller 2*) may now provide the higher appeal courts with further perspectives on a case. However, a lack of information will continue to stymie the courts' ability to provide appropriate review even where confidentiality is not a question. In *Northumbria*, for example, judges will not have heard evidence about the comparative effectiveness

[110] Lord Mustill described it as 'a penetration into Parliament's exclusive field of legislative activity far greater than any that has been [previously] contemplated': *ex parte Fire Brigades Union*, above n 47 at 544 (Lord Keith) and 562 (Lord Mustill).

[111] *R v Secretary of State for Education, ex parte Begbie* [2000] 1 WLR 1115, [82] (Laws LJ).

of CS gas and baton rounds in dealing with serious public disorder as opposed to more traditional policing methods.

Second, the courts are limited in the sorts of evidence they can admit or take into account because some decisions are 'beyond the constitutional competence assigned to the courts under our conception of the separation of powers'.[112] Even if the court in *Northumbria* could have considered the evidence on comparative effectiveness, would it really be right for judges to take the measure of that balance? As Lord Hoffmann has said, in a much-quoted passage, national security decisions 'require a legitimacy which can be conferred only by entrusting them to persons responsible to the community through the democratic process'.[113]

The Value of Executive Autonomy

Critics of the expanding role of the courts have suggested that descriptions of the prerogative as 'a relic of a past age' (Lord Reid) are deeply misleading about the continuing need for 'an efficient, unified and democratic executive'.[114] Prerogative is not a 'stubborn stain' to be washed out; it is a feature of the system, not a bug. In *Miller 1*, Lord Reed (dissenting) spoke of the 'value of unanimity, strength and dispatch' in using the treaty-making power.[115] That would be undermined by over-intrusive courts. This point was also recognised by the majority, who thought the prerogative *not* 'anomalous or anachronistic': 'There are important areas of governmental activity which, today as in the past, are essential to the effective operation of the state and which are not covered, or at least not completely covered, by statute.'[116]

Executive autonomy is certainly important. Balancing that against appropriate controls is one of the core themes of this book. However, we make two points. First, in some contexts the executive's hand is strengthened by more clearly representing a democratic consensus, demonstrated through the exercise of democratic controls in Parliament. This has driven some of the recent reforms to treaty-making (see chapter eight). Analogously, judicial supervision of the limits of the prerogative legitimises its use by publicly demonstrating that it cannot be abused, for instance by intruding on individuals' rights.

Second, the democratic demands to supervise the exercise of the prerogative have increased. As a result, the prerogative no longer consists, as Albert Venn

[112] *Shergill v Khaira* [2014] UKSC 33, [42] (Lord Sumption); *cf Rahmatullah (No. 2) v Ministry of Defence* [2017] UKSC 1, [57].

[113] *Secretary of State for the Home Department v Rehman* [2001] UKHL 47, [62]; *cf* Laws LJ in *Al Rawi v The Security Service* [2011] UKSC 34, [147] and *Marchiori v Environment Agency* [2002] EWCA Civ 3, [38].

[114] T Endicott, *The Stubborn Stain Theory of Executive Power* (Policy Exchange, 2017), 3; *Burmah Oil Co*, above n 18 at 101 (Lord Reid).

[115] *Miller* [2017], above n 20 at [160].

[116] ibid at [49].

Dicey wrote, of 'large powers which can be exercised and constantly are exercised, free from Parliamentary control'.[117] War powers, treaty-making, and even (for a short time) dissolution have all fallen within the expanding democratic oversight of Parliament, to greater and lesser extents. Moreover, Parliament is better equipped than it has ever been to take on that scrutiny, armed with resources, advisers, committees and other structures. It is perhaps, then, little surprise to see its role asserted more forcefully by the Supreme Court in the *Miller* cases.

'Politics by Other Means'

It is often said that the courts have become 'politicised' and that the expanding scope of judicial review, particularly of the prerogative, has merely enabled activists to pursue 'politics by other means'. Certainly, it would be hard to deny the political background of the claimants in cases like *Molyneaux*, *Rees-Mogg*, or *McCord*. It is sometimes added that reliance on the courts is anti-democratic: judges themselves have even been called 'enemies of the people'.[118]

To some degree, this challenge revisits the argument about 'constitutional competence'. Yet the more specific challenge here is that the courts improperly displace the scrutiny of *Parliament*, not decision-making by the government. Blackstone justified the non-justiciability of the prerogative on the basis that the appropriate forum for its control is Parliament.[119] However, in *Miller 2* the constitutional principle recognised was '*parliamentary* accountability'. In *Miller 1*, the majority relied on '*parliamentary* sovereignty'. By enforcing those principles, the courts aimed to bolster – not detract from – Parliamentary scrutiny.

Nevertheless, there are two challenges going forwards. First, if the courts use other constitutional principles beyond those connected to the role of Parliament in order to limit the prerogative, they do risk making value judgments that might more properly be addressed by Parliament. Second, there may come a point at which the courts must decide whether Parliament can ever remove judicial supervision of the limits of the prerogative by using an 'ouster clause'. The Supreme Court has already decided that an ouster clause is not fully effective in wholly removing judicial scrutiny of *statutory* bodies.[120] The question is much less likely to arise with the prerogative, but – inspired by *Miller 2* – some campaigners may wish to challenge a future dissolution of Parliament, which the Dissolution and Calling of Parliament Act attempts to make entirely non-justiciable.[121]

[117] AV Dicey, *Introduction to the Study of the Law of the Constitution*, 9th edn (London, Macmillan, 1939), 465.

[118] J Slack, 'Enemies of the People: Fury over out of touch judges who have declared war on democracy by defying 17.4m Brexit voters and who could trigger constitutional crisis' *Daily Mail* (London, 4 November 2016).

[119] W Blackstone, *Commentaries on the Laws of England*, vol 1 (London, S Sweet, 1836), 251, 257-8.

[120] *Privacy International*, above n 39.

[121] Dissolution and Calling of Parliament Act 2022, s 3.

Judicial vs Parliamentary Controls

Courts, unlike Parliament, can only address the cases in front of them. Their form of control over the prerogative is entirely reactive. Furthermore, legal answers are inevitably black or white, while Parliament promotes compromises. Partly, this is why judicial review has become so popular among campaigning groups: it can provide more instant, headline-grabbing results. However, from a system-wide perspective, judicial oversight has its limitations. Courts are 'animated by a combination of abstract reasoning and moral value-judgment, which at first sight appears to embody a higher model of decision-making than the messy compromises required to build a political consensus in a Parliamentary system'.[122]

As Thomas Poole has put it,

> … just because an area becomes more amenable to judicial oversight it does not necessarily follow that the underlying problem is solved. The juridical situation might be clearer, but what was a hard case remains a hard case, the reason of state questions it raises still likely to prove difficult to resolve.[123]

This danger is to some extent averted while the courts continue to view parliamentary sovereignty (and accountability) as central to their exercise of control. Mark Elliott has called this a 'principle of legality' for the prerogative.[124] The principle of legality in statutory construction 'means that Parliament must squarely confront what it is doing and accept the political cost'.[125] By throwing the government's decisions in *Miller 1* and *Miller 2* back into the parliamentary arena, the Supreme Court could be said to use judicial controls to strengthen parliamentary ones.

Conclusion

This chapter cannot serve as a comprehensive compendium of the law on the limits and judicial control of the prerogative. However, we have attempted to identify the major tools used by the courts in policing executive autonomy, and some of the difficulties they have in articulating the nature and scope of those tools. As a closing observation, we note a danger in a chapter such as this one – that 'the prerogative' is treated as a unitary concept, devoid of context. That is neither helpful nor representative of the ways in which the courts approach judicial review. Each prerogative power – and each use of each prerogative power – bears with

[122] J Sumption, 'The Limits of Law' (Sultan Azlan Shah Lecture, Kuala Lumpur, 20 November 2013).

[123] T Poole, *Reason of State: Law, Prerogative and Empire* (Cambridge, Cambridge University Press, 2015), 266.

[124] M Elliott, 'A new approach to constitutional adjudication? Miller II in the Supreme Court' (*Public Law for Everyone*, 24 September 2019) www.publiclawforeveryone.com/2019/09/24/the-supreme-courts-judgment-in-cherry-miller-no-2-a-new-approach-to-constitutional-adjudication.

[125] *R v Secretary of State for the Home Department, ex parte Simms* [2000] 2 AC 115, 131 (Lord Hoffmann).

it its own historical baggage, factual circumstances, statutory interactions and constitutional concerns. Part of the confusion over, for example, the legacy of *De Keyser* stems from that almost infinite variety. That is why we have addressed the prerogative powers in the earlier parts of this book in the distinct ways appropriate to them. Yet – as we have set out in this chapter – one of the constant themes is the interaction between political and legal controls on those powers. In the next chapter, we examine the role of Parliament in controlling prerogative powers. It is only through understanding both sides of the coin that the ongoing legal debate about the proper scope for executive autonomy can fully be understood.

18

The Role of Parliament

Introduction

Chapter seventeen, on the relationship between the prerogative and the courts, recorded how over the last 30 years, judges have gradually increased their scrutiny of the prerogative through a series of rulings extending its justiciability. This chapter, on the prerogative and Parliament, records a similar story but with a twist in the tail: in the last five years, the executive has fought back, reversing some of Parliament's earlier gains.

Until then, the story of recent years was one of Parliament steadily acquiring more and more control over different prerogative powers, in particular over the war-making power and the power of dissolution. The nature and degree of that control varies from one power to another, and the record of Parliament's battles with the executive for control of the prerogative can be divided into four distinct periods. In the first phase, right up until the twenty-first century, the dominance of the executive meant that Parliament had only a very limited role in regulating the prerogative. The second phase began in 2004, when the House of Commons Public Administration Select Committee embarked upon a sustained campaign (in its own words) to 'tame the prerogative'. That campaign started to yield results when Gordon Brown became Prime Minister in 2007, with further inroads into the prerogative in the third phase after the coalition came into power in 2010. The fourth phase, which has unfolded in the last five years, has seen Theresa May and Boris Johnson roll back some of those achievements.

The first part of this chapter records those four phases, of Parliament gradually acquiring more control over different aspects of the prerogative, and of the executive beginning to fight back. The second part provides more detail about the struggle for greater parliamentary control of each of the prerogative powers, before assessing the effectiveness of that control. What difference has Parliament made? Does Parliament have the will, the time, the institutional capacity, and the expertise to exercise effective control over the prerogative powers?

The Dominance of the Executive (1689–2000)

The relationship between Parliament and the prerogative owes its origins to the prolonged struggle for power in the seventeenth century that was eventually won by Parliament. Sovereign authority now belonged to Parliament. Prerogative power, once ascribed to the monarch by divine right and common law recognition, continued to exist by the tacit permission of Parliament.[1] It might have been expected that Parliament would legislate to assume control of the prerogatives. But such authority was merely transferred from the monarch to his or her ministers. As David Yardley explained:

> The leaders of the majority in the House of Commons found it extremely convenient to have these great powers in their hands, unfettered by formal safeguards, and naturally their party supporters were content that they should retain the powers. Equally the opposition in Parliament would not press strongly for their abolition or reduction because they hoped in their turn to become the ruling group by the effluxion of time, when the powers would be of the greatest assistance to them also.[2]

Executive authority over the prerogative was thus preserved into the twentieth century. The power to summon, dissolve, or prorogue Parliament, and important powers over foreign affairs, including the power to declare war, enter into treaties, and acquire territory, remained exercisable by, or on the advice of the Prime Minister. The conferment of honours was similarly exercised on the advice of the Prime Minister (though from 1923, he was advised by the Political Honours Scrutiny Committee) and the judicial prerogative of mercy was exercisable on the advice of the Home Secretary. Although Parliament retained the theoretical ability to alter, abridge, or abolish the prerogatives,[3] oversight was limited in practice. The executive was not required to seek prior approval for the exercise of the prerogative, nor were ministers bound to inform Parliament of their intent.[4]

Arising by practice, convention, and in some cases statute, particular provisions were adopted in relation to certain prerogatives so as to allow Parliament the opportunity for consultation. It had been practice since the 1890 cession of Heligoland to Germany to seek parliamentary approval to cede territory. The Ponsonby Rule, established in 1924, required the government to lay treaties before Parliament for a period of 21 days before they could be ratified.[5] After the Bill of Rights 1689 precluded the keeping of an army in peacetime without the consent of Parliament, it had become custom for Parliament to authorise the maintenance of the armed forces through an annual (now quinquennial) Army Act.

[1] J Chitty, *A Treatise on the Law of the Prerogatives of the Crown* (London, Butterworths, 1820), 5.

[2] DCM Yardley, 'The Primacy of the Executive in England' (1967) 21 *Parliamentary Affairs* 155, 156.

[3] For example, the Crown Proceedings Act 1947 partially abolished immunities enjoyed by the Crown under the prerogative. Later, the Fixed-term Parliaments Act 2011 abolished the prerogative power of dissolution.

[4] ECS Wade and GG Phillips, *Constitutional and Administrative Law*, 9th edn (London, Longman, 1977), 234; HW Clarke, *Constitutional and Administrative Law* (London, Sweet and Maxwell, 1971), 87.

[5] From 1981, the Ponsonby Rule did not apply to bilateral double taxation treaties. In accordance with the spirit of the Ponsonby Rule, it was confirmed that Parliament would be provided with the opportunity to consider such agreements through the statutory requirement that the draft of any Order in Council providing for double taxation would require approval by affirmative resolution. See *Hansard*, HC Deb Vol 4, col 82W (6 May 1981).

These limited incursions should not mask the overall reality, that parliamentary oversight of the prerogatives remained seriously inadequate. In 1977, Emlyn Wade and George Phillips expressed their dissatisfaction as follows:

> One consequence of the survival of the prerogative is that a particular power may not be subject to parliamentary or judicial safeguards that would be considered appropriate if the power was being conferred afresh by legislation upon the Government. Why, for example, should Parliament not have a formal right to be asked to approve treaties which the Government has concluded? And why should the prerogative to issue and withdraw passports not be subject to formal safeguards for the citizen? It has evidently been more convenient for successive Governments to retain prerogative powers in their ancient legal form than to modernise them.[6]

Parliamentary scrutiny was limited in other ways, for example at Question Time. There existed 'a number of issues on which Ministers conventionally decline to provide information', many of which concerned the prerogative.[7] Matters pertaining to the dissolution of Parliament and the grant of honours were out of order. The government declined to answer questions on the disposition and weaponry of the armed forces, government contracts, and judicial appointments. When departmental select committees were established in 1979, it was hoped that they would provide more forceful scrutiny. Then still in their infancy, select committees made no attempt to probe the prerogative.

But, if select committees initially were reticent, individual parliamentarians were less so, until the 1980s and 1990s saw a series of Private Member's Bills introduced by prominent backbenchers to challenge the executive's use of the prerogative. The first to show interest was Tony Benn, who argued in 1982 that the prerogative constituted a 'major reversal of the advances that we made towards democracy, even allowing for the fact we hadn't in any case completed the democratic process begun in the seventeenth century'.[8] With the support of the Campaign Group of Labour MPs,[9] Benn introduced the Reform Bill 1985 and the Crown Prerogatives (House of Commons Control) Bill 1988. The Bills were designed to transfer to the Speaker of the House of Commons the responsibility for advising the monarch on the dissolution of Parliament, formation of government, declaration of war, signature and ratification of treaties, public appointments, and all other executive powers not conferred by statute, subject to assent from the Commons.

Neither Bill had any prospect of success, and both were dropped at second reading.[10] But they began to change the terms of constitutional debate: Blackburn commented that the Bills represented a 'new strand of constitutional thought on

[6] Wade and Phillips, above n 4 at 234.
[7] H Barnett, *Constitutional and Administrative Law*, 2nd edn (London, Cavendish, 1998), 202.
[8] T Benn, *Parliament, People and Power: Agenda for a Free Society* (London, Verso, 1982), 44.
[9] Campaign Group of Labour MPs, *Parliamentary Democracy and the Labour Movement* (London, 1984).
[10] *Hansard*, HC Deb Vol 79, col 1253 (24 May 1985); *Hansard*, HC Deb Vol 129, col 1109 (16 March 1988).

the royal power of dissolution'.[11] And they led to further proposals for reform. Bills for fixed-term Parliaments were proposed in the Commons by Tony Banks in 1992, and Jeff Rooker in 1994. In 1994, the Treasury and Civil Service Committee advocated for regulation of the civil service to be placed on a statutory footing. In 1996, Lord Lester presented the Treaties (Parliamentary Approval) Bill to the Lords. In 1999, Tam Dalyell introduced the Military Action Against Iraq (Parliamentary Approval) Bill.[12] These individual Private Member's Bills had no more prospect of success than Tony Benn's earlier attempts did, but they paved the way for the more systematic campaign led by Tony Wright in the first decade of the twenty-first century.

A Sustained Campaign: PASC Paves the Way for Brown's Reforms (2000–10)

Tony Wright was the highly effective chair of the Public Administration Select Committee (PASC), whose main function was to scrutinise the Cabinet Office, but with a wider brief across the whole of the civil service. Under his chairmanship, PASC embarked upon a sustained campaign to tame the prerogative, publishing a steady stream of detailed reports on every aspect of the prerogative over the next two decades (recorded in Table 1 below). After 2015, PASC became the Public Administration and Constitutional Affairs Committee (PACAC). When Bernard Jenkin was appointed chair in 2010, he maintained the Committee's interest in the prerogative, as did William Wragg, who became chair in 2019.

Many of PASC's reports were topical, starting in 2002 with the reform of the House of Lords when it was still part of the government's agenda; and later turning its focus to war powers after the parliamentary vote approving the allied invasion of Iraq in March 2003. But, over the years, PASC and PACAC have covered every aspect of the prerogative, including topics such as the scrutiny and ratification of treaties, the conferral and revocation of passports and honours, and the regulation of the civil service, as can be seen from the long list of reports in Table 1.

PASC's opening salvo was its 2004 report entitled *Taming the Prerogative: Strengthening Ministerial Accountability to Parliament*, in which the committee sought to constitutionalise those prerogatives under which 'Ministers still have very wide scope to act without parliamentary approval'.[13] This included the making and ratification of treaties, deployment and use of the armed forces, and the granting and revocation of passports. Annexed to the report was a draft Ministers of

[11] R Blackburn, 'The Dissolution of Parliament: The Crown Prerogatives (House of Commons Control) Bill 1988' (1989) 52 *Modern Law Review* 837, 837.

[12] As the Bill concerned the Royal Prerogative, ministers were able to prevent the Bill from being debated through advising the denial of Queen's consent. For details, see chapter six.

[13] Fourth Report from the House of Commons Public Administration Select Committee, *Taming the Prerogative: Strengthening Ministerial Accountability to Parliament* HC 422 (2003–04), 7.

Table 1 Reports published by PASC and PACAC on the prerogative powers between 2000–2021

Date	Report	Scope
Feb 2002	The Second Chamber: Continuing the Reform	Appointments to the Lords
Jan 2004	A Draft Civil Service Bill: Completing the Reform	Regulation of the civil service
March 2004	Taming the Prerogative: Strengthening Ministerial Accountability to Parliament	War Powers; Treaties; Passports; Wider Review of the Royal Prerogative
July 2004	A Matter of Honour: Reforming the Honours System	Honours
March 2007	Politics and Administration: Ministers and Civil Servants	Regulation of the civil service (and the role of Special Advisers)
June 2008	Constitutional Renewal: Draft Bill and White Paper	Regulation of the civil service; War Powers; Treaties; Passports; Wider Review of the Royal Prerogative
Dec 2007	Propriety and Peerages	Honours; Appointments
Aug 2012	The Honours System	Honours
Sept 2013	Truth to Power: How Civil Service Reform Can Succeed	Regulation of the civil service
July 2016	Better Public Appointments: The Grimstone Review on Public Appointments	Public Appointments
Dec 2018	The Role of Parliament in the UK Constitution (Interim Report): The Status and Effect of Confidence Motions and the Fixed-term Parliaments Act 2011	Dissolution
Aug 2019	The Role of Parliament in the UK Constitution: Authorising the Use of Military Force	War Powers
Nov 2018	A Smaller House of Lords	Appointments to the Lords
Sept 2020	The Fixed-term Parliaments Act 2011	Dissolution; Prorogation
July 2021	Dissolution and Calling of Parliament Bill. (No report: PACAC concerns raised in correspondence with the Minister for the Constitution and Devolution)[14]	Dissolution; Prorogation
Forthcoming	The Scrutiny of International Treaties and other international agreements in the 21st century	Treaties

[14] Letter from William Wragg to Chloe Smith (21 July 2021); See also Letter from Chloe Smith to William Wragg (7 September 2021).

the Crown (Executive Powers) Bill which had been drafted by the Committee's Specialist Adviser, Professor Rodney Brazier, to ensure that the ratification of treaties and decisions to engage in armed conflict were subject to approval by both Houses. Brazier had hoped that the draft Bill 'would provide a possible template for later parliamentary work on other executive powers',[15] such as those recognised by, but omitted from the 2004 report due to overlapping interests: the regulation of the civil service, conferral of public appointments, and granting of honours.

Although PASC's strengthened role for Parliament was rejected by the Blair government in a bland response in 2004,[16] the climate changed dramatically when Gordon Brown became Prime Minister in 2007. Within a week of taking office, Brown published a Green Paper declaring his intention to build on PASC's earlier proposals.[17] This was followed by a 2008 White Paper and draft Bill, that set out plans to reform the prerogative war powers, treaties, passports, public and judicial appointments, and regulation of the civil service.[18] We related in chapter three how Brown's ambitious plans, announced with much fanfare, were gradually attenuated until all that survived in the Constitutional Reform and Governance Act 2010 (CRAG), passed in the last days of his premiership, was a provision to put the Civil Service Commission on a statutory basis, as well as codification of the Ponsonby Rule on the ratification of treaties. Further action had been promised: a draft Commons resolution on war powers,[19] comprehensive legislation on passports,[20] and additional measures on the dissolution and recall of Parliament. On dissolution, Brown had proposed that the Prime Minister should be required to obtain the approval of the Commons before seeking a dissolution; on recall, that the Speaker should be able to recall the House on receiving a request from over half the MPs.[21]

Further Regulation of the Prerogative under the Coalition (2010–15)

When the Conservative-Liberal Democrat coalition was formed after the 2010 election, fixed-term Parliaments became one of the main items in their programme for government. Although the immediate purpose was to shore up the coalition, ministers emphasised two wider objectives: to limit the power of the executive, which was too dominant in relation to the legislature; and to remove the right

[15] ibid at 30.

[16] Department for Constitutional Affairs, *Government response to the Public Administration Select Committee's Fourth Report of Session 2003–04: Taming the Prerogative: Strengthening Ministerial Accountability to Parliament* (Cm 6187, 2004), 4–5.

[17] Ministry of Justice, *The Governance of Britain* (Cm 7170, 2007).

[18] Ministry of Justice, *The Governance of Britain – Constitutional Renewal* (Cm 7342, 2008).

[19] ibid at para 37.

[20] ibid at para 38.

[21] ibid at para 39.

of a Prime Minister to choose the date of the next election for partisan advantage. The Fixed-term Parliaments Act 2011 (FTPA) went far further than anything Brown had proposed, by wholly transferring the power to dissolve Parliament from the executive to the legislature. In so doing, it abolished the prerogative power of dissolution. The Act provided for five-year fixed terms, with a provision in section 2 for a mid-term dissolution by a two-thirds vote, or following a successful no confidence motion; but again by statute not under the prerogative. As stated in section 3(2), 'Parliament cannot otherwise be dissolved.' This was a huge constitutional change, recognised as such by the Conservative Party in their 2015 manifesto, which recorded the achievement as 'an unprecedented transfer of Executive power'.

The other development under the coalition was further regulation of the war-making power. Gordon Brown had proposed a formal parliamentary resolution, setting out the process Parliament should follow before approving deployment of the armed forces but made no further progress before leaving office. The coalition government soon had to address the issue in March 2011 with the deployment of forces in Libya. Although a parliamentary debate was held after the bombing of Libya had commenced, the government acknowledged the existence of a convention that normally there should be a prior debate, and undertook to observe the convention except in cases of emergency. The test came in August 2013, when David Cameron wanted to engage in bombing in Syria, but was narrowly defeated by 272 to 285 votes. As a result of the vote, the government dropped its plans.[22] A year later the government again sought parliamentary approval for action against ISIS in Iraq in September 2014, and on this occasion the House supported the proposed deployment by 524 votes to 43.[23] The following year, the government sought parliamentary approval to extend the bombing of ISIS to Syria, and in December 2015, the House again approved the proposed action by a large majority.[24] These successive precedents enabled commentators to state with increasing confidence that there was now an established convention that the government would not deploy the armed forces overseas without prior recourse to Parliament.[25]

[22] Shortly after David Cameron informed President Barack Obama of the outcome of the vote, Obama decided to seek authorisation from Congress. See B Rhodes, 'Inside the White House during the Syrian Red Line Crisis' (*The Atlantic*, 3 June 2018) www.theatlantic.com/international/archive/2018/06/inside-the-white-house-during-the-syrian-red-line-crisis/561887/.

[23] *Hansard*, HC Deb Vol 585, col 1360 (26 September 2014).

[24] *Hansard*, HC Deb Vol 603, cols 323–499 (2 December 2015).

[25] G Phillipson, "Historic' Commons' Syria vote: the constitutional significance (Part I)' (*UK Constitutional Law Association Blog*, 19 September 2013) www.ukconstitutionallaw.org/2013/09/19/gavin-phillipson-historic-commons-syria-vote-the-constitutional-significance-part-i/; See also G Phillipson, "Historic' Commons' Syria vote: the constitutional significance (Part II – the way forward) (*UK Constitutional Law Association Blog*, 29 November 2013) www.ukconstitutionallaw.org/2013/11/29/gavin-phillipson-historic-commons-syria-vote-the-constitutional-significance-part-ii-the-way-forward/; G Phillipson, 'Voting on Military Action in Syria: A Reply' (*UK Constitutional Law Association Blog*, 2 December 2015) www.ukconstitutionallaw.org/2015/12/02/gavin-phillipson-voting-on-military-action-in-syria-a-reply/.

The Pendulum Swings Back: Reassertion of Executive Dominance (2016–21)

Optimism amongst constitutional experts or parliamentarians about the prospect of taming the prerogative proved short lived, because in the Parliaments which followed, Theresa May and Boris Johnson reasserted executive control in three important respects. The first was over the war-making power. In April 2018, Theresa May authorised military action in Syria without seeking prior parliamentary approval. She subsequently explained the reasons why Parliament was not consulted: the need to protect planned operations, guard shared intelligence, preserve collaboration with allies, and provide humanitarian relief. But, in so doing, she carved out such broad exceptions to the convention that it was questionable whether it still existed. The subsequent parliamentary debate did nothing to clarify the role of Parliament in relation to war powers; and PACAC's 2019 proposal to codify the core convention in a resolution was rebuffed by the government. Whether the convention still exists, and in what modified form, is discussed further in chapter seven.

The second respect in which the executive ultimately reasserted control was over the ratification of treaties. The statutory procedure prescribed in CRAG for parliamentary consideration of treaties did not match up to the political exigencies of Brexit. There is not space here to describe the many twists and turns of the Brexit Parliament in which the government could not construct a majority for its flagship policy. Suffice it to say that initially Parliament tightened up the CRAG requirements by passing (against the government's wishes) Dominic Grieve's amendment to the European Union (Withdrawal) Bill 2018 to ensure that ratification of the withdrawal agreement required a positive resolution of the Commons, or a 'meaningful vote'. But after Theresa May's failure to secure a positive resolution for her agreement, and Boris Johnson's landslide victory in 2019, the requirement for a meaningful vote was repealed by section 31 of the EU (Withdrawal Agreement) Act 2020, and the possibility of parliamentary delay under Part 2 of CRAG was removed by section 32. Thanks to the new government's huge majority, the EU (Withdrawal Agreement) Act 2020 was passed within weeks and with minimal parliamentary scrutiny. A year later, in December 2020, the government agreed the Trade and Cooperation Agreement (TCA) with the EU without the Commons having had a formal debate on the substance of the UK's negotiating position. The implementing Bill was passed in one day, providing Parliament with very little time to scrutinise either the treaty or its implementing legislation.

The third, and most dramatic respect in which the executive reasserted control was over the power of dissolution. Boris Johnson had tried to break the Brexit deadlock in Parliament by holding an early election, but had failed three times to secure the two-thirds majority required under the Fixed-term Parliaments Act (FTPA) for a mid-term dissolution. The December 2019 election was consequently authorised by side stepping the FTPA through the Early Parliamentary General Election Act 2019. Following these difficulties, the 2019 Conservative Party manifesto promised to 'get rid of the Fixed Term Parliaments Act', which had 'led to paralysis at a time the country needed decisive action'. In December 2020, the government published the draft Fixed-term Parliaments Act 2011 (Repeal) Bill to fulfil this commitment. In the words of the government's foreword:

> The draft Fixed-term Parliaments Act 2011 (Repeal) Bill delivers on this commitment. In doing so, the Bill makes express provision to revive the prerogative power to dissolve Parliament. This means once more Parliament will be dissolved by the Sovereign, on the advice of the Prime Minister. This will enable Governments, within the life of a Parliament, to call a general election at the time of their choosing.[26]

The government was thus quite explicit about wishing to transfer the power of dissolution from Parliament back to the Prime Minister. Despite PACAC's earlier recommendation that 'there should not be a return to Executive dominance of election calling',[27] and lukewarm support from the parliamentary joint committee established to review the FTPA, the government persisted and the Dissolution and Calling of Parliament Act was passed in March 2022 with only minimal changes when compared with the draft Bill. Of the three respects in which the government has reasserted control in recent years, this is the most important, representing a significant shift of power from Parliament back to the executive.

War Powers

The second part of this chapter provides more detail about the struggle for greater parliamentary control of each of the prerogative powers. In relation to each power, we ask first about the formal status of Parliament's role: is it enshrined in statute; in convention; or something looser? And second, how effective has Parliament been in controlling the exercise of the prerogative powers?

We start with war powers, for there are few political decisions more important than going to war. After the invasion of Iraq in 2003, parliamentary committees conducted several inquiries in order to consider how to ensure that the government could not embark on military action without the approval of the House of Commons (see chapter seven). Three possible mechanisms were proposed, in ascending order of stringency:

- an informal convention based upon precedent (starting with the Commons vote approving the planned invasion of Iraq in 2003);

[26] Cabinet Office, *Draft Fixed Term Parliaments Act 2011 (Repeal) Bill* (CP 322, 2020).

[27] Sixth Report from the House of Commons Public Administration and Constitutional Affairs Committee, *The Fixed-term Parliaments Act 2011* HC 167 (2019–21), para 18.

- a formal parliamentary convention embodied in a resolution of the House of Commons, (as favoured by the House of Lords Constitution Committee);[28] and
- legislation setting out the conditions the government would need to satisfy before it could wage war (as proposed by the PASC).[29]

Several backbenchers sought to introduce legislation following PASC's 2004 report. The Armed Forces (Parliamentary Approval for Participation in Armed Conflict) Bill was introduced by Neil Gerrard in 2005, and again by Clare Short later that year. Michael Meacher introduced the Waging War (Parliament's Role and Responsibility) Bill in 2006. The Bills attempted to introduce the statutory requirement that prior parliamentary approval was necessary for participation in armed conflict, but retrospective approval was sufficient in times of urgency. Wary of the effect that statutory displacement of the prerogative might have on the need to act flexibly, the House of Lords Constitution Committee advocated instead a formal convention embodied in a Commons resolution that the government must seek parliamentary approval to engage in armed conflict.[30]

The Blair government remained unpersuaded even by this lesser form of control,[31] but in 2007 the new Prime Minister Gordon Brown proposed that 'On an issue of such fundamental importance, the government should seek the approval of the House of Commons for significant, non-routine deployments of the Armed Forces into armed conflict.'[32] The Brown government subsequently opted for a parliamentary resolution, setting out in detail the processes Parliament should follow before approving deployment of the armed forces; and appended a draft resolution to their White Paper.[33] Scrutinising the proposals, the Joint Committee on the Draft Constitutional Renewal Bill criticised the definition of a 'conflict decision' that had been included in the draft resolution, and PASC was even more critical, in particular of the Prime Minister's proposed ability to control the information which would be made available to Parliament prior to the debate.[34] The Brown government made no further progress before it left office in May 2010.

Legislation was ruled out because it just raised too many difficult questions: how to define the sort of military action that would trigger parliamentary involvement; under what circumstances the government could circumvent Parliament on grounds of urgency; and what were the risks of involving the courts. In addition,

[28] Fifteenth Report from the House of Lords Constitution Committee, *Waging War: Parliament's Role and Responsibility* HL 236-I (2005–06).

[29] House of Commons Public Administration Select Committee, above n 14.

[30] House of Lords Constitution Committee, above n 28 at para 108.

[31] Department for Constitutional Affairs, *Government Response to the House of Lords Constitution Committee's Fifteenth Report of Session 2005–06: Waging War: Parliament's role and response* (Cm 6923, 2006).

[32] Ministry of Justice, above n 17 at para 26.

[33] Ministry of Justice, above n 18 at para 215.

[34] *First Report from the Joint Committee on the Draft Constitutional Renewal Bill* HL 166-I HC 551-I (2007–08), paras 470–478; Tenth Report from the House of Commons Public Administration Select Committee, *Constitutional Renewal: Draft Bill and White Paper* HC 499 (2007–08), para 72.

when modern warfare is rapidly changing with the development of new threats like cyber-attacks, there was also the difficulty of future-proofing. When PACAC revisited the subject in 2019, it concluded: 'While the involvement of Parliament at the earliest opportunity is vital, any statutory formalisation of this expectation would create new risks, given the difficulty of legislating for all possible contingencies.'[35]

But, under Cameron's premiership, successive instances of the government seeking parliamentary approval (see page 275) suggested there was a recognised convention that the government would not deploy the armed forces overseas without prior recourse to Parliament.[36] The convention was acknowledged in the Cabinet Manual, albeit in terms which left the government with a degree of discretion and flexibility.[37] The key moment was in 2013, when the Commons voted against intervention, and Cameron responded that the 'Government will act accordingly'.[38] But, in 2018, Theresa May called the convention into question by authorising military action against Syria without seeking prior parliamentary approval. May explained that there were four reasons why Parliament was not consulted, seemingly indicating four exceptions to the convention: the need to protect the effectiveness of planned military operations, to guard shared intelligence, to preserve collaboration with allies, and to provide humanitarian relief under international law.[39]

This episode underlined the weakness of relying on informal conventions. Adherence to conventions depends on political will: the willingness of the executive to follow the convention; and the willingness of Parliament to sanction the government when it fails to do so. In theory, Parliament thus retains the ability to regulate the operation of the war powers convention through the exertion of political pressure. Recognising Parliament's role in scrutinising her decision, May pronounced 'I am absolutely clear, Mr Speaker, that it is Parliament's responsibility to hold me to account for such decisions, and Parliament will do so.'[40]

But Parliament did not. Following the airstrikes, leader of the opposition Jeremy Corbyn introduced a motion on 17 April 2018 'That this house has considered Parliament's rights in relation to the approval of military action by British Forces overseas.'[41] Yet, this was only a 'take note' motion under Standing Order 24 which did not allow for a vote: it was thus difficult for Parliament formally to express disapproval of May's failure to observe the convention. On whether we still have a war powers convention, Strong has observed:

> [The] question of whether a war powers convention exists, depends on three contingent factors; whether ministers accept a convention exists, whether MPs believe a convention

[35] Twentieth Report from the House of Commons Public Administration and Constitutional Affairs Committee, *The Role of Parliament in the UK Constitution: Authorising the Use of Military Force* HC 1891 (2017–19), paras 134 and 69–83.

[36] Phillipson, above n 25.

[37] Cabinet Office, *The Cabinet Manual*, 1st edn (2011), para 5.38.

[38] *Hansard*, HC Deb Vol 566, col 1556 (29 August 2013).

[39] *Hansard*, HC Deb Vol 639, cols 205–208 (17 April 2018).

[40] *Hansard*, HC Deb Vol 639, col 42 (16 April 2018).

[41] *Hansard*, HC Deb Vol 639, col 192 (17 April 2018).

> exists, and whether MPs are willing to enforce a convention that they believe in but that ministers do not accept. These factors cannot entirely be divorced from their immediate institutional and ideational contexts; what MPs believe depends at least in part on what their predecessors believed, for example, while their willingness to enforce a convention depends on party-political calculations as well as the specific substantive issues at stake.[42]

Without tighter parliamentary enforcement of the war powers convention, it risks becoming optional, as in Canada. With no formal convention requiring the government to consult the Commons in Ottawa, the Canadian government has chosen to consult Parliament only when it suits them. For example, parliamentary consultation was used to deflect accountability for the unpopular military engagement in Afghanistan in 2007 and 2008, and to divide the opposition against air strikes on the Islamic State.[43] Summarising the effect of this pattern of occasional consultation, Lagassé observes that 'Rather than augmenting the Commons' control over military deployments, Canada's war power reforms have strengthened the Executive's position vis-à-vis Parliament.'[44]

In 2019, PACAC revived its campaign to formalise Parliament's role. Acknowledging the difficulties in legislating for all possible contingencies and exceptions, PACAC suggested that a resolution recognising the core convention should be approved. In addition, PACAC emphasised that the Commons 'must have access to as much of the information as possible so it can carry out effective scrutiny of the Government's use of military force'.[45] Where information is confidential, PACAC recommended that the Intelligence and Security Committee, or a similar committee bound by secrecy, should be provided with full access in order to 'inform and reassure the House of Commons on the scope of the action proposed by the Government'.[46] In response to the committee, the government offered a bland reply, illustrating yet again the institutional weakness of Parliament, and the difficulties of relying upon a convention whose contours have never been sufficiently clear:

> The Government believes that the current arrangements strike an appropriate balance between respecting the role of Parliament in relation to the authorisation of military force, and allowing the Government to act flexibly as circumstances demand.[47]

[42] J Strong 'Did Theresa May Kill the War Powers Convention? Comparing Parliamentary Debates on UK Intervention in Syria in 2013 and 2018' (2021) 00 *Parliamentary Affairs* 1, 17.

[43] P Lagassé, 'Parliament and the War Prerogative in the United Kingdom and Canada: Explaining Variations in Institutional Change and Legislative Control' (2017) 70 *Parliamentary Affairs* 280, 281.

[44] ibid.

[45] House of Commons Public Administration and Constitutional Affairs Committee, above n 35 at para 131.

[46] ibid at para 132.

[47] First Special Report from the House of Commons Public Administration and Constitutional Affairs Committee, *Government Response to the Committee's 20th Report of Session 2017–19: The Role of Parliament in the UK Constitution: Authorising the Use of Military Force* HC 251 (2017–19), 11.

Treaties

Parliament's role in ratifying treaties is enshrined in Part 2 of the Constitutional Reform and Governance Act 2010 (CRAG), which codified the Ponsonby Rule. Under CRAG, the government cannot ratify a treaty unless it has first laid the signed treaty (along with an explanatory memorandum) before Parliament for 21 sitting days. CRAG also gave the House of Commons a new power: if during that statutory pause it passes a resolution that a treaty should not be ratified, another 21 sitting day delay to ratification is triggered – and this process may be repeated. In contrast, a resolution passed by the House of Lords against ratification merely requires the government to think again and produce a further explanatory statement as to why the treaty should be ratified.

Neither House has yet passed a resolution against ratification of a treaty under these provisions. There are several possible reasons: the all-or-nothing nature of such a vote; the difficulty of finding time when most parliamentary time is controlled by the government; or simply a lack of interest. But interest in treaties has greatly increased as a result of Brexit: because of the surge in trade and other agreements which the UK now has to negotiate; and because of the growing awareness of how little control Parliament has over such negotiations. This has led to greater interest in treaties amongst certain select committees and has renewed discussion about whether Parliament should have a more systematic approach to the scrutiny of treaties.

The House of Lords has shown much greater interest in establishing a dedicated mechanism than the Commons. The Lords Secondary Legislation Committee was active in scrutinising non-EU related treaties, but in January 2019, the Lords European Union Committee assumed oversight of Brexit-related rollover treaties, producing 22 reports pertaining to over 50 treaties.[48] The Lords Constitution Committee in 2019 recommended establishment of a dedicated treaty committee that could create a 'natural home and possible clearing house within Parliament for all treaty-related activity'.[49] This could give rise to a number of benefits. First, such a committee could negotiate new arrangements for the provision of information about treaties under negotiation. Second, it could result in a greater number of parliamentarians with experience of treaty scrutiny. Third, the committee could increase the involvement of devolved legislatures in the treaty-making process. Fourth, a notable deficiency of CRAG could be addressed through empowering a treaty committee with the power to request debates on specific treaties.[50]

The Australian Joint Select Committee on Treaties (JSCOT) serves as an example of how a dedicated treaty committee could operate. Introduced by the Howard

[48] A Lang, *How Parliament treats treaties* (House of Commons Library Briefing Paper 9247, June 2021), 29.

[49] ibid at para 62.

[50] J Barrett, 'Treaties beyond the EU' in UK in a Changing Europe, *Parliament and Brexit* (UK in a Changing Europe, 2020), 47.

government in 1996 to address the democratic deficit present in the treaty making process, JSCOT reviews treaty texts and accompanying reports, presents a report to Parliament and recommends whether the treaty should be ratified. But, as JSCOT possesses no power to scrutinise treaties prior to signature, concerns of a democratic deficit continue. In 2015, JSCOT released recommendations to address these issues, including ensuring parliamentary access to draft treaty text, and improving parliamentary consultation during negotiations (see chapter fifteen).[51]

The most recent development in the UK, following the recommendation of the House of Lords Constitution Committee, is the creation in March 2020 of the House of Lords International Agreements Sub-Committee (IAC), which was upgraded to a full Select Committee in 2021. Its remit is to consider the negotiation, conclusion, and implementation of all treaties and international agreements presented to Parliament. Although the IAC has increased information sharing between Parliament and the government, its substantive effect remains to be seen. The Lords has few powers under CRAG, and even the Commons has only a power of delay. For parliamentary scrutiny to be more effective, CRAG would need to be strengthened in several respects. First, and most importantly, CRAG should be amended to require parliamentary approval of treaties – a 'meaningful vote' similar to that required by the Grieve amendment to the European Union (Withdrawal) Act 2018. Second, it should require the government to provide time for a debate and vote. Third, Parliament should have more of a role when the government is negotiating treaties, which is the stage when changes could be made. Fourth, CRAG should be extended to cover treaty amendments, withdrawals and derogations. Not all these changes would necessarily require legislation: the procedural changes could be made through Standing Orders, or government undertakings. But without some strengthening of its formal role, parliamentary scrutiny of treaties seems likely to continue to have only limited effectiveness.

Dissolution

Chapter five related the story behind the introduction of the Fixed-term Parliaments Act 2011, and of the Johnson government's plans to repeal the Act and restore the prerogative power of dissolution. The FTPA certainly had its flaws, having been rushed through Parliament in the first year of the Conservative-Liberal Democrat coalition, with no prior consultation or pre-legislative scrutiny. That is why, in the final stages of the FTPA's passage, Parliament inserted a statutory requirement for the Act to be reviewed in 2020. Parliament tried hard to influence the statutory review: earlier in 2020, the House of Lords Constitution Committee and PACAC both initiated inquiries of their own. PACAC's report, published in

[51] Parliament of Australia Senate Foreign Affairs, Defence and Trade References Committee, *Blind Agreement: reforming Australia's treaty-making process* (2015).

September 2020, laid down some clear markers for the joint committee to review, arguing that it would be unfair to restore the right of an incumbent to time an election for electoral advantage, and that parliaments should normally run for a full term, with elections at scheduled times.[52]

This defence of the principles behind the FTPA will have been unwelcome to the government who were already intent on restoring the prerogative. Only one member of PACAC, and one member of the House of Lords Constitution Committee were subsequently chosen by the Prime Minister to be part of the statutory review. The review was conducted by a parliamentary joint committee composed of 14 MPs and six members of the Lords, and was chaired by former Conservative Chief Whip Lord McLoughlin. Most of the evidence received by the committee supported the retention of the FTPA with amendments, rather than outright repeal. As a result, the committee's report devoted almost equal space to the FTPA and how it might be amended, in case Parliament prefers to go down that route at some time in the future. The committee recommended the possibility of three main amendments to the FTPA: replacing the Commons supermajority threshold for triggering an early general election with a simple Commons majority; requiring any early election motion to stipulate when polling day would take place; and removing from the statute the no-confidence mechanism by which an election could be triggered. This would have simplified the dissolution rules; reduced the risk of gridlock; and enabled questions of confidence to be governed by constitutional convention rather than statute.

The joint committee was equally critical of the government's draft Bill, which would repeal the FTPA, and restore the prerogative power of dissolution. But the draft Bill went beyond simple restoration of the previous system, by adding an ouster clause to prevent any judicial oversight of the power, and a statement of Dissolution Principles (which were subsequently dropped) enabling the Prime Minister to advise rather than request a dissolution. The committee was strongly critical of both features of the draft Bill, but ultimately felt obliged to support the repeal of the FTPA because both major parties had given clear commitments to repeal the FTPA in their 2019 manifestos.

On several key issues, however, the committee's report went against the weight of evidence received. The main recommendation on which this happened was on the central issue of whether dissolution should be decided by the executive or by Parliament. As the committee acknowledged, 'Retaining a role for the House of Commons commanded a great deal of support in evidence to this Committee as well as PACAC and the Constitution Committee.'[53] The committee also acknowledged that retaining a vote for the Commons would resolve two other central concerns: it would protect the monarch from controversy; and it would ensure that the decision to dissolve was non-justiciable, obviating the need for any ouster

[52] House of Commons Public Administration and Constitutional Affairs Committee, above n 27.

[53] *First Report from the Joint Committee on the Fixed-Term Parliaments Act* HC 1046 HL 253 (2019–21), para 84.

clause. It is disappointing that a parliamentary committee was not braver in asserting a stronger role for the legislature, and when the issue surfaced again in debates on the Dissolution and Calling of Parliaments Bill, Parliament once again felt constrained by the manifesto commitment to repeal the FTPA; the Bill becoming an Act of Parliament in March 2022.

Regulation of the Civil Service

Parliament can take much of the credit for putting regulation of the civil service on a statutory basis. In the late twentieth century concerns about politicisation and the need to protect the core values of the civil service led to increasing demands that it be placed upon a statutory footing. The parliamentary campaign began with the 1994 report of the Treasury and Civil Service Committee, and was continued by PASC in its 2004 report *A Draft Civil Service Bill: Completing the Reform*. The campaign eventually reached fruition under the premiership of Gordon Brown in Part 1 of CRAG.

Parliament should have emerged triumphant, but it was to prove a rather hollow victory. The hope was that embedding the core values of the civil service in primary legislation and putting the Civil Service Commission on a statutory basis would restore the authority of the civil service, and strengthen the hands of officials in speaking truth to power. It is true that giving the Civil Service Commission a statutory basis has enabled it to ensure that civil service appointments continue to be on merit, after fair and open competition. So, the worst of politicisation has been avoided; but as we record in chapter nine, the decade since the enactment of CRAG has seen further politicisation in other respects, resulting in the civil service becoming even more marginalised. CRAG has provided no defence against that. The legislation was essentially conservative, in that it codified what had previously been in Orders in Council, providing a statutory foundation for the Civil Service Commission and core civil service values, but not much more.

The key provision contained in section 3(1) CRAG provides that the Minister for the Civil Service has the power to manage the civil service. This role, by convention, falls to the Prime Minister. It gives the Prime Minister wide ranging powers: to reshape, abolish or merge government departments; to appoint and dismiss senior officials; to decide on the members of the Civil Service Commission.[54] Parliament has been largely silent, save for the occasional protest from former mandarins in the House of Lords, and critical reports from PACAC, which the government has easily brushed aside.[55] It is hard to see what more Parliament could do, when it is

[54] Note that the appointment of the Civil Service Commissioners is subject to the constraints in the Constitutional Reform and Governance Act 2010, sch 1, paras 1–3. For further details, see chapter nine.

[55] Fifth Special Report from the House of Commons Public Administration Select Committee, *Truth to Power: How Civil Service reform can succeed: Government Response to the Committee's Eighth Report of Session 2013–14* HC 955 (2013–14).

the way the government has exercised its powers that is called into question, rather than the powers themselves: as in so many other fields, it is hard to legislate for good conduct.

Public Appointments

One of Gordon Brown's lasting achievements was not one that was realised through a change in the law (as with the ratification of treaties, or the regulation of the civil service), but through a change in political practice which has since developed into a convention. The change was his announcement that in future the executive's nominee for senior public appointments should be subject to a pre-appointment hearing with the relevant select committee. As recounted in chapter ten, the House of Commons Liaison Committee negotiated with the Cabinet Office to agree upon over 50 positions that would be subject to this procedure, including the major constitutional watchdogs and regulators. Although non-binding, the conclusions reached by select committees in pre-appointment hearings have had a significant influence on public appointments. Since their inception in 2007, committee reports from pre-appointment hearings have resulted in candidates not being appointed, as well as withdrawing and resigning.[56]

Parliament has also succeeded in obtaining a power of veto over certain positions: the Comptroller and Auditor General, Parliamentary Ombudsman, Office for Budgetary Responsibility, chair of the UK Statistics Authority, and Information Commissioner. But those were all one-off decisions. Parliament has been less successful in persuading the government that it should have a power of veto over whole categories of public appointments, for example those where independence from the executive is crucial to the role (such as constitutional watchdogs). The Commons Liaison Committee made a bold attempt to do so in 2011, suggesting that appointments be divided into three distinct categories. First-tier posts should require a joint appointment by government and Parliament, second tier posts should be subject to an effective veto, and for the remainder, holding a pre-appointment hearing should be at the discretion of the committee.[57] The recommendations were not adopted, but a similar proposal was recently floated by the Committee on Standards in Public Life.[58]

By contrast, parliamentary influence over the use of the prerogative to make appointments to the Lords remains much weaker. The House of Lords Appointments Commission (HoLAC) was created under the prerogative in 2000 to recommend the appointment of independent peers. Noting that the 'intention

[56] R Hazell, 'Improving Parliamentary Scrutiny of Public Appointments' (2019) 72 *Parliamentary Affairs* 223, 223.

[57] First Report from the House of Commons Liaison Committee, *Select Committees and Public Appointments* HC 1230 (2010–12).

[58] Committee on Standards in Public Life, *Upholding Standards in Public Life* (2021), paras 5.20–5.22.

was always to create a Statutory Appointments Commission', PASC advocated for the statutory anchoring of the Commission in 2007.[59] This would have clarified the remit of the Commission and provided that the requirements for entry to the Lords were clear, widely agreed, and of unquestionable legitimacy.[60] In 2018, PACAC returned to the topic in order to support the Lord Speaker's Committee on the Size of the House's proposals on reducing the size of the Lords, but received an equally non-committal government response.[61] Chapter ten records how, in the absence of statutory protection, the role of HoLAC has been undermined; first by reducing the number of crossbench appointments that could be recommended by the Commission under David Cameron; then by ignoring the Commission's vetting advice under Boris Johnson. In the absence of statutory protection, the Commission remains vulnerable to being marginalised in this way. And if it continues to be seen by the Prime Minister as an irritant, there is a risk that HoLAC could even be abolished.

Honours

In 2004, PASC recommended that an independent Honours Commission should be established in order to address the politicisation of the honours system.[62] The proposal was to establish the commission by statute, in the hope that the body would have been 'anchored in and scrutinised by Parliament'.[63] Rather than adopt PASC's recommendations, the government proceeded to implement a number of suggestions made by Sir Hayden Phillips to bring a stronger independent element into the system (see chapter thirteen). This included reforming the Honours Committees to introduce a majority of non-civil service members, and appointing an independent chairperson to each expert committee.[64] Although both Tony Blair and Gordon Brown had made commitments neither to add nor to subtract any names from the list of recommendations provided by the Main Honours Committee,[65] these changes did not go far enough in the eyes of PASC. In 2012, PASC returned to the issue, strongly criticising the establishment of a new Parliamentary and Political Honours Committee and the presence of each of the Chief Whips from the three main political parties on it. PASC recommended

[59] Second Report from the House of Commons Public Administration Select Committee, *Propriety and peerages* HC 153 (2007–08), para 115.

[60] ibid at para 135.

[61] Twelfth Special Report from the Public Administration and Constitutional Affairs Committee, *Government Response to the Committee's Thirteenth Report: A Smaller House of Lords* HC 2005 (2017–19).

[62] Fifth Report from the House of Commons Public Administration Select Committee, *A Matter of Honour: Reforming the Honours System* HC 212-I (2003–04), para 161.

[63] ibid at para 165.

[64] Cabinet Office, *Reform of the Honours System* (Cm 6479 2005), 5.

[65] Ministry of Justice, above n 17 at para 85.

removal of the Prime Minister's role in providing strategic direction for the honours system, and again advocated for the creation of an Independent Honours Commission.[66] The government rejected both proposals. Later in 2012, PASC returned to the subject once again but must have known it would gain no satisfaction other than having the last word.[67]

Passports

Despite Gordon Brown's pledge to 'remove the prerogative in relation to passports',[68] any mention of passports was omitted from the draft Constitutional Renewal Bill in 2008. Having identified passports as requiring early legislative action just four years earlier, PASC urged the government to introduce legislation before the next session.[69] But when the Brown government ran out of parliamentary time to do so and the coalition government failed to pick up the baton, parliamentary interest faded. It was confirmed in 2013 that as 'there is no statutory right to have access to a passport', the decision to 'issue, withdraw, or refuse a British passport' remains entirely at the discretion of the Home Secretary.[70] A consequence of this is that the rules on the issue of passports are contained in occasional statements by the Home Secretary, with no parliamentary input: the rules are not even set out in secondary legislation (see chapter twelve).

Legislation should be perfectly possible. In other Westminster realms, the prerogative to confer and withdraw passports has been placed on a statutory basis. In New Zealand, the Parliament legislated to enact the Passports Act 1992, and in Australia the Passports Act 2005. The legislation confers a legal entitlement to a passport upon the citizen, and provides an exhaustive list of rules governing the issue of passports. Under such systems, there is very little discretion to refuse the granting of a passport save in the circumstances approved by Parliament.[71]

Conclusion

This chapter has considered the role of Parliament in regulating the prerogative. In the last 20 years that role has grown, thanks largely to the campaign initiated

[66] Second Report from the House of Commons Public Administration Select Committee, *The Honours System* HC 19 (2012–13), para 68.

[67] Seventh Report from the House of Commons Public Administration Select Committee, *The Honours System: Further Report with the Government Response to the Committee's Second Report of Session 2012–13* HC 728 (2012–13).

[68] Ministry of Justice, above n 18 at para 247.

[69] House of Commons Public Administration Select Committee, above n 34 at para 91.

[70] *Hansard*, HC Deb Vol 561, col 69W (25 April 2013).

[71] P Scott, 'Passports, the Right to Travel, and National Security in the Commonwealth' (2020) 69 *International & Comparative Law Quarterly* 365, 376.

by PASC to tame the prerogative, the changes introduced by Gordon Brown in 2007–10, and further changes under the 2010–15 coalition. But, in the last five years, some of those changes have been rolled back, defying the simplistic assumption that once Parliament had assumed greater control over a prerogative power, it could not be taken back.

The overall assessment has to be that Parliament has not been very successful in getting a tighter grip on the prerogative. Of all the areas reviewed in the second half of this chapter, it is only in relation to the war-making power, the ratification of treaties, the regulation of the civil service and the conferral of public appointments that Parliament has made any impression; and some of those gains have been transitory. The seeming convention that Parliament would be consulted about military action evaporated when Theresa May ignored it in 2018. Neither House has yet exercised the statutory power in CRAG to pass a resolution against ratifying a treaty. The statutory protections provided for the civil service in Part 2 of CRAG have not prevented further politicisation in Whitehall. Only pre-appointment scrutiny hearings can be regarded as a lasting success, and a check against favouritism in public appointments; although one not recognised by select committee chairs, who tend to regard the hearings as a waste of time.

There are several reasons why parliamentary control of the prerogative has not been more sustained or effective. One is simply the lack of political will: politicians like Tony Wright are rare exceptions, and most parliamentarians have shown little interest in the prerogative. Another is lack of awareness: most parliamentarians were not aware of the importance of treaties until Brexit – which has changed all that. A third factor is limited institutional capacity and expertise, illustrated in Parliament's lack of interest (until recently) in developing the capacity to scrutinise treaties. A fourth is the unreliability of shifting conventions, seen in Parliament's attempts to regulate the war-making power. A fifth is the complexity of the underlying issues of the prerogative, illustrated again by the war power. After a sustained campaign, led by several different select committees, what hampered their efforts was the growing recognition of the difficulty of the government sharing sensitive intelligence about planned operations and the difficulty of crafting a resolution which was sufficiently watertight but also flexible to deal with emergencies.

Executive resistance to greater parliamentary control tends to vary depending on the importance of the power in question: it is no coincidence that the war-making power and the power of dissolution have seen the greatest executive pushback. But that does not explain the continuing resistance to codification of the prerogative power over lesser matters such as passports. Unlike the process of codifying the war powers convention, there cannot be serious difficulty in drafting a clear set of criteria for the issue and withdrawal of passports. It remains a puzzle why Parliament has not insisted on codification of the Home Secretary's policy. To show how it could be done, PACAC could take the initiative and produce a draft Passports Bill, just as PASC produced a draft Civil Service Bill in 2004.

That leads us to the final reason why Parliament has not been more effective in regulating the prerogative, which we might call institutional confidence.

Most parliamentarians would not regard it as their job to draft a Passports Bill: that is seen as a matter for government, which has the expertise, and the responsibility to do so. And after several decades of growing parliamentary confidence and effectiveness, well charted by Meg Russell and others,[72] the combination of Brexit followed by Covid-19 has seen a re-assertion of executive dominance, in legislation by decree, control of parliamentary time, and many other respects.[73] It is too early to say whether this new period of executive dominance will outlast the Johnson government; but so long as it does last, parliamentary regulation of the prerogative will remain fragile and liable to further reversals.

[72] M Russell and P Cowley, 'The Policy Power of the Westminster Parliament: The "Parliamentary State" and the Empirical Evidence' (2016) 29 *Governance* 121.

[73] M Russell, R Fox, R Cormacain and J Tomlinson, 'The marginalisation of the House of Commons under Covid has been shocking; a year on, parliament's role must urgently be restored' (*Constitution Unit Blog*, 21 April 2021) www.constitution-unit.com/2021/04/21/covid-and-parliament-one-year-on/; Twentieth Report from the House of Lords Secondary Legislation Scrutiny Committee, *Government by Diktat: A Call to return Power to Parliament* HL 105 (2021–22); Twelfth Report from the House of Lords Delegated Powers and Regulatory Reform Committee, *Democracy Denied? The urgent need to re-balance power between Parliament and the Executive* HL 106 (2021–22).

19

Conclusions

> Framers and developers of constitutional frameworks confront an inherent tension between the need to grant powers to the executive and the competing interest in limiting the extent of such powers in the name of the rule of law.
>
> Margit Cohn (2015)[1]

Prerogative, Past, Present and Future

This book is sub-titled *The Prerogative, Past, Present and Future*, but our treatment of those three time periods has not been equal. We have dipped into the past to explain the historical background; but our main focus has been on the present and the future. This concluding chapter will continue in the same vein, summarising recent developments, analysing the present position, and turning to the future towards the end of the chapter.

Where we have written about the past, it has mostly been about the last 30–40 years. These have seen huge changes, with tighter regulation of the prerogative by the courts, and by Parliament, alongside a process of greater codification. That applies to the personal prerogatives of the monarch as well as to prerogative powers of the executive, and this process of tighter regulation will be the main theme running through this chapter. But it has been an incremental process, in fits and starts, with two steps forward, one step back: reactive as much as proactive, driven by external events as much as changing constitutional norms. These include events like the invasion of Iraq, the changing nature of modern warfare, and the growing importance of international treaties: external factors which have also driven developments in Australia, Canada and New Zealand, where there have been equally big changes in the prerogative just in the last 20 years, described in chapter fifteen.

This final chapter is mainly about the prerogative powers of the executive, not the personal prerogatives of the monarch. But these too have recently been the subject of tighter regulation. Having been shrouded in mystery and regulated only through conventions understood by a chosen few, those conventions have been

[1] M Cohn, 'Non-Statutory Executive Powers: Assessing Global Constitutionalism in a Structural-Institutional Context' (2015) 64 *International & Comparative Law Quarterly* 64, 67.

codified in chapters one and two of the Cabinet Manual,[2] and the prerogative power of dissolution abolished by statute in the Fixed-term Parliaments Act 2011 (FTPA). Here too there is ebb and flow, with the FTPA being repealed and the prerogative power of dissolution restored, in the Dissolution and Calling of Parliament Act 2022. Conventions will remain the most important guide to the monarch's exercise of her prerogative powers, and of all the constitutional actors the monarch is the most constrained, not by hard or even soft law, but by the weight of convention, which allows little room for manoeuvre. Nevertheless, the fuzziness of the monarch's reserve powers, as the ultimate guardian of the constitution, can itself act as a significant potential constraint on others, in particular the Prime Minister (see part two).

The Prerogative is an Important Part of Executive Power

The overarching narrative of tighter regulation can easily lead to an assumption that prerogative powers are inherently undesirable and need to be more tightly controlled. That is the 'stubborn stain' theory, that the prerogative is a relic of a bygone age which needs to be expunged from any self-respecting modern constitution.[3] Implicit in the theory is a mistrust of executive power, and belief that all executive power needs to be tightly controlled. Although we support the Westminster view of the constitution (discussed further below), we do not share the instinctive mistrust of executive power. It is important in any system of government to have an executive with powers of 'unanimity, strength and despatch', as described by William Blackstone. The prerogative is an important source of such powers. Nor are they minor or obscure powers: there are few powers more important than the power to make war, or to enter into international agreements. What is important is to acknowledge the positive reasons for a strong executive, and the equally strong reasons for comparable accountability: 'we can only understand the extent of the executive power – and the ways in which it ought to be limited and constrained – if we understand its constitutional value'.[4]

Margit Cohn has developed a sophisticated comparative analysis of the nature and justification of executive power:

> Despite their problematic nature, non-statutory powers have always been on the menus of executives in democratic Western States. Such powers have gone by different names: prerogative, residual, inherent, autonomous, unilateral, presidential … The arguments for broad and flexible executive power draw on law's limitations and on expediency. Essentially, no text can supply a basis for all possible contingencies … Further, executives are best placed to respond to fast-moving, ever-changing realities.[5]

[2] Cabinet Office, *Cabinet Manual*, 1st edn (2011).
[3] T Endicott, *The Stubborn Stain Theory of Executive Power* (Policy Exchange, 2017).
[4] ibid at 3.
[5] Cohn, above n 1 at 69.

Cohn's study of non-statutory executive power in the UK, the US and Israel concludes that such powers 'have long pedigrees and are well-embedded in the constitutional practice of at least three Western democracies'. Her subsequent writing explores in great depth the nature of such powers, the risk of their abuse, and how they are best controlled.[6]

Our own comparative chapters have shown the need for a degree of executive autonomy in all political systems. Chapter sixteen showed how many aspects of the prerogative equate to reserve powers in countries with written constitutions: powers enabling the executive to act without the legislature, or even to override the legislature. In some of those countries the executive enjoys more autonomy than that enjoyed by the British government under the prerogative – the war-making power in France and the US being one example. This is not just a policy choice; chapter sixteen also showed that it is an inevitable consequence of drafting. All constitutions have gaps and silences, being high level texts. Even where detail is provided in subsequent legislation, that still leaves a wide margin of discretion for the executive.[7]

Traditionally, the Prerogative has been Regulated by Convention and not Law

In *Law of the Constitution*, Dicey described conventions as 'rules intended to regulate the exercise of the whole of the remaining discretionary powers of the Crown, whether these powers are exercised by the King himself or by the Ministry'.[8] This book has provided plenty of examples: the conventions guiding the monarch's choice of Prime Minister (chapter four), the Lascelles principles regulating the power of dissolution (chapter five), and the Ponsonby Rule on laying treaties before Parliament prior to ratification (chapter eight). Conventions are unwritten rules of governmental morality. Their strength is that they can evolve and adapt to changing circumstances; their weakness is that they are unenforceable – they work only so long as political actors consider them to be binding.

The book also contains examples of apparent conventions which ultimately lacked that binding quality: the proportionality principle in appointments to the House of Lords, violated by David Cameron and Boris Johnson (chapter ten); the requirement to consult the House of Commons before engaging in military action overseas, ignored by Theresa May (chapter seven). One reason for proposing stronger measures, typically through codification in soft law or hard law, is that conventions are flouted. But codification may also be proposed simply for greater

[6] M Cohn, *A Theory of the Executive Branch: Tension and Legality* (Oxford, Oxford University Press, 2021).

[7] M Foley, *The Silence of Constitutions* (London, Routledge, 1989).

[8] AV Dicey, *Introduction to the Study of the Law of the Constitution*, 9th edn (London, Macmillan, 1939), 426.

transparency: the Cabinet Manual was not initially compiled to prevent abuse, but to explain the rules on government formation – including the continuity convention, the caretaker convention, and the confidence convention (chapter four). But codes of conduct may also become instruments of accountability: Amy Baker says of the Ministerial Code that 'the media and members of Parliament have … used it as a strict code of conduct by which to judge and regulate ministerial behaviour'.[9] In a similar vein, Andrew Blick observes that publication of the Cabinet Manual was 'likely to increase awareness of those conventions it describes amongst those who are expected to adhere to them … and amongst those who might pass judgement on constitutional behaviour'.[10]

Even when incorporated in a code, conventions remain largely unenforceable save in the political realm.[11] There is a simplistic spectrum, in terms of rising enforceability and durability, of convention to soft law to hard law. It is true that unwritten conventions are the most easily flouted; and soft law codes like the Ministerial Code can be – and have been – changed by a new Prime Minister.[12] But codification in statute is not always more durable: the provisions in the Constitutional Reform and Governance Act 2010 (CRAG) for ratifying treaties failed the stress test of Brexit, and the FTPA has proved transitory. By comparison, the practice (now a convention?) of parliamentary pre-appointment scrutiny hearings has proved more enduring (chapter ten). So ultimately whether a convention or practice continues to be observed depends on continuing political consensus about its value: how to forge and maintain that consensus is something we return to below.

The Prerogative is Gradually Becoming More Regulated: By the Courts, by Parliament, by Codification, and by Specialist Watchdogs

The narrative running throughout this book, and through this final chapter, is one of the prerogative gradually becoming more regulated. As we said at the start, the direction of travel is not all one way: in the courts as in Parliament there has been

[9] A Baker, *Prime Ministers and the Rule Book* (London, Politico, 2000), 104.

[10] A Blick, 'The Cabinet Manual and the Codification of Conventions' (2014) 67 *Parliamentary Affairs* 191, 198.

[11] On the enforceability of conventions, see F Ahmed, R Albert and A Perry, 'Judging constitutional conventions' (2019) 17 *International Journal of Constitutional Law* 787; In *FDA v The Prime Minister* [2021] EWHC 3279 (Admin), the court recognised that several of the more political conventions in the Ministerial Code were not justiciable, but ruled that the Code itself was justiciable.

[12] In 2015, David Cameron omitted the duty on ministers to comply with international law and treaty obligations: J Halliday, 'Ministerial code: No 10 showing contempt for international law' *The Guardian* (London, 26 October 2015). A list of subsequent changes made by successive Prime Ministers can be found in H Armstrong and C Rhodes, *The Ministerial Code and the Independent Adviser on Ministerial Interests* (House of Commons Library Briefing Paper 03750, August 2021).

ebb and flow, but the overall trend over the last 30–40 years has been to make the prerogative more transparent, more accountable, and to reduce the breadth of executive discretion. That is the trend described in chapter seventeen, about the changing role of the courts, in landmark cases like *Council of Civil Service Unions v Minister for the Civil Service* (*GCHQ*), *R v Secretary of State for the Home Department ex parte Fire Brigades Union*, *R (Miller) v Secretary of State for Exiting the European Union* (*Miller 1*) and *R (Miller) v The Prime Minister* (*Miller 2*).[13] And it is the trend described in chapter eighteen, about the growing interest of Parliament in seeking greater control over war powers, treaties and public appointments. It is a trend visible in the gradual process of codification, into both soft law and hard law. And it is a trend visible in the creation of a whole new cadre of constitutional watchdogs, each designed to regulate a particular aspect of the prerogative.

Tighter Regulation by the Courts

The next four sections provide more detail about the four main ways in which the prerogative has become more tightly regulated, starting with the courts. The courts have always reserved the right to define the existence and scope of prerogative powers, going back to the *Case of Proclamations* in 1610.[14] But traditionally they had been reluctant to go further and rule on its exercise. That changed dramatically with the *GCHQ* case in 1985, when the House of Lords held that 'the controlling factor in determining whether the exercise of prerogative power is subject to judicial review is not its source but its subject matter'.[15] Only prerogative powers that fell into certain excluded categories, including 'high policy', were to be non-justiciable.[16] Lord Roskill gave an indicative list of powers that would continue to be non-justiciable, but even that has not proved sacrosanct: for example, the prerogative of mercy has since proved to be an exception, with judicial review now extending to most exercises of the pardon power (see chapter eleven).

The next incursion into the prerogative came ten years later, with the *Fire Brigades Union* case in 1995, which has been said to espouse the principle that the prerogative 'cannot frustrate the purpose of a statute or a statutory provision, for example by emptying it of content or preventing its effectual operation'.[17] But the biggest shock came with the two Brexit cases brought by Gina Miller: not just because they were such high profile defeats for the government, but because they

[13] *Council of Civil Service Unions v Minister for the Civil Service* [1985] AC 374; *R v Secretary of State for the Home Department ex parte Fire Brigades Union* [1995] 2 AC 513; *R (Miller) v Secretary of State for Exiting the European Union* [2017] UKSC 5; *R (Miller) v The Prime Minister; Cherry v Advocate General* [2019] UKSC 41.

[14] *Case of Proclamations* (1610) 77 ER 1352.

[15] *Council of Civil Service Unions*, above n 13 at 407 (Lord Scarman).

[16] ibid at 418 (Lord Roskill).

[17] *ex parte Fire Brigades Union*, above n 13; *Miller* [2017], above n 13 at [51].

broke new ground legally (see chapter seventeen). In *Miller 1*, about triggering Article 50 of the Treaty on European Union, the Supreme Court asserted that the executive required parliamentary authorisation to make such a great constitutional change: it could not rely on the prerogative alone. In *Miller 2*, the court found that the prerogative power of prorogation could not be used to undermine the fundamental role of Parliament, in scrutinising government and holding it to account.

These two cases mark a notable shift in the way in which the courts approach the prerogative. The government was clearly dismayed, not just at its defeat, but at the uncertainty which might flow from the courts' approach, based more on fundamental principles than previous case law: what further constitutional principles might be invoked in future cases? It led the government to ask the Independent Review of Administrative Law in 2019 to consider 'whether the legal principle of non-justiciability requires clarification';[18] but the panel advised 'leaving questions of justiciability to the judges'.[19] It is unlikely there will be many further cases like *Miller 1* or *Miller 2*; but if a future government is tempted to sideline Parliament, they offer a salutary reminder that the courts will stand up for Westminster.

Tighter Regulation by Parliament

Tighter regulation of the prerogative by Parliament is a phenomenon just of the last 20 years. Interest in the House of Commons was sparked initially by the sustained campaign led by the House of Commons Public Administration Select Committee (PASC) to tame the prerogative, boosted by the support shown by Gordon Brown in 2007–10, and further boosted by the series of votes on military deployments under the 2010–15 coalition. But, despite the breadth of PASC's campaign, it is only in relation to war powers, treaties, and public appointments that Parliament has made any impression; and some of those gains have been transitory. The convention that Parliament would be consulted about military action, which appeared to consolidate under David Cameron, was considerably watered down by Theresa May in 2018. As for treaties, neither House has yet exercised the statutory power in CRAG to pass a resolution to delay ratification. Only pre-appointment scrutiny hearings can be regarded as a lasting success, a further small check against favouritism in public appointments.

Chapter eighteen identified several reasons why parliamentary control of the prerogative has not been more sustained or effective. One is simply lack of political will: politicians like PASC's chairman Tony Wright are rare exceptions. Another is lack of awareness: most parliamentarians were not aware of the importance of treaties – until Brexit. A third is the unreliability of shifting conventions, illustrated in Parliament's attempts to regulate the war making power. A fourth is

[18] Independent Review of Administrative Law, *Terms of Reference* (2020), para 2.
[19] *Report from the Independent Review of Administrative Law* (CP 407, 2021), paras 2.98, 2.100.

the complexity of the underlying issues, illustrated again by the war power, with the changing nature of modern warfare, and the difficulties of sharing sensitive intelligence.

A final factor is Parliament's limited institutional capacity and lack of leadership. Unlike the executive, which is tightly organised, with clear collective decision-making procedures, Parliament is the reverse, with multiple different sources of power and authority. It is hard to provide strategic leadership when the Leader of the House, the Speaker of the Commons, and the House of Commons Commission can all claim a share in the management of the institution; to say nothing of the need for coordination with the House of Lords.[20] Added to this is the problem of executive domination: the main priority of the Leader of the House is to advance the government's business rather than maximise parliamentary scrutiny. So it is no wonder that it has taken Parliament a long time to develop the capacity to scrutinise treaties, in the new International Agreements Committee (chapter eight); and no surprise that it was the House of Lords, with no government majority, rather than the Commons which has done so.

Tighter Regulation through Codification

The third way in which the prerogative has become more tightly regulated is through codification. This has taken a variety of different forms, with varying degrees of effectiveness. There is the obvious distinction between soft and hard law codification; but even when the prerogative is regulated in statute, regulation is not necessarily much tighter – it depends on the content of the regulatory regime. The strongest examples of codification in statute are the series of Acts passed to regulate the intelligence agencies: starting with the Security Service Act 1989, which put MI5 on a statutory footing; and then the Intelligence Agencies Act 1994, which did the same for GCHQ and MI6. Subsequent legislation has strengthened and then consolidated the network of Commissioners who scrutinise their operations. Chapter nine described how the statutory regime has transformed the agencies' status and accountability. Under the prerogative their activities did not fall under the normal rule of law, and the aggrieved citizen had no recourse against an organisation which did not officially exist. By contrast, the new statutory framework has introduced Judicial Commissioners to approve the issue of warrants, together with an overarching Investigatory Powers Commissioner and Tribunal, as well as parliamentary oversight through the Intelligence and Security Committee. Codification has greatly tightened the regulatory regime.

[20] B Yong, 'Exposing the hidden wiring of Parliament' (*UK Constitutional Law Association Blog*, 10 January 2022), www.ukconstitutionallaw.org/2022/01/10/ben-yong-exposing-the-hidden-wiring-of-parliament/. See also B Yong, 'The Governance of Parliament' in A Horne and G Drewry (eds), *Parliament and the Law* (Oxford, Hart Publishing, 2018); D Judge and C Leston-Bandeira, 'The Institutional Representation of Parliament' (2018) 66 *Political Studies* 154.

But codification does not invariably do so. Chapter nine also described the new statutory framework for the civil service introduced by Part 1 of CRAG 2010. In this case, codification has made little difference. The main reason for placing the civil service on a statutory footing was growing concerns about politicisation and the need to protect its core values. But since then concerns about politicisation have continued, and if anything increased: the statutory basis has done little to protect the position of senior civil servants. A similar judgement can be passed on Part 2 of CRAG, which codified the Ponsonby Rule on the ratification of treaties. Here too, codifying what had previously been a convention has made little difference: that partly reflects a weakness in the statutory regime, but partly a weakness in Parliament itself in being slow to develop stronger scrutiny machinery.

The FTPA illustrates a different kind of weakness, namely vulnerability to political change. At the time the FTPA appeared to be a strong form of codification, abolishing the prerogative power of dissolution and replacing it with a statutory regime in which early dissolution could only be decided by a formal vote in the House of Commons. But the FTPA was rushed through in the first year of the coalition government, with no Green or White Paper, and no attempt to build cross-party support: come the 2019 election, both Labour and the Conservatives were committed to its repeal, subsequently implemented in the Dissolution and Calling of Parliament Act 2022.

The reversibility of the FTPA illustrates a different lesson of codification, namely the need to build consensus if it is to endure. That applies to codification in soft law as well as hard law. The drafting of the Cabinet Manual, which occurred at the same time as the FTPA, adopted a very different, consensus building approach. The Cabinet Office consulted constitutional experts about early drafts of key chapters, then a draft of the whole was published for wider consultation; it was then scrutinised by three parliamentary committees and their comments taken into account before the final version was published in October 2011.[21]

The House of Lords Constitution Committee has recommended that a similar process be followed when the Cabinet Manual is revised and updated.[22] That will provide an opportunity to try to broker a consensus draft of the war powers convention (codified at paras 5.36-38 of the 2011 Cabinet Manual), and a consensus draft of the Lascelles principles (codified at para 58 of the 2010 draft). It may not be possible to reach complete agreement between government and Parliament; and in the case of the Lascelles principles, the Palace will also need to be consulted, since it is the reserve power of the monarch which is being codified. Ultimately, the Cabinet Office and Prime Minister will have to come to a conclusion: the Cabinet

[21] For an account of the process, see the Preface to the Cabinet Manual: Cabinet Office, *The Cabinet Manual*, 1st edn (2011), iv-v. For the draft Cabinet Manual and comments received, see Cabinet Office, Cabinet Manual (*HM Government*, 14 December 2010) www.gov.uk/government/publications/cabinet-manual.

[22] Sixth Report from the House of Lords Constitution Committee, *Revision of the Cabinet Manual* HL 34 (2021–22).

Manual is a statement by the executive of its understanding of how the conventions operate.

Tighter Regulation by Specialist Watchdogs

The fourth strand to tighter regulation is through the creation of specialist watchdogs. This is a novel development, not yet recognised in the literature. Five different prerogative powers are now regulated by specialist watchdogs, all created in the last 30 years. Their role and functions vary, some being supervisory, some advisory, and some decision making: but in different ways they all serve to restrict executive autonomy. The area which has become most closely regulated is public appointments, with the creation of the Commissioner for Public Appointments (OCPA) in 1995, the House of Lords Appointments Commission (HoLAC) in 2000, and the Judicial Appointments Commission (JAC) in 2005. The first two are themselves creatures of the prerogative; the JAC is created by statute, and is much the most powerful of the three. That is mainly because of the way its functions are defined in the Constitutional Reform Act 2005: the Lord Chancellor is left with no effective discretion, and the JAC has become de facto an appointing rather than advisory body.[23] By contrast, OCPA and HoLAC are purely advisory, and as related in chapter ten, OCPA's role has been reduced, as has that of HoLAC. But both bodies have served to restrict executive discretion: in its first 15 years, HoLAC screened out 17 nominations as part of its vetting for propriety; while OCPA remains a guardian of the principle of fair and open competition, calling ministers out when they fail to observe the principle in practice.

The next set of specialist watchdogs are those which supervise the intelligence agencies. After a proliferation of separate watchdogs, these were merged into a single Investigatory Powers Commissioner in 2017, together with Judicial Commissioners who ensure a double lock process before the issue of warrants for the most intrusive investigatory powers. Again, executive discretion is significantly curtailed. No longer are warrants issued simply by the Home Secretary; and before embarking on any operation the intelligence agencies have to engage in detailed legal analysis of whether it meets tests of proportionality and necessity, knowing that the Commissioner and Tribunal can oversee the use of their powers.

The other prerogative powers regulated by specialist watchdogs are the grant of honours, the prerogative of mercy, and the dismissal of ministers. These can be dealt with more briefly. Following a review in 2005, honours are now awarded following the recommendations of ten subject committees, reporting to the Main Honours Committee. The main historical roles of the royal prerogative of mercy have been gradually superseded by statutory criminal appeals, and the creation

[23] G Gee, R Hazell, K Malleson and P O'Brien, *The Politics of Judicial Independence in the UK's Changing Constitution* (Cambridge, Cambridge University Press, 2015), ch 7.

in 1995 of the Criminal Cases Review Commission. The dismissal of ministers remains a matter for the Prime Minister, but since 2006 he has been advised by the Independent Adviser on Ministers' Interests.[24]

There is continuing debate about the independence of these various watchdogs, with the Committee on Standards in Public Life (CSPL) pressing for some of them to be given greater security by being put on a statutory basis. In the final report of its *Standards Matter 2* review, the committee concluded:

> … the degree of independence in the regulation of the Ministerial Code, public appointments, business appointments, and appointments to the House of Lords falls below what is necessary to ensure effective regulation and maintain public credibility. The Committee recommends that the government gives a statutory basis to the Independent Adviser on Ministers' Interests, the Public Appointments Commissioner … as well as to the codes they regulate, through new primary legislation. The Committee believes a statutory House of Lords Appointments Commission should be considered as part of a broader House of Lords reform agenda …[25]

There are Still Important Gaps, where the Prerogative Remains Unregulated, or Insufficiently Regulated

Despite the tighter regulation described above, there remain important gaps where the prerogative remains unregulated, or insufficiently regulated. These range from serious gaps to minor ones, from gaps in the law to gaps in parliamentary procedure, to the need for stronger conventions. This illustrates the great variety of prerogative powers, and the need for tailored solutions rather than a one-size-fits-all approach, a point returned to below. Previous chapters about the individual prerogative powers have identified suitably tailored proposals for reform, which are summarised in the table below.

There is not space to discuss the nuance of each of these recommendations; readers are referred back to the individual chapters for the thinking which lies behind them. But it is worth drawing out certain themes which run through all the recommendations. First is the Westminster versus Whitehall view of the constitution (see chapter one). On dissolution and prorogation, the war making power, and the ratification of treaties, we come down firmly on the side of Westminster. Dissolution and prorogation should not be triggered solely by the executive, but subject to a parliamentary vote; the unstable convention about parliamentary approval of military deployment needs to be formalised in a resolution of the House of Commons; and Parliament needs closer involvement in the negotiation and ratification of treaties.

[24] The Independent Adviser has conducted seven investigations, listed in Armstrong and Rhodes, above n 12 at 30–7.

[25] Committee on Standards in Public Life, *Upholding Standards in Public Life* (November 2021), 8.

Table 1 Recommendations for tighter regulation of the Prerogative

Chapter	Topic	Recommendations
4	Appointment and Dismissal of Ministers	Investiture vote in House of Commons. Put Independent Adviser on Ministers' Interests on statutory basis.
5	Dissolution, Prorogation, and Recall of Parliament	By vote of House of Commons, not decision of Prime Minister alone.
7	War-Making Power	Codification of convention by Resolution of House of Commons.
8	Treaties	Prevent Parliament being presented with a fait accompli. Share information before and during negotiations. Give Parliament control over time for debate.
10	Public Appointments	Put Commissioner for Public Appointments and House of Lords Appointments Commission on statutory basis.
11	Mercy	More transparent reporting. Mandatory advice before exercising power. Enhanced institutional supervision.
12	Passports	Codify criteria for issue and withdrawal in statute. Appeals mechanism.
13	Honours	Independent Honours Commission.
14	Inquiries	Statutory inquiry should be default procedure.

The second connecting theme is the need for greater independence of some of the specialist watchdogs. As recommended by the CSPL, three watchdogs – the House of Lords Appointments Commission, the Commissioner for Public Appointments, and the Independent Adviser on Ministers' Interests – all need to be put on a statutory basis. The Honours Committees also need to become completely independent, and free from prime ministerial intervention. A third theme is the need for greater transparency, and accountability, which runs through all the recommendations: from the negotiation of treaties, to exercise of the prerogative of mercy, to the issue and withdrawal of passports. A final theme is the need for further codification: for most of these recommendations to happen, it would require codification – in statute, in changes to Standing Orders, in tightening of the Cabinet Manual and the Ministerial Code.

The Prerogative can Never be Fully Codified

Although further codification is required, complete codification of the prerogative is unachievable. That was the clear lesson from the Brown government, which started with the ambition that 'in general the prerogative powers should be put on a statutory basis'.[26] Two years later, after trawling Whitehall to compile a comprehensive list of all the prerogative powers, the government concluded that complete codification was neither feasible nor desirable. In some cases, such as the conduct of diplomacy or regulation of the armed forces, it was because statutory and prerogative powers were so intertwined that it was impossible to disentangle them. In others, such as emergency powers, it was desirable to keep the prerogative for extreme emergencies where immediate action was required.[27]

We have come to similar conclusions; as eventually did the House of Commons Public Administration and Constitutional Affairs Committee (PACAC).[28] The prerogative is too sprawling and varied to be susceptible to one-size-fits-all solutions. Even in this lengthy book we have not dealt with all the prerogative powers: we have omitted the power of confiscation, detaining enemy aliens, legislating for overseas territories, the grant of charters, and more.[29] Several of the prerogative powers we have covered would benefit from tighter regulation in statute; but others merely require changes in soft law codes, or in parliamentary procedure. And codification should not be seen as an end in itself: chapter eight showed that codification of the Ponsonby Rule has not strengthened parliamentary scrutiny of treaties, and chapter nine found that putting the civil service onto a statutory basis in CRAG has not stemmed creeping politicisation.

Codification of an open-ended prerogative into an equally open-ended statutory power does little to reduce the fuzziness of the law: as we saw with Part 1 of CRAG (see chapter nine). Cohn describes 'reliance on fuzzy law as a central strategy for the retention of executive dominance over and under law'.[30] She warns that 'Executive action in the absence of a clear authorisation to act … carries a higher potential for unchecked abuse.'[31] But she also reminds us that non-statutory executive powers, such as the prerogative in the UK or executive orders in the US, represent only one form of fuzziness. Constitutions are typically open-ended and inevitably fuzzy. Statutes can also be open-ended, grant extensive discretion, or allow wide delegation: those who recommend codification need to think hard about the content of the new law – otherwise the risk is that codification merely replicates the fuzziness of the prerogative.

[26] ibid at para 24.

[27] Ministry of Justice, *The Governance of Britain: Review of the Executive Royal Prerogative Powers, Final Report* (October 2009).

[28] In 2004, PASC advocated legislation to control the war making power: Fourth Report from the House of Commons Public Administration Select Committee, *Taming the Prerogative: Strengthening Ministerial Accountability to Parliament* HC 422 (2003–04), para 56. In 2019, PACAC concluded that legislation was undesirable, recommending a resolution of the House instead: Twentieth Report from the House of Commons Public Administration and Constitutional Affairs Committee, *The Role of Parliament in the UK Constitution: Authorising the Use of Military Force* HC 1891 (2017–19), para 81.

[29] For a more comprehensive list of prerogative powers, see Ministry of Justice, above n 27 at 31–4.

[30] Cohn, above n 6 at 255.

[31] ibid at 257.

Conclusion: The Endless Tug of War between Government, Parliament and the Courts

This final chapter has summarised how the last 30–40 years have seen gradually tighter regulation of the prerogative by Parliament, by the courts, and by specialist watchdogs. On a Whig view of history it might be thought that process would steadily continue; but the Johnson government has provided a stark reminder that reform of the prerogative is not all one way. In a vigorous reassertion of executive power, it has reversed previous reforms such as the FTPA, pushed back against judicial review, and undermined constitutional watchdogs.

We said in chapter one that the underlying issue in all the debates about the prerogative is about power: how much autonomy the executive should have to wield that power; with what degree of supervision (if any) from Parliament or the courts; or (more rarely) from the monarch. If our conclusions in part two are accepted, the monarch would not be expected to exercise any real supervisory power, because dissolution and prorogation should be a matter for the House of Commons; but the monarch remains the ultimate guardian of the constitution, with deep reserve powers in the event of constitutional emergencies.

As for the courts, they also uphold the constitution *in extremis*, which is perhaps the best way of understanding their rulings in *Miller 1* and *Miller 2*, when they reminded the government of the importance of two fundamental constitutional principles: parliamentary sovereignty, and the executive's accountability to Parliament. Such interventions by the courts are likely to be very rare, and for day-to-day supervision of the prerogative we must look to Parliament. But for Parliament to be effective requires political will and institutional leadership, both of which are in short supply. It also requires the right structures, and resources: an encouraging recent sign is the willingness of the House of Lords to create dedicated machinery to scrutinise treaties. But we have to be realistic in our expectations of Parliament, so long as it remains dominated by the executive.

Despite those difficulties, it is in Parliament that the main tug-of-war over the prerogative will be played out. It is a tug-of-war endlessly fought in other countries between executive and legislature, as we saw in chapters fifteen and sixteen. And even if in future the Whig (or Westminster) view prevails, and more prerogative powers are codified, the tug-of-war will still continue: the fascination of the prerogative, as of reserve powers in other systems, is that they never reach a steady state.

BIBLIOGRAPHY

Books and Journal Articles

Ahmed, F, Albert, R and Perry, A, 'Judging Constitutional Conventions' (2019) 17 *International Journal of Constitutional Law* 787.

Andeweg, R, 'Constitutional Functions in the Netherlands' in Hazell, R and Morris, B (eds), *The Role of Monarchy in Modern Democracy: European Democracies Compared* (Oxford, Hart Publishing, 2020).

Andrew, C, *The Defence of the Realm: The Authorised History of MI5* (London, Penguin, 2010).

Bagehot, W, *The English Constitution*, 2nd edn (London, 1872).

Bai, J and Hobbs, H, 'Appointing Attorneys-General to the High Court: A Case for Reform' (2017) 42 *Alternative Law Journal* 286.

Baker, A, *Prime Ministers and the Rule Book* (London, Politico, 2000).

Baker, J, *The Oxford History of the Laws of England: Volume XI 1483-1558* (Oxford, Oxford University Press, 2003).

Baker, J, *The Reinvention of Magna Carta 1216-1616* (Cambridge, Cambridge University Press, 2017).

Baker, J, *Introduction to English Legal History*, 5th edn (Oxford, Oxford University Press, 2019).

Bamforth, N, 'Political Accountability in Play: the Budd Inquiry and David Blunkett's resignation' [2005] *Public Law* 229.

Banno, J, *The Establishment of the Japanese Constitutional System* (London, Routledge, 1992).

Barnett, H, *Constitutional and Administrative Law*, 2nd edn (London, Cavendish, 1998).

Beattie, JM, 'The Royal Pardon and Criminal Procedure in Early Modern England' (1987) 22 *Historical Papers* 9.

Beer, J, *Public Inquiries* (Oxford, Oxford University Press, 2020).

Benn, T, *Parliament, People and Power: Agenda for a Free Society* (London, Verso, 1982).

Bennion, F, 'Modern Royal Assent Procedure at Westminster' (1981) 2 *Statute Law Review* 133.

Birch, AH, *Representative and Responsible Government: An Essay on the British Constitution* (London, Allen & Unwin, 1964).

Black, J, *Parliament and Foreign Policy in the Eighteenth Century* (Cambridge, Cambridge University Press, 2004).

Blackburn, R, 'The Dissolution of Parliament: The Crown Prerogatives (House of Commons Control) Bill 1988' (1989) 52 *Modern Law Review* 837.

Blackburn, R, 'Monarchy and the Personal Prerogatives' [2004] *Public Law* 546.

Blackstone, W, *Commentaries on the Laws of England*, vol 1 (London, S Sweet, 1836).

Blackstone, W, *Commentaries on the Laws of England*, vol 4 (London, 1769).

Blick, A, 'The Cabinet Manual and the Codification of Conventions' (2014) 67 *Parliamentary Affairs* 191.

Blom-Cooper, L, *Public Inquiries: Wrong Route on Bloody Sunday* (Oxford, Hart Publishing, 2017).

Bogdanor, V, *The Monarchy and the Constitution*, (Oxford, Oxford University Press, 1995).

Boyron, S, *The Constitution of France: A Contextual Analysis* (Oxford, Hart Publishing, 2012).

Bracton, H, *On the Laws and Customs of England*, vol 2 (Samuel Thorne tr, Cambridge, Harvard University Press, 1968).

Bradley, AW, Ewing, K, and Knight, C, *Constitutional and Administrative Law*, 17th edn (Harlow, Pearson, 2018).

Bradley, AW, 'Police powers and the prerogative' [1988] *Public Law* 298.

Brazier, R, 'Royal Assent to Legislation' (2013) 129 *Law Quarterly Review* 184.
Brazier, R, *Choosing a Prime Minister: The Transfer of Power in Britain* (Oxford, Oxford University Press, 2020).
Brown, G, My *Life, Our Times* (London, Vintage, 2018).
Cameron, CM, *Veto Bargaining: Presidents and the Politics of Negative Power* (Cambridge, Cambridge University Press, 2000).
Chen, M, 'A Constitutional Revolution? The Role of the New Zealand Parliament in Treaty-Making' (2001) 19 *New Zealand Universities Law Review* 448.
Chezenko, G, 'Fixing What Ain't Broke: The New Norm of Fixed-Date Elections in Canada' (2017) 8(3) *Mapping Politics* 83.
Chitty, J, *A practical treatise on the Criminal Law* (London, Butterworth & Sons, 1819).
Chitty, J, *A Treatise on the Law of the Prerogatives of the Crown* (London, Butterworths, 1820).
Chrimes, SB, *English Constitutional Ideas in the Fifteenth Century* (Cambridge, Cambridge University Press, 1936).
Clarke, HW, *Constitutional and Administrative Law* (London, Sweet and Maxwell, 1971).
Clayton, M, 'The Old English *Promissio regis*' (2008) 37 *Anglo-Saxon England* 91.
Clokie, HM and Robinson, JW, *Royal Commissions of Inquiry; The Significance of Investigations in British Politics* (Stanford, Stanford University Press 1937).
Cobbett, W, *Parliamentary History of England*, vol 14 (London, TC Hansard, 1813).
Cohn, M, 'Non-Statutory Executive Powers: Assessing Global Constitutionalism in a Structural-Institutional Context' (2015) 64 *International & Comparative Law Quarterly* 64.
Cohn, M, *A Theory of the Executive Branch: Tension and Legality* (Oxford, Oxford University Press, 2021).
Coke, E, *The Third Part of the Institutes of the Laws of England* (London, M Flesher, 1644).
Comyns, J, *A Digest of the Laws of England*, vol 7, 5th edn (Anthony Hammond ed, London, Strachan, 1822).
Congdon, P, 'In a Fix: Fixed-Term Parliaments in the Australian States' (2013) 41 *Federal Law Review* 265.
Copeland, G, 'When Congress and the President collide' (1983) 45 *Journal of Politics* 696.
Côté, C, 'Federalism and Foreign Affairs in Canada', in Bradley, C (ed), *The Oxford Handbook of Comparative Foreign Relations Law* (Oxford, Oxford University Press, 2019).
Cox, N, 'The Royal Prerogative in the Realms' (2007) 33 *Commonwealth Law Bulletin* 611.
Cox, N, *The Royal Prerogative and Constitutional Law: A Search for the Quintessence of Executive Power* (Oxford, Routledge, 2020).
Craig, R, 'Casting Aside Clanking Medieval Chains: Prerogative, Statute and Article 50 after the EU Referendum' (2016) 79 *Modern Law Review* 1019.
Craig, R, and Phillipson, G, 'Protecting National Security by Breaking the Law? Prerogative, Statute and the Powers of MI5' (2021) *Modern Law Review* 1.
Cranston, R, 'Lawyers, MPs and Judges' in Feldman, D (ed), *Law in Politics, Politics in Law* (Oxford, Hart Publishing, 2015).
Danesi, SL, 'Tabling and waiting: a preliminary assessment of Canada's treaty-tabling policy' (2014) 20 *Canadian Foreign Policy Journal* 189.
De Smith, SA, *The New Commonwealth and its Constitutions* (London, Stevens & Sons, 1964).
Devlin, R and Dodek, A, 'The Achilles heel of the Canadian judiciary: the ethics of judicial appointments in Canada' (2017) 20 *Legal Ethics* 43.
Dicey, AV, *Introduction to the Study of the Law of the Constitution*, 9th edn (London, Macmillan, 1939).
Diplock, K, 'Passports and Protection in International Law' (1946) 32 *Transactions of the Grotius Society* 42.
Dodek, A and Cairns Way, R, 'The Supreme Court of Canada and Appointment of Judges in Canada' in Oliver, P, Macklem, P and Des Rosier, N (eds), *The Oxford Handbook of the Canadian Constitution* (Oxford, Oxford University Press, 2017).
Dunworth, T, 'The Influence of International Law in New Zealand: Some Reflections' in Morris, C, Boston, J and Butler, P (eds), *Reconstituting the Constitution* (Heidelberg, Springer, 2011).

Eldridge, RD and Katsuhiro, M, *The Japan Self-Defense Forces Law* (Cambridge Scholars Publishing, 2019).
Ewing, KD, 'Prerogative, Judicial Review and National Security' (1985) 44 *Cambridge Law Journal* 1.
Feldman, D, Bailey, D and Norbury, L, *Bennion, Bailey and Norbury on Statutory Interpretation*, 8th edn (LexisNexis Butterworths, 2020).
Fikfak V and Hooper, HJ, *Parliament's Secret War* (Oxford, Hart Publishing, 2018).
Fleming, T and Schletier, P, 'Prorogation: Comparative Context and Reform' (2021) 74 *Parliamentary Affairs* 964.
Fleming, T, 'Parliamentary Procedure under Theresa May: Nothing has Changed?' (2021) 74 *Parliamentary Affairs* 943.
Foley, M, *The Silence of Constitutions* (Oxford, Routledge, 1989).
Fortescue, J, *De Laudibus Legum Angliae* (Andrew Amos ed, London, Butterworths, 1825).
Fortescue, J, *De Natura Legis Naturae*, vol 1 (Lord Clermont ed, 1869).
Fortescue, J, *The Difference between an Absolute and a Limited Monarchy* (Charles Plummer ed, Oxford, Oxford University Press, 1885).
Gearty, C, 'The Courts and Recent Exercises of the Prerogative' (1987) 46 *Cambridge Law Journal* 372
Gee, G, Hazell, R, Malleson, K and O'Brien, P, *The Politics of Judicial Independence in the UK's Changing Constitution* (Cambridge, Cambridge University Press, 2015).
Goldsworthy, J, *Parliamentary Sovereignty: Contemporary Debates* (Cambridge, Cambridge University Press, 2010).
Gooch, RK, *Governments of Continental Europe*, 1st edn (New York, Macmillan, 1940).
Gordon, R, '*Entinck v Carrington* [1765] Revisited: All the King's Horse' in Juss, S and Sunkin M (eds), *Landmark Cases in Public Law* (Oxford, Hart Publishing, 2017).
Hadfield, B, 'Judicial Review and the Prerogative Powers of the Crown' in Sunkin, M and Payne, S (eds), *The Nature of the Crown: A Legal and Political Analysis* (Oxford, Oxford University Press, 1999).
Hamilton, A, 'The Federalist No 69' in Hamilton, A, Madison, J and Jay, J, *The Federalist Papers* (Ian Shapiro ed, New Haven, Yale University Press, 2009).
Handsley, E and Lynch, A, 'Facing up to Diversity? Transparency and the Reform of Commonwealth Judicial Appointments 2008-13' (2015) 37 *Sydney Law Review* 187.
Handsley, E, '"The judicial whisper goes around": Appointment of Judicial Officers in Australia' in Malleson, K and Russell, P, *Appointing Judges in an Age of Judicial Power: Critical Perspectives from Around the World* (Toronto, University of Toronto Press, 2006).
Hansen, ME, 'The Government and the Prime Minister More than Primus Inter Pares' in Christiansen, P, Elklit, J and Nedergaard, P, *The Oxford Handbook of Danish Politics* (Oxford, Oxford University Press, 2020).
Harris, BV, 'A Judicial Commission for New Zealand: a good idea that must not be allowed to go away' [2014] *New Zealand Law Review* 383.
Hathaway, O, 'Presidential Power over International law: Restoring the Balance' (2009) 119 *Yale Law Journal* 140.
Hatsell, J *Precedents of Proceedings in the House of Commons*, vol 3, 2nd edn (London, T Payne, 1796).
Hawkins, W, *A Treatise of the Pleas of the Crown*, vol 2 (John Curwood ed, London, S Sweet, 1824).
Hazell, R, 'Improving Parliamentary Scrutiny of Public Appointments' (2019) 72 *Parliamentary Affairs* 223.
Hazell, R and Morris, B (eds), *The Role of Monarchy in Modern Democracy: European Democracies Compared* (Oxford, Hart Publishing, 2020).
Helboe Pederson, H, 'The Parliament (FOLKETINGET): Powerful, Professional, and Trusted?' in Christiansen, P, Elklit, J and Nedergaard, P, *The Oxford Handbook of Danish Politics* (Oxford, Oxford University Press, 2020).
Hillmer, N and Lagassé, P, 'Parliament will decide: an interplay of politics and principle' (2016) 71 *International Journal* 328.
Hirobumi, I, *Commentaries on the Constitution of the Empire of Japan*, (Tokyo, Igirisu-Hōritsu Gakko, 1889).

Houben, M, *International Crisis Management: The approach of European states* (London, Routledge, 2005).
Howarth, D, 'Westminster versus Whitehall: What the Brexit Debate Revealed About an Unresolved Conflict at the Heart of the British Constitution' in Doyle, O, McHarg, A and Murkens, J (eds), *The Brexit Challenge for Ireland and the United Kingdom* (Cambridge, Cambridge University Press, 2021).
Hunard, ND, *King's Pardon for Homicide Before AD 1307* (Oxford, Clarendon Press, 1969).
Hutton, M, Natzler, D, Hamlyn, M, Lee, C, Mawson, C, Poyser, C, Samson, E and Lawrence, K, *Erskine May: Parliamentary Practice*, 25th edn (LexisNexis Butterworths, 2019).
Ireton, E, 'The Ministerial Power to Set Up a Public Inquiry: Issues of Transparency and Accountability' (2016) 67 *Northern Ireland Legal Quarterly* 209.
Ireton, E, 'How Public is a Public Inquiry?' [2018] *Public Law* 277.
Iwasaw, Y, *International Law, Human Rights, and Japanese Law: The Impact of International Law on Japanese Law* (Oxford, Oxford University Press, 1998).
Jackson, DM, *The Crown and Canadian Federalism* (Toronto, Dundurn, 2013).
Jennings, I, *Cabinet Government* (Cambridge, Cambridge University Press, 1959).
Joseph, P, *Constitutional and Administrative Law in New Zealand*, 4th edn (Thomson Reuters, 2014).
Joseph, R, *The War Prerogative: History, Reform and Constitutional Design* (Oxford, Oxford University Press, 2013).
Judge, D, and Leston-Bandeira, C, 'The Institutional Representation of Parliament' (2018) 66 *Political Studies* 154.
Keene, E, 'The Treaty-Making Revolution of the Nineteenth Century' (2012) 32 *The International History Review* 475.
Keir, DL, *The Constitutional History of Modern Britain 1485–1937* (London, A and C Black, 1938).
Kelly, P and Bramston, T, *The Dismissal: In the Queen's Name* (Melbourne, Viking, 2015).
Kennedy, L, *Wicked Beyond Belief: The Luton Murder Case* (London, Granada, 1980).
Kerr, J, *Matters for Judgement: An Autobiography* (London, Macmillan, 1978).
Knapp, A and Wright, V, *The Government and Politics of France*, 5th edn (London, Routledge, 2006).
Koh, HH, 'Presidential Power to Terminate International Agreements' (2018) 128 *Yale Law Journal* 432.
Krunke, H, 'The Monarch's Constitutional Functions in Denmark' in Hazell, R and Morris, B, *The Role of Monarchy in Modern Democracy: European Monarchies Compared* (Oxford, Hart Publishing, 2020).
Ku, C and Jacobsen, HK, *Democratic Accountability and the Use of Force in International Law* (Cambridge, Cambridge University Press, 2009).
Lacey, H, *The Royal Pardon: Access to Mercy in the Fourteenth-Century* (York, York Medieval Press, 2009).
Lachs, PS, 'Advise and Consent: Parliament and Foreign Policy under the Later Stuarts' (1975) 7 *Albion* 41.
Lagassé, P, 'The Crown's Powers of Command-in-Chief: Interpreting Section 15 of Canada's Constitution Act, 1867' (2013) 18 *Review of Constitutional Studies* 189.
Lagassé, P, 'Parliament and the War Prerogative in the United Kingdom and Canada: Explaining Variations in Institutional Change and Legislative Control' (2017) 70 *Parliamentary Affairs* 280.
Lansing, P, 'Freedom to Travel: Is the Issuance of a Passport an Individual Right or a Governmental Prerogative' (1981) 11 *Denver Journal of International Law & Policy* 15.
Lauriat, B, '"The Examination of Everything" – Royal Commissions in British Legal History' (2010) 31 *Statute Law Review* 24.
Levy, R, 'Pardons and Amnesties as Policy Instruments in Contemporary France' (2007) 36 *Crime & Justice* 551.
Lewis, K, *Kingship and Masculinity in Medieval England* (London, Routledge, 2013).
Lim, PJ, 'Reforming Canada's war prerogative' (2020) 26 *Canadian Foreign Policy Journal* 345.
Locke, J, *Essay concerning the True Original, Extent and End of Civil Government*, 4th edn (London, 1713).

Lockwood, TJ, 'A History of Royal Commissions' (1967) 5 *Osgoode Hall Law Journal* 172, 182.
Loughlin, M, 'The Silences of Constitutions' (2018) 16 *International Journal of Constitutional Law* 922.
Lovik, M, 'The Constitutional Court Reviews the Early Dissolution of the West German Parliament' (1983) 7 *Hastings International and Comparative Law Review* 79.
Low, S, 'The Foreign Office Autocracy' (1912) 91 *Fortnightly Review* 1.
Lucraft, M (ed), *Archbold: Criminal Pleading, Evidence and Practice* (Sweet & Maxwell, 2021).
Lukes, S, *Power: A Radical View*, 2nd edn (Hampshire, Palgrave Macmillan, 2005).
Macdonald, NA and Bowden, JWJ, 'No Discretion: On Prorogation and the Governor General' (2011) 34 *Canadian Parliamentary Review* 7.
Makower, A, 'Queen's Consent' (2019) 87 *The Table: The Journal of the Society of Clerks-at-the-Table in Commonwealth Parliaments* 35.
Mance, J, 'Justiciability' (2018) 67 *International & Comparative Law Quarterly* 739.
Mansfield, H, *Taming the Prince: The Ambivalence of Executive Power* (New York, Free Press, 1989).
Marshall, G, *Constitutional Conventions: The Rules and Forms of Political Accountability* (Oxford, Oxford University Press, 1984).
Mason, D, 'Deliberative democratising of Australian treaty making: putting into context the significance of online access to the treaty process' (2016) 24 *Journal of Law, Information and Science* 1.
McConnell, M, *The President Who Would Not Be King: Executive Power Under the Constitution* (New Jersey, Princeton University Press, 2020).
McGee, D, *Parliamentary Practice in New Zealand*, 4th edn (Mary Harris and David Wilson eds, Auckland, Oratia, 2017).
McHarg, A, 'The Supreme Court's Prorogation Judgment: Guardian of the Constitution or Architect of the Constitution?' (2020) 21 *Edinburgh Law Review* 88.
McKeown, M and Thomson, S, 'Sources of Law and the UK Honours System' (2012) 14 *Scots Law Times* 81.
Mills, A, 'Judicial Pushback – National Airports Policy Grounded' (2020) 79 *Cambridge Law Journal* 208.
Montesquieu, C, *L'Espirit des Lois* (Thomas Nugent tr, London, J Nourse, 1777).
Moore, C, *Crown and Sword: Executive power and the use of force by the Australian Defence Force* (Acton, ANU Press, 2017).
Morton, FL and Snow, D (eds), 'Judicial Recruitment and Selection' in *Law, Politics and the Judicial Process in Canada* (Calgary, University of Calgary Press, 2018).
Mulherin, PE, 'War-Power Reform in Australia: (Re)considering the Options' (2020) 66 *Australian Journal of Politics and History* 633.
Nelson, B, 'The Role of Government and Parliament in the Decision to Go to War' (2015) 63 *Papers on Parliament* 1.
Neville, C, 'The beginnings of royal pardon in Scotland' (2016) 42 *Journal of Medieval History* 559.
Norton, P, 'A Temporary Occupant of No.10? Prime ministerial succession in the event of the death of the incumbent' [2016] *Public Law* 18.
Novak, A, *Comparative Executive Clemency: The Constitutional Pardon Power and the Prerogative of Mercy in Global Perspective* (Abingdon, Routledge, 2016).
Craig, P, 'Epilogue: *Miller*, the Legislature and the Executive' in Juss, S and Sunkin M (eds), *Landmark Cases in Public Law* (Oxford, Hart Publishing, 2017).
Palmer, G, 'Judicial Selection and Accountability: Can the New Zealand System Survive?' in Gray, BD and McClintock, RB (eds), *Courts and Policy: Checking the Balance* (Wellington, Brookers, 1995).
Parry, G, 'Foreign Policy and the Parliament of 1576' (2015) 34 *Parliamentary History* 62.
Payne, S, 'The Royal Prerogative' in Sunkin, M and Payne, S (eds), *The Nature of the Crown: A Legal and Political Analysis* (Oxford, Oxford University Press, 1999).
Perry, A, 'The Crown's Administrative Powers' (2015) 131 *Law Quarterly Review* 652.
Perry, A, 'Pardons' in Sobel, D and Wall, S (eds), *Oxford Studies in Political Philosophy*, vol 8 (Oxford, Oxford University Press, 2021).
Phillipson, G and Young, A, 'Would Use of the Prerogative to Denounce the ECHR "Frustrate" the Human Rights Act? Lessons from Miller' [2017] *Public Law* 150.

Phillipson, G, 'A dive into deep constitutional waters: Article 50, the prerogative and parliament' (2016) 79 *Modern Law Review* 1064.
Pimlott, B, *The Queen: Elizabeth II and the Monarchy* (London, Harper Collins, 2001).
Ponsonby, A, *Democracy and Diplomacy: A Plea for Popular Control of Foreign Policy* (London, Meuthen, 1915).
Ponting, C, *The Right to Know: The Inside Story of the Belgrano Affair* (London, Sphere Books, 1985).
Poole, T, *Reason of State: Law, Prerogative and Empire* (Cambridge, Cambridge University Press, 2015).
Poole, T, 'The Strange Death of Prerogative in England' (2018) 43 *University of Western Australia Law Review* 42.
Redlich, J, *The Procedure of the House of Commons*, 3 vols (London, Constable, 1908).
Riley, T, 'Something Weird: An Examination of Parliamentary Involvement in New Zealand's Treaty-making Process' (2018) 5 *Public Interest Law Journal of New Zealand* 11.
Russell, M, *The Contemporary House of Lords: Westminster Bicameralism Revived* (Oxford, Oxford University Press, 2013).
Russell, P and Sossin, L (eds), *Parliamentary Democracy in Crisis* (Toronto, University of Toronto Press, 2009).
Sapienza, A, *Judicial Review of Non-Statutory Executive Action* (Alexandria NSW, The Federation Press, 2020).
Schwartz, B and Wade, HWR, *Legal Control of Government: Administrative Law in Britain and the United States* (Oxford, Clarendon Press, 1972).
Scott, P, *The National Security Constitution* (Oxford, Hart Publishing, 2018).
Scott, P, 'Passports, the Right to Travel, and National Security in the Commonwealth' (2020) 69 *International & Comparative Law Quarterly* 365.
Sedley, S, 'The Sound of Silence: Constitutional Law Without a Constitution' (1994) 110 *Law Quarterly Review* 270.
Sedley, S, *Lions Under the Throne: Essays on the History of English Public Law* (Cambridge, Cambridge University Press, 2015).
Seldon, A, *The Impossible Office? The History of the British Prime Minister* (Cambridge, Cambridge University Press, 2021).
Sibley, NW, 'The Passport System' (1906) 7 *Journal of the Society of Comparative Legislation* 32.
Smith, ATH, 'The Prerogative of Mercy, the Power of Pardon and Criminal Justice' [1983] *Public Law* 398.
Smith, E, 'Is Foreign Policy Special?' (2020) 41 *Oxford Journal of Legal Studies* 1040.
Smith, E, Lang, A and Bjorge, E, 'Treaties, Parliament and the constitution' [2020] *Public Law* 508.
Smith, R, 'Political Functions of the Monarch in Norway' in Hazell, R and Morris, B, *The Role of Monarchy in Modern Democracy: European Monarchies Compared* (Oxford, Hart Publishing, 2020).
Stephenson, P, 'The Relationship between the Royal Prerogative and Statute in Australia' (2021) 44 *Melbourne University Law Review* 1001.
Stöckmann, J, 'The First World War and the Democratic Control of Foreign Policy' (2020) 249 *Past & Present* 121.
Straw, J, 'Abolish the Royal Prerogative' in A Barnett (ed), *Power and the Throne: The Monarchy Debate* (London, Vintage, 1994).
Straw, J, *Aspects of Law Reform: An Insider's Perspective (The Hamlyn Lectures)* (Cambridge, Cambridge University Press, 2013).
Strong, J, 'Did Theresa May Kill the War Powers Convention? Comparing Parliamentary Debates on UK Intervention in Syria in 2013 and 2018' (2021) 00 *Parliamentary Affairs* 1.
Thomas, J, 'The Future of Public Inquiries' [2015] *Public Law* 225.
Torpey, J, *The Invention of the Passport: Surveillance, Citizenship and the State* (Cambridge, Cambridge University Press, 2000).
Twomey, A, '*Miller* and the Prerogative' in Elliott, M, Williams, J and Young, A (eds), *The UK Constitution After Miller: Brexit and Beyond* (Oxford, Hart Publishing, 2017).
Twomey, A, *The Veiled Sceptre: Reserve Powers of Heads of State in Westminster Systems* (Cambridge, Cambridge University Press, 2018).

Twomey, A, 'The Prerogative and the Courts in Australia' (2021) 3 *Journal of Commonwealth Law* 55.
Wade, ECS and Phillips, GG, *Constitutional and Administrative Law*, 9th edn (London, Longman, 1977).
Wade, HWR and Forsyth, C, *Administrative Law*, 4th edn (Oxford, Oxford University Press, 2004).
Wade, HWR, *Constitutional Fundamentals* (London, Stevens & Sons, 1980).
Ward, R, 'Baton Rounds and Circulars' (1988) 47 *Cambridge Law Journal* 155.
Watt, G, 'The Coronation Oath' (2017) 19 *Ecclesiastical Law Journal* 325.
Wheeldon, J, 'Constitutional Peace, Political Order or Good Government? Organizing Scholarly Views on the 2008 Prorogation' (2014) 8 *Canadian Political Science Review* 102.
Wheeler, G, 'Royal Assent in the British Constitution' (2016) 132 *Law Quarterly Review* 495.
White, S, 'Keeping the Peace of the Realm' (2021) 42 *Adelaide Law Review* 101.
Williams, DW, 'British Passports and the Right to Travel' (1974) *International & Comparative Law Quarterly* 642.
Williams, G, 'High Court Appointments: the need for reform' (2008) 30 *Sydney Law Review* 161.
Williams, J, 'Prerogative Power after *Miller*: An Analysis in Four E's' in Elliott, M, Williams, J and Young, A (eds), *The UK Constitution After Miller: Brexit and Beyond* (Oxford, Hart Publishing, 2017).
Williams, PM, *Crisis and Compromise: Politics in the Fourth Republic*, 3rd edn (London, Longman, 1958).
Wilson, R, 'Portrait of a Profession Revisited' (2003) 81 *Public Administration* 365.
Wilson, R, *Five Days to Power: The Journey to Coalition Britain* (London, Biteback, 2010).
Woolf, H, Jowell, J, Donnelly, C and Hare, I, *De Smith's Judicial Review*, 8th edn (London, Sweet & Maxwell, 2018).
Yardley, DCM, 'The Primacy of the Executive in England' (1967) 21 *Parliamentary Affairs* 155.
Yong, B and Hazell, R, *Special Advisers: Who They Are, What They Do and Why They Matter* (Oxford, Hart Publishing, 2014).
Yong, B, 'The Governance of Parliament' in Horne, A and Drewry, G (eds), *Parliament and the Law* (Oxford, Hart Publishing, 2018).
Zines, L, 'The Inherent Executive Power of the Commonwealth' (2005) 16 *Public Law Review* 279.

Reports

Armstrong, H and Rhodes, C, *The Ministerial Code and the Independent Adviser on Ministers' Interests* (House of Commons Library Briefing Paper 03750, August 2021).
Armstrong, H, *Honours: History and reviews* (House of Commons Library Briefing Paper 02832, February 2017).
Australasian Institute of Judicial Administration, *Suggested Criteria for Judicial Appointments* (2015).
Barnard, B, *Open, Meritocratic and Transparent: Reforming Civil Service Appointments* (Policy Exchange, 2021).
Barrett, J, 'Treaties beyond the EU' in *Parliament and Brexit* (UK in a Changing Europe, 2020).
Bennett, S, *House of Representatives Fixed Terms: Barriers to Implementation* (Australian Parliamentary Library Research Paper 15 2008–09, November 2008).
Broinowski, A, *How does Australia go to War? A call for accountability and change* (Australians for War Powers Reform, 2015).
Campaign Group of Labour MPs, *Parliamentary Democracy and the Labour Movement* (London, 1984).
Conservative Democracy Task Force, *Power to the People: Rebuilding Parliament* (2007).
Conservative Party, *Strong Leadership. A Clear Economic Plan. A Brighter, More Secure Future* (2015).
Conservative Party, *Get Brexit Done: Unleash Britain's Potential* (2019).
Conservative Party of Canada, *Stand Up for Canada: Federal Election Platform* (2006).
Constitution Unit, *Monitor 76* (London, Constitution Unit, 2020).

Council of Europe Committee of Legal Advisers on Public International Law, *Expression of Consent by States to be Bound by a Treaty: Analytical Report and Country Reports* (Strasbourg, Council of Europe, 2001).

Cowie, G, *Non-statutory public inquiries* (House of Commons Library Briefing Paper SN02599, November 2021),

Dawson, J, *Covert Human Intelligence Sources (Criminal Conduct) Bill 2019–2021* (House of Commons Library Briefing Paper 9012, October 2020).

Ekins, R and Gee, G, *Reforming the Lord Chancellor's Role in Senior Judicial Appointments* (Policy Exchange, 2021).

Endicott, T, *The Stubborn Stain Theory of Executive Power* (Policy Exchange, 2017).

Evans, P, *Braking the Law: Is there, or should there be, an Executive Veto in the UK Constitution?* (London, Constitution Unit, 2020).

Finnis, J, *The Unconstitutionality of the Supreme Court's Prorogation Judgment* (Policy Exchange, 2019).

Gill, M and Dalton, G, *Ten Questions the proposed Commissioner for Public Appointments must answer* (Institute for Government, 2021).

Gill, M, Clyne, R and Dalton, G, *Ten Questions the proposed Commissioner for Public Appointments must answer* (Institute for Government, 2021).

Harris, J, *Legislating for a Civil Service* (Institute for Government, 2013).

Hazell, R and Paun, A (eds), *Making Minority Government Work: Hung Parliaments and the Challenges for Westminster and Whitehall* (London, Constitution Unit, 2009).

Hazell, R, *Fixed Term Parliaments* (London, Constitution Unit, 2010).

Hazell, R, Cogbill, A, Owen, D, Webber, H and Chebib, L, *Critical Friends: the Role of Non-Executives on Whitehall Boards* (London, Constitution Unit, 2018).

Jarrett, T, *The Independent Inquiry into Child Sexual Abuse and background* (House of Commons Library Briefing Paper 07040, August 2016).

JUSTICE, *Going Abroad: A Report on Passports* (London, Brown & Son, 1974).

Kelly, R, *Recall of Parliament* (House of Commons Library Briefing Paper 1186, 2021).

Labour Party, *New Labour: Because Britain Deserves Better* (1997).

Labour Party, *It's Time for Real Change* (2019).

Lagassé, P, *Accountability for national defence: Ministerial responsibility, military command and parliamentary oversight* (Institute for Research on Public Policy, 2010).

Lang, A, *Parliament's Role in Ratifying Treaties* (House of Commons Library Briefing Paper 5855, February 2017).

Lang, A, *How Parliament treats treaties* (House of Commons Library Briefing Paper 9247, June 2021).

Lloyd, T, Jones, N and Davies, M, *The Lloyd Inquiry: independent public inquiry on Gulf War Illnesses* (London, 2004).

Lodge, G, Kalitowski, S, Pearce, N and Muir, R, *Accountability and Responsiveness in the Senior Civil Service: Lessons from Overseas* (London, Institute for Public Policy Research, 2013).

Maddox, B, *Reform at the Centre of Government* (Institute for Government, 2020).

McKeown, D and Jordan, R, *Parliamentary involvement in declaring war and deploying forces overseas* (Parliament of Australia Parliamentary Library Background Note, March 2010).

Paun, A, Harris, J and Magee, I, *Permanent Secretary Appointments and the Role of Ministers* (Institute for Government, 2013).

Russell, M and Semlyen, T, *Enough is Enough: Regulating Prime Ministerial Appointments to the Lords* (London, Constitution Unit, 2015).

Schleiter, P, Belu, V and Hazell, R, *Forming a government in the event of a hung parliament: The UK's recognition rules in comparative context* (London, Constitution Unit, 2016).

US Congress, *Trade Promotion Authority Act (TPA)* (Congressional Research Service IF10038, December 2020).

Wagner, W, Peters, D and Glahn, C, *Parliamentary War Powers Around the World, 1989–2004: A New Dataset* (Geneva, Geneva Centre for the Democratic Control of Armed Forces, 2010).

Wilson, R, *Tomorrow's Government (RSA Lecture)* (London, Constitution Unit, 2007).

Blogs and Newspaper Articles

Adams, T, 'Royal Consent and Hidden Power' (*UK Constitutional Law Association Blog*, 26 January 2013).

Atkins, G, 'A cross-party parliamentary commission is the best way to build lasting social care reform' (*Institute for Government*, 25 November 2019).

Auditor Tantum, 'The Veto of the Crown', *Fortnightly Review* (London, September 1913).

Balls, K, 'Sajid Javid quits as No 10 takes control' *The Spectator* (London, 13 February 2020).

Barber, N, 'Can Royal Assent be Refused on the Advice of the Prime Minister?' (*UK Constitutional Law Association Blog*, 25 September 2013).

Bathurst, WL, 'At the Court at Buckingham Palace, the 21st day of May' *The London Gazette* (London, 1855).

Bayer, J, 'Germany: New law against right-wing extremism and hate crime' (*Inforrm*, 24 April 2021).

BBC, '16 Irish republicans received royal pardons since 2000' (*BBC News*, 25 March 2015).

BBC, 'Theresa May's Conservative Conference Speech: Key Quotes' (*BBC News*, 2 October 2016).

BBC, 'London Bridge attack: Steven Gallant up for early release after confronting knifeman' (*BBC News*, 18 October 2020),

Blitz, J and Croft, J, 'Parliament the winner in prorogation case, say lawyers' *Financial Times* (London, 24 September 2019).

Booth, R, 'Secret papers show extent of senior Royals' veto over bills' *The Guardian* (London, 14 January 2013).

Braverman, S, 'People we elect must take back control from people we don't. Who include the judges' (*ConservativeHome*, 27 January 2020).

Bright, M, 'Why did Howard release two dangerous gangsters?' *The Observer* (London, 13 February 2005).

Buckingham Palace, 'Counsellors of State' (*The Royal Family*).

Buckler, C, 'Secret royal pardons granted to NI paramilitaries' (*BBC News*, 10 June 2014).

Burns, T, 'The House of Lords is too large: party leaders must put aside short-term interests and agree plans to reduce its numbers' (*Constitution Unit Blog*, 25 June 2021).

Calvert, J, Abuthnott, G and Calver, T, 'New Tory sleaze row as donors who pay £3m get seats in House of Lords' *Sunday Times* (London, 6 November 2021).

Carrell, S and Evans, R, 'Scottish government refuses to publish details about Queen's secret lobbying' *The Guardian* (London, 29 July 2021).

Carrell, S, Evans, R, Hughes, A and Pegg, D, 'Queen vetted 67 laws before Scottish Parliament could pass them' *The Guardian* (London, 28 July 2021).

Chalmers, M, 'Parliament's decision on Syria: pulling our punches' (*Royal United Services Institute*, 30 August 2013).

Civil Service World, 'PM in rare veto of permanent secretary job' (*Civil Service World*, 5 December 2012).

Corera, G, 'Inside the government's secret data room' (*BBC News*, 15 December 2021).

Craig, P, Dickson, B, Douglas-Scott, S, Elliott, M, Hickman, T, Howarth, D, King, J, Le Sueur, A, Masterman, R, McCrudden, C, McHarg, A, O'Cinneide, C, Pannick, P, Phillipson, G, Poole, T, Prosser, T, Rose, D, Russell, M, Sunkin, M, Thomas, R and White, H, 'Royal Assent: A Letter to The Times' *The Times* (London, 3 April 2019).

Detmold, M, 'The Proper Denial of Royal Assent' (*UK Constitutional Law Association Blog*, 5 September 2019).

Dominiczak, P, Swinford, S and Hope, C, 'Revealed: seven peerages blocked after failing vetting process' *Daily Telegraph* (London, 6 August 2015).

Donaghy, R, 'We must address the scrutiny gap in Brexit-related international agreements' (*PoliticsHome*, 28 October 2019).

Durrant, T, 'No 10 should give up its control of special advisers' (*Institute for Government*, 18 November 2020).

Ekins, R, 'Constitutional Government, Parliamentary Democracy and Judicial Power' (*Policy Exchange*, 5 April 2019).

Elliott, M, 'Can the Government veto legislation by advising the Queen to withhold royal assent?' (*Public Law for Everyone*, 21 January 2019).

Elliott, M, 'A new approach to constitutional adjudication? Miller II in the Supreme Court' (*Public Law for Everyone*, 24 September 2019).

Faulks, E, 'Parliament has the right to reverse judicial decisions, but governments must be careful not to undermine the important role the courts play as a check and balance in our constitution' (*Constitution Unit Blog*, 27 August 2021).

Fikfak, V and Hooper, HJ, 'Whither the War Powers Convention? What Next for Parliamentary Control of Armed Conflict after Syria?' (*UK Constitutional Law Association Blog*, 20 April 2018).

Fine, S, 'Chief Justice hits back at Prime Minister over claim of improper call' *The Globe and Mail* (London, 2 May 2014).

Finnis, J, 'Only one option remains with Brexit – prorogue Parliament and allow us out of the EU with no deal' *Daily Telegraph* (London, 1 April 2019).

Foot, T, 'A Note on the Creation of Peers' (*Constitution Unit*, 30 January 2021).

Fraser, M and Barratt, P, 'Going to war is a matter for Parliament' *The Australian* (8 September 2014).

Goddard, J, 'New Lords Appointments: December 2020' (*House of Lords Library*, 19 January 2021).

Goldsmith, P, 'International agreements affect us all. They deserve to be scrutinised' (*Prospect Magazine*, 12 Feb 2021).

Gouglas, A and Brans, M, 'UK Extended Ministerial Offices: On the Road to Cabinetisation' (*Constitution Unit Blog*, 9 February 2016).

Groves, J, 'Boris Blasts: Who Runs Britain?' *The Daily Mail* (London, 25 September 2019).

Halliday, J, 'Ministerial code: No 10 showing contempt for international law' *The Guardian* (London, 26 October 2015).

Hazell, R, 'What happens when the Prime Minister is incapacitated?' (*Constitution Unit Blog*, 9 April 2020).

Herbert, AP, 'Pageant of Parliament' *Punch* (vol 186, 27 June 1934).

Hestermeyer, H, 'Parliament and treaty-making: from CRAG to a meaningful vote?' (*Constitution Unit Blog*, 14 March 2019).

Hickman, T, 'Quashing Orders and the Judicial Review and Courts Act' (*UK Constitutional Law Association Blog*, 26 July 2021).

Hogarth, R, 'Jonathan Jones' resignation points to wider questions about breaking international law' (*Institute for Government*, 8 September 2020).

Honeycombe-Foster, M, 'Boris Johnson slams judges but confirms Parliament will return after court rules his suspension was unlawful' (*PoliticsHome*, 24 September 2019).

Hooper, HJ, 'The Principle of Legality and Prerogative Power after the Third Direction Case' (*UK Constitutional Law Association Blog*, 26 April 2021).

Howarth, D, 'Westminster versus Whitehall: Two Incompatible Views of the Constitution' (*UK Constitutional Law Association Blog*, 10 April 2019).

Human Rights Watch, 'Syria: A Year On, Chemical Weapons Attacks Persist' (*Human Rights Watch*, 4 April 2018).

Institute for Government, 'Public Inquiries' (*Institute for Government*, 21 May 2018).

Jones, G and Blick, A, 'The PM and the centre of government from Blair to Cameron' (*LSE Blog*, 21 May 2010).

King, J, 'Can Royal Assent to a Bill be withheld if so advised by Ministers?' (*UK Constitutional Law Association Blog*, 5 April 2019).

Lagassé, P, 'On Crown Consent' (*Phillipe Lagassé*, 13 August 2013).

Lascelles, A, 'Dissolution of Parliament: Factors in Crown's Choice' *The Times* (London, 2 May 1950).

London Gazette (30 September 2021, 63488).

Ludlam, S, 'The Australian parliament must have the power to decide if we go to war' *The Guardian* (London, 17 July 2014).

Lynch, A, 'Judicial Appointments in Australia – Reform in Retreat' (*UK Constitutional Law Association Blog*, 26 May 2014).
Macleod, I, 'The Tory Leadership' *The Spectator* (London, 17 January 1964).
Maguire, P, 'Dominic Cummings moves No 10 staff to heart of Whitehall' *The Times* (London, 13 August 2020).
Mason, R, 'Boris Johnson's speech to the Tory party conference' *The Guardian* (London, 2 October 2019).
McHarg, A and Young, A, 'The Resilience of the (*Old*) British Constitution' (*UK Constitutional Law Association Blog*, 8 September 2021).
McKie, D, 'How Ministers exercise Arbitrary Power' *The Guardian* (London, 6 December 2000).
Mohdin, A, 'Boris Johnson sabotage letter to EU would break law' *The Guardian* (London, 9 September 2019).
Morris, N, 'Boris Johnson intends to pack House of Lords with Brexiteers to correct pro-Remain bias' (*iNews*, 26 August 2019).
Mountfield, R, 'Politicisation and the Civil Service' (*Understanding the Civil Service*, 2002).
Murphy, P, 'Why it matters that so many senior civil servants are quitting under Boris Johnson' (*The Conversation*, 2 September 2020).
Newton-Dunn, T, 'Squatter Holed up in No 10' *The Sun* (London, 8 May 2010).
Normington, D, 'The five reasons I'm concerned about plans to overhaul the public appointments process' (*Civil Service World*, 21 March 2016).
Payne, S and Parker, G, 'Relations between Johnson and cabinet secretary fray over Cummings ties' *Financial Times* (London, 28 May 2021).
Pegg, D and Evans, R, 'Queen lobbied for change in law to hide her private wealth' *The Guardian* (London. 7 February 2021).
Pegg, D and Evans, R, 'Queen lobbied for changes to three more laws, documents reveal' *The Guardian* (London, 8 February 2021).
Peplow, A, 'Withdrawal from the ECHR after Miller – A Matter of Prerogative?' (*UK Constitutional Law Association Blog*, 28 February 2017).
Phillipson, G, "Historic' Commons' Syria vote: the constitutional significance (Part I)' (*UK Constitutional Law Association Blog*, 19 September 2013).
Phillipson, G, "Historic' Commons' Syria vote: the constitutional significance (Part II – the way forward) (*UK Constitutional Law Association Blog*, 29 November 2013).
Phillipson, G, 'Voting on Military Action in Syria: A Reply' (*UK Constitutional Law Association Blog*, 2 December 2015).
Public Law Project, 'High Court rules: Gove broke the law' (*Public Law Project*, 9 June 2021).
Remeikis, A, 'Labor vows to restore penalty rates and address gender pay gap – as it happened' *The Guardian* (London, 18 December 2018).
Rhodes, B, 'Inside the White House during the Syrian Red Line Crisis' (*The Atlantic*, 3 June 2018).
Riddell, P, 'By Prime Ministerial Appointment: the PM and Permanent Secretaries' (*Institute for Government*, 17 October 2014).
Rowley, T and Marsden, S, 'Jimmy Savile could be stripped of knighthood, says David Cameron' *The Times* (London, 9 October 2012).
Rozenberg, J, 'Things can only get better: Dominic Raab struggles to say the right thing' (*A Lawyer Writes*, 8 October 2021).
Ruddick, G and Butler, S, 'Philip Green agrees to pay £363m into BHS pension fund' *The Guardian* (London, 28 February 2017).
Russell, M, 'Boris Johnson's 36 new peerages make the need to constrain prime ministerial appointments to the House of Lords clearer than ever' (*Constitution Unit Blog*, 31 July 2020).
Russell, M, Fox, R, Cormacain, R and Tomlinson, J, 'The marginalisation of the House of Commons under Covid has been shocking; a year on, Parliament's role must urgently be restored' (*Constitution Unit Blog*, 21 April 2021).

Russell, M, Phillipson, G and Schleiter, P, 'The Dissolution and Calling of Parliament Bill: Why the House of Commons should retain control over dissolution' (*Constitution Unit Blog*, 8 September 2021).

Seaward, P, 'The Veto' (*History of Parliament Trust Blog*, 15 April 2019).

Shipman, T and Wheeler, C, "Sack me if you dare,' Boris Johnson will tell the Queen' *The Sunday Times* (London, 6 October 2019).

Slack, J, 'Enemies of the People: Fury over out of touch judges who have declared war on democracy by defying 17.4m Brexit voters and who could trigger constitutional crisis' *Daily Mail* (London, 4 November 2016).

Stanley, M, 'The Westminster Model – Summary' (*Understanding the Civil Service*).

Straw, J, 'Michael Shields: press release by the Justice Secretary' *The Times* (London, 9 September 2009).

Sydney Morning Herald, 'MPs must debate troop deployments: Leahy' *The Sydney Morning Herald* (17 June 2010).

Taylor, M, 'Parliamentary Confirmation of Ministerial Nominations' (*UK Constitutional Law Association Blog*, 11 March 2021).

The Iraq Inquiry, 'Inquiry Costs' (*National Archives*).

The Spectator, 'M. Doumergue's Problems' *The Spectator* (London, 26 October 1934).

Theil, S, 'An Aversion to Weimar: German Constitutional Hesitance on Dissolving the Bundestag' (*UK Constitutional Law Association Blog*, 23 November 2017).

Thomas, A, 'It is not right to appoint a politician to lead the Civil Service Commission' (*Institute for Government*, 9 December 2021).

Turnbull, A, 'Valedictory Lecture' *The Guardian* (London, 27 July 2005).

Varuhas, J, 'Remedial Reform Part 1: Rationale' (*UK Constitutional Law Association Blog*, 3 November 2021).

Varuhas, J, 'Remedies Reform Part 2: Discretionary Factors' (*UK Constitutional Law Association Blog*, 9 November 2021).

Watt, N, Mason, R and Hopkins, N, 'Blow to Cameron's authority as MPs rule out British assault on Syria' *The Guardian* (London, 30 August 2013).

Watts, J, 'Speaker of House of Lords warns Theresa May against appointing new peers to get Brexit bills passed' *The Independent* (London, 6 January 2017).

Whitbourn, M, 'Review considers shake-up of federal judicial appointments' *The Sydney Morning Herald* (3 May 2021).

Wikipedia, 'List of United States presidential vetoes' (*Wikipedia*, 20 December 2021).

Wikipedia, 'Prorogation in Canada' (*Wikipedia*, 6 April 2021).

Williams, G, 'Integrity must rule process of judging conduct of judges' *The Australian* (14 February 2021).

Williams, J, 'Miller and the Human Rights Act 1998: can the Government withdraw the UK from the ECHR by the royal prerogative?' (*Public Sector Blog*, 28 February 2017).

Yong, B, 'Exposing the hidden wiring of Parliament' (*UK Constitutional Law Association Blog*, 10 January 2022).

Speeches and Productions

Bartlett, M, 'King Charles III' (2014).

Bercow, J, 'Opening up the Usual channels: next steps for reform of the House of Commons' (Hansard Society, London, 11 October 2017).

Brown, G, 'Speech to Charter 88' (Charter 88, London, 12 July 1997).

Debré, M, 'Speech before the Council of State' (Paris, 27 August 1958).

Gove, M, 'The Privilege of Public Service' (Ditchley Annual Lecture, Oxford, 27 June 2020).

Graham, J, 'This House' (2012).

Koizumi, J, 'Press Conference' (8 August 2005).
McClelland, R, 'Judicial Appointments Forum' (Bar Association of Queensland Annual Conference, Gold Coast, 17 February 2008).
Mitterand, F, 'L'entrietien télévisé du president de la République' (Le Monde, Paris, 16 July 1993).
O'Donnell, G, 'Cabinet Secretary Speech on the Cabinet Manual' (Constitution Unit, London, 26 February 2011).
Sumption, J, 'The Limits of Law' (Sultan Azlan Shah Lecture, Kuala Lumpur, 20 November 2013).

Government and Parliamentary Publications

Armstrong, R, *The Duties and Responsibilities of Civil Servants in relation to Ministers* (1985).
Armstrong, R, *Supplementary memorandum to the House of Lords Constitution Committee* HL 107 DCM1 (8 February 2011).
Australian Government Attorney-General's Department, *Judicial Appointments: Ensuring a strong, independent and diverse judiciary through a transparent process* (2010).
Australian Judicial System Advisory Committee, *Report to the Constitutional Commission* (1987).
Australian Law Reform Commission, 'Review of Judicial Impartiality – Terms of Reference' (Australian Government, 11 September 2020).
Australian Law Reform Commission, *Judicial Impartiality: Consultation Paper* (CP 1, April 2021).
Balladur, E, *Une Ve République plus démocratique – Comité de reflexion et de proposition sur la modernisation et le rééquilibrage des institutions de la Ve République* (Department of Legal and Administrative Information, 29 October 2007).
Buckland, R, *Oral evidence to the House of Commons Public Administration and Constitutional Affairs Committee* HC 829 (8 December 2020).
Cabinet Office, 'Governance' (*The Honours System of the United Kingdom*).
Cabinet Office, *The Civil Service: Taking forward Continuity and Change* (Cm 2748, 1995).
Cabinet Office, *A Draft Civil Service Bill: Consultation Document* (Cm 6373, 2004).
Cabinet Office, *Review of the honours system* (2004).
Cabinet Office, *Three Years of Operation of the Reformed Honours System* (2008).
Cabinet Office, *Chapter 6: Elections and Government Formation (DRAFT)* (February 2010).
Cabinet Office, *The Cabinet Manual – Draft* (December 2010).
Cabinet Office, *The Second Report on the Operation of the Honours System* (2011).
Cabinet Office, *The Cabinet Manual*, 1st edn (2011).
Cabinet Office, *Government Response to the House of Lords Constitution Committee, Political and Constitutional Reform Committee and Public Administration Select Committee on the Cabinet Manual and Committee Reports of Session 2010-12* (Cm 8213, 2011).
Cabinet Office, *Goodwin Knighthood Decision* (HM Government, 31 January 2012).
Cabinet Office, *Inquiries Guidance* (2012).
Cabinet Office, *The Report of the Detainee Inquiry* (December 2013).
Cabinet Office, *Civil Service Reform Plan: One Year On* (2013).
Cabinet Office, *Guide to Making Legislation* (July 2014).
Cabinet Office, *The Third Report on the Operation of the Reformed Honours System* (2014).
Cabinet Office, *Code of Conduct for Special Advisors* (2016).
Cabinet Office, *Governance Code on Public Appointments* (2016).
Cabinet Office, 'Having honours taken away (forfeiture)' (December 27 2017).
Cabinet Office, *Ministerial Code* (2019).
Cabinet Office, *The Fourth Report on the Operation of the Honours System* (2019).
Cabinet Office, *Annual Report on Special Advisers 2020* (2020).
Cabinet Office, *Draft Fixed Term Parliaments Act 2011 (Repeal) Bill* (CP 322, 2020).
Cabinet Office, *Annual Report on Special Advisers 2021* (2021).

Cabinet Office, *Declaration on Government Reform* (2021).
Cabinet Office, *Government Response to the Joint Committee on the Fixed-Term Parliament Act Report* (CP 430, 2021).
Canadian House of Commons Standing Committee on National Defence, *Canada's Role in International Peace Operations and Conflict Resolution* (May 2019).
Chancellor of the Duchy of Lancaster, *Government's Response to the Report from the House of Lords Select Committee on the Public Service* (Cm 4000, 1998).
Civil Service Commission, *Annual Report and Accounts 2010-11* (HC 1180, 2011).
Civil Service Commission, *Annual Report and Accounts 2014-15* HC 251 (2015).
Civil Service Commission, *Annual Report and Accounts 2019-20* HC 455 (2020).
Civil Service Commission, *Written evidence to the House of Commons Public Administration Select Committee* (CSR 24) HC 74 (2012-13).
Commissioner for Public Appointments, *Annual Report 2011-12* (2012).
Committee on Standards in Public Life, *Standards in Public Life* (Cm 2850-I, 1995).
Committee on Standards in Public Life, *Reinforcing Standards: Review of the First Report of the Committee and Standards in Public Life* (Cm 4557-I, 2000).
Committee on Standards in Public Life, *Defining the Boundaries within the Executive: Ministers, Special Advisers and the permanent Civil Service* (Cm 5775, 2003).
Committee on Standards in Public Life, 'CSPL statement on PACAC's report on public appointment process' (2016).
Committee on Standards in Public Life, *Standards Matter 2: The Committee's Findings* (June 2021).
Committee on Standards in Public Life, *Upholding Standards in Public Life* (November 2021).
Criminal Cases Review Commission, *Annual Report and Accounts 2010/11* (HC 1225, July 2011).
Criminal Cases Review Commission, *Annual Report and Accounts 2020/21* (HC 404, July 2021).
Crown Law Office, *Judicial Protocol* (April 2014).
Day, J, 'Memo to the Prime Minister' (Jp 115, 29 August 2013).
Department for Business, Energy and Industrial Strategy, *Post Office Horizon IT inquiry 2020: terms of reference* (22 September 2021).
Department for Constitutional Affairs, *Government response to the Public Administration Select Committee's Fourth Report of Session 2003-04: Taming the Prerogative: Strengthening Ministerial Accountability to Parliament* (Cm 6187, 2004).
Department for Constitutional Affairs, *The Lord Chancellor's Judiciary Related Functions: Proposals (the Concordat)* (2004).
Department for Constitutional Affairs, *Report on the UK Government's Inter-Departmental Review of the UK's Position under various International Human Rights Instruments* (July 2004).
Department for Constitutional Affairs, *Government Response to the House of Lords Constitution Committee's Fifteenth Report of Session 2005-06: Waging War: Parliament's role and responsibility* (Cm 6923, 2006).
Department for International Trade, *Processes for making free trade agreements after the United Kingdom has left the European Union* (CP 63, February 2019).
Exiting the European Union Committee, *Parliamentary Scrutiny and approval of the Withdrawal Agreement and negotiations on a future relationship* HC 1240 (2017-19).
Folketinget, *Folketinget – The Danish Parliament* (Christiansborg Palace, October 2013).
Foreign, Commonwealth and Development Office, *Treaties and Memoranda of Understanding (MOUs): Guidance on practice and procedures* (November 2021).
Fritchie, I, *Memorandum to the House of Commons Public Administration Select Committee* HC 122-I (2005).
Gladstone, D, *Memorandum to the House of Commons Public Administration Select Committee* HC 422 MPP04 (May 2003).
Government of Canada, 'Policy on Tabling of Treaties in Parliament' (Department of Foreign Affairs and International Trade Treaty Law Division, November 2020).
Grimstone, G, *Better Public Appointments: A Review of the Public Appointments Process* (Cabinet Office, 2016).

Hallett, H, *The Report of the Hallett Review: An Independent Review into the On the Runs Administrative Scheme* (HC 380, July 2014).
Harman, H, *Memorandum from the Leader of the House of Commons* (M58) (February 2008).
Hazell, R and Russell, M, *Written evidence to the Joint Committee on the Fixed-Term Parliaments Act* HC 1046 HL 253 FTP0003 (December 2020).
Hazell, R, *Written evidence to House of Commons Political and Constitutional Reform Committee* HC1023 GFE0004 (16 February 2015).
HM Government, *The Coalition: our programme for government* (2010).
HM Government, *Memorandum of Understanding and Supplementary Agreements Between the United Kingdom Government, the Scottish Ministers, the Welsh Ministers, and the Northern Ireland Executive Committee* (October 2013).
HM Government, *Civil Service Code* (2015).
HM Government, *The Government Response to the Annual Report on the Operation of the Terrorism Acts in 2015 by the Independent Reviewer of Terrorism Legislation* (Cm 9489, 2017).
HM Government, *Government Response to the Constitution Committee Report: Parliamentary Scrutiny of Treaties* (July 2019).
HM Government, *Transparency Report: Disruptive Powers 2018/19* (CP 212, March 2020).
Home Office, 'Inquiry launched into issues raised by Couzens conviction' (5 October 2021).
House of Commons Digital, Culture, Media and Sport Committee, *Pre-appointment hearing for Information Commissioner* HC 260 (2021-22).
House of Commons Home Affairs Select Committee, *Counter-terrorism: Foreign Fighters* HC 993 (2014-15).
House of Commons Justice Committee, *Constitutional Reform and Renewal* HC 923 (2008-09).
House of Commons Justice Committee, *Constitutional processes following a general election* HC 396 (2009-10).
House of Commons Justice Committee, *Criminal Cases Review Commission* HC 850 (2014-15).
House of Commons Liaison Committee, *Select Committees and Public Appointments* HC 1230 (2010-12).
House of Commons Liaison Committee, *Pre-Appointment Hearings* HC 2307 (2017-19).
House of Commons Liaison Committee, *The Effectiveness and Influence of the Select Committee System* HC 1860 (2017-19).
House of Commons Modernisation Committee, 'Press Notice' (11 October 2007).
House of Commons Modernisation Committee, *Revitalising the Chamber: the role of the back bench Member* HC 337 (2006-07).
House of Commons Northern Ireland Affairs Committee, *The administrative scheme for "on-the-runs"* HC 177 (2014-15).
House of Commons Political and Constitutional Reform Committee, *Parliament's role in conflict decisions* HC 923 (2010-12).
House of Commons Political and Constitutional Reform Committee, *Parliament's role in conflict decisions: a way forward* HC 892 (2013-14).
House of Commons Political and Constitutional Reform Committee, *The Impact of Queen's and Prince's Consent on the Legislative Process* HC 784 (2013-14).
House of Commons Political and Constitutional Reform Committee, *Government formation post-election* HC 1023 (2014-15).
House of Commons Public Administration and Constitutional Affairs Committee, *The Strathclyde Review: Statutory Instruments and the power of the House of Lords* HC 752 (2015-16).
House of Commons Public Administration and Constitutional Affairs Committee, *Appointment of the Commissioner for Public Appointments* HC 869 (2015-16).
House of Commons Public Administration and Constitutional Affairs Committee, *The Role of Parliament in the UK Constitution: Authorising Military Force* HC 1891 (2017-19).
House of Commons Public Administration and Constitutional Affairs Committee, *Government Response to the Committee's Thirteenth Report: A Smaller House of Lords* HC 2005 (2017-19).

House of Commons Public Administration and Constitutional Affairs Committee, *Government Response to the Committee's 20th Report of Session 2017-19: The Role of Parliament in the UK Constitution: Authorising the Use of Military Force* HC 251 (2017-19).

House of Commons Public Administration and Constitutional Affairs Committee, *A Public Inquiry into the Government's response to the Covid-19 pandemic* HC 541 (2019-21).

House of Commons Public Administration and Constitutional Affairs Committee, *The Fixed-term Parliaments Act 2011* HC 167 (2019-21).

House of Commons Public Administration and Constitutional Affairs Committee, *Appointment of William Shawcross as Commissioner for Public Appointments* HC 662 (2021-22).

House of Commons Public Administration Select Committee, *Special Advisers: Boon or Bane* HC 293 (2000-01).

House of Commons Public Administration Select Committee, *Government by Appointment: Opening up the Patronage State* HC 165 (2002-03).

House of Commons Public Administration Select Committee, *A Draft Civil Service Bill: Completing the Reform* HC 128-I (2003-04).

House of Commons Public Administration Select Committee, *A Matter of Honour: Reforming the Honours System* HC 212-I (2003-04).

House of Commons Public Administration Select Committee, *Taming the Prerogative: Strengthening Ministerial Accountability to Parliament* HC 422 (2003-04).

House of Commons Public Administration Select Committee, *Government by Inquiry* HC 51-I (2004-05).

House of Commons Public Administration Select Committee, *Politics and Administration: Ministers and Civil Servants* HC 122 (2006-07).

House of Commons Public Administration Select Committee, *Constitutional Renewal. Draft Bill and White Paper* HC 499 (2007-08).

House of Commons Public Administration Select Committee, *Propriety and peerages* HC 153 (2007-08).

House of Commons Public Administration Select Committee, *The Honours System* HC 19 (2012-13).

House of Commons Public Administration Select Committee, *The Honours System: Further Report with the Government Response to the Committee's Second Report of Session 2012-13* HC 728 (2012-13).

House of Commons Public Administration Committee, *Truth to Power: How Civil Service reform can succeed* HC 74 (2013-14).

House of Commons Public Administration Select Committee, *Truth to Power: How Civil Service reform can succeed: Government Response to the Committee's Eighth Report of Session 2013-14* HC 955 (2013-14).

House of Commons Treasury and Civil Service Committee, *The Role of the Civil Service* HC 27-I (1993-94).

House of Commons Work and Pensions and Business Innovation and Skills Committee, *BHS* HC 54 (2016-17).

House of Lords Appointment Commission, *Annual Report 2013-2015* (2015).

House of Lords Appointment Commission, 'Two new non-party-political peers' (24 February 2021).

House of Lords Committee on the Inquiries Act 2005, *The Inquiries Act 2005: post-legislative scrutiny* HL 143 (2013-14).

House of Lords Constitution Committee, *Waging War: Parliament's role and responsibility* HL 236-I (2005-06).

House of Lords Constitution Committee, *Constitutional Reform and Governance Bill* HL 98 (2009-10).

House of Lords Constitution Committee, *The Cabinet Manual* HL 107 (2010-11).

House of Lords Constitution Committee, *Constitutional arrangements for the use of armed force* HL 46 (2013-14).

House of Lords Constitution Committee, *Constitutional implications of coalition government* HL 130 (2013-14).

House of Lords Constitution Committee, *Parliamentary Scrutiny of Treaties* HL 345 (2017-19).
House of Lords Constitution Committee, *A Question of Confidence? The Fixed-term Parliaments Act 2011* HL 121 (2019-21).
House of Lords Delegated Powers and Regulatory Reform Committee, *Democracy Denied? The urgent need to re-balance power between Parliament and the Executive* HL 106 (2021-22).
House of Lords European Union Committee, *Scrutiny of international agreements: lessons learned* HL 387 (2017-19).
House of Lords European Union Committee, *Treaties considered on 12 February 2019* HL 287 (2017-19).
House of Lords European Union Committee, *Treaty scrutiny: working practices* HL 97 (2019-21).
House of Lords International Agreements Committee, *Working Practices: One Year On* HL 75 (2021-22).
House of Lords Liaison Committee, *Review of House of Lords investigative and scrutiny committee activity in 2019-20* HL 103 (2019-21).
House of Lords Liaison Committee, *Review of investigative and scrutiny committees: strengthening the thematic structure through the appointment of new committees* HL 193 (2019-21).
House of Lords Procedure Committee, *Report* HL 29 (2019-21).
House of Lords Secondary Legislation Scrutiny Committee, *Government by Diktat: A Call to return Power to Parliament* HL 105 (2021-22).
House of Lords, 'The Third Report on the Dignity of a Peer' in *Reports from the Lords Committees touching The Dignity of a Peer of the Realm*, vol 2 (London, 1829).
Independent Review of Administrative Law, *Terms of Reference* (2020).
Independent Review of Administrative Law, *Review* (CP 407, 2021).
Independent Reviewer of Terrorism Legislation, *The Terrorism Acts in 2013* (2014).
Independent Reviewer of Terrorism Legislation, *The Terrorism Acts in 2015* (2016).
Institute for Government, *Written evidence to the House of Commons Political and Constitutional Reform Committee* HC 1023 GFE0003 (16 February 2015).
Intelligence and Security Committee of Parliament, *UK Lethal Drone Strikes in Syria* (HC 1152, 26 April 2017).
Iraq Inquiry, *The Report of the Iraq Inquiry*, vol 1 (HC265 I, 2016).
Joint Committee on Fixed-Term Parliaments Act, *Report* HC 1046 HL 253 (2019-21)
Joint Committee on Human Rights, *Protocol No. 14 to the European Convention on Human Rights* HL 8 HC 106 (2004-5).
Joint Committee on Human Rights, *Review of International Human Rights Instruments* HL 99 HC 264 (2004-05).
Joint Committee on Human Rights, *The Government's policy on the use of drones for targeted killing* HL 141 HC 574 (2015-16).
Joint Committee on Human Rights, *Human Rights Protections in International Agreements* HC 1833 HL 310 (2017-19).
Joint Committee on the Draft Constitutional Renewal Bill, *Report* HL 166-I HC 551-I (2007-08).
Law Council of Australia, *Policy on the Process of Judicial Appointments* (June 2021).
Lord Speaker's Committee on the Size of the House, *Third Report* (2019).
Ministry of Defence and Foreign and Commonwealth Office, *War Powers and Treaties: Limiting Executive Powers* (Cm 7239, 2007).
Ministry of Justice, *Government Response to the Report of the House of Lords Select Committee on the Inquiries Act 2005* (Cm 8903, 2014).
Ministry of Justice, *The Governance of Britain* (Cm 7170, 2007).
Ministry of Justice, *The Governance of Britain – Constitutional Renewal* (Cm 7342, 2008).
Ministry of Justice, *The Governance of Britain: Review of the Executive Royal Prerogative Powers: Final Report* (2009).
Ministry of Justice, 'Royal pardon for WW2 code-breaker Dr Alan Turing' (*HM Government*, 24 December 2013).

Ministry of Justice, *Review of the Parole Board Rules and Reconsideration Mechanism* (CP 29, February 2019).
Ministry of Justice, *Root and branch review of the parole system* (2020).
Ministry of Reconstruction, *Report of the Machinery of Government Committee* (London, 1918).
National Audit Office, *Investigation into government-funded inquiries* (HC 836, May 2018).
National Offender Management Service, *Sentence Calculation – Determinate Sentenced Prisoners* (2015).
New Zealand Cabinet Office, *Cabinet Manual*, 6th edn (2017).
New Zealand Parliament Regulations Review Committee, *Inquiry into regulation-making powers that authorise international treaties to override provisions of New Zealand enactments* (12 March 2002).
New Zealand Parliament Senate Foreign Affairs, Defence and Trade Committee, *Report on the agreement between New Zealand and Singapore on a closer economic partnership* (588 NZPD 6329–6357, 2000).
Northcote, SH and Trevelyan, CE, *Report on the Organisation of the Permanent Civil Service* (London, 1854).
Office of Parliamentary Counsel, *Queen's or Prince's Consent* (September 2018).
Office of the Commissioner for Federal Judicial Affairs Canada, 'Judicial Advisory Committees – Guidance for Judicial Advisory Committee Members' (*Government of Canada*, October 2016).
Office of the Commissioner for Federal Judicial Affairs Canada, 'Statistics regarding Judicial Applicants and Appointees' (*Government of Canada*, 28 October 2020).
Parliament of Australia Joint Standing Committee on Treaties, *A history of the Joint Standing Committee on Treaties: 20 years* (Report 160, March 2016).
Parliament of Australia Joint Standing Committee on Treaties, *Strengthening the Trade Agreement and Treaty-Making Process in Australia* (Report 193, August 2021).
Parliament of Australia Senate Foreign Affairs, Defence and Trade References Committee, *Blind Agreement: Reforming Australia's Treaty-making Process* (2015).
Parliament of Australia Senate Legal and Constitutional Affairs References Committee, *Australia's Judicial System and the Role of Judges* (December 2009).
Parliament of Australia Senate Legal and Constitutional References Committee, *Trick or Treaty? Commonwealth Power to Make and Implement Treaties* (November 1995).
Prime Minister's Office, *Chemical weapon use by Syrian regime: UK government legal position* (29 August 2013).
Privy Council Office, *Manual of Official Procedure of the Government of Canada* (Ottawa, Government of Canada, 1968).
Quentin-Baxter, A, *Review of the Letters Patent 1917 Constituting the Office of Governor-General of New Zealand* (Cabinet Office, Wellington, 1980).
Royal Commission on Capital Punishment, *Report* (Cmd 8932, September 1953).
Royal Commission on Criminal Justice, *Report* (Cm 2263, 1993).
Royal Commission on Reform of the House of Lords, *A House for the Future* (Cm 4534, 2000).
Royal Commission on the Reform of the House of Lords, *A House for the Future* (Cm 4534, January 2000).
Scottish Government, *Scotland's Role in the Development of Future UK Trade Arrangements* (August 2018).
Scottish Government, *A Fairer, Greener Scotland: Programme for Government* 2021-22 (September 2021).
Select Committee on the Civil List, *Report* HC 529 (1971-72).
Smith, C, *Oral evidence to the House of Commons Public Administration and Constitutional Affairs Committee* HC 376 (23 June 2021).
St prp nr 5, *Om Norges tiltredelse av De Forente Nasjoner* (Oslo, Utenriksdepartementet, 1945).
The Anthony Grainer Inquiry, *Report into the Death of Anthony Grainger* (HC 2353, 2019).
Trump, D, 'Presidential Veto Message to the Senate for SJ Res 68' (White House, 6 May 2020).
Twomey, A, *Oral evidence to the Joint Committee on the Fixed-Term Parliaments Act* HC 1046 HL 253 (21 January 2021).

US Department of Justice, 'Clemency Statistics' (*US Department of Justice*, 2 February 2022).
US Department of State, *Joint Statement Issued by Partners at the Counter-ISIL Coalition Ministerial Meeting* (3 December 2014).
Watmore, I, *Oral evidence to the House of Commons Public Administration and Constitutional Affairs Committee* HC 1314 (16 March 2021).
Welsh Assembly External Affairs and Additional Legislation Committee, *International agreements: a suggested approach to engagement and scrutiny* (October 2019).

Communications

Letter from Jonathan Stephens to Frank Field (17 January 2017).
Letter from Peter Riddell to Lord Evans (7 October 2020).
Letter from Boris Johnson to Lord Bew (21 December 2020).
Letter from William Wragg to Chloe Smith (21 July 2021).
Letter from Chloe Smith to William Wragg (7 September 2021).

Archival Material

'Events leading to the resignation of Mr Heath's administration 4 March 1974' TNA PREM 16/23.
Letter by Mr De Winton (Law Officers' Department) to Lord Bridges (5 September 1972) TNA PREM 15/1183.
Draft Letter by No 10 Downing Street (Prime Minister's Office) to Mr McWhirter (21 September 1972) TNA PREM 15/1183.
Letter from Alan Lascelles to Michael Adeane (3 May 1950) Royal Archives PS/PSO/GVI/C/320/37.

INDEX

www.ingramcontent.com/pod-product-compliance
Ingram Content Group UK Ltd.
Pitfield, Milton Keynes, MK11 3LW, UK
UKHW020237290926
15470UKWH00002B/587

9 781509 951444